How to Cheat in Maya 2026

How to Cheat in Maya 2026 is more than a software manual—it's a complete guide to working smarter, animating faster, and thinking like a professional. This edition covers Maya's latest tools and features; but more importantly, it focuses on real-world workflows and the creative process behind great animation. You'll find not just the how, but also the why, behind each technique, helping you build intuition and confidence in your craft. Whether you're learning the ropes or refining your skills, this book is designed to remove friction, streamline your process, and let you focus on what matters most: crafting compelling animated performances.

Featuring advice, strategies, and best practices for:

- Configuring optimal Maya settings
- Testing and mastering your rigs
- Avoiding and overcoming common animation pitfalls
- Harnessing the power of Constraints, Layers, and Cycles
- Employing physics, anatomy, and psychology to push your facial animation and polish to the next level

New to this Edition:

- Maya updates and upgrades to the Graph Editor, Time Slider, Time Slider Bookmarks, Dope Sheet, Light Editor, Ghosting, Blue Pencil, and more
- Four new character rigs added to the *How to Cheat in Maya* series
- All new interlude articles covering everything from AI, the animation industry, selecting schools, to demo reels
- "Tempo" is a workflow so revolutionary, we're calling it The Thirteenth Principle!

Kenny Roy began his career in 1997 as a dustbuster on cel-animated features. He's gone on to animate some of the most memorable characters on screen, from *King Kong to Scooby Doo*. Over more than a 25-year career, he has taught animation in-person and online and has been a speaker at conferences and seminars around the globe. Kenny currently operates November Games in New Zealand where he lives with his wife and two sons.

Genevieve Freckelton is an animator and instructor. Genevieve started her career in TV commercials and network news, then moved on to feature films and television. Her credits include: *Tron: Legacy* and *The Adventures of Kami and Big Bird*. Genevieve has been teaching undergraduate character animation in Autodesk Maya for over 10 years. Currently, Genevieve is teaching animation at De Anza College in Cupertino, California.

How to Cheat in Maya 2026

Tools & Techniques for Animators

Sixth Edition

Kenny Roy and Genevieve Freckelton

CRC Press
Taylor & Francis Group
Boca Raton London New York

CRC Press is an imprint of the
Taylor & Francis Group, an **informa** business

Designed cover image: Tamaryn Roy

Sixth edition published 2026
by CRC Press
2385 Executive Center Drive, Suite 320, Boca Raton, FL 33431, U.S.A.

and by CRC Press
4 Park Square, Milton Park, Abingdon, Oxon, OX14 4RN

CRC Press is an imprint of Taylor & Francis Group, LLC

First edition published by Focal Press 2009
Fifth edition published by Routledge 2018

Library of Congress Cataloging-in-Publication Data
Names: Roy, Kenny, author. | Freckelton, Genevieve, author.
Title: How to cheat in Maya 2026 : tools & techniques for animators / Kenny Roy and Genevieve Freckelton.
Description: Sixth edition. | Boca Raton, FL, U.S.A. : CRC Press, 2026. |
Includes bibliographical references and index.
Identifiers: LCCN 2025022878 (print) | LCCN 2025022879 (ebook) | ISBN 9781032883373
(hardback) | ISBN 9781032883090 (paperback) | ISBN 9781003537267 (ebook)
Subjects: LCSH: Maya (Computer file) | Computer animation--Computer programs.
| Computer graphics--Computer programs.
Classification: LCC TR897.72.M39 R693 2026 (print) | LCC TR897.72.M39 (ebook)
LC record available at https://lccn.loc.gov/2025022878 LC ebook record available at
https://lccn.loc.gov/2025022879

ISBN: 978-1-032-88337-3 (hbk)
ISBN: 978-1-032-88309-0 (pbk)
ISBN: 978-1-003-53726-7 (ebk)

DOI: 10.1201/9781003537267

Typeset in Avenir Book Font
by KnowledgeWorks Global Ltd.

Publisher's note: This book has been prepared from camera-ready copy provided by the authors.

Contents

03 THE THIRTEENTH PRINCIPLE

04 MAXIMIZING YOUR RIGS

05 GRAPH EDITOR

09 CAMERA

10 CYCLES

11 FACIAL ANIMATION

Acknowledgments

KENNY ROY

First and foremost, my deepest thanks to my wife, Tamaryn: the brilliant designer behind this edition. Her work has made this the most visually striking and well-organized *How to Cheat in Maya* yet. She has the rare gift of seeing through chaos to uncover clarity and beauty, and even when the subject matter is dense, she shapes our ideas into something effortlessly elegant.

A heartfelt thank you to my coauthor, Genevieve. Your tenacity is the reason this edition exists at all, and your relentless work ethic is the reason it got finished. You lit the spark to start it and kept the momentum alive to see it through. I couldn't have done it without you.

And finally Sean Connelly, for the opportunity to come back to the How to Cheat series, and for your incredible support over the years.

Cheers.

GENEVIEVE FRECKELTON

I want to thank Dave, Mom, Stef, and my family for all their encouragement. You guys gave me the support to balance it all and reach my goals. I can always count on you for feedback, proofreading and advice, anytime, anywhere. I love you all.

To Kenny, I have never known someone who can juggle so many projects so successfully, and the fact that you just said yes to taking on one more without hesitation is crazy to me, but I am glad you did. Thank you so much for writing this book with me.

Thank you, Tamaryn, for taking on all that work to help us. It was so exciting to see that first chapter laid out. The book looks beautiful.

To my mentors and instructors that helped me along the way, thank you for giving back and sharing your time and knowledge. To all my students, past and present, you're my inspiration and you made me a better teacher. It's so rewarding watching you create and grow. I hope this book serves as a resource for animators and aspiring animators to keep practicing and learning.

Resource Acknowledgments

JOSH SOBEL

fRigging Awesome Studios

We would both like to sincerely thank Josh Sobel of FriggingAwesome.com for the use of Kayla Bot in our example files. It's a truly awesome rig, built with animators in mind. Josh is an accomplished technical animator and rigger with credits that include *Big Hero 6*, and *Ice Age: Collision Course*. The great news for our readers is, Josh's shop is absolutely chock-full of amazing rigs for you! Please give his gumroad a visit, and support him:

https://friggingawesome.gumroad.com

RAMÓN ARANGO

We would like to recognize Ramón Arango for providing the Mannequin rigs featured throughout this book. Ramón is an accomplished animator known for his work on projects like the award-winning film *Nimona*, and acclaimed short films *Entergalactic* (2017) and *The Edge* (2020). Beyond his film credits, Ramón is also a skilled rigger and modeler. His expertise made it possible to bring our examples to life with professional-quality character setups using his versatile Mannequin rigs. Thank you, Ramón, for sharing your tools and talent with us.

We encourage readers to support Ramón's work by visiting his site and exploring more of his fantastic character rigs:

https://ramonarango.gumroad.com

Interview Acknowledgments

We would like to extend our heartfelt appreciation to Isaí Calderón for participating in an interview available on our Discord channel. Isaí's extensive experience as a Senior Animator and Technical Animator includes notable contributions to films such as *Kong: Skull Island*, *Ms. Marvel*, *The Witches* (2020), and *Wonder Woman 1984* . His insights into the animation industry and the stories he's shared have significantly enriched our community's understanding. Thank you, Isaí, for sharing your time and knowledge with us.

We'd also like to thank Dave Vasquez for his interview, also available on the Discord. Dave is a seasoned animator with over 13 years in feature animation, including 9 years at Blue Sky Studios. His impressive film credits include *Luck*, *Nimona*, *Spies in Disguise*, *Ferdinand*, *Ice Age: Collision Course*, *The Peanuts Movie*, *Rio 2*, *Epic*, *Arthur Christmas*, *The Smurfs*, *Yogi Bear*, and *Alvin & The Chipmunks: The Squeakquel*. Currently, Dave serves as a Senior Cinematic Animator at Riot Games. Thank you, Dave, for sharing your time and expertise with us. Our community is better for it!

How to Cheat

In years past, the *How to Cheat in Maya* series was written to be a resource for learning the shortcuts and tricks that professional animators use on the job. We focused on developing examples that took a concept to near completion, then letting the reader make the final tweak to solidify their understanding. The intention was to inspire readers to continue to learn animating in Maya by giving them an opportunity to make choices and complete animations they were perhaps years from being able to do themselves. The format worked in part because access to quality online tutorials was still limited.

When an update to the series was proposed, the question of where this series fits in the Age of YouTube and online learning had to be answered. What was true back in 2014 is not true a decade later; tutorials are free, abundant, and high quality. What has changed though is the quality of answers one can find for overall operation of software. Artificial Intelligence (AI) articles have taken over the internet, replacing simple, handy guides with awkwardly-worded Frankenstein's monsters. Maya forums and user groups have closed, online communities have been segmented, and even active Discords need to have at least one person with the answer be online to be helpful. We see a gap, and we aim to fill it.

This 2026 update to *How To Cheat In Maya* represents a shift to a format that is geared towards being a handbook for animators to keep by their desk as they learn the craft and start their careers. We have collated all of the necessary knowledge to avoid snags when animating, as well as assembled an exhaustive list of shortcuts and cheats that the pros use to keep you sailing along in your journey. We emphasize proper scene and rig setup, shortcuts and hotkeys, and provide an entire section of dozens of the most common issues that professionals encounter regularly.

We hope the book will be your on-the-job guide for proper Maya usage that you turn to in a pinch, rather than get lost online sifting through 10-year-old forum posts and AI articles.

Thank you for purchasing this book. We hope it helps, and we're looking forward to seeing you shine!

Using This Book

This book is organized to be read through with Maya open, and chapter files at the ready. Follow along with the walkthroughs whenever you see a screenshot with instructions to do so. Most menus are magnified in the walkthroughs for readability, so when you see a zoomed-in screen, you will know the important information being displayed is a menu item or button.

All the chapter files are available on the Official *How to Cheat in Maya* Discord Server. Once there, download them from the #resources channel.

JOIN HERE

https://discord.gg/656FTUg6yS

Discord

Callouts

We also wanted to make it easy to categorize the information in your head as you go through, and to also refer back to the book as you animate. Keep an eye out for these callouts as you read:

CHEAT

These are the main points from the section that you should remember and keep with you as you work. If you remember anything, remember these tips.

FUN FACT

These are interesting tidbits perhaps not related to Maya, but are things that great animators keep in the back of their mind as they work. We're always thinking about the world around us, and incorporating anatomy, acting, directing, music, visual art, etc. into our animations.

WATCH OUT!

Finally, these are things that you should NOT do, remember to avoid and you'll be in good shape.

DON'T FORGET

Anything that you need to remember to check, settings that have to be configured properly, or material we covered earlier that comes back into play will be put here. Forgetting to follow these tips can lead to negative results like lost work. From turning on Incremental Save, to setting your project before you work, these will save you time and hassle.

1 BEFORE YOU START

Welcome to Maya! Before beginning, let's take some time to set up the software. It is highly recommended to get a three-button mouse, because many basic Maya functions make use of all three buttons. If using a stylus and tablet, make sure the stylus has a middle mouse button equivalent. We will abbreviate mouse buttons in this way:

- **LMB:** Left mouse button
- **MMB:** Middle mouse button
- **RMB:** Right mouse button

CHEAT

Mac users with two buttons can use Command + LMB in place of the middle mouse button, but acquiring a three-button mouse is a better option.

WHERE TO START

Maya creates a default project folder the first time the program is run.

- **Windows:** C:\Users\{YOUR_USER_NAME}\Documents\maya\projects\default
- **Linux:** /home/{YOUR_USER_NAME}/maya/project/default
- **Mac:** /Users/{YOUR_USER_NAME}/Documents/maya/projects/default

Inside the default folder are a set of subfolders that will store everything needed to create animation, models, and VFX. Maya always looks in the project folders for files by default. When clicking File > Open, Maya will look in the Scenes folder, the SourceImages folder for textures, and the Assets folder for rigs and props, and so on.

Every studio has a project and file structure that works with its production pipeline. At the novice level, it is fine to work within the default project folder, or you may be instructed to make new project folders per class or per assignment.

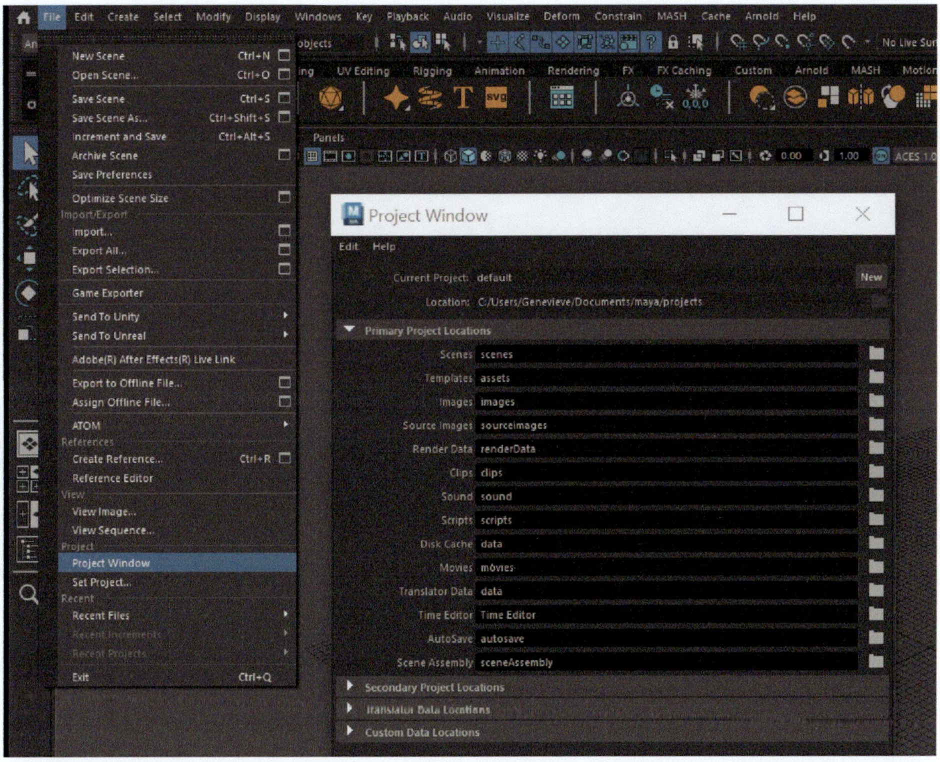

To make a new project, go to File > Project Window > New. Once there are multiple projects, Maya must be told which project is the current project, to save files in the proper folders. Go to File > Set Project, under Directory, choose the current project and click Set.

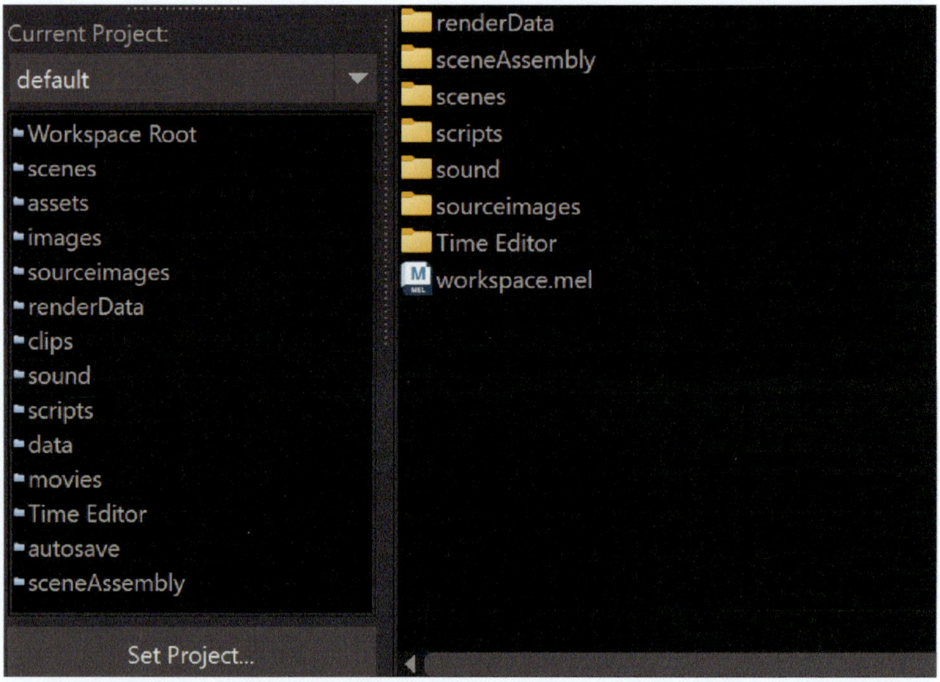

The File > Open menu contains a File Browser. On the lower-left side sits the Current Project panel. There is a scroll view where all of the folders in the current project can be accessed. There is also another Set Project button to change the current project.

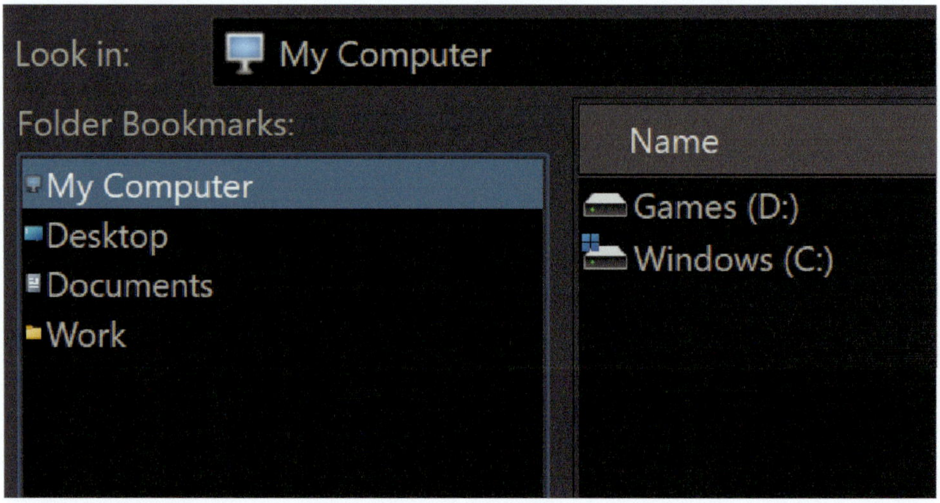

On the upper-left side, there is a Folder Bookmarks panel. To make a bookmark shortcut, just drag the item into the Folder Bookmarks panel. To remove a bookmark, RMB and choose Remove.

While working on an animation, it might be necessary to access the preference and scripts folders. Go to:

- **Windows:** C:\Users\{YOUR_USER_NAME}\Documents\maya\2026
- **Linux:** {YOUR_USER_NAME}/maya/2026
- **Mac:** /Users/{YOUR_USER_NAME}/Library/Preferences/Autodesk/maya/2026

Inside are the folders: prefs, presets, and scripts. Maya created these folders the first time it was launched. Prefs stores every customization to Maya. Presets stores saved settings like render presets. Scripts stores scripts like plug-ins, custom tools, and character rig extras.

On occasion, Maya's preferences can get corrupted. If this happens, close Maya, delete the prefs folder (make a backup file if needed,) then re-launch Maya. This will force Maya to create a new prefs folder with everything set to default. The old folder can be thrown away unless there is specific information to keep.

Preferences are stored locally. Meaning, when using a different computer, your preferences will not automatically be there. Either spend a few minutes setting up preferences or copy your prefs folder to each new computer with a thumb drive.

FILE NAMING

Studios will have a set naming convention to work within their pipeline. At the student level, the instructor may have specific instructions on how to name files.

Universal best practice in naming files is to use an underscore instead of spaces in the name; blank spaces in a file name can cause problems with the operating system. Within Maya, spaces are also forbidden in object naming, so using an underscore is a good habit to develop. Avoid special symbols, especially multiple periods/decimal points between words. Mac users, make the file extensions visible.

Example: name_info_V001.ma

Using version numbering syntax allows us to change the name of the file by simply changing the version number. At any time, a short note can be included within the file name.

FUN FACT

Yes, a file name can be too long. The max length for a file name in Windows is 256 characters and 255 for Mac.

SAVING FILES

Maya scenes have two file types, Maya ascii (.ma) text and Maya binary (.mb) numbers. Ascii files are larger but can be edited in a text editor. Binary are more compressed files that cannot be edited. Which should be used? At a studio, the pipeline will determine what format is in use. At the student level, unless the instructor states otherwise, ascii is best — it is fairly easy to learn how to troubleshoot a broken file, and the saved file size is negligible. Once the file is saved in one format, attempting to switch formats can be problematic or simply result in an error message.

Save by going to File > Save Scene or hotkey Ctrl + S. Saving a scene this way will continually overwrite the original file. This is not the recommended practice in the industry. What if there is a need to go back to an earlier version? Or the file gets corrupted? To protect the time and effort put into the scene, save multiple versions of the scene file.

Incremental saving means renaming the file and making another copy of it. Go to File > Save Scene As or hotkey Ctrl + Shift + S. I recommend incremental saving. Get in the habit of hitting Ctrl + Shift + S whenever a significant change is made to a scene, before executing a command, or running a script in Maya. Before long, it becomes a habit. This gives better control of when to save and what to name a file.

Maya has an Increment and Save option under the File menu. This is not the recommended option because it does not allow a change to the name of the file, instead it adds numbers: ex. .0001.ma or mb to the end of the current file. This occasionally causes problems on Macs to have two decimals in a file name.

AutoSave is a built-in incremental save. If the computer is unstable or you are a beginner and just don't trust yourself, use AutoSave. The drawback to AutoSave is it saves based on time and not progress made. Another drawback is the scenes will be numbered, so it is not as easy to jump back to a specific point in a scene's progress.

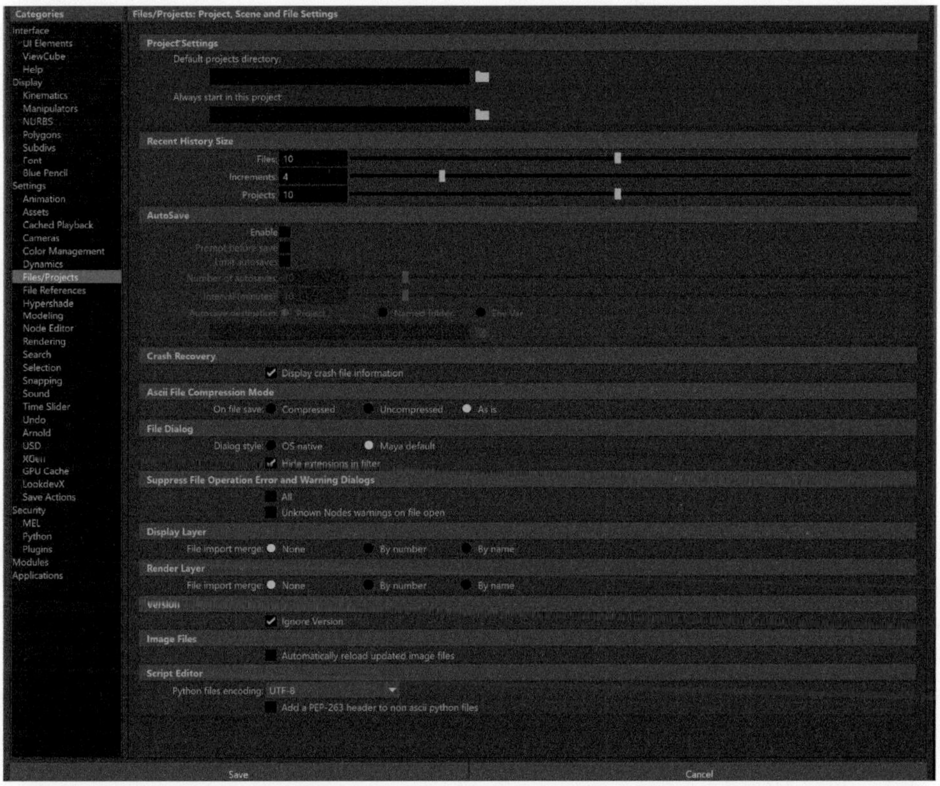

Go to Windows > Setting/Preferences > Preferences. Go down the list to Files/Projects and go to the AutoSave section. Check the Enable box and choose from options like interval time.

Crash Recovery is a tool offered in Maya. It automatically saves a crashing file with the option to re-open it. The success of Crash Recovery depends on why Maya crashed. When it opens a recovered file, it will execute the last command. If that command caused the crash, it will crash again. Instead, saving incrementally makes it possible to go back to the last good version of a scene.

COMMON SETTINGS

On a personal computer, preferences only need to be set once. At school or a studio with high project turnover, it may be necessary to reconfigure Maya preferences on every computer you use.

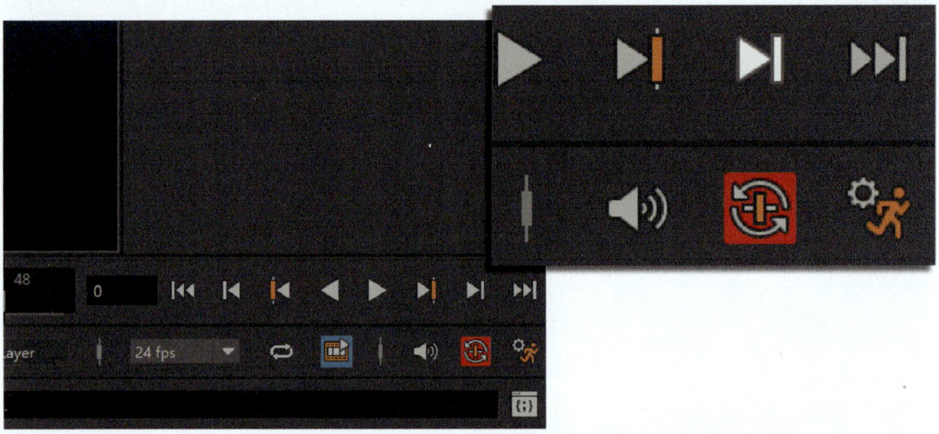

First go to the bottom-right corner and click the Time Slider preferences shortcut, the orange man with a gear.

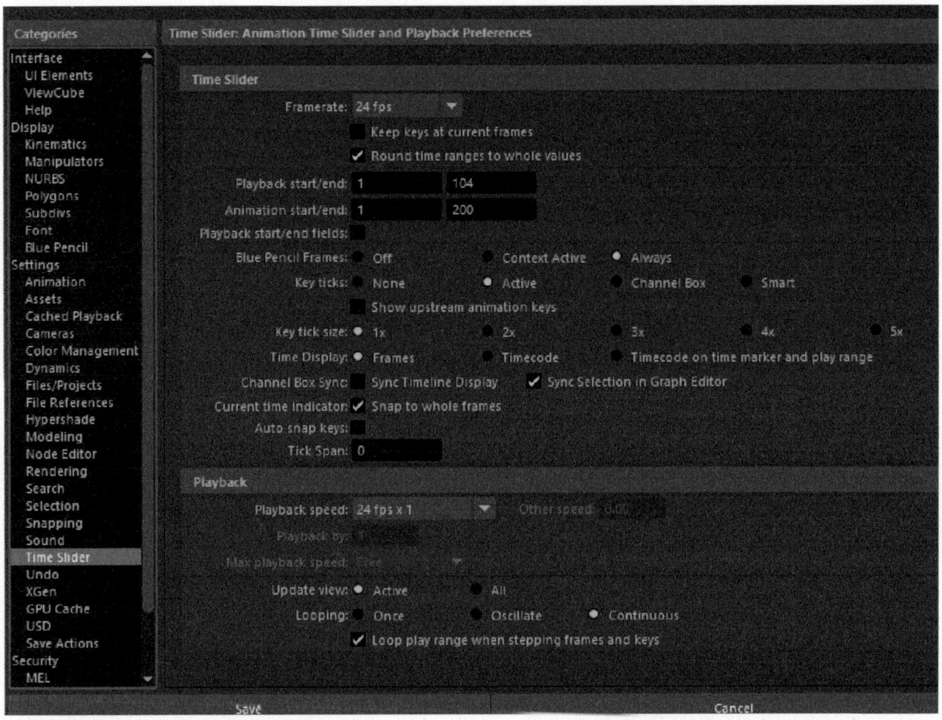

Look at Framerate. It should be set to 24 fps. This is the industry standard for animation. Next, we want to make sure the animation will play at 24 fps. Go down to the Playback section and make sure Playback Speed is set to 24 x 1. This will force the computer to play the scene as close to 24 fps as possible.

Cached Playback is a tool to make Maya playback faster. It saves the screen draws in a cache and only redraws what has been changed. This can be a powerful tool when working in heavy scenes and simulations. However, sometimes it is overkill for simple scenes and beginning animators. The cache will take up memory and will need to be flushed out. Also, the Playback Cache can have unintended effects, like causing temporary visual effects of 'baked on' black shadows on rigs with older materials.

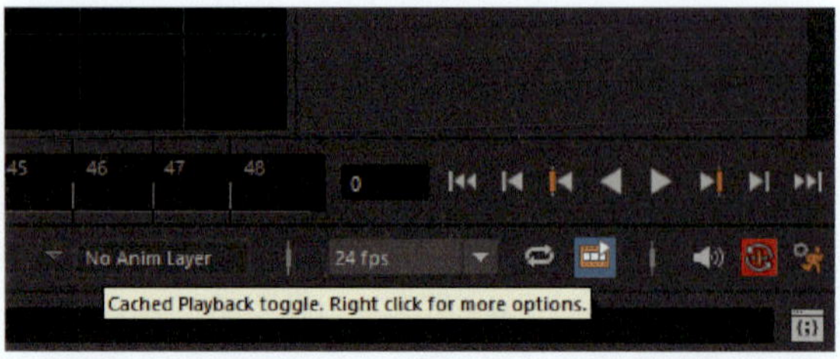

It is recommended for beginning animators to turn off Cached Playback. Just click the icon so that it is not highlighted.

If you want to use Cached Playback, there are a few settings to check. RMB on the icon and go to Cached Playback Preferences. Make sure the % of RAM is 70% or less. Check the box for Stop caching at memory limit. Set Cache fill to Playback so it is not constantly caching as you are trying to work. Finally, set Background fill direction to Forward From Animation Start so constraints or simulations calculate correctly.

WORKSPACE

Over time, animators develop a preferred workspace layout. It is highly recommended for new users to keep the workspace set to the default General layout as you learn.

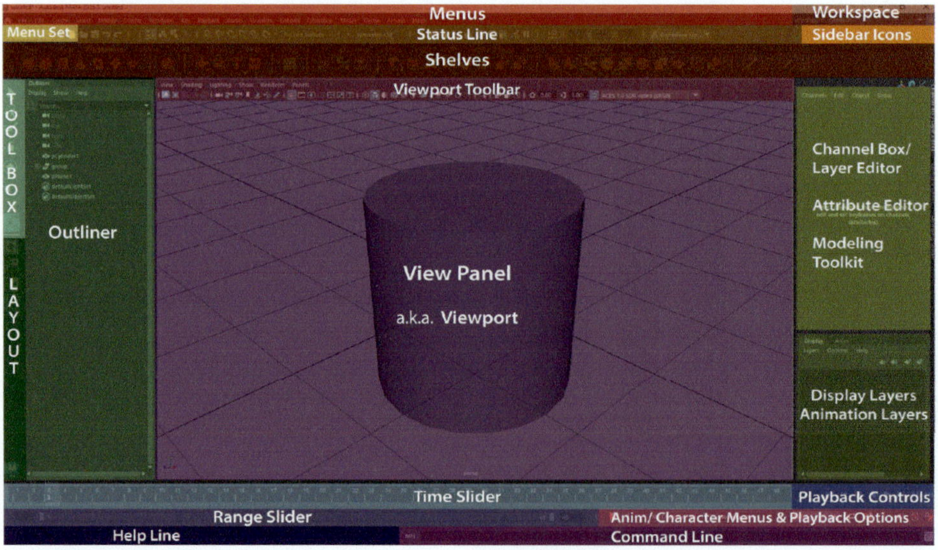

Diagram of Maya General workspace

By default the Maya workspace is set to tear off and dock all the available panels anywhere. This offers a lot of freedom for advanced users. Beginning animators may get frustrated by docking, undocking, closing and losing panels when you don't know how to fix the workspace. Locking the workspace panels is recommended.

The padlock icon is in the upper-right-hand corner. Click it so that it is highlighted blue. This will lock the workspace, so panels cannot be accidentally torn off and docked in random places.

There is a pre-made Animation workspace which works well on large monitors but may feel cramped on laptop screens because the view panel is shrunk to fit the Graph Editor underneath. Clicking on the side tabs will minimize the Graph Editor. Click again on the tabs over the Time Slider to restore the Graph Editor. Pros generally prefer to keep the Graph Editor as a free-floating panel that can be moved anywhere and minimized while not in use. However, launching the Graph Editor as a free-floating panel through menus is not efficient.

To fix the workspace layout, go to the Workspace pull-down menu and select Reset Current Workspace.

1 BEFORE YOU START

To quickly access the Graph Editor, assign it to a shelf button or hotkey.

To make a shelf button for any menu item:

1. Open the shelf where the new button will be placed, or make a new shelf. To make a new shelf, click the gray gear to the left of the shelves.
2. Navigate to the item in the menu and place the cursor over it.
3. Press Ctrl + Shift + RMB.
4. Once the button is made, RMB to edit or delete.
5. To move a button on a shelf, use MMB drag.

To assign a hotkey to launch the Graph Editor:

1. Go to Windows > Settings/ Preference > Hotkey Editor.
2. Go to Edit Hotkeys for: open dropdown menu.
3. Choose Menu items.
4. Go to Common > Windows > Animation Editors > Graph Editor.
5. Locate a gray unassigned key on the keyboard that will serve as the new hotkey.
6. Type in this key in the input box and click Save.

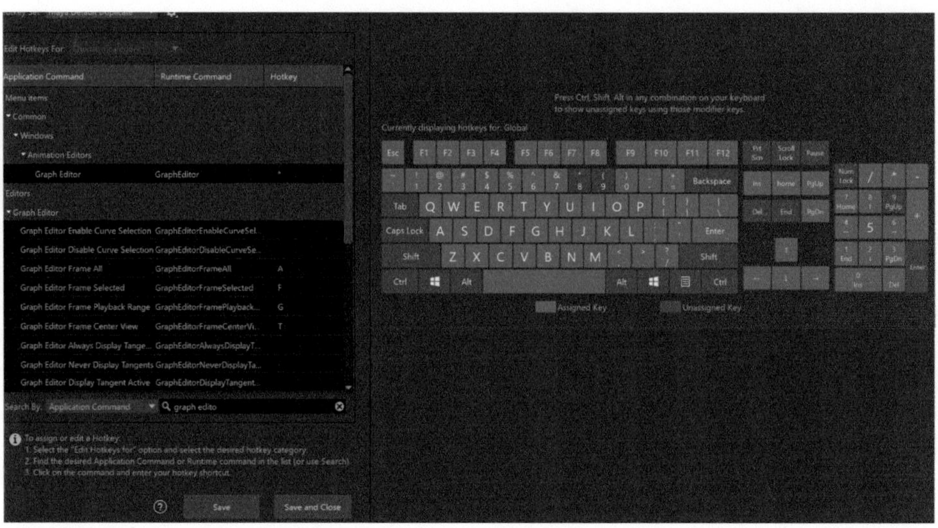

Hotkey Editor

COMMON HOTKEYS

General		
Ctrl + S	Save Scene	Saves scene by overwriting file
Ctrl + Shift + S	Save Scene As	Saves scene under new name
Ctrl + Z	Undo	Undoes last action
Ctrl + Y	Redo	Redoes last action
Ctrl + O	Open	Opens scene
Ctrl + N	New	Creates new scene
F1	Maya Help	Opens browser to Autodesk Maya Help
Ctrl + F	Find	Types in tool to find
Camera		
Alt + LMB	Tumble	Orbits the camera around selection
Alt + MMB	Pan	Drags camera
Alt + RMB	Zoom	Zooms camera in or out
A	Frame All	Frames everything
F	Frame Selection	Frames only selected objects
Shift + A or F	Multi-panel	Framing applied to all views
Home	Reset Camera	Moves camera back to default view
[	Undo View	Jumps back to previous camera position
]	Redo View	Jumps forward to camera position
Ctrl + Space	Full Screen	Sets active panel to full screen, toggle off
Shift + Alt + mouse button	Movement Constraint	Will constrain movement in horizontal or vertical on tumble and pan
Navigation in Viewport		
Spacebar (short)	Toggle Viewport	Toggles 1 panel to 4 panel viewport layout
Spacebar (long)	Hotbox	Floating menu with access to all menus
RMB	Marking Menu	Floating menu with relevant options
LMB		Click off to side on nothing to deselect all
+	Enlarge	Makes manipulator handles larger
-	Shrink	Makes manipulator handles smaller
Alt + 1	Toggle Curves	Hides/ Shows NURBS curves (often Rig controls)

Alt + 2	Toggle Polys	Hides/ Shows polygons (rig & props meshes)
Alt + 4	Toggle ImagePlane	Hides/ Shows image plane
4	Wireframe	Toggles display to wireframe
Alt + 5	Wireframe/Shaded	Toggles display to wireframe on shaded
5	Shaded	Toggles display to shaded
6	Texture	Toggles display texture preview
7	Lights	Toggles display lights preview
Shift + H	Show	Shows selection
Ctrl + Shift + H	Hide	Hides selection
Shift + I	Isolate	Toggles displays only selected items
Ctrl + M	Hide Menus	Toggles display active menu
Alt + B	Change Background	Switches background preset colors
\ + RMB	2D Pan/ Zoom	Pan/ zoom the viewport, not the camera
Translations		
Q	Select Tool	Selection mode
W	Move Tool	+ Shift to constrain direction
E	Rotate Tool	+ Shift to constrain direction
R	Scale Tool	+ Shift to constrain direction
Alt + D	De-select	De-selects all
G	Repeat Command	Repeats last command
Y	Repeat Tool	Repeats last tool
MMB on Menus	Repeat	Repeats last menu item chosen
Alt + Arrow key	Nudge 1 Pixel	Move 1 pixel up, down, left, right
Arrow key	Pick Walk	Moves selection to next component
Animation		
Ctrl + R	Create Reference	Brings in Rigs/ Environments as referenced objects
S	Save Key	Saves a key on all keyable attributes
Shift + W	Save Move Key	Adds translate keys and changes curve
Shift + E	Save Rotate Key	Adds rotate keys and changes curve
Shift + R	Save Scale Key	Adds scale keys and changes curve

Alt + I	Insert Key	Inserts key with no change to curve
Ctrl + Shift +W	Save Move Key	Inserts move key without changing curve
Ctrl + Shift +E	Save Rotate Key	Inserts rotation key without changing curve
Ctrl + Shift + R	Save Scale Key	Inserts scale key without changing curve
.	Next Key	Moves indicator to next key on Time Slider
,	Previous Key	Moves indicator to prev key on Time Slider
Ctrl + Alt + .	Select Next Key	Moves to and selects next key
Ctrl + Alt + ,	Select Prev Key	Moves to and selects prev key
Alt + .	Next Frame	Moves to next frame
Alt + ,	Prev Frame	Moves to prev frame
LMB Time Slider	Scrub W/ Update	Scrubs Time Slider and plays animation
MMB Time Slider	Scrub No Update	Scrubs Time Slider and does not update animation
LMB + Shift Time Slider	Selection Range	Selects a range of frames to move or scale, RMB for more options
K + Drag	Virtual Time Slider	Drags in viewport to scrub timeline without Time Slider
Alt + V	Play	Plays animation, and toggles to stop
Time Slider Bookmarks		
Alt + T	Time Slider Bookmark	Creates bookmark on Time Slider and opens Create Bookmark Editor
Alt + Shift + T	Time Slider Bookmark	Makes bookmark - no name or color, can edit after
Ctrl + double-click	Select Frames	Selects frames within bookmark
| (vertical bar)	Frame Bookmark	Sets the playback range to range of current bookmark.
: (colon)	Frame Previous Bookmark	Sets range slider before bookmark
" (quotation mark)	Frame Next Bookmark	Sets range slider after bookmark
Alt + \ (backslash)	Unframe	Resets playback range back
' (apostrophe)	Step Forward	Bookmarks selection step forward
; (semicolon)	Step Back	Bookmarks selection step backwards
Ctrl + drag (middle)	Move Bookmark	Repositions bookmark on Time Slider
Ctrl + drag (side edge)	Resize Bookmark	Resizes the bookmark range

Graph Editor Navigation		
Alt + Z	Undo	Undoes view change
Alt + Y	Redo	Redoes view change
T	Center View	Centers view on current time
Alt + / (forward slash)	Snap	Snaps Time Marker to selected key
1	Absolute	True view of Curves
2	Stacked	Curves scaled and stacked to fit view
3	Normalized	Curves scaled to the same size to fit view
H	Lock	Locks curve channel
J	Unlock	Unlocks curve channel
D	Auto Tangent	Sets curve to Auto Tangent
9	Move Left	Moves key(s) left
0	Move Right	Moves key(s) right
Ctrl + Alt + , (comma)	Previous	Selects previous key
Ctrl + Alt + . (period)	Next	Selects next key

- **Rapid Double Click Tip**
  Rapid Double Click on any icon and it will open additional settings. It will open the Tool Settings for the translation tools in the Toolbox, or options settings for Shelf items.
- **RMB on any Shelf icon will open a menu.**
  Open will open the options panel for the chosen item. Edit, Edit Popup and Delete modify the shelf button.
- **Tool button vs. Apply button Tip**
  In the options panel for a tool, the first button/ tool button will execute the tool and close the option box. The Apply button will execute the tool but keep the options panel open. The Apply button is useful if the tool will be used repeatedly.
- **Enter**
  Press Enter to complete a tool or command. Certain tools require the user to press Enter to finish the operation, and exit the tool. Input boxes - press Enter when finished entering data to exit the input field. If Enter does not get you out of the tool mode, hit Q to go to Selection mode.

TOOL SETTINGS

In Maya world space, Y is the up / down axis. The X axis is always displayed in red, Y axis is green, and Z axis is blue. Manipulators with handles like Move and Scale will have the handles displayed in the positive direction. Clicking directly on the manipulator handles will constrain movement to that one axis. Clicking in the center of the manipulator is free translations in X, Y and Z.

By default the tools are set to world space. Sometimes, it might be necessary to translate an object in the direction it is oriented.

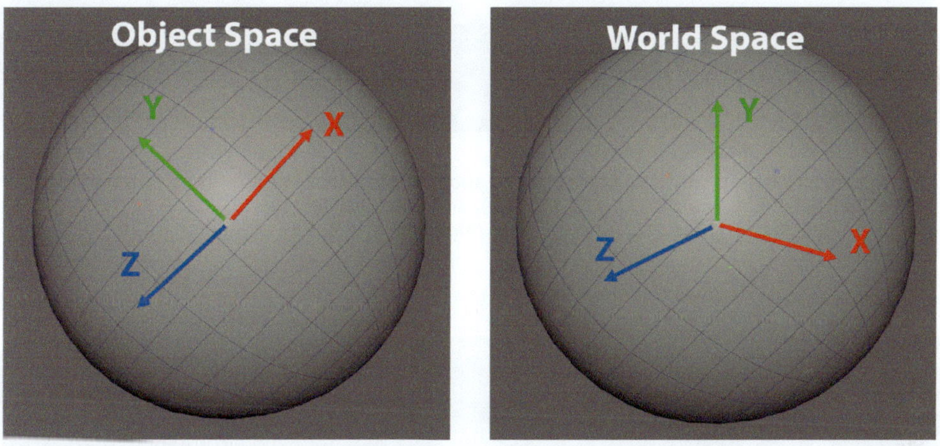

Double-click the tool and change Axis Orientation to Object space. Additionally, the tools can be aligned to Component, Parent, Normal, Rotation Axis, Live Object Axis, and Custom.

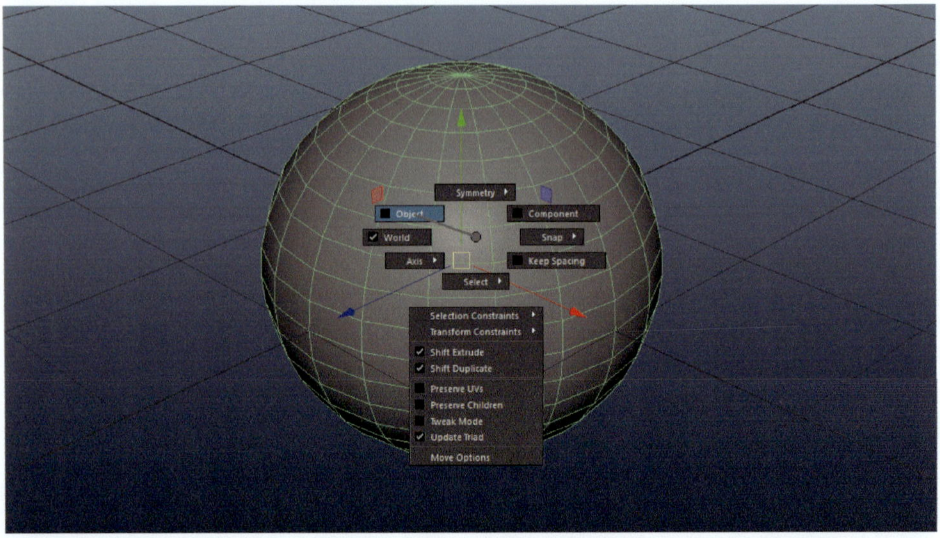

The quickest way to change the manipulator space is to hold down the transform hotkey (W for translate, E for Rotate, and R for Scale), and LMB drag on the object. A hotbox will appear, and the space can be chosen by releasing the hotkey while highlighting the selection.

DON'T FORGET

Most professionals hone their workspace, hotkeys, and menus over time. Don't be worried about setting up Maya perfectly when you begin learning. It will be obvious which tools you need to start streamlining and creating shelves and hotkeys as you go.

2 PRINCIPLES

THE 12 PRINCIPLES

The 12 principles of animation, developed and refined by Disney's original animators, serve as a foundation for making technical and performance decisions. They are not rigid rules but flexible guidelines for crafting engaging and visually appealing animation. While these concepts may seem simple, they work together to shape even the most complex performances on screen. Adapting them for use in Maya requires some interpretation, and this chapter provides a clear breakdown of these principles, along with practical guidance on applying them to your own work.

SQUASH AND STRETCH

Considered by many to be one of the most essential animation principles, Squash and Stretch infuses characters and objects with flexibility and life. It ensures that as forms move and deform, their overall volume remains consistent. Sometimes, this effect is driven by physical impact, like a ball compressing when it bounces. In character animation, squash and stretch takes on broader roles; enhancing anticipation, exaggerating movement, and adding visual appeal.

For instance, a character preparing to leap might compress their spine, causing their body to bulge outward. As they launch, their form elongates, stretching thin while maintaining volume. This principle can convey tension — such as a character straining to reach something overhead — or emotion, like fear, when a character curls into a tight ball to avoid danger. Observing squash and stretch in professional animation and real life reveals how this deceptively simple technique enhances the illusion of life in every movement.

CHEAT

Squash and Stretch can be put into your animation even if a rig is not built to support it; in later chapters, we'll discuss using advanced tools like lattices to correct silhouette and make shape changes like Squash and Stretch.

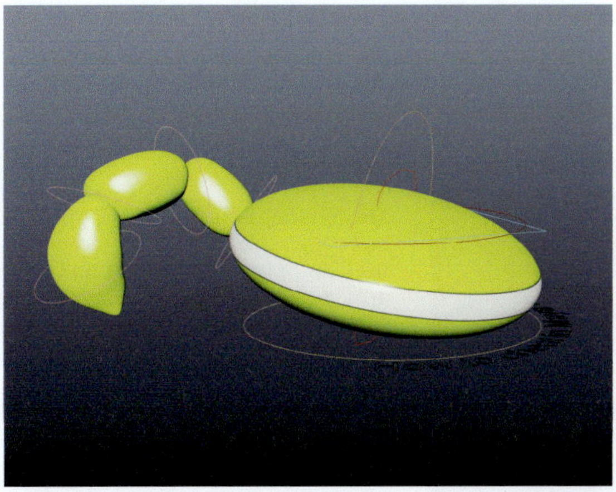

This ball is squashed down, projecting tension and energy before release.

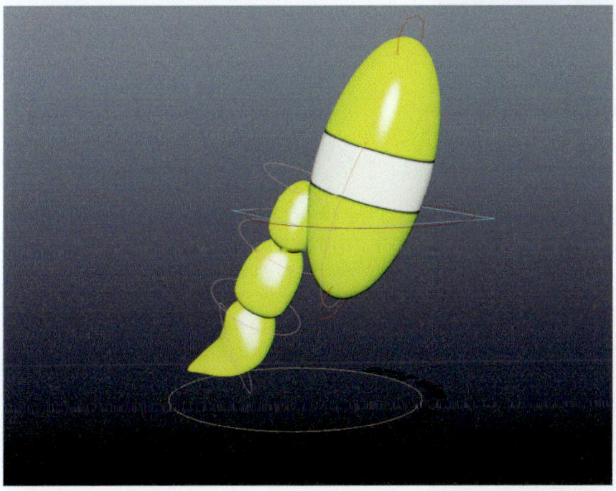

As the ball takes off, it stretches up and forward. The energy in the jump is emphasized by the rapid shape change. This principle shows up over and over again in animation.

It is not only bouncing balls and squishy characters that are subject to this animation principle. On the contrary, it is clever application of squash and stretch within the body posing that sets apart really energetic, dynamic animation.

For creatures, look to the spine to get a lot of the squash and stretch into your animation; quadrupeds especially have miles of room in their flexible spines to imbue this principle.

With humans and humanoids, the limbs do much more work, but as much as ducking and stretch is possible, it will take clever use of silhouette to give the impression of volume in your pose.

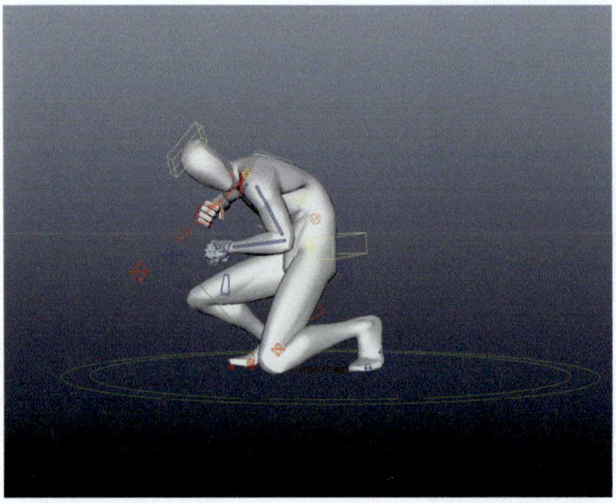

This character is all wound up! Look how the posing, including the use of foreshortening on the arm, combines to give a compact silhouette, even with a bony character like a human.

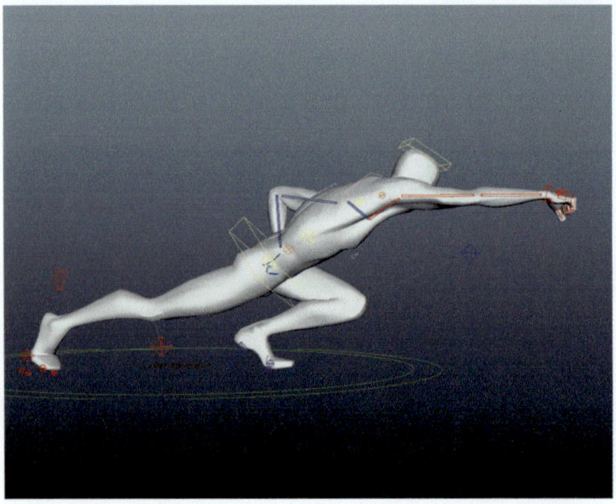

The character springs forward, firing that line of action straight forward and stretching their whole body to do so! This kind of contrast makes for very high energy animation.

In a lot of ways, it is the contrast in posing that really sells squash and stretch. Be sure to emphasize this when applying this principle to your animation.

ANTICIPATION

Anticipation is the technique of preparing both the character and the audience for an action. It often involves a small, preliminary movement in the opposite direction of the main motion. Since animation relies heavily on physicality, anticipation is crucial for achieving believable movement. A character must bend their knees before jumping, just as a pitcher must draw their arm back before throwing. This principle mirrors real-life physics, making it an essential tool for creating natural, convincing motion.

Humans are wired to track movement by noticing anticipation first and then predicting the direction of motion. Animators can use this to guide the audience's focus, ensuring their attention is drawn to the right part of the screen at the right moment.

Beyond its role in motion, anticipation also refines character performance. Disney legend Eric Goldberg ties anticipation directly to thought, reinforcing that a well-anticipated action feels intentional. When a character winds up for a punch, it signals planning and forethought. In contrast, a sudden, unanticipated motion feels reflexive or accidental. Think of Wile E. Coyote pulling his arm back before swinging a mallet at the Road Runner — his movement is deliberate, emphasizing his intent. But when the mallet unexpectedly bounces back and smashes him in the face, his head snapping backward is purely reflexive, highlighting the lack of anticipation in his reaction.

By carefully controlling anticipation in animation, you can define whether a character is thinking, planning, and acting with intent - or simply reacting to the world around them.

CHEAT

Anticipation and Squash and Stretch go hand in hand. Look for opportunities to add an amount of either principle whenever you employ the other.

Ah, the classic wind up for a great "zip out". A staple of animation! But this pose is so recognizable only because we've seen a character blast away in movies and TV shows for the better part of a century, and this anticipation pose tells a story.

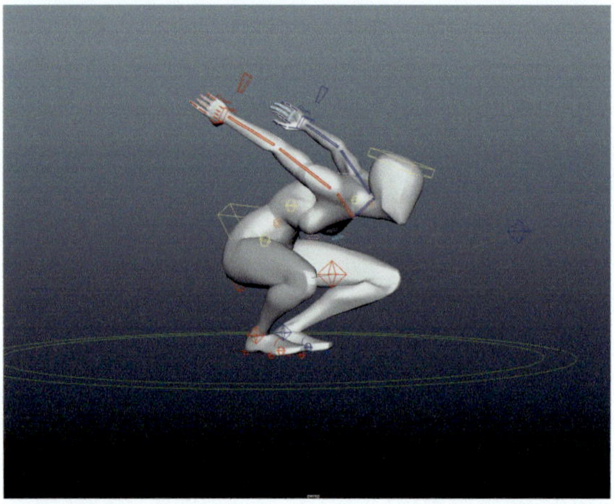

What is this character doing? We recognize the moment before a huge jump because we can see the power being built up by the anticipation. Sometimes, the anticipation is as clear as the motion.

CHEAT

Maya is extremely versatile, so take advantage early in your work to try multiple stagings of a scene. Reference your characters in, create a bunch of cameras, and have a play. The pros do!

STAGING

Staging is a cornerstone of animation that blends artistic composition, cinematography, and storytelling clarity. It involves framing the camera to best capture the action, planning movement to direct the viewer's focus, and ensuring the character's performance reads clearly within the scene. Simply put, staging is how you construct and present the visual narrative.

Effective staging begins in the planning phase. Thumbnail sketches help define strong poses early, allowing for thoughtful composition before animation begins. If drawing isn't your strength, relying on photo or video references can provide crucial cues for blocking out action. At this stage, staging is about ensuring that character movement and scene layout clearly communicate the intended motion and emotion.

As the shot progresses, staging becomes more dynamic. Can all the planned poses be achieved smoothly in motion? Do camera angles and layout adjustments enhance clarity or introduce confusion? Staging isn't just about still images; it means considering how screen elements evolve over time. Composition, silhouette clarity, and spatial relationships all play a role in guiding the viewer's eye to the most important parts of the scene.

Even in the final animation stages, staging remains critical. Where will the audience's attention naturally fall in each frame? If the animation is well executed, the focal point should always be clear. Beyond animation alone, staging influences downstream processes such as lighting, visual effects, and editing, all of which reinforce what the audience sees and feels. A well-staged shot isn't just visually appealing; it enhances the storytelling, ensuring every moment lands with maximum impact.

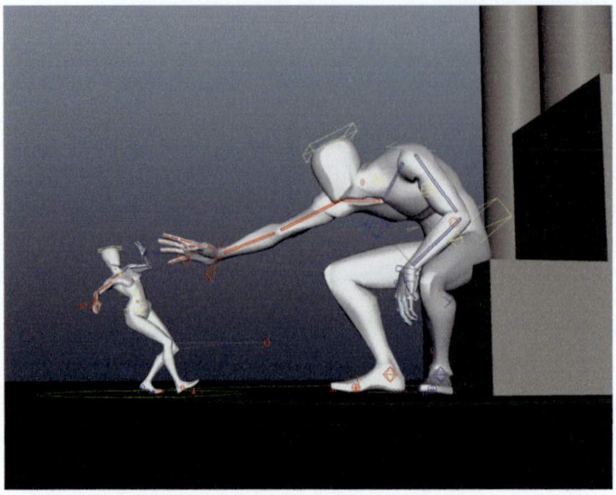

This is quite a dynamic and energetic scene. However, the camera angle and positioning of the characters is letting down the potential this has to be dynamic and exciting.

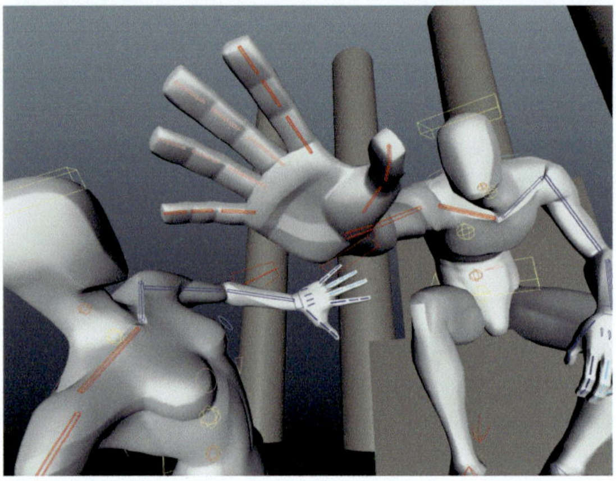

What a difference staging can make! The same scene setup, but with camera angle, focal length, posing, and a bit of forced perspective raise the entire stakes of the shot.

CHEAT

Animating straight ahead is much more straightforward (pun intended) with Auto Key turned on. And similarly, creating key poses for your pose-to-pose blocking is best approached (at least as you are learning) by using the S key (set key) on your full-body controls.

STRAIGHT AHEAD AND POSE-TO-POSE

This principle defines the two primary approaches to blocking animation. Straight ahead animation involves creating poses sequentially, advancing frame by frame without predefined key poses. This method mirrors stop-motion animation, where each frame must be captured before moving forward. Pose-to-pose animation, on the other hand, starts with key poses that define the overall motion. The timing is refined by adjusting spacing between these poses, making it a more flexible and nonlinear approach.

Each method has its strengths. Straight ahead animation is ideal for dynamic, mechanical, or fluid motion because it allows for a more natural sense of movement. When animating something unpredictable like an overlapping antenna, it is difficult to predict where each frame will land without working through the motion organically. This approach ensures the movement remains natural and reactive.

Pose-to-pose animation is best suited for character-driven performances. Key poses define the storytelling beats, and timing adjustments help refine emotional clarity. In performance animation, strong posing is essential for clear body language, ensuring the character's intent is readable. Without deliberate key poses, the emotional core of the animation can be lost.

This sequence was blocked with a Pose-to-Pose workflow. The ball was positioned, and posed with its controls to hit the key beats of anticipation, launch, height of the jump, and landing.

This sequence uses a hybrid approach. Now that the ball is blocked in, we need to animate the tail. This makes much more sense to do straight ahead.

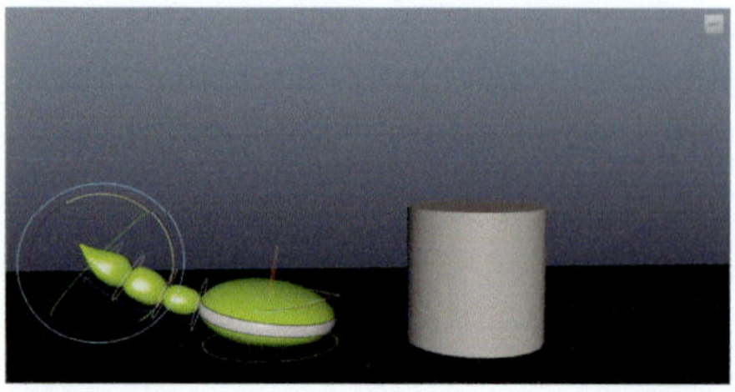

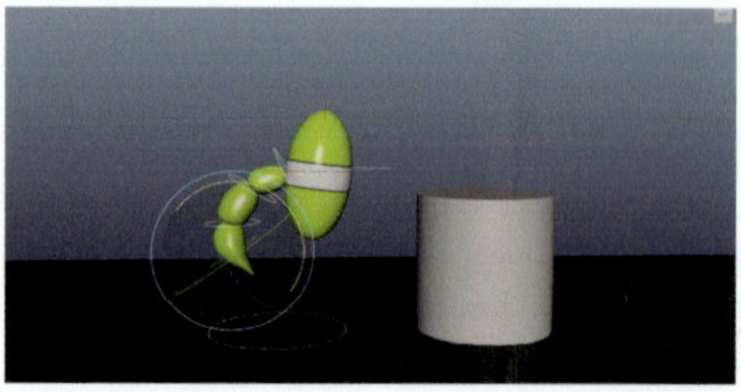

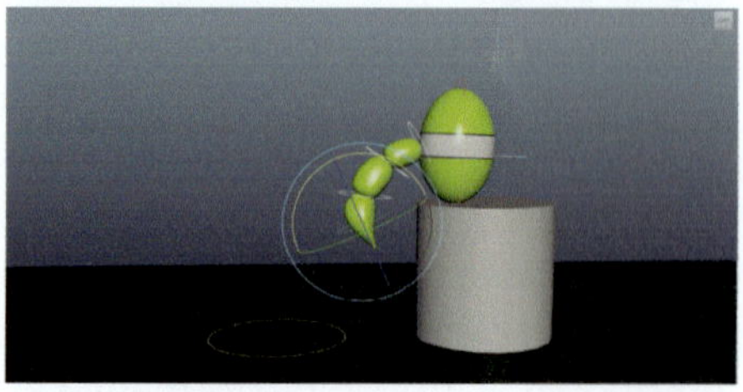

Now, with all of the tail controls selected, and auto key on, we step through the animation a few frames at a time, and add the tail overlap.

With this done, this small sequence has the benefit of both approaches; full-body posing done with Pose-to-Pose and a fluid tail done after the main posing with a Straight Ahead approach.

One way to tell if you are using either approach is if you are using many controls, or only a few. Also, if you are jumping around on the Time Slider, or moving a few frames forward at a time. In both cases, the former is Pose to Pose, and the latter is Straight Ahead!

OVERLAPPING ACTION AND FOLLOW-THROUGH

These two related principles enhance the natural quality and fluidity of movement. Both stem from physics, with the shared fundamental truth that objects require energy to start moving and to come to a stop. Overlap occurs when parts of an object or character lag behind the primary motion, while follow-through happens when motion overshoots its intended stopping point before settling.

Overlap adds a sense of flexibility and organic motion to a character. When a character swings an arm, the wrist lags slightly behind the main movement, creating a more natural look. Subtle overlap in the spine during a walk cycle conveys a relaxed demeanor, while exaggerated spinal overlap can make a character seem slouched or dejected. This principle plays a crucial role in expressing mood and personality through body language.

Follow-through emphasizes weight and momentum. A heavier character or object requires more energy to stop, which can be shown through overshooting movements or secondary reactions. A large character might take an extra step or sway slightly after coming to a stop, reinforcing their mass.

This character has just leapt off of this box; their arms are relaxed and by their side.

As they begin to fall, the arms start to lag behind, or overlap the action of the body. This would affect all parts of their body, and accessories, like belts, capes, etc.

As they approach the ground, the leg begins to extend to meet the impact. The arms continue to overlap.

At the moment of impact, the arms are fully behind, and the body transitions to Follow-Through. Why? The inertia of the body will continue to drive his weight down and toward the ground.

All of that momentum makes the arms and spine fly forward, and the motion follows through past the planted feet. This transition is essential for the audience to believe the physics of a motion like this.

When properly applied, Overlap and Follow-Through really sell the weight and physicality of an action. People are naturally aware of the effect inertia has on the body and on objects, and so subtle issues stand out to audiences.

CHEAT

Overlap generally is applied when a motion is happening, and follow-through takes over when the action stops.

SLOW-IN, SLOW-OUT

Also known as Ease-In and Ease-Out, this principle controls how objects accelerate and decelerate in animation. Instead of moving at a constant speed, most objects and characters gradually gain speed when starting a motion (slow-out) and gradually lose speed when coming to a stop (slow-in). This makes movement feel more natural and visually appealing.

In Maya's Graph Editor, this principle is represented by curves with smooth, flattened tangents. A bouncing ball provides a clear example: as it reaches the peak of its arc, it slows down before reversing direction, which is visible as a flattened section of the curve. However, slow-in and slow-out are not universal rules — certain movements require abrupt direction changes instead.

For example, when a ball impacts the ground, its motion shifts instantly due to the impact, so there should be no easing at the moment of contact. Similarly, in a running animation, the foot accelerates as it moves but hits the ground with force, meaning its movement does not ease in when making contact. A common mistake is applying flat tangents everywhere, assuming that all motion should ease in and out. True mastery of this principle comes from knowing when to use easing and when to create sharp transitions.

Maya's Motion Trail Editor makes it extremely easy to visualize spacing and determine when Slow-In and Slow-Out should be applied.

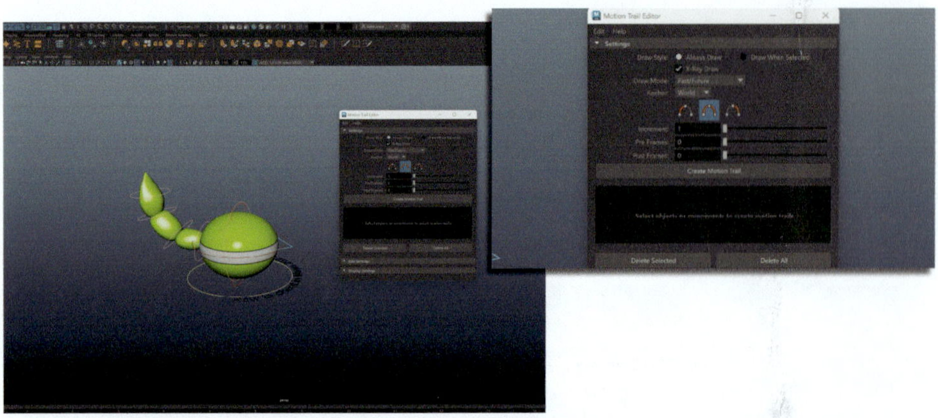

Open SlowInSlowOut.ma. Switch to the animations menu set by pressing F4, and open the Motion Trail Editor by going to Visualize > Motion Trail Editor.

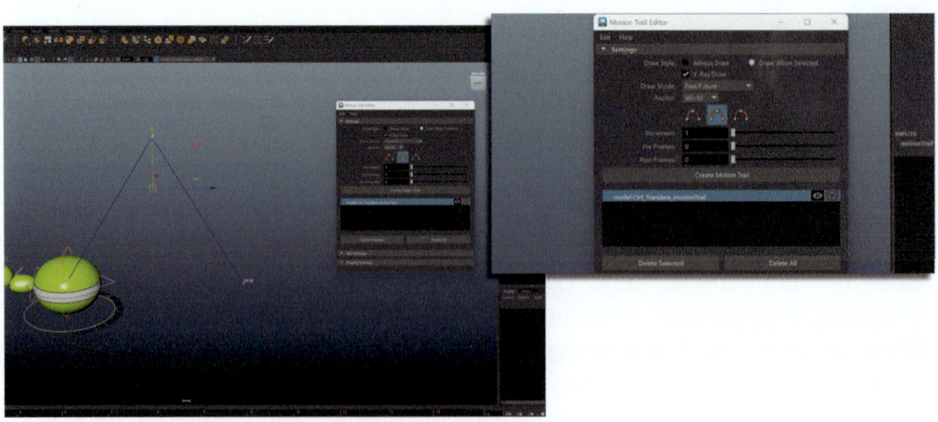

Select the Ctrl_Translate. Leave all the options default in the Motion Trail Editor and click Create Motion Trail. It should look like the above.

Notice how the ball moves up and down linearly, with no easing to the Translate Y curve. This is not typically the curve that you will receive when blocking, but truthfully the default smooth curve that we get out of Maya when blocking is not much better. Knowledge of proper easing is required to then stretch the rules, and even break them.

If we open the Graph Editor, we can see that the keys are linearly interpolated. Let's select the key at the top of the jump.

The graph editor shows the jump has been keyed with linear interpolation. We know intuitively that a ball changes direction smoothly from rising to falling, but we don't know the animation term Slow-In and Slow-Out is what is at play until we create motion like this ourselves.

Now, let's make a few adjustments here. With the top key selected on the Translate Y curve, click on the Flat Tangents button at the top of the Graph Editor toolbar.

FUN FACT

There is such a thing as Fast In, and Fast Out, and they are what you think! The keys leading into and out of the moment the ball hits the ground would be described as Fast In and Fast Out, but these terms are not often used in production, as notes like "Make the impact harder!" usually suffice.

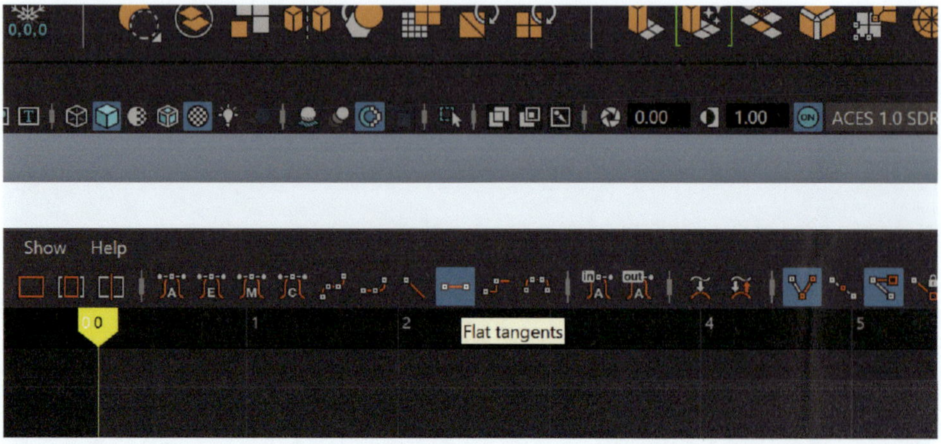

The flatter the tangent, the less the motion, so perfectly flat tangents in the middle of the animation represent a Slow-In and Slow-Out.

The effect on the Motion Trail we've created should be pretty apparent. Now there is a nice ease to the top of the jump.

Notice the nice ease of this jump. We've gone ahead and adjusted the tangents on f0 and f12 as well, to give some more speed and impact to the moment of contact.

In essence, most of the principles refer back to laws of motion. In this case, the main body movements are affected by gravity, which slows the body as it goes up, and slowly changes direction and accelerates as it falls.

ARCS

Early animators noticed that most natural movements follow curved trajectories rather than straight lines. This observation led to the animation principle of Arcs, which ensures motion feels organic rather than robotic. To maintain fluidity in animation, it is crucial to track motion paths and avoid linear, jagged movements. While it is important to check arcs from all angles, the most critical viewpoint is the camera view — since that is what the audience will see.

A common mistake is focusing only on major body controls, such as the root, hand IK, foot IK, and head. Many animators track arcs only on these key areas, which can create inconsistencies elsewhere in the body. True polish comes from analyzing the entire figure and understanding how forces flow through the character. Every joint, limb, and secondary motion contributes to the overall appeal of an animation.

Still a great resource for studying force and dynamic posing is *Force: Dynamic Life Drawing for Animators* by Michael Mattesi. Recommended for years in the *How to Cheat in Maya* series, this book explores how to create energy and flow within a pose — skills that translate directly into crafting smoother arcs in motion.

Let's take a look at arcs as they apply to a common animated moment that appears in TV, Film, and especially in Games: swinging an object.

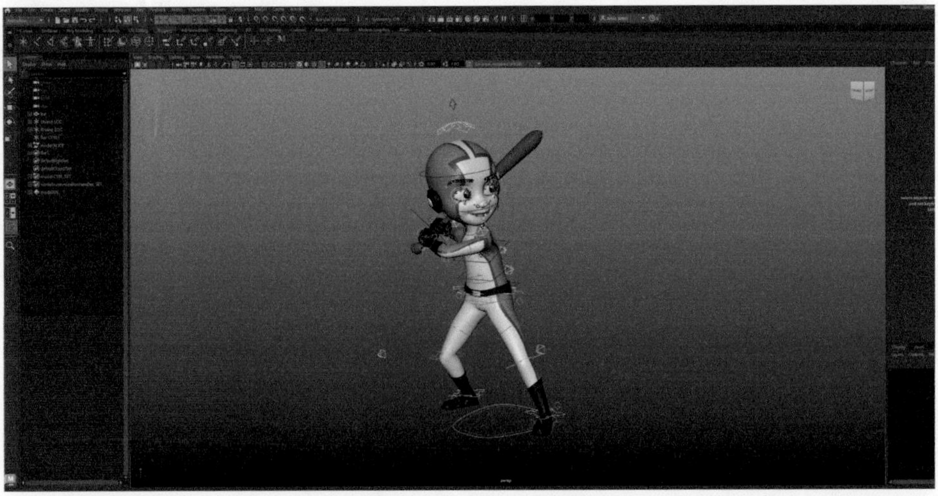

Open Arcs.ma. Here we have a blocked swing of a baseball bat. The animation is not finished, but we can demonstrate Arcs with this motion.

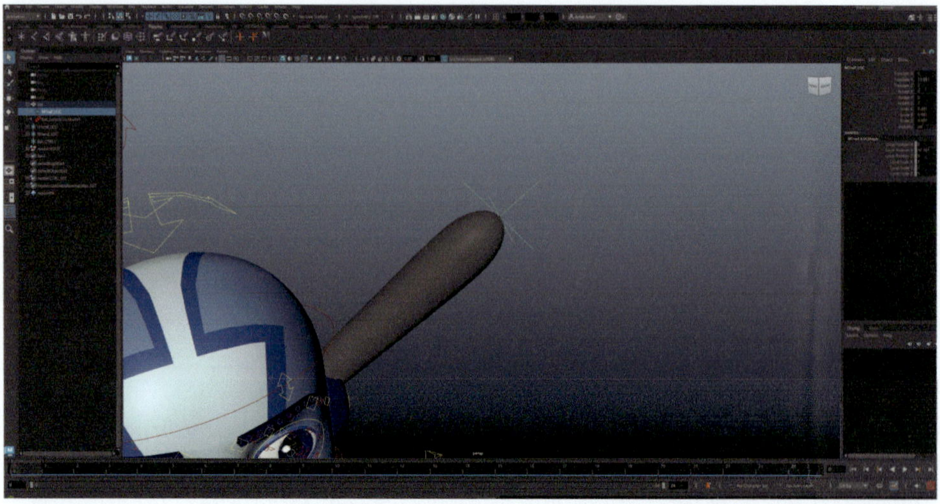

Select the locator called MTrail_LOC that is parented to the top of the bat.

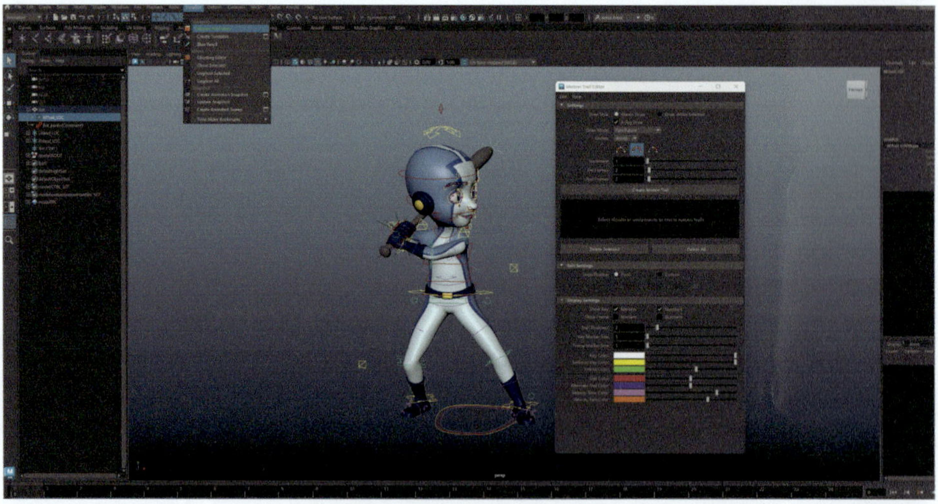

In the Animation menu set (F4), go to Visualize > Motion Trail Editor.

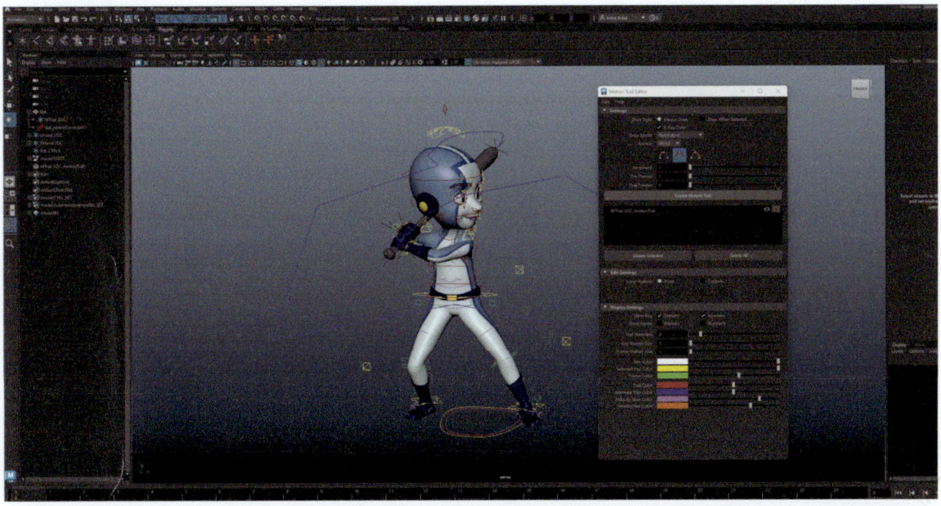

Leave all options at default and click on Create Motion Trail. A motion trail should appear like above.

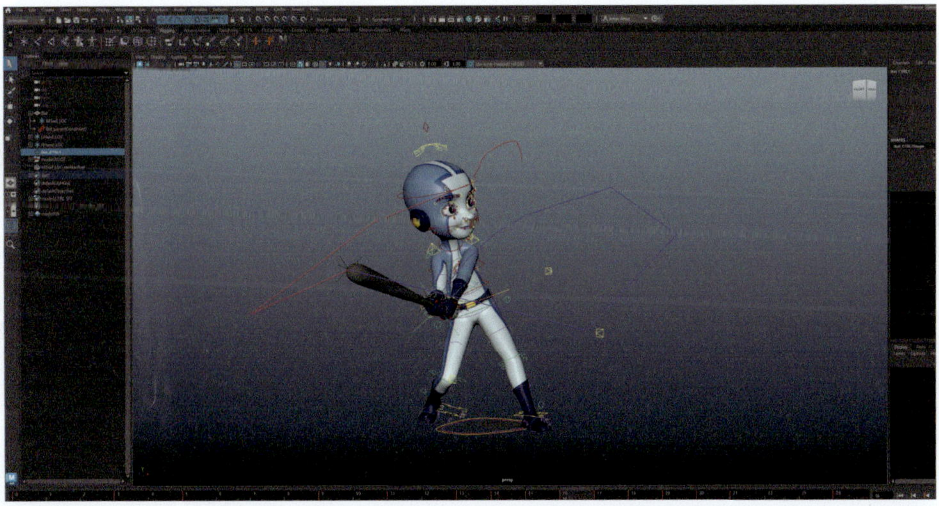

Yikes! The bat really has a nasty bump in its arc on frame 16. This may not stand out very much when played back but pro animators will correct it, knowing audiences can feel this bad arc.

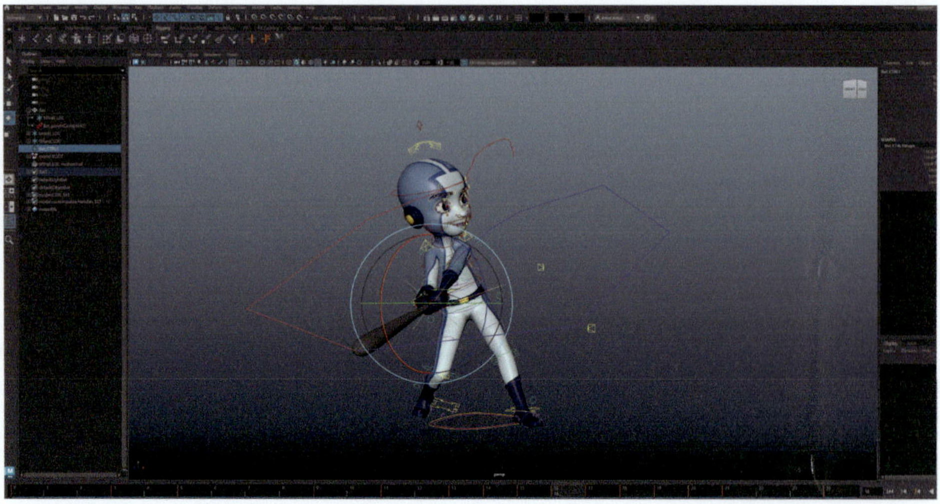

Select the locator called Bat_CTRL1, and rotate it in world space downward in the Rotate X direction on frame 16. There we go! Play the animation back, and you'll see a major improvement!

DON'T FORGET

Motion Trails are only editable if the object they are created from has translation keys on it. In this case, a separate locator was created and parented to the top of the bat to show its outermost arc. If we'd tried to add the trail to the bat itself, the trail would appear near the handle.

SECONDARY ACTION

This principle adds depth and subtext to a scene by introducing additional movements that support the primary action. Secondary actions do not distract from the main performance but instead enhance it by revealing more about the character's emotions, state of mind, or personality.

For example, if a character sharpens a pencil while complaining about their boss, the sharpening is a secondary action that reinforces their frustration. If a character casually runs their hand through their hair while turning from a mirror with a wink, the hand movement adds confidence and charm to an otherwise simple turn.

There is no strict limit to how much secondary action can be used, especially for human characters, who constantly multitask. However, balance is key; too many layered movements can clutter the animation and dilute its impact. The most skilled animators use secondary action to "color" a performance, adjusting pose, timing, and spacing to fit the subtext of a scene.

Consider a woman ironing clothes while looking out a window. If her husband enters and tells her their son has died in war, her ironing continues — but her hands tremble, her posture stiffens, and her movements become unsteady. The subtle changes in the ironing transform it into a window into her emotions. Now, imagine the same woman receiving different news; she just found out she is pregnant, but she hasn't told her husband yet. This time, when he casually asks about her day, her ironing might speed up with excitement, or she might pause briefly, staring at the tiny onesie she is ironing before responding. These variations in secondary action re-define the scene's meaning without altering a single word of dialogue.

A walk is just a walk, even with personality. Kayla looks happy and confident, but is there more to this story?

CHEAT

At a studio, animators will be asked to take on a huge variety of shots, most of which are described as very run-of-the-mill. In other words, it is your task to brainstorm some Secondary Action that you can use to plus-up your shots. Use this as an opportunity to shine!

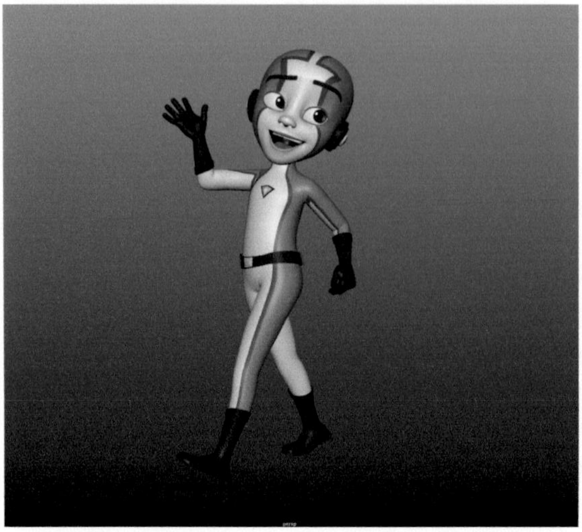

What a difference some Secondary makes! Kayla's little gesture solidifies her chipper demeanor and doesn't distract from her primary motion of the walk.

EXAGGERATION

Exaggeration is one of the most powerful yet frequently misunderstood animation principles. Many novice animators assume that exaggeration means simply making movements bigger and more extreme, but true exaggeration is about clarifying and enhancing the message of a scene. It does not automatically make animation more cartoony; it makes it more expressive.

The key is targeted exaggeration. Find the core idea of your scene and amplify the elements that reinforce it. If a character gets pricked by a pin, exaggerating the timing and spacing of their sudden reaction makes the pain feel sharper. If a character is startled by a spider, stretching their legs away from their torso can push the sense of fear. In both cases, the exaggeration is focused on a single aspect of the animation; trying to exaggerate everything at once (posing, timing, weight, composition) would create unnecessary complexity and weaken the impact.

Good animation in Maya should be lean and efficient, with minimal keyframes that allow for easy adjustments.

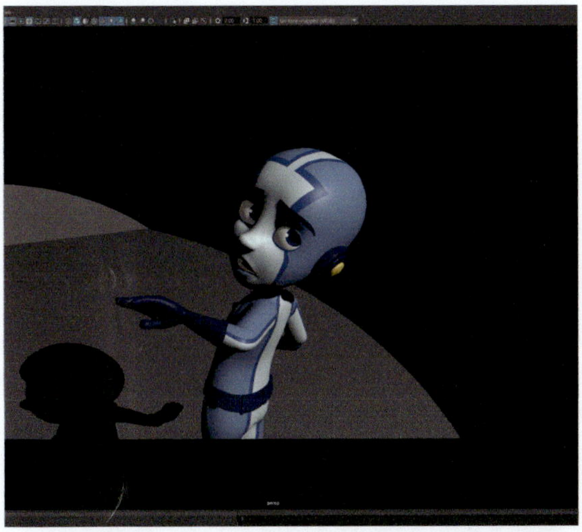

How spooky! Whatever is sneaking up on Kayla, it sure could use a little push in the right direction to sell the danger!

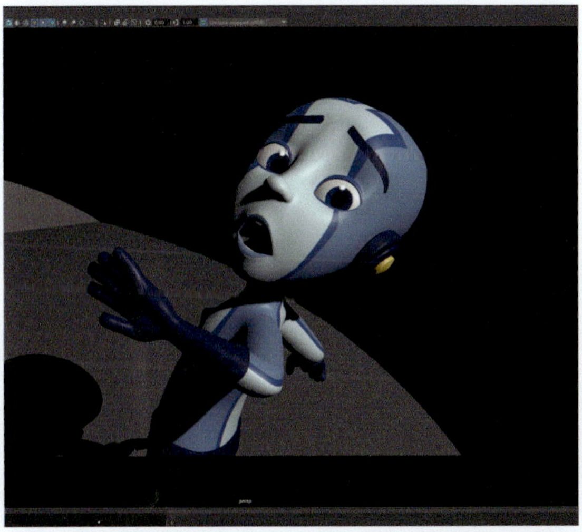

With a little push, the moment really pops. A little bit of over-the-top brow raise, exaggerated stretch in the spine, and the face pose given just a few tweaks make this scary moment all the stronger.

In some ways, to animate is to exaggerate. We use it a little in everything we do. Knowing when to use it and when to hold back is an essential skill of great animators.

SOLID DRAWING

At first glance, solid drawing might seem irrelevant to computer-generated (CG) animation. Since Maya is a 3D animation paradigm, what role does drawing play? In reality, this principle remains just as crucial in digital animation as it was in traditional cel animation. It reinforces core artistic skills such as posing, perspective, form, volume, and force. Ignoring these fundamentals can result in stiff, lifeless animation that lacks appeal.

In traditional animation, every frame had to be carefully drawn to maintain consistent proportions and perspective. Animators relied on simple construction techniques, ensuring each drawing followed a clear line of action, balanced weight, and strong silhouette. In CG, Maya helps maintain character consistency, but it does not guarantee strong posing or appealing motion. It is still up to the animator to avoid distortions, awkward perspectives, and unintended deformations.

A common mistake in CG is relying too much on the rig without understanding how its controls affect the model. Poorly tested rigs, improper use of controls, or careless posing can push a character off-model, making them look unnatural. While Maya can handle technical aspects like volume preservation, it is the animator's responsibility to maintain clear posing and a sense of weight.

CHEAT

Look for 'cartoony' controls on your rigs for ways to exaggerate poses and movements. They might be called bendy, stretchy, or even overdrive. And in 99 out of 100 cases, any scale channels available on body parts are there for exaggeration purposes!

The Kayla Rig is extremely versatile, chock-full of macro- and micro-controls to give animators amazing range for acting choices. This still frame looks like it could be from the middle of an expressive monologue.

But be careful! Many animators take the controls provided and push them too far. Just because there is range in the rigging, does not mean that the model falls within Solid Drawing.

Solid Drawing could be said to be even more applicable to 3D animation. Why? In hand-drawn animation, nothing came for free. Animators needed fundamental drawing skills to complete their work. When drawing itself was the entry-point to moving pictures, improving this core skill meant greater and greater understanding of the principle of Solid Drawing. In 3D though, we as animators need to make a conscious effort to remember this principle.

APPEAL

Appeal is such a broad and fundamental concept in animation that an entire book could be written on the subject alone. It goes beyond simply making things look "good" and instead focuses on creating visuals that are engaging, clear, and compelling. While this chapter cannot cover appeal in its entirety, we can examine some of its most significant contributors:

- **Strong Posing and Silhouettes:** A well-crafted pose is the foundation of appeal. Characters should have clear, dynamic silhouettes that instantly communicate action, emotion, and personality. Avoid awkward angles where limbs blend into the body or where foreshortening causes key details to disappear. A pose should be readable at a glance, even in thumbnail form.
- **Thoughtful Staging and Composition:** Appeal is not just about the character, it is also about how they are framed within the shot. A well-composed scene directs the viewer's eye to the most important elements while maintaining balance and visual interest. Avoid cluttered backgrounds that compete with the character, and use staging to reinforce the narrative.
- **Expressive Timing and Spacing:** Motion itself contributes to appeal. Well-paced timing creates rhythm, clarity, and entertainment value. Snappy, exaggerated movements add excitement, while slower, deliberate actions build tension and emotion. Avoid robotic or evenly spaced motion, as it quickly becomes dull and predictable.
- **Avoiding "Twinning" and Over-Symmetry:** Perfect symmetry can make a character feel unnatural and stiff. In nature, nothing is completely symmetrical, and appealing poses reflect that. Twinning, where both arms, legs, or facial features mirror each other, should be avoided. Asymmetry adds realism and personality to animation.
- **Personality and Subtext:** A character's appeal is not just visual — it is also tied to their personality and the emotions they convey. Every movement and expression should reflect their unique traits. A slight tilt of the head, a carefully timed glance, or a subtle shift in weight can add layers of depth and meaning.

An alternative cover design for this book. We opted for the one you see now, but isn't this one also appealing?

Appeal is the result of all of the artistic choices of an animator working together in unison. It is a balance of design, motion, composition, and storytelling. While there is no single formula for achieving it, consistently analyzing your work, getting feedback, and studying great animation will help sharpen your ability to create visually engaging and emotionally resonant performances.

CHEAT

The audience knows best! The absolute best advice you can get on animation is from the people you are trying to entertain. So, ask your family, friends, and strangers on the internet for feedback on your work constantly. You will feel your work improving as the reactions get more and more excited!

TIMING

Timing is not just a principle; it is the core of animation itself. It dictates when an action happens and how long it lasts, shaping everything from movement to emotion. Beyond making motion feel believable, timing plays a crucial role in storytelling. The right pauses, holds, and beats between actions can communicate more than movement alone ever could.

In character animation, timing is what makes an audience feel a performance. A well-timed hesitation can reveal uncertainty, while a lingering pause after failure can deepen the impact of a loss. It is easy to become so focused on mechanics that we forget timing is a storytelling tool as much as a technical one.

The way an action plays out over time can define a character's personality, mood, or intent. Think about how Buzz Lightyear whips and snaps into position, with military-like precision, compared to how loose and relaxed Woody is. There's no mistaking which toy is new to this world and taking his job too seriously, and which toy is a seasoned professional completely comfortable in his role. The perfect application of the principle of Timing directed the animator's choices with these character portrayals.
If Anticipation is thought, then Timing is thought in motion.

While this book does not provide a full curriculum on timing, we will experiment with Timing by adjusting a scene with Kayla turning around, terrified when she hears something behind her. Through a very simple adjustment, we can see two completely different directions for the shot.

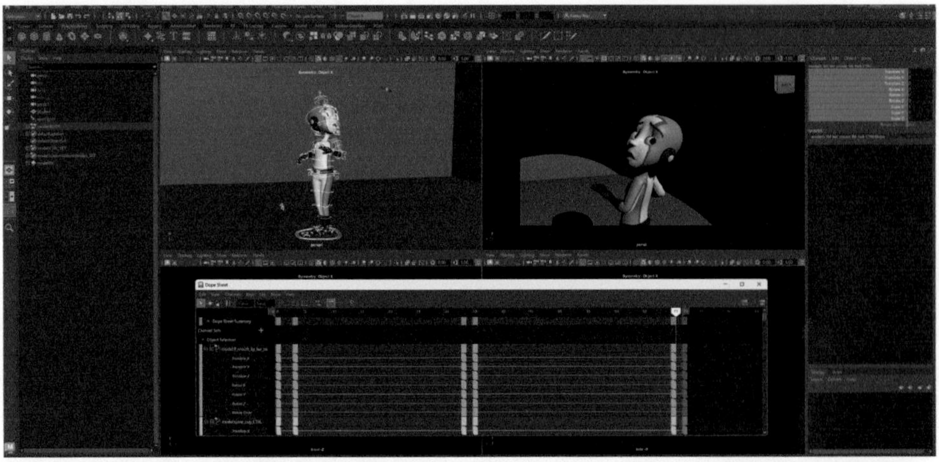

Open Timing.ma. Change your Selection Mask to Curves only, and select all of Kayla Bot's controls. Finally, open the Dope Sheet by going to Windows > Animation Editors > Dope Sheet.

This simple blocked scene has only three copied pairs in it, represented by the six key ticks at the top of the Dope Sheet that are arranged in three closely timed groups. For the purposes of this example, these copied pairs can be re-timed to create dramatically different effects.

Play the animation back, and see how the scene is timed currently to convey the idea that Kayla hears something and immediately starts slowly turning around. What drives that timing choice? Perhaps the animator wanted to convey her terror building as she turns to see what made the sound.

But, what if this was a misunderstanding on the part of the animator, and the direction is different? Imagine the direction was supposed to be building the tension by having the camera move in on the unsuspecting Kayla, and a sound triggers her to turn quickly in surprise!

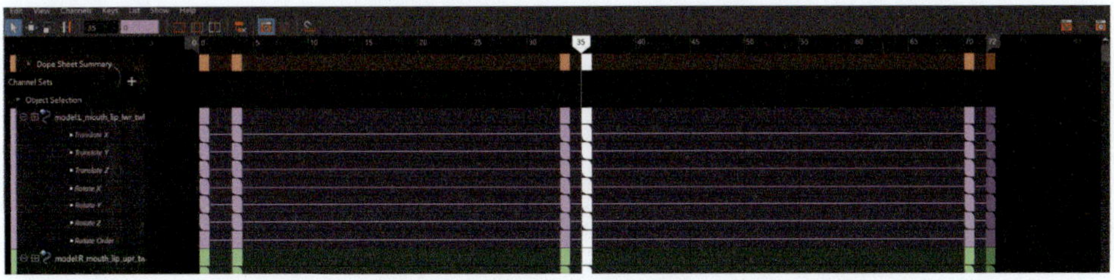

With all of the controls still selected, select the key in the Dope Sheet in the row labled "Dope Sheet Summary" that is on frame 35. These ticks in the Dope Sheet Summary represent ALL of the keys in the Dope Sheet. When you click it and press W to move, all of the keys beneath it should be highlighted white.

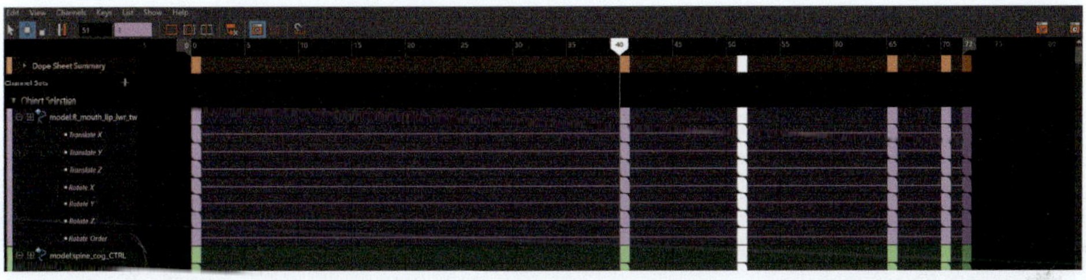

Ignoring the first and last keys in the scene, arrange the 2nd, 3rd, and 4th Dope Sheet Summary keys to be on frames 40, 51, and 65, respectively. Play back the animation.

A completely different performance emerges from just a simple adjustment of the timing. The intention, character thought process, and reaction all changed dramatically from tweaking the timing. With practice, this workflow of trying different timings can be incorporated into your blocking and you can achieve fast results with minimal work.

DON'T FORGET

The terms Timing and Spacing are sometimes used interchangeably but they mean different things. Timing is WHEN an action happens. It's the starting, speed, duration, and halting of motion to emphasize and support the performance. Spacing is HOW the action happens. It's how the positioning of the objects and posing of the characters throughout the visual scene space impact that timing decision, control the arcs, and affect the director's decisions.

AI

Before motion capture was omnipresent in animation, industry veterans quaked at the thought of their jobs being replaced by a technology looming on the horizon. We've been here before. Throughout history, technological advances have made us painfully aware of just how tenuous our control is over our livelihoods. So, as the field of generative AI starts to garner mainstream attention, we should be aware of the impact it will have on our craft. The pace has been astonishing; in only a few years, generative AI went from soupy images of 100-toothed ghouls looking simultaneously ecstatic and tortured, to video and illustrations nearly indistinguishable from the real thing. As of writing, early generative video examples bear striking resemblance to reality, and it's just going to get better. It can be dangerous to opine at the early stages of a technology, as time will prove you either prescient, or panicked. But I'm going to go for it!

Take note that the ethics of internet scraping, copyright and ownership, and environmental impact of training AI models are not part of this discussion. I would snap it out of existence had I the chance, but we can all only do our part.

In the early days of mocap, the general concern was that animators would lose their jobs because a studio could fire all their animators and then simply mocap all the performances in a film or TV show. This caused great alarm, because it framed the technology as a replacement for both current standards and means of production.
I was of the opposite opinion; mocap would create jobs. And it did. We saw many shows, films, games, etc. all come to fruition solely because of the availability of mocap. On a vast majority of projects to this day (when millimeter and millisecond mocap is the norm), animators are still hired to clean up the work. In addition, animators are needed to hand-key all non-human characters, and when a shot is too dangerous for actors to perform. More to the point, mocap created an ecosystem where new entrants to the industry could consider using the technology to initiate a project that was previously too expensive.

A producer with a small budget who wanted to do a film with many digital humanoid characters could now do it; before, a studio would turn them away. In most cases, lowering the technological bar for low-end entrants to an industry creates jobs.
My prediction is that we are going to continue to see AI illustration and video expand to take over the lowest tiers of advertising and media campaigns. We'll see generative AI animation continue to iterate, and it will be able to produce more and more stable results and more character consistency over a span of a few shots. Tools are emerging that can generate humanoid motion data for

skeletons, and correct for weight and pose of hand-keyed motion according to libraries of human motion data. These will evolve into tools that even the lay-user can pilot to produce acceptable results for human motion.

What we will not see, at least soon, are fully rendered results stable enough to be tweaked on a per-pixel or per-frame basis. For now, these models are only capable of rearranging pixels based on prompts that draw from massive data sets to create a fancy "likeliest neighboring pixel" image or video. Even low-end TV episodic animation requirements are too strict for this methodology of generation.
Until a supervisor can look at an animation of a puppy jumping over a daisy and say "make it 5 frames longer, and make him smile and wink when he lands", these tools aren't ready for primetime. If you tried that today with prompting, you would be generating for hours as the cub does hundreds of various jumps and winks (or doesn't wink) at various wrong times. For an animator, those tweaks would be a few minutes of work.

What I believe we ARE going to see are things like online marketing companies that already churn out 100 videos a month starting to mix in AI animated content, small restaurant chains adding an animated version of their restaurant's mascot in their commercials, local news having an animated character in their announcement of the yearly local blood drive. In all of the above examples, there were no animators employed to do this work before AI.
The ability to have animated content was never in the budget. In other words, these are new entrants attracted by generative AI, not high-end vfx and animation companies replacing artists with machines. Jobs lost: 0.
Unfortunately, the same cannot be said for concept artists and visual artists. Even texturing has been infiltrated. As of the time of writing (which is a lifetime away from publishing on the scale of technology), there are artists lamenting their workplaces integrating AI into the pipeline, job postings for AI prompt writers, and major companies being caught using gen AI in ads
I can only imagine in another year how much the technology is going to improve, at the expense of visual artists' livelihood. Hopefully, the models can be retrained to attribute work, and pay artists a share of the platform proceeds, like Spotify. But I digress.

Being afraid of technology is hardly serving, but similarly being ignorant to its impact can mean being left behind. I don't think the sky is falling for animators, but at the same time we should try to meaningfully engage and assist our still-image brethren in the overarching fight against unethical AI.

3 THE THIRTEENTH PRINCIPLE

ANIMATING WITH TEMPO

What Is Tempo?

For novice animators and working professionals facing ever-tightening deadlines, it is imperative to know how to best start an animation to set it up for success. Over the course of many years observing students and juniors in learning and studio settings, it is apparent that many workflows taught in schools fall short when it comes to creating an overall awareness of the lifespan of a shot. In other words, animators following workflows carried over from cel animation are not seeing the forest for the trees.

Let's take a brief step back and describe the origins of the typical 3D character animation workflow and how it evolved.

In the beginning, "key" animators were tasked with drawing key frames. Then, an in-betweener filled in the missing frames based on timing directions provided on the page. It is important to note that aside from "flipping" (putting pages between your fingers and rapidly turning them), timing could not be accurately checked as the animator worked. Instead, they waited until the drawn frames were shot onto film, the film developed, and then projected a day or so later. "Dailies" got their name literally from the fact that the film shooting and developing process could only take place on a daily basis. As keyframing was a senior's task, timing itself was understood to be an intuitive process, not an iterative one. So, to create what would hopefully become great timing, animators pored over extremely thoughtfully drawn, exaggerated, dynamic poses. Posing was everything.

With the invention of video, animators around the world were ecstatic; one could block out a sequence in the morning and watch it back that afternoon. Timing choices started to get more experimental, dynamic, and groundbreaking. The 90s Disney masterpieces kicked off the incorporation of digital filmmaking techniques and 3D imagery. The computer was becoming a major part of the cel animation workflow, but it was in 1995 with Pixar's *Toy Story* that the world changed forever; 3D animation finally stood on its own.

Animators could suddenly create an entire performance digitally, in a medium (computer) featuring instantaneous playback. Even the process of rendering a preview that took a few minutes was a 99.9% savings of time compared to 2D workflows. The point is, animators were suddenly unshackled from trying to inflect interesting timing to a shot by relying on initial posing to guide the shot all the way through to finish.

Unfortunately though, the 3D renaissance didn't mean traditional animation methods were completely re-evaluated. On the contrary, either out of reverence or deference, old master's cel animation workflows were religiously guarded. Adherence to cel workflows (and the resulting pain of forcing this workflow on a computer) were worn as badges of honor.

Creating key poses in 3D and then in-betweening like a cel animator is like making the lid for a clay pot before you even shape it. It's like putting three teaspoons of salt into a mixing bowl when inventing a brand new dish, before you can taste any of the ingredients in combination. It's like deciding the exact spot on stage a dancer will land after the final leap, before you've choreographed the first step.

To summarize, with cel animation, posing necessarily carried a huge burden of communicating timing to the in-betweeners because the technology to iterate timing choices did not exist. When the computer arrived, we failed as an industry to reassess this approach. The results? Two generations of 3D animators fighting themselves by posing complex rigs as their "blocking" phase. Animators focused too closely on generating thumbnails they follow religiously to the final version of the shot. Storyboards lacking camera awareness, and reference video replacing nearly the entire early exploration phase of a shot during which dynamic movement is found. Novice animators are led to believe that by strictly adhering to these setup steps, their shots will turn out great, so it's no wonder many beginners quit when their shots fall short of expectation after spending so much effort on planning. The precious hours in the early life of a shot are when we are supposed to freely experiment and hone in on the perfect timing for a shot.

These hours are being lost.

What is apparent to teachers is these planning steps all lack a jumping-off point for creating amazing timing that will last through the lifespan of an animation. This is really unfortunate, because by working so closely to the shot in the beginning, following a rigid workflow that is primarily pose-based, animators set themselves up for huge difficulty without even realizing it.

After years of experimenting with a breakthrough approach, it was time to officially codify "Tempo" — a blocking workflow with so much power that it is boldly presented as **The Thirteenth Principle.**

HOW TO ANIMATE WITH TEMPO

The premise is simple: establish absolutely the strongest timing foundation as early as possible. Ignore posing. In fact, ignore the rig; strip the shot down to pure motion. Regardless of your comfort level and expertise in Maya, start with a humble cube.

Using a cube as a stand-in for your character allows you to concentrate entirely on establishing the raw movement through space without being bogged down by foot placement, deformation issues, or controller management. In this stage, your sole focus is on when and where the character moves; the beats of the shot, the spacing between those beats, and the energy of the action.

Set the Tempo: Identify the major storytelling moments in the shot. If it's a jump, this means takeoff, peak, and landing. If it's a punch, it's anticipation, impact, and follow-through. Set these broad moments using only translation keys on the cube.

Refine the Timing: Play the animation frequently and make big changes without fear of breaking anything. Shift keys around, adjust spacing, and experiment with different pacing choices. The goal is to make the movement feel right before committing to anything else. Since you are using a cube and not a full character rig and can press Alt+V to playback in-panel, even the tiny amount of time it takes to playblast is saved.

Introduce Contact and Follow Through: Even without limbs, you can indicate weight shifts, impacts, and reactions. If a character is landing, does the cube settle slightly? If they come to a stop, does it overshoot by a few frames before stabilizing? These are small but crucial details that give the movement believability before any posing happens.

Iterate Until It Feels Right: This is the most important step. Because there are no poses, no breakdowns, and minimal keys, every adjustment is easy. You are free to test new rhythms, exaggerate timing choices, or tweak the spacing, all without destroying a carefully posed rig.

Only once the timing is locked in should you reference the character rig and start posing. Then, you are simply building on an already solid foundation rather than fighting to correct timing issues after the fact. The Tempo phase is where you refine the soul of the movement, ensuring that every action feels natural, intentional, and alive.

The Guillotine

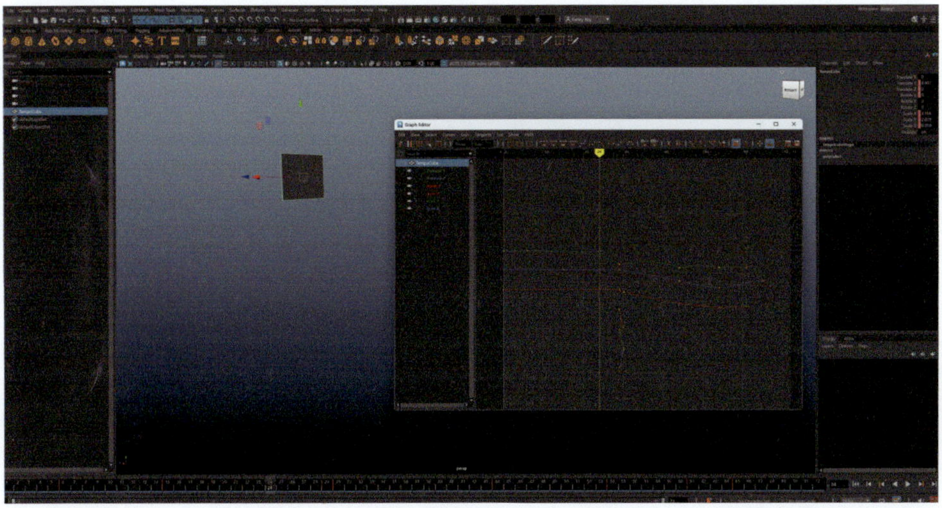

Open Guillotine.ma. Open the Graph Editor and see how few keys are in the scene.

In this very simple scene, we demonstrate how economical you can be with your keys when using Tempo. The shot is simple; a guillotine blade starts at the top of the screen, releases, and comes sliding down. It hits the bottom and lops the head off its victim. The head goes popping into the air and tumbling down onto the ground below, bouncing a few times before settling.

There's a few fun Tempo tricks going on here. First, the cube represents two different animated objects in the scene, the blade and the head. Second, with so few keys, it's quite simple to adjust the entire timing of the shot.

Using the Graph Editor, take a few moments to try to elongate the start of the blade falling — maybe you want to create an even bigger moment of tension as it starts to move, giving the audience a chance to realize what is about to happen.

Try to change the shot to have the severed head do a very plateaued pause in the air — perhaps this is the climax of a comedy, when the robot villain delivers his catch-phrase as his head pops up into the air. Adjusting the arc of the cube Translate Y to be flat achieves this. The takeaway here is that with an extremely simple start to your scene, experimenting with timing using the Graph Editor is simple and powerful.

Legitimate timing explorations are possible even with as few as a dozen keyframes.

If this is your first time using Tempo, it might feel strange editing sparse keys to attempt to change the entire feeling of a shot. The truth is, blocking a shot by conventional methods typically means that one's mindset is geared towards copying thumbnails and reference video, and it can feel pretty strange to be animating without a rig. How freeing is it though, to be finalizing timing as your first step? And, can you imagine now how simple it would be to replace these objects with your thumbnail poses?

WATCH OUT!

To show all the keys in the scene, we are using the Stacked View in the Graph Editor (Press the 2 key with Graph Editor Open). This may not look like your Graph Editor if you are in Normal View.

The Golf Swing

Let's continue with examples of how well Tempo can make honing in on the beats of your shot quick and easy.

Like before, we'll start with just a humble cube. The idea is to have the cube timed to clearly delineate the beats of the shot. For this shot, we're going for comedic effect; a golfer approaches the ball at the beginning of the scene, takes two tiny practice swings, wiggles their hips, and then goes for the drive. Important for this scene is a little bit of distinction between the little tiny practice swings (even as small as they are, they should not be identical). This is very easy to play with when blocking with Tempo. Then, the little hip wiggle signals to the audience that the golfer is gearing up for something. Before we can guess what that is, they really wind up and give the ball a huge smack.

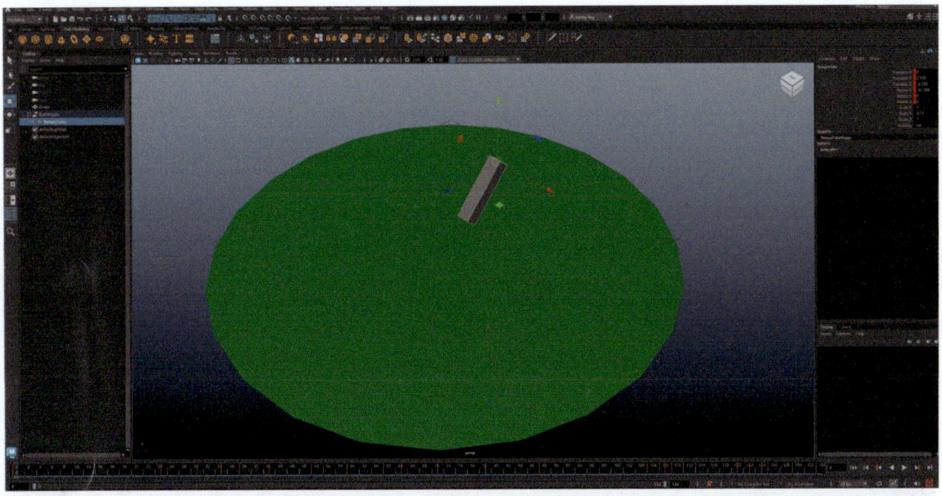

Open Golf.ma. Play back the animation, seeing if the beats called out in the paragraph above are clear.

Hopefully, imagining the character doing all of the actions we described is straightforward. Though it's only a few keys again, this Tempo pass has everything needed for an animator to now come along and pose the rig according to reference and thumbnails, timed as directed here.

The Graph Editor isn't the only tool that is great for making broad adjustments and experimenting early. The Dope Sheet is equally powerful for re-timing large sections as it is for making frame-by-frame adjustments to a Tempo pass.

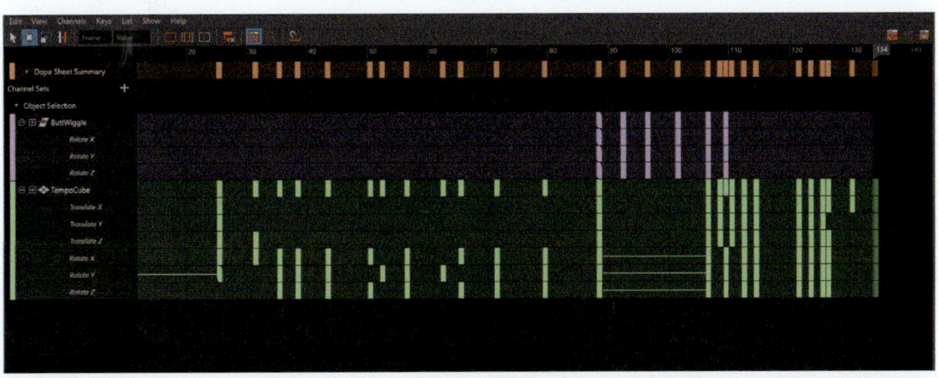

Select all of the objects in the Outliner, and open the Dope Sheet by clicking Windows > Animation Editors > Dope Sheet. Notice how sparse the scene is?

The really cool thing about the Dope Sheet is how it lets you select all keys on a frame and move them, at greater speed and efficiency than the Time Slider. Even scaling entire sections using the Scale tool in the Dope Sheet enables lightspeed workflow.

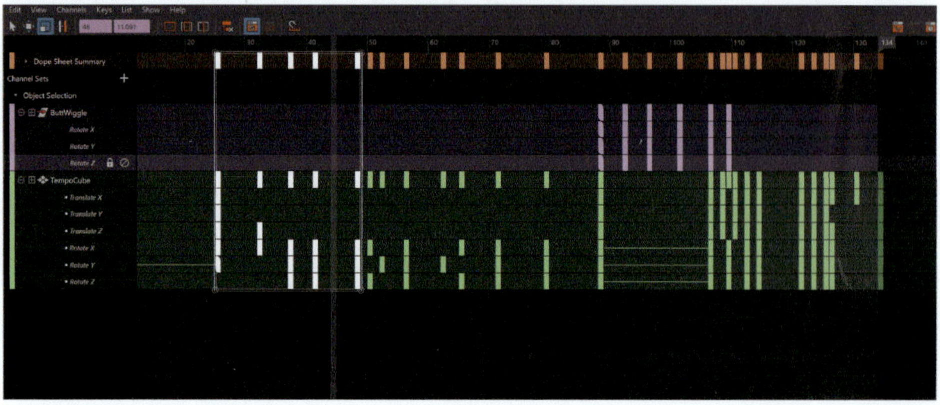

The scale tool is super powerful in the Dope Sheet — retiming entire sections in just a few clicks.

What you may have noticed is that there is another object with keys in the scene: ButtWiggle. This aptly named group node was added to make the section of the little anticipation hip shake easy to add and edit. It's not uncommon when using Tempo to have a few parent nodes to make moments like this easy to create. No rigger is looking over your shoulder making sure you have not broken something! Take a fearless approach to the Tempo Workflow.

Using the Dope Sheet, spend some time adjusting the duration and spacing of the beats of this scene. But here's what you should do to build on your understanding from the last exercise: do not decide in advance what effect you are going for before you move some keys around. Grab entire sections and scale them. Lengthen the swing by 20 frames. Cut it by 15. Make rapid edits, and then play back the animation to see the effect. Become an audience to your own work.

Perhaps you are starting to get a sense of play with Tempo? That is good. Doing this properly will train you to be more flexible with your workflow, and able to experiment to find happy accidents. All before touching a single character control.

DON'T FORGET

It's not about the cleanliness of the keys. Animate frame by frame if you need to; nothing needs to be smoothed or polished. Tempo provides a framework for quick and accurate timing, nothing more.

Sneaking Scared

Let's get a little more advanced. So far, we've looked at extremely simple timed scenes that have quite an indicative set piece or prop that telegraphs a lot of the action. The guillotine and golf club do some heavy lifting. What about a scene that has very little of that? Not every shot relies on such tell-tale moments.

Tempo is great for scenes like the below: a character sneaking around, noticing a booby trap, getting scared and running off. These types of scenes suffer greatly with some traditional workflows for a few reasons:

1. The key poses that one might thumbnail for this shot might have body mechanics such as footfalls to consider, and without meticulous planning (or an innate sense of how to time the beats amidst complex body mechanics), the thumbnails might bear little resemblance to the poses you end up with. In the fight between thumbnail poses and great timing, the loser is almost always great timing.
2. Blocking slowly moving characters (especially against camera movement) is notoriously fraught with peril. How many breakdowns are not enough? How many is too many? If done first with a character rig, blocking a slow moving section almost always turns out putting the animator in a position to wrestle with mistimed moments.
3. The fallback for these types of shots is heavy video reference. While reference is absolutely our recommendation, it is meant to be used as a guide and not a template. If all of your beats are set by your video reference and then 'pushed' later, it is the opposite direction of the flow of information that animation is meant to go in. In other words, we are supposed to discover incredible timing, fall in love with it, and then use video reference to 'fill in the blanks' of the beats we've established.

Let's take a look at the scene and see how Tempo creates a really solid timing foundation for us to then fill with great posing, silhouette, and secondary.

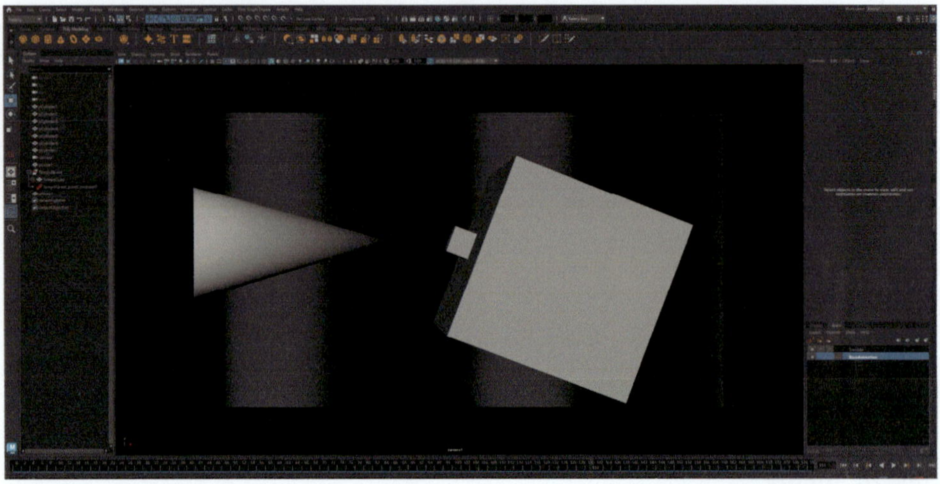

Open Sneak.ma. Play the Tempo pass back and imagine how you could fill this scene in with poses quite simply.

It might come as no surprise that this scene took less than 30 minutes to throw together. There are sections with some frame-by-frame happening (in the scramble out of frame), and that's ok. As long as the impression you are aiming for is clear, there are no rules! Key with abandon.

There's another nice little setup happening in this scene: the camera move. It's easy to get deep in the weeds when trying to block a camera move against the character movement. The problems begin when trying to set accurate footfalls, then figuring out how the character will keep up with the camera move. The problems continue as you try to keep beats delineated, but there is timing you've set at the start which may not be compatible with these beats. On and on, the problems mount, and tracking camera shots can make you burn out. With Tempo, you just keep cracking at the timing, making sure to keep keys sparse as you initially work out the movement. Refine as you go, and use all the tools at your disposal to improve the communication of the beats.

This scene has another nice little trick with Animation Layers as well.

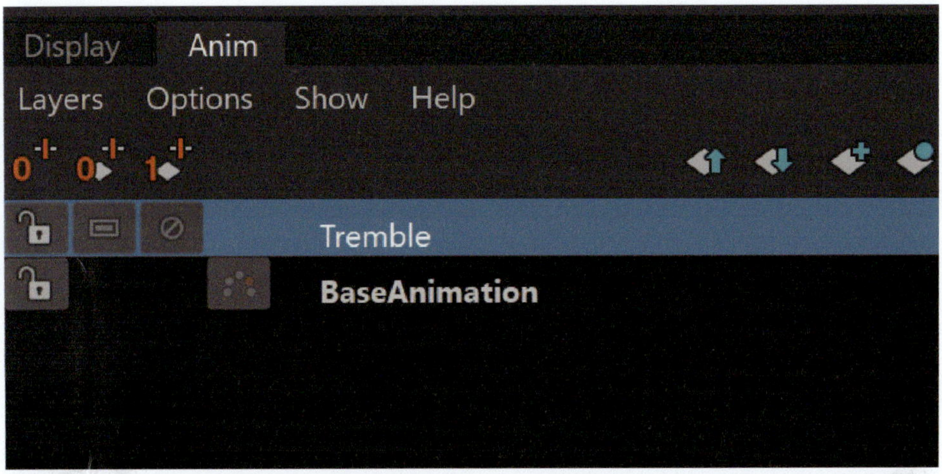

Select the Tremble animation layer in the Anim tab of the Channel Box / Layer Editor.

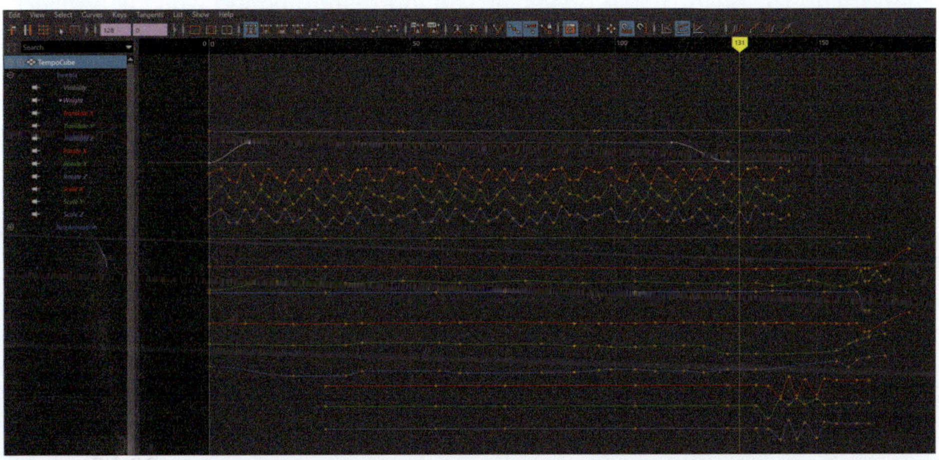

Open the Graph Editor. Notice there are keys in this layer and they are noisy. Also notice there are keyframes on the Weight attribute.

Recall that the beats of this scene were sneaking, noticing the trap, and then skittering off. We do not want to lose those beats, which is common when trying to incorporate small movements into blocking. So to preserve the beats and make it easier to dial this texture in later, we use an animation layer. This would be over the top for a blocking pass normally, but fine for a Tempo pass. You may also notice that the weight is not keyed at 1 — this is because the trembling was keyed willy-nilly, then toned down to the more subtle level it is now.

Animation Layers put the ability to really try out some crazy ideas early on in your shot! Throw some crazy experiments into a layer, and toss it out if it's no good. You can only have happy accidents, if you have a lot of accidents to begin with...

Slip on Ice

Animation is like fishing. If you always start by dropping your hook in the water just in front of you, and try to push it toward the fish, you will never quite get there. However, if you cast your line past the fish, and slowly reel it in, you will find the perfect spot to catch the big one. As animators, we struggle sometimes to "push" the work to the point of it being great. Could it be that this is purely the result of a workflow based on "inputting" our poses from reference and thumbnails all in a row (directly in front of us), then trying to "push" these poses into an interesting timing while wrangling with the rig and scene?

To find that beautifully pushed timing, our contention is that the process cannot simply be to start at zero and have the lifespan of the shot be "pushing" endlessly. There needs to be some "pull". And to have a moment where one has to pull back, you need to first go too far. Tempo allows you to shoot for the moon as your first step. It provides the freedom to explore uncharted territory with your timing. So let loose!

In our last shot to examine Tempo, we're going to look at a shot that has a really pushed moment, to demonstrate just how important finding the extremes early in the shot can be for amazing timing. The beats are:

- A character is running in the snow
- They run onto a frozen lake and slide to a slow stop
- They think they are safe and venture a step
- But their feet fly out from underneath them, and they smack onto their back.

Open Ice.ma and play the Tempo pass. By now you are familiar with what this is meant to communicate, so you should be able to clearly read the beats as described above.

One of the first decisions made was on what frame the character arrives at the ice. Once that was set (frame 57), we back out of that moment with some great, poppy, plateaued arcs on the running section.

This scene is simple but it demonstrates a lot. Let's talk about the exaggerated entrance and run cycle to the pond. When the scene begins, the character is off-screen. We went with a large leap onto screen to create an impact. This was tweaked with a single key on the Translate X channel. Find it on frame 15, and play around with the value and tangent and see if you find a new effect that you like better.

Notice how the advice was not to first think about an effect you'd like, then try to achieve it! We are specifically saying to play with the keys and watch the results without judgment, experimenting around and learning to make big changes to timing early in your shot!

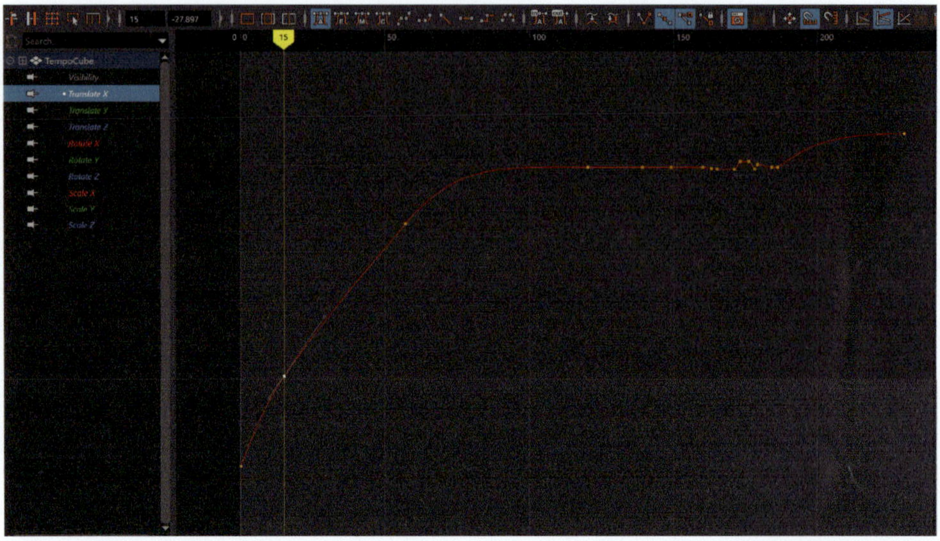

This one keyframe establishes the energy of the shot right out of the gate. Think about how much opportunity there is to make radical timing adjustments to the shot if you stay in the Tempo pass for a while playing around!

Let's discuss how we treated the scramble. There's obviously no feet in this shot, but we added a little bit of a trick to the scene to create some frenetic energy as the character starts slipping. Look in the Outliner for the Feet object. This is merely a group that is keyed Visibility off during the first part, then keyed visible as the character takes a careful step. Inside this group, there are boxes with some looping animation going every which way. The intended effect is to have the viewer "feel" there are feet slipping out from underneath them. Is this meant to be a guide for posing? No, on the contrary, this is an addition that is meant specifically to remind the animator later about the goals for the scramble beat. Namely, keep the limbs flailing as the character whips around off-balance before finally flipping backward into the air. The final poses for the limbs during this wild moment will bear no resemblance to what was set here, only the timing.

CHEAT

Create as many objects as you want to help sell the beats. Squash, stretch, flip, slide, bend and break your geometry to get the perfect foundation as best you can. Just like these silly little feet sell the frantic nature of the slip and fall, you are unbridled when it comes to your shots when animating with Tempo!

This group is packed with cheats to give the impression of the character's frantic scramble to keep balance. Use of Post-Infinity Curve interpolation, stepped keys on the group parent to reorient the moving cubes, and animated visibility. Tempo is amazing for cartoony exploration because cheats like those applied here save hours and hours of posing.

The shot has a clear foundation, snappy timing, and interesting beats that can be filled with dramatic posing and great silhouette. By now, it should be readily apparent just how much flexibility and versatility animating with Tempo can be.

CHEAT

Since Tempo uses a cube or other helper object to create the motion, Motion Trails work naturally with this workflow for setting great arcs early!

WHAT WE'VE LEARNED

The Tempo workflow fundamentally reshapes how animators should approach a shot. Rather than treating timing as something that emerges from posing, Tempo prioritizes timing as the foundation and builds everything else on top of it. This shift eliminates many of the common struggles animators face when working in CG: floaty movement, weak accents, stiff blocking, and overly constrained animation that lacks energy.

Here's why Tempo is a superior approach compared to traditional pose-first blocking:

1. **Stronger Timing Decisions from the Start**
   Timing is the lifeblood of good animation, yet many animators only start addressing it once their blocking is nearly complete. The problem? By that point, changing timing requires redoing entire sequences of animation. Tempo eliminates this issue by letting you explore the perfect timing first, ensuring that everything flows naturally before committing to complex poses.
2. **Fewer Revisions and Less Wasted Effort**
   One of the biggest inefficiencies in CG animation is the constant re-blocking of shots due to weak timing choices. Animators often pose their shots meticulously, only to realize later that something feels wrong; but at that stage, revising means fighting existing animation, wrangling a spaghetti Graph Editor, all while struggling to maintain clarity. With Tempo, you finalize the rhythm of the shot early, dramatically reducing the need for later revisions.
3. **Eliminating the "Rig Struggle" Early On**
   Anyone who has animated complex CG rigs knows the pain of fighting the rig instead of animating. Too many shots start with an animator wrestling a character into the right pose, rather than exploring the motion itself. Tempo sidesteps this completely; by using a simple helper object, you remove rig complexity entirely and focus purely on how the movement feels.
4. **More Freedom to Experiment**
   When you start with poses, you're already locking yourself into a specific performance before knowing if it truly works. Tempo keeps the early stages of animation fluid, letting you iterate quickly, try different beats, and refine ideas without being restricted by existing poses. This results in more creative, dynamic movement because you're free to play with motion rather than build from rigid posing.

5. **Reducing Over-Reliance on Reference Video**
   While reference video is a powerful tool, many novice animators become too dependent on it by treating it as a rigid roadmap rather than a guide. They key poses are based purely on what they see in their video, without understanding why the movement works. Tempo allows animators to establish strong timing first, then apply reference selectively, ensuring that the movement is crafted rather than mimicked.
6. **Encouraging a More Natural Feel**
   One of the most common critiques of CG animation is that it can feel too clean and mechanical: overly interpolated, mathematically spaced, and lacking the organic imperfections that make movement feel alive. Tempo helps fix this by allowing animators to craft the rhythm of a shot first, ensuring the motion feels dynamic before adding in the details.

FINAL THOUGHTS: THE POWER OF TEMPO

For decades, animators have inherited workflows that were designed for a different medium with different limitations. Pose-based blocking worked in 2D animation because there was no way to iterate timing efficiently. But in CG, where instantaneous feedback is possible, there is no reason to treat timing as something that emerges late in the process.

Tempo represents a fundamental shift in how we approach animation; one that prioritizes the single most important aspect of a shot: movement over time. By integrating Tempo into your workflow, you are freeing yourself from unnecessary struggles. You are no longer trapped by early decisions, no longer reworking shots endlessly, and no longer forcing yourself to make poses work that were never timed properly in the first place.

The best animators in the world are not the ones who simply make beautiful poses; they are the ones who understand how to sculpt time itself. Tempo is the key to doing exactly that.

So start your next shot not by posing, but by moving. Let the rhythm dictate the energy. Let the motion tell the story. Because when you get the timing right, everything else falls into place.

Begin By Testing

Test your rigs before starting animation! Rig testing means going through all the controls to get an idea of what's available, where controls are located, and what the limits are. At large studios, rigs and naming conventions will be standardized for the most part. But as a student or a contract animator, you will come across many rigs and they will all be different. I've come across rigs labeled in French, Portuguese, and Turkish. All rigs will have similar parts, but rigging controls can vary widely in their appearance, locations and organization, so it's up to you to familiarize yourself before work begins.

REFERENCE YOUR RIG!

Always reference the rig into the scene. Do not open or import rigs into a working scene.

What's wrong with opening or importing? It inserts a copy of the rig file directly into the scene file. Every time you save, you are making a copy of the scene file and rig file. The animation will be directly on the copied rig file. This will be a problem if the rig needs to be swapped out. Animation will have to be copied over to the controls of the new rig manually or by script. Also, it will greatly increase the file size.
When referencing a rig into a parent scene, it does not embed the rig file, but instead it makes a pointer to the original rig file in the project folder. This reference point allows for easy reloading, swapping, or replacing the rig without losing any animation. In professional environments, referencing the rig is required because rig updates do happen during production after animation has begun. If anything happens to break the rig, the original rig file will not be affected, and the reference can be reloaded. The scene files with references are much smaller. Heavy complex set and environment models will also be referenced into a parent scene to keep the scene files small. It gives the animators the flexibility to load and unload assets as needed and other artists the ability to keep working while animation has begun.

To reference a rig, go to File > Create Reference, or hotkey Ctrl + R, and use the File Browser to navigate to the rig file in the project assets folder.

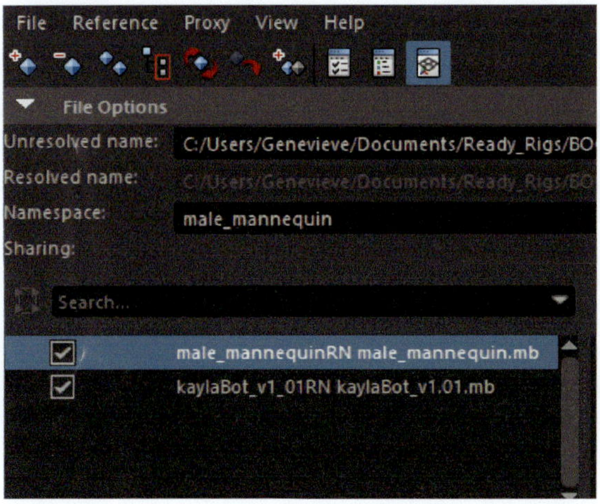

Go to File > Reference Editor to manage the referenced rigs. The rigs will be listed with a check box next to them. Unload a reference without losing any information or animation by unchecking the box. Then re-check to load.

Under the Reference menu, there are options to load, replace, remove, and lock referenced files. Replacing the rig is useful if there is an updated version of the rig with a different namespace. Replacing the rig can often fix issues where the rig has been unintentionally altered or broken.

WATCH OUT!

Do not change the name of the rig file! Maya will reference the newly named rig, but it will not connect the animation that points to a rig with a different namespace. This can be fixed with editing namespaces or sometimes replacing the rig. However, it is easier for everyone if you do not change the name of the rig.

4 MAXIMIZING YOUR RIGS

CONTROLS AND ANATOMY

Everyone has been observing people and animals all their life. The audience will feel when the weight and body mechanics are incorrect. They may not be able to articulate why a movement seems wrong. Maybe they can't even identify a single thing that looks wrong, but subconsciously they can recognize something that either doesn't look right or feel right. The last thing we want to do as animators is break the audience's suspension of disbelief and take them out of the story.

As animators, we need a fundamental understanding of anatomy and physics. Even cartoony animation is just impossibly extreme exaggerations of a character's body to match the natural movements and properties of different materials and objects. For example, if I stretch my character like a rubber band, I am still respecting the physics of a real rubber band. There is still an understanding of weight, gravity, physics, and volume to make your cartoony animation appealing and entertaining.

Most rigs are constructed to function like the real skeletons of humans or animals. This allows animators to move the character like their real-world counterparts. However, in 3D, we can move the joints in infinite ways that we can't do in nature. With a good understanding of anatomy, you can make believable motion, but also know when and how to break the rules for effect.

Finally, the most important thing when approaching rig controls is we have to make it look like all parts of the body are working together.

Breaking the Rig

Because our characters are virtual puppets in a computer, we can move them in ways that cannot be done in the real world. Breaking the rig happens when we move a control to the point where the geometry pinches, twists, tears, intersects, turns inside out, or the controls and connected controls become non-functional. It is usually visually obvious and quite unappealing. The rig has been pushed too far and it must be fixed. Sometimes a different approach to the controls is needed to get a similar pose.
Going off model is where the controls have been moved in such a way that the physical features or appearance of the character has changed. It could be something about the pose being unflattering or unappealing. You can go off model without breaking the rig.

Let's Talk About Joints.

We are going to boil down a lot of scientific and medical knowledge to simplify joint movement for animators.

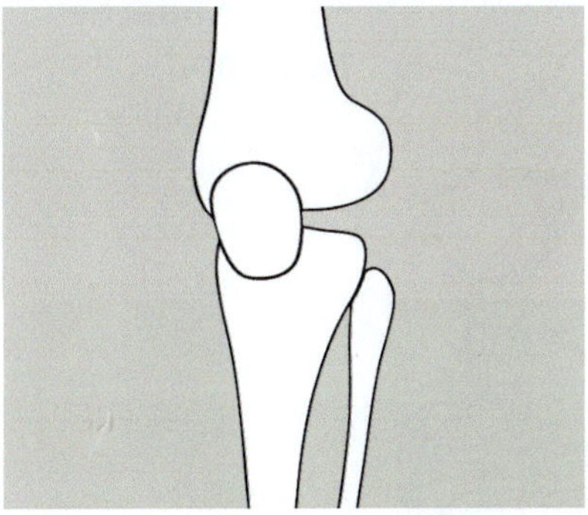

Hinge — a hinge swings back and forth in one direction. Examples of a hinge are jaw, elbows, and knees.

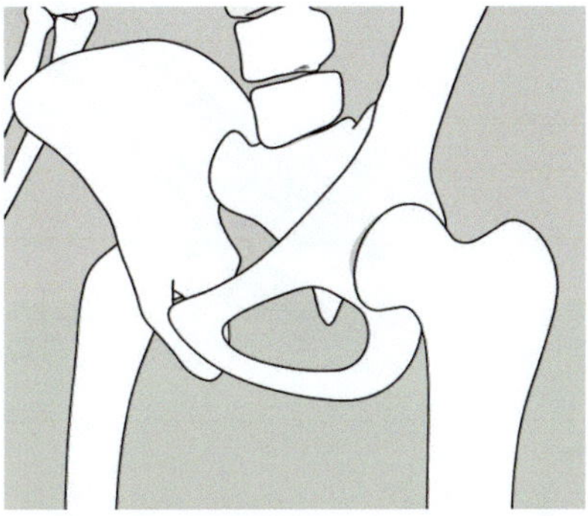

Ball — a ball joint fits in a rounded socket and has a large range of rotation. Examples of ball joints are the shoulders and hips.

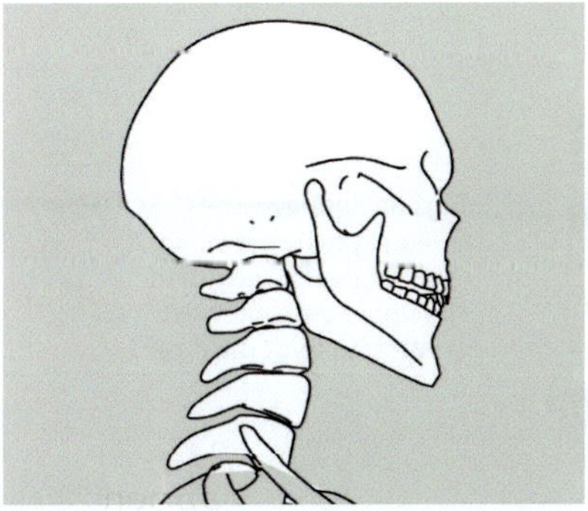

Pivot — a pivot joint sits on an axis and so it can swivel. An example of a pivot joint is the skull sitting atop the spine.

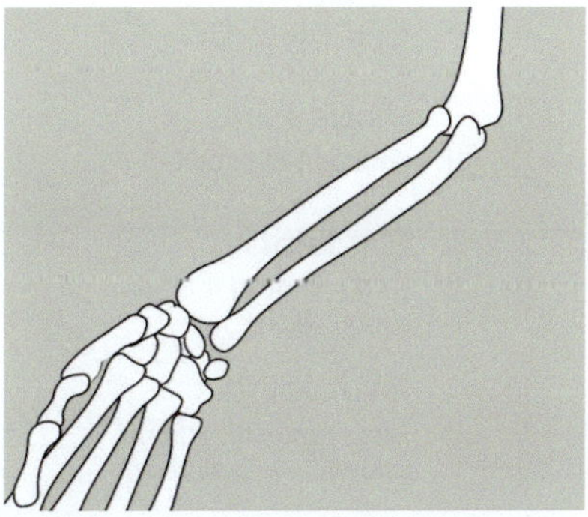

Gliding — gliding joints are a group of multiple types of joints (saddle, planar, and condyloid) that function like hinges but have limited rotation. Examples of gliding joints are spine, wrists, ankles, fingers, and toes.

CHEAT

In order to 'stay on model' professional animators have character sheets that are created by testing the rigs before production. The sheets contain information like how far you can push the controls before the appearance is off. It may also contain information about style guides on facial expressions to keep the rig on character.

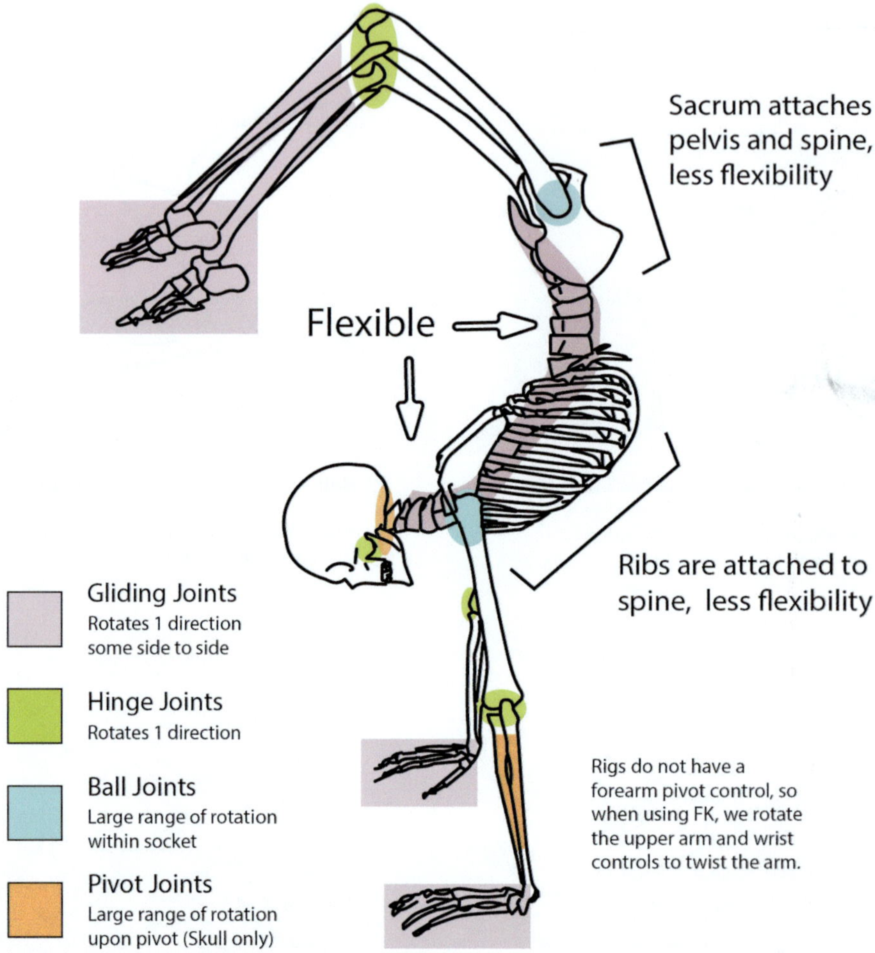

FUN FACT

Why don't we have an elbow cap? We actually do, the hard rounded end of the Ulna bone is called the Olecranon. Where the free floating kneecap functions as a pivot point to help us carry our weight on two legs, the fused olecranon serves as a pivot point that assists the rotations of the forearm.

Root or Center of Gravity

The root of the character is where we will put most of the body translation. The upper and lower body connects to the root; therefore, the root moves the whole body. The root is located at the center of gravity (COG). For humans standing on two feet, the center of gravity is around the pelvis/ base of the spine and top of the hips. The COG changes when we move. For example, if I want to stand on one leg, I must shift my COG over the supporting foot so I won't fall over. If I pick up a box and hold it against my chest, it moves the COG out between the box and my torso.

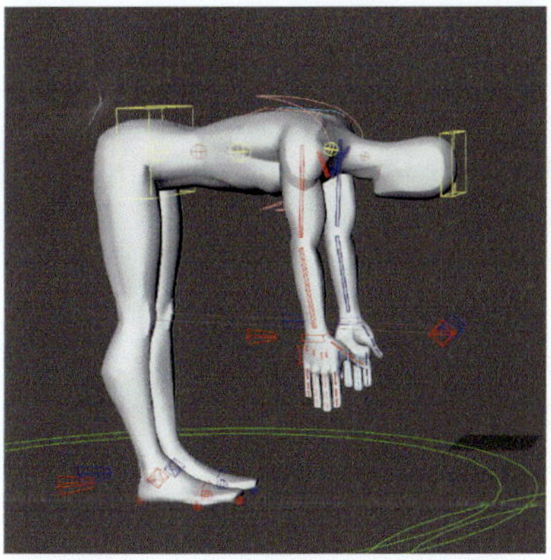

Bend pose made by rotating only the root control. IK legs pulled straight and knees popped backward. Torso is too stiff and straight. Nowhere to offset body parts for a natural looking pose or movement.

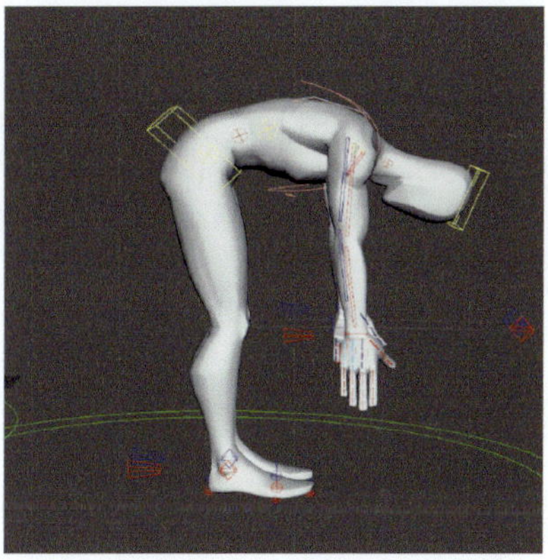

Bend pose made by distributing rotation on hips, root, spine, neck, and head. IK legs retain soft bend at the knee. Torso controls can be offset to create natural looking movement with overlap through the spine.

It may be tempting to make large rotations on the root, but if you do, then the body parts are not working together. Doing a front bend by rotating only the root a large amount, will pull on the inverse kinematics (IK) legs and move the entire spine over in one stiff piece. Instead, do a smaller rotation on the root, rotate the hips, and rotate the controls along the spine. This will give you a more natural looking pose and allow for offsetting the spine controls.

Head and Neck

When turning the head, put the majority of the rotation on the head control. The neck bends and the head turns (pivots). Putting all the twist on the neck control, it will pull on the geometry of the shoulders and upper chest. Some rigs have multiple neck controls. If that is the case, the twist can be distributed up the neck with increased rotation on the head and upper neck control.

Shoulder

Moving the arms starts from the shoulders and goes down the arm. The shoulder control is between the neck and top of the arm. It may be called the shoulder, shrug, clavicle (collarbone) or scapula (shoulder blade) control. This control should have limited rotation movement, like a shoulder shrug. It lifts the top of the arm. The collarbone and shoulder blade prevent the arms from traveling too far in front of or behind the rib cage.

When raising the character's arm overhead, lift the shoulder shrug control first, then rotate the upper arm control. Trying to use the upper arm control only will lead to pinched geometry at the top of the arm and an unrealistic looking pose.

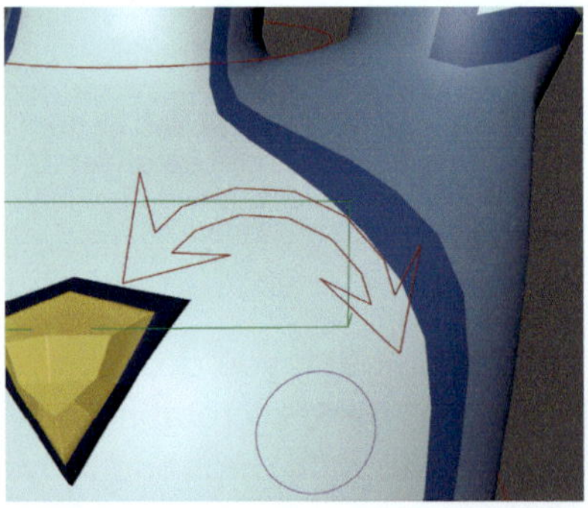

Arm raised with shoulder control for better posing

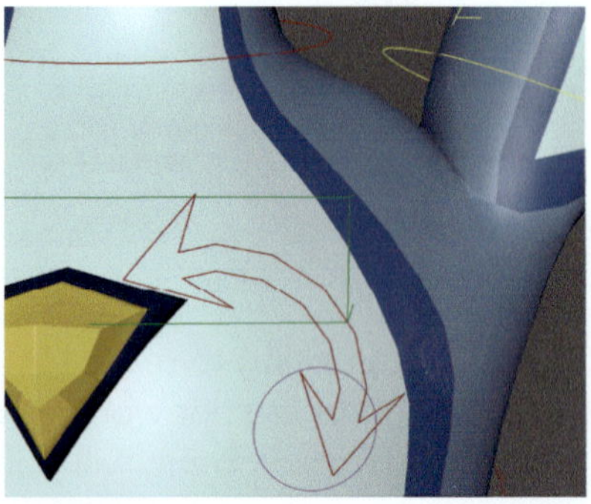

Arm raised without shoulder control results in pinching

FUN FACT

How are cats liquid? Their clavicles and scapulas are free floating, so they can squeeze through any space that is big enough for their head.

Arms

The forward kinematics (FK) arm will have a large range of movement from the top arm control (ball joint). The elbow should rotate in one direction (hinge joint). Want to bend the arm in a certain direction? Twist it from the top arm control, instead of rotating in multiple directions at the elbow. The elbow tends to angle down when bent. The IK arm will be positioned by rotating and translating the IK control at the wrist. Position the elbow pole vector low when using IK arms.

Wrists and Hands

The rig's wrist will have a very large range of rotation. This makes up for the fact that animation rigs do not have forearm pivot rotation that real people do. An unfortunate side effect is it's very easy to make the wrist look broken. Try to avoid bending the wrist 90° or more. The wrist is made up of seven bones and cannot actually bend at a right angle.

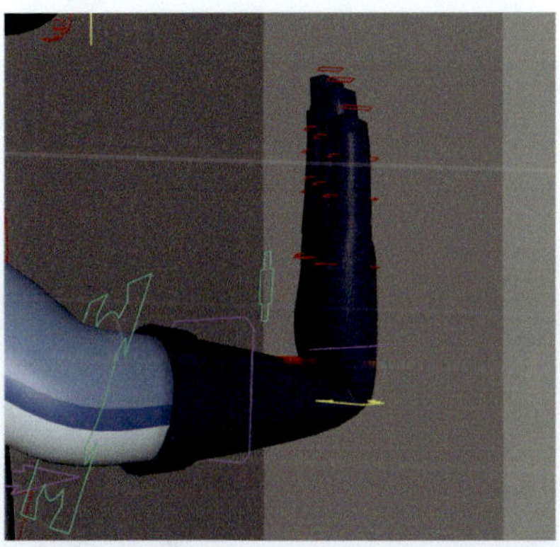

Broken Wrist: Geometry pinched and distorted

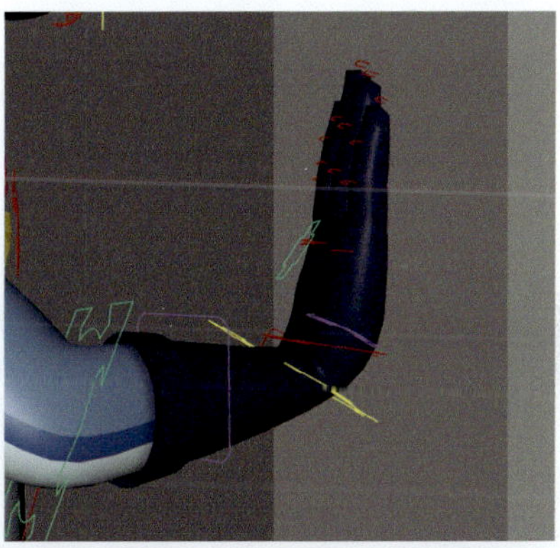

Healthy Wrist: Pose distributed through wrist, palm, and fingers. Use hand and finger IK if available.

Modelers and Riggers will have the hand and fingers flat, straight, and spread out. This bind pose is terrible for animators. If the hands are not a focal point of storytelling, pose them in a simple shape. Imagine the hand is in a mitten, group the fingers, and give them a slight curl. Your fingers start deep in the palm of your hand. When spreading or grouping fingers, look for base finger controls in the palm and use those. Beware, complex hand shapes can be very visually distracting, so only use them with purpose.

Legs

Your character's legs will most likely be set to IK, to keep your feet on the ground. Move the legs by translating the IK foot control. The IK knees should be aligned with the foot direction. There is usually an attribute to set the knee pole vector to follow the feet and sometimes the hips. However, in the case that the legs are set to FK, pose from the top of the leg (ball joint) down to the knee (hinge), then ankle (gliding joint), and to the feet.

Feet

IK feet have special foot roll controls to make the feet appear to have solid contact with the ground. It is important to use the roll controls on the ground and the rotation control when the foot is up in the air. Rotating a foot on the ground will result in the foot going through the ground plane. There will be a variation of heel roll and toe roll, maybe even a ball roll. The foot can be rocked side to side. There will also be pivots to spin the foot on the toes, ball, or heel.

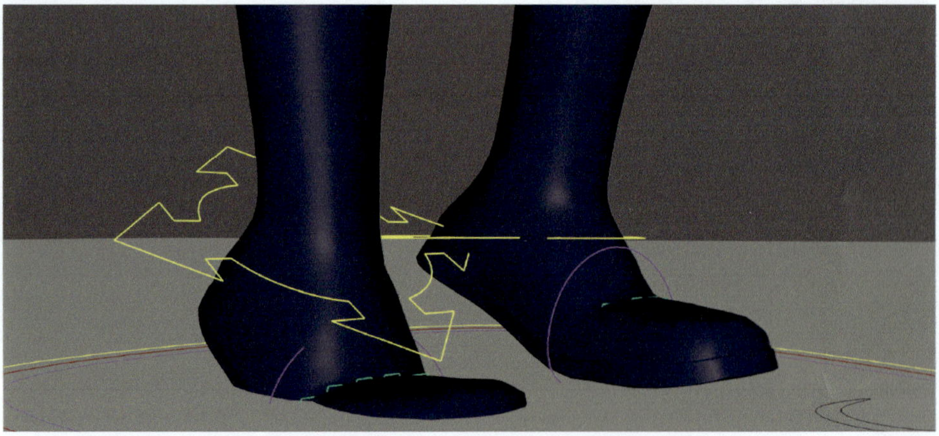

On the left, we see the Leg IK Control rotated to lift heel resulting in the foot intersecting the floor. On the right, the Ball Roll attribute lifts the heel while keep the toes on the floor.

It may be tempting to Y rotate the foot on the ground because it won't cut through the floor. However, if the Y rotation pivot is in the middle of the foot and not at an anatomically correct location, the rotation will not be right.

In conclusion, our job as animators is to make it look like all body parts are connected and working together.

Some rigs have dozens of controls. Some feature film rigs can have hundreds of controls. Riggers often add many controls just to cover any unforeseeable situation. Animators don't need to use every control on the rig, but you do need to approach the controls in an organized way.

Master Control

All rigs will have a master control found at the feet of the character.
This control can have many names such as Global, World, Main, Master, All, Placement Control, etc. This master control will be the parent of all the other controls on the body.

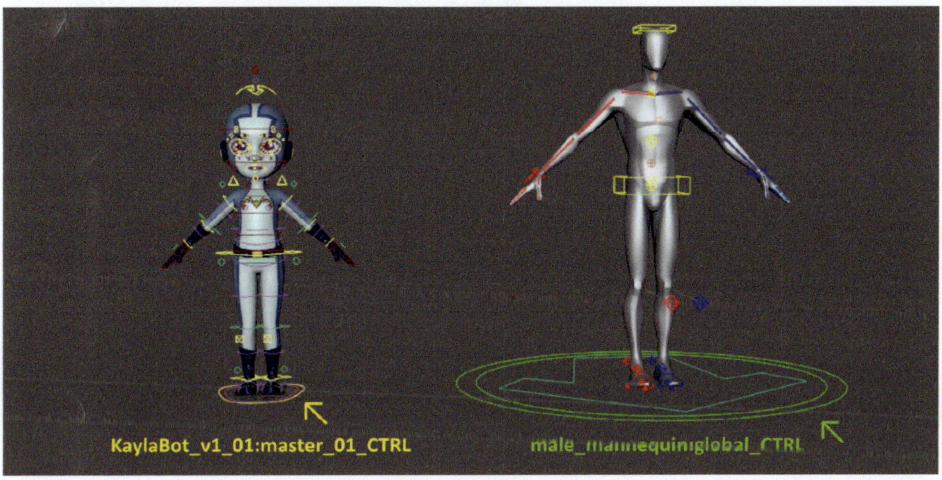

All rigs will have a control at the feet/floor that all other controls are grouped under. If there are multiple master controls, it will be the outermost rig.

Select the master control and look in the Channels Box; often there are many extra attributes.

CHEAT

One of the attributes to look for is scale. The control may be called Size, Global Scale, or XYZ Scale. To scale the character, it is very important to find the global scale option off the master control because it will ensure all the rig controls scale uniformly and nothing will break.

Avoid putting animation on the master control. It establishes the world space for the rig. IK controls will be influenced by this world space. Making the master control move will cause the IK controls to move with it. This makes the feet slide all over the floor. It will make it impossible to create the illusion that the 3D feet have weight and make solid contact with the 3D floor if the master control is moving.

What is the master control for? In most situations, we use the master control to position the character in the set or environment. Then we leave the master control alone, especially in feature animation. There are always exceptions to the rule. You can constrain the master control to a moving object like a car or bike. Game engines will use the master control to move the character in the environment while walk or run cycles are looping. We can even measure the stride length in a stationary cycle and apply it to the master control to make a stationary cycle move forward without visible foot slipping. This method would not be used on main characters, but may be appropriate for games or background characters.

DON'T FORGET

When given two different sized rigs, it is a safer practice to scale the smaller rig up to match the larger one. Scaling a large rig down may cause issues if some of the rigging is dependent on distances.

Macro- vs. Micro-controls

Macro means large, think of it as one control to influence a large group of controls or a large region of the character. For example, a hand macro-control is one control that allows you to pose all the fingers at once. It groups together and overrides all the individual controls across every finger. Micro-means a single control that drives one thing. An example for a micro-control is the third joint on the left index finger. It's just one control that rotates the tip of the finger. It is possible to put animation on the macro-control and additional animation on all the micro-controls within. In most rigs, this results in an additive effect. For example, 20° of rotation on the finger macro, and 20° rotation on the individual finger controls will result in the fingers curled 40°.

ORGANIZING CONTROLS

The top-level controls or macro-controls are the large body parts or body part groups: root/ cog, spine group, neck, head, shoulder, upper arm, elbow, wrist, hand group, hips, upper leg, knee, ankle, and foot group. These are the controls we want to use in the first blocking pass.

Mid-level controls are smaller body parts: fingers, toes, jaw, mouth, eyes, brows, ears, nose, hair group, and larger clothing items. These controls may be used for blocking or blocking plus.

Fine controls are even smaller body parts: cheeks, nostrils, lips, brow regions, eyelids, tongue, teeth, regions of the feet, hands and hair, and smaller clothing details like collars or belts. These controls are used for refining and polishing.

Polishing controls can correct, modify, or push poses: bend/ bow, stretch, twist, volume, lip zip, breath, muscle deformers, and squash/ stretch.

Technical controls: FK/IK switches, visibility switches, extra attribute switches, rotation orders, pole vectors, head/ body part alignment, anti-pop, pinning, locking, following, aim controls, subcontrols, pivot controls, and rig space switches.

The top-level rig controls will be visible and easily accessible. The other controls may or may not be hidden. Rigs vary, but often the extra controls can be made visible with an attribute found on the master control. Sometimes, the extra controls can be located along the head, torso, or limbs. For example, the fine facial controls may have a switch found on the head control. Go through the rig and locate where everything is before you start animating.

Which Controls to Start?

We want to block with a relatively small group of controls. It's much easier to select and edit 20 controls vs. 200 controls. Start with the top level controls first.

- For a full-body shot, block with the largest body parts, IK legs, hip, root, spine, neck, head, shoulders, arms, and wrists.
- For a face close-up, block with the face macros, eye and brow groups, jaw, lips and corners and cheek groups.
- For a hand detail, start with the hand macro before moving to the individual finger controls.

Start at the center of the body, the COG, or root and work your way out. Work from largest controls or body parts, then mid-level controls. The blocking may include some technical controls like IK/FK switching depending on the situation. Once blocking is approved, you can move on to smaller body/ face parts. The polishing stage will include the fine level controls for refining the poses and solving any problem areas.

Keying every control on the rig during blocking will result in hundreds of extraneous keys. Items like hair may be a simulation or may be hand-keyed. But we need to finish the movements of the body to know where the hair will be going. Keying all the little detail items, like the hair controls in blocking, will result in deleting it all later. Skip the fine, micro-, tweaking, or polishing controls in the blocking stages. Take a moment to hide the extra/ polishing controls before starting blocking.

The intention of the first blocking pass is to put in enough information for the Lead or Director to see the direction you're going and envision the final shot. Don't spend too much time putting in detailed information, because you will be asked to make changes to the shot.

CHEAT

Some rigs have the ability to hide minor controls, as riggers understand they can get in the way or get accidentally keyed in blocking. Look for switches on main body parts to enable / disable minor controls.

1st Level:

Top Level Macro-Control — Moves the entire brow and corresponding controls

2nd Level:

Brow Regions — Use to shape brows

3rd Level:

Brow Interstitial — Use to make all brow regions flow together

4th Level:

Brow Tweak — Final step, use to polish brow shapes or troubleshoot any problem areas

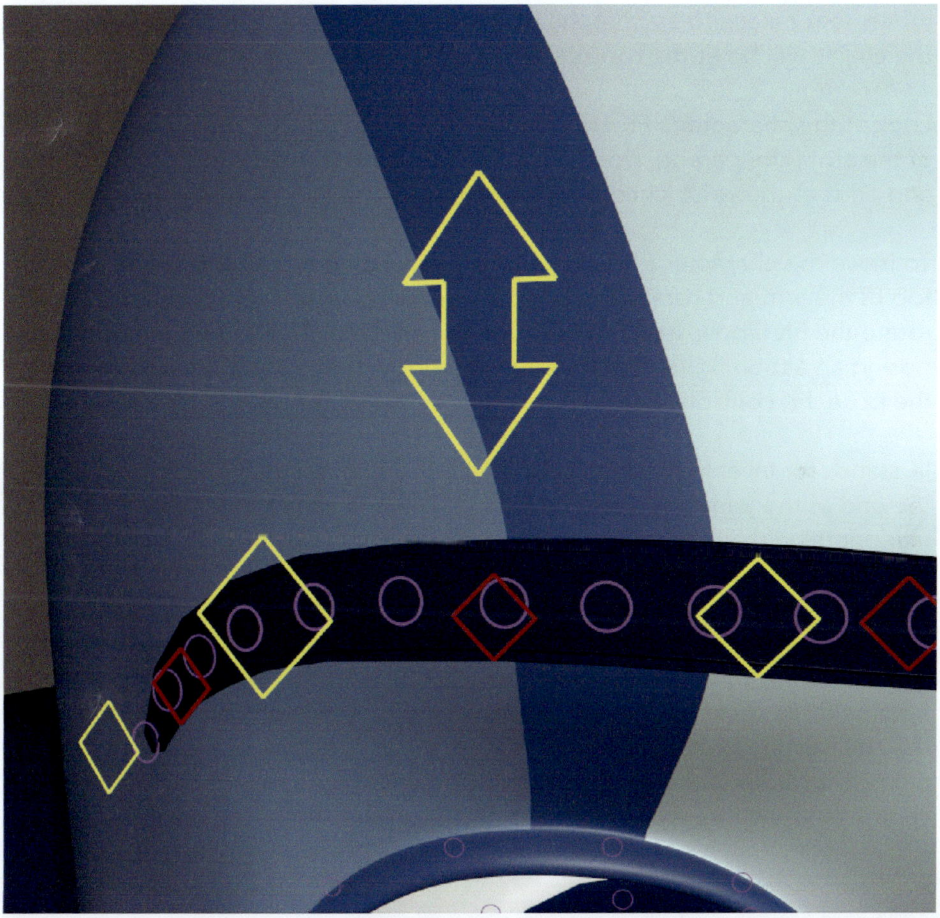

FK AND IK

The rig doesn't have one skeleton inside. It has several. Most rigs have a minimum IK, FK, and bend/bow skeleton. There could be even more than that, like a ribbon system skeleton. Each skeleton has a specific purpose and behaviors that are desirable. While animating, we often need to switch between these skeletons.

FK stands for Forward Kinematics. The skeleton in the rig is made up of chains of joints. The chains have a beginning and an end. Forward movement means to start at the beginning of the chain. The beginning of the chains will be at the root/center of the body and radiates out.

Look at the character's FK arm. The joint chain in the arm starts at the top of the arm (the parent), goes down to the elbow (child of the top of the arm), and ends at the wrist (child of the elbow).

To move the character's FK arm, do not translate the controls. Go to the top of the arm and rotate the FK control, then go down the hierarchy and rotate the FK elbow, and finally rotate the FK wrist. Think of FK animation like posing an action figure, each part of the body needs to be rotated to make the pose. FK controls function like our own skeleton.

IK stands for Inverse Kinematics. We affect the joints backward by selecting the end of the joint chain and moving it. Think of animating IK like a marionette with strings or a puppet with rods, you pull or push the hands and feet closer or further from the body to make the pose.

To move the character's IK arm, select the control at the wrist, translate and rotate. Move the wrist closer to the body, and the elbow will bend automatically to compensate. To control the direction the elbow is bending, use the floating control behind the elbow. This is called a pole vector and helps to aim the elbow or knee joint point when the chain folds. The pole vector can be set to world space, or to follow the shourlder, hand, etc.

CHEAT

There are no standardized controls in the world of 3D rigging. However, FK controls are usually circles. IK controls are often wireframe boxes but can be a wide range of shapes.

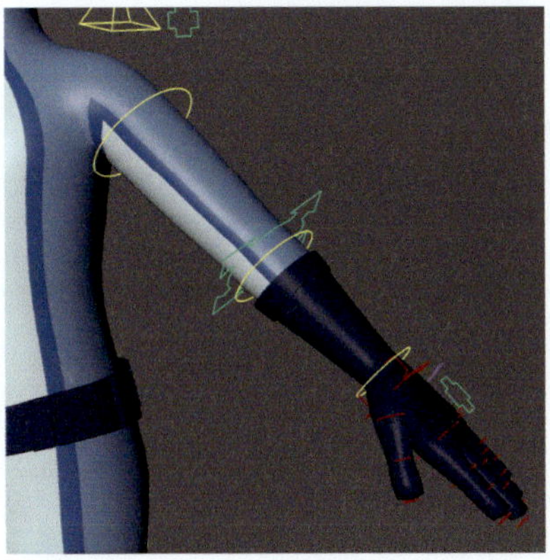

FK — Rotate

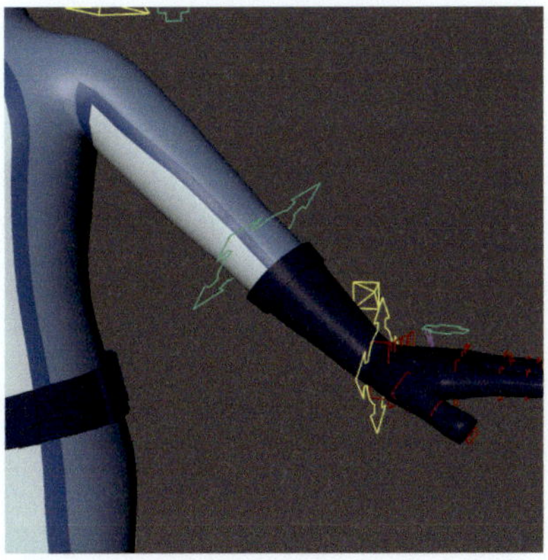

IK — Rotate and Translate

FK controls should be rotated for realistic motion. Some rigs may have FK controls with translate and scale channels. These should be used for cartoony animation with bend, stretch, and volume systems; otherwise, the rig will tear apart. If you do not intend to do this style of animation, it's recommended to lock the translate and scale channels by selecting with the Ctrl key, RMB, and choosing Lock attribute.

WHEN TO USE FK VS. IK

FK moves with the body. For a natural-looking arm swing that moves with the torso, use FK. If a character is swinging their feet over a ledge, use FK legs. For a natural-looking backbend, use the FK spine. However, since FK controls will inherit movement from the body, FK is the wrong choice when we need to make body parts freeze in space.

IK does not move with the body. To make a body part look like it is making solid contact with a surface, like a foot on the floor, or a hand on a table, or the back leaning on the wall, use IK. Can you make natural-looking arm swings with an IK arm? Yes, but Motion Trails will need to trace the path of the arm to make sure it makes nice arcs. IK can look disconnected from the body if the body parts don't move together. If the IK control gets too far away from the body, the chain snaps straight causing an 'IK pop.' Take extra care with IK to keep up the illusion that the entire body is connected and moving together.

One more situation that calls for IK is when the character's hand or foot is constrained to follow an object and gets its position data from that object. Constraints with the IK will affect the entire arm. Trying to constrain a FK control will only affect the single joint, leading it to tear away from the rest of the chain.

TECHNICAL CONTROLS

FK/IK Switch

To access FK and IK controls, there are usually switches near the arms, legs and spine. The rig has multiple skeletons inside of it. When switching from FK to IK, any animation on the FK controls are still there, but that skeleton is hidden and is being overridden by the IK system. You will need to line up the body parts when switching so that there is no 'pop' in position. If using a high-end rig, it may have controls to match the FK and IK positions exactly. If not, you will have to do it manually or use a third-party tool.

Most rigs toggle the visibility of their FK and IK controls. For example, set the arm to FK, then the IK controls will be automatically hidden to avoid confusion. However, the same is not always true for spines. Plenty of professional rigs have both the FK and IK spines visible and active at the same time. For beginning animators, this can cause confusion, or worse you'll accidentally start counter-animating the spine controls against each other. To avoid this confusion, it's recommended to pick either the FK or IK spine. Then search the rig controls for an option to hide the controls you do not need. If there is no convenient way to hide the controls, put them on a Display Layer and turn off visibility.

Space Controls

The master control of the rig serves as the rig's world space. For example, if the IK feet are set to world space and the character's root is moved up and down, the feet stay on the floor level and will not move until directly animated. If the feet are set to hip space, and the character is moved up and down, the feet will inherit that motion and move through the floor.

Space controls are useful for managing these relationships. For instance, if the knee pole vector is set to world space and the character is moved, the pole vector must also be manually moved and keyed to stay aligned. If the pole vector is instead set to foot space, it will follow the foot automatically, maintaining proper orientation in front of the knee.

These controls are sometimes labeled as Follow controls. Eyes may have an aim control that locks their direction. When the aim control is stationary in world space, the eyes can appear unnaturally fixed. A more natural result is achieved by setting the aim to follow the head and animating the eyes to look at a specific target.

Pinning Controls

Pinning controls are often found at the elbows and knees when using IK. If you want the character to put their elbow on the table and rest their head on the hand then use pinning controls. We can keep the hand from moving by using IK, but to keep the elbow on the table, we pin it. It locks the elbow joint to an override control or the elbow pole vector control. Pole vectors often stretch out the arm. You will need to move the elbow pole vector to the table, and then it will look like the character is leaning on their elbow. Some rigs will have the option to set the elbow or knees to the Master Control space which functions like pinning.

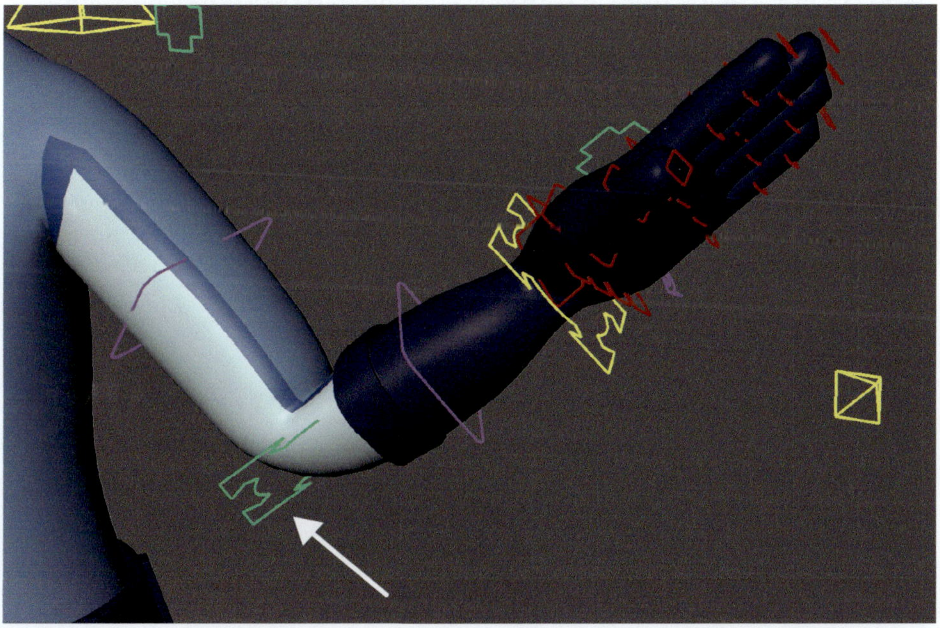

Set the elbow override to Master Control space to pin elbow to one location.

Stretch, Volume, and Anti-Pop

If the rig is set up for cartoony animation, it will have the ability to stretch and preserve volume. You can't throw out all physics and reality when doing cartoony animation. When we do a cartoon stretch, the characters' body should get longer and narrow. When we do a cartoony squash, the body should get short and wide. We use stretch and volume together to achieve this effect. The anti-pop controls work in a similar way. If the IK control is moved too far from the body, the limb snaps straight. Anti-pop adds some stretch to the limbs to soften the snap. When doing realistic animation, make sure the audience can't see the limbs stretching and shrinking because it is distracting and breaks the illusion.

Bend/Bow

Bend and bow controls are multiple controls on the arms and legs and elsewhere that allow the limbs to be bent in many places. Bend controls can be used in two ways. They can be used to do little polishing corrections like folding the character's arms across the chest and solving the intersections. Bend controls can be used in cartoony animation to bend stretched limbs in multiple directions, like the character is made of rubber.

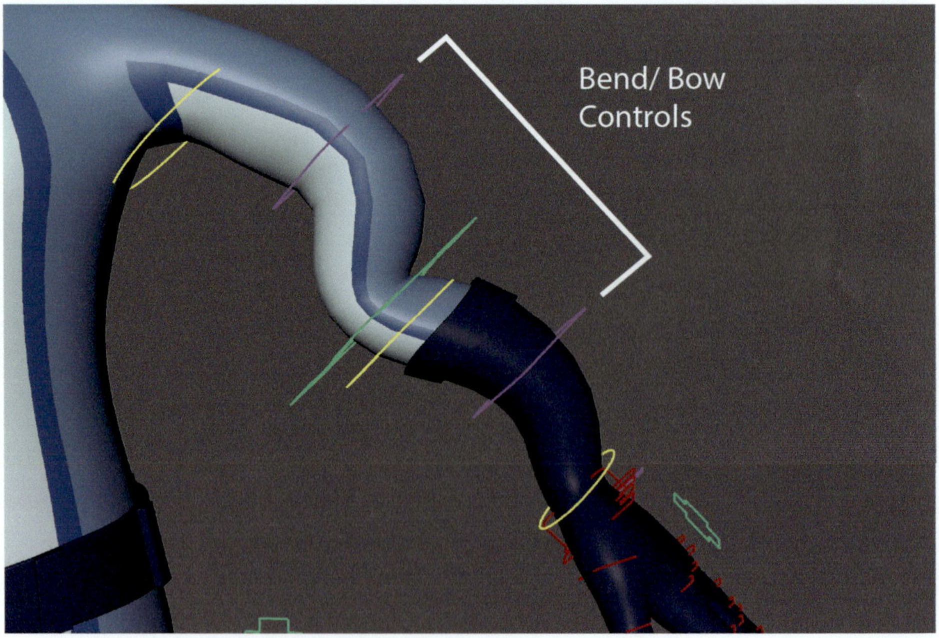

Subcontrols

Subcontrols are duplicate rig controls. They're usually used for problem-solving like constraints or changing pivot points or solving rotation order/gimbal lock issues. They can be used to add polish or layer animation. For example, having animation on the COG and additional animation on the sub-COG. Unfortunately, it is very easy to accidentally select subcontrols, or worse start to counter-animate with them. Hide the subcontrols. Do not use them during animation blocking. Start with a clean, efficient blocking pass on the top-level controls first.

Reset the Rig

The rig arrives in a bind pose, either T-stance or A-stance with arms out at a 45° angle. The rigger should have frozen the transformations on the rig controls to Translate = 0, Rotate = 0, and Scale = 1. Sometimes, we want to quickly return the rig to a default bind pose, but every control has new transformation values that will need to be zeroed. To reset a rig, first look at the rig and see if it comes with a Reset command built into a picker button, or a shelf button. If it does, use that. Next, if using a third-party plug-in like a pose library, make a button with the bind pose saved to quickly reset the rig.

Here are two methods for resetting the controls:

First, select the controls by going to Select > All by Type > NURBS curves. Do not select with a camera-based marquee because it will not select hidden controls. Go to the Channels and type 0 in all Translate and Rotate channels. If anything needs a scale reset, type 1 in the Scale channels.

Want to store poses with no Character Sets or Pose Library plug-in? Expand the frame range of the shot to f-200 or more. You can save a bind pose on f-199 or a casual standing pose on f-198, etc. Then copy the poses when needed. Beware sometimes negative frames before the shot are used to rampup simulations, so be sure to store poses well out of that range.

What if selecting All by Type did not give you the option of all translate, rotate, or scale channels? Sometimes using select all by type, Maya will land on a random last control that does not have all channels available. Instead, try this second method with the Attribute Spread Sheet.

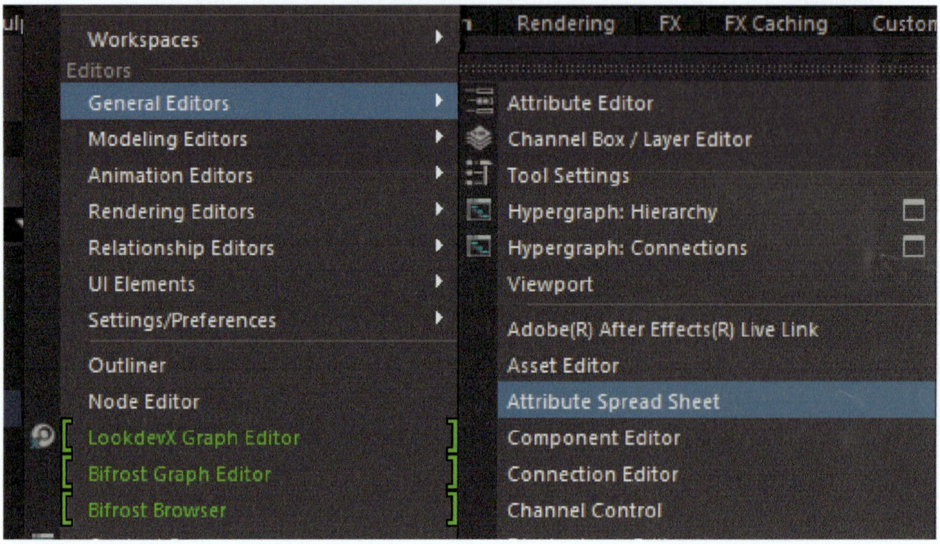

Again, select All by Type > NURBS Curves again and go to Windows > General Editors > Attribute Spread Sheet.

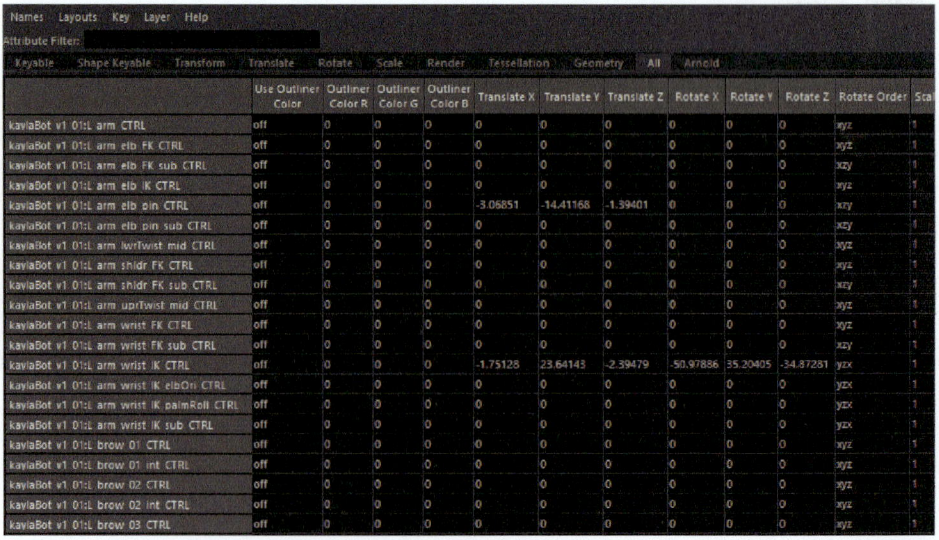

	Use Outliner Color	Outliner Color R	Outliner Color G	Outliner Color B	Translate X	Translate Y	Translate Z	Rotate X	Rotate Y	Rotate Z	Rotate Order	Scal
kaylaBot v1 01:L arm CTRL	off	0	0	0	0	0	0	0	0	0	xyz	1
kaylaBot v1 01:L arm elb FK CTRL	off	0	0	0	0	0	0	0	0	0	xyz	1
kaylaBot v1 01:L arm elb FK sub CTRL	off	0	0	0	0	0	0	0	0	0	xzy	1
kaylaBot v1 01:L arm elb IK CTRL	off	0	0	0	0	0	0	0	0	0	xyz	1
kaylaBot v1 01:L arm elb pin CTRL	off	0	0	0	-3.06851	-14.41168	-1.39401	0	0	0	xzy	1
kaylaBot v1 01:L arm elb pin sub CTRL	off	0	0	0	0	0	0	0	0	0	xzy	1
kaylaBot v1 01:L arm lwrTwist mid CTRL	off	0	0	0	0	0	0	0	0	0	xyz	1
kaylaBot v1 01:L arm shldr FK CTRL	off	0	0	0	0	0	0	0	0	0	xyz	1
kaylaBot v1 01:L arm shldr FK sub CTRL	off	0	0	0	0	0	0	0	0	0	xzy	1
kaylaBot v1 01:L arm uprTwist mid CTRL	off	0	0	0	0	0	0	0	0	0	xyz	1
kaylaBot v1 01:L arm wrist FK CTRL	off	0	0	0	0	0	0	0	0	0	xyz	1
kaylaBot v1 01:L arm wrist FK sub CTRL	off	0	0	0	0	0	0	0	0	0	xzy	1
kaylaBot v1 01:L arm wrist IK CTRL	off	0	0	0	-1.75128	23.64143	-2.39479	-50.97886	35.20405	-34.87281	yzx	1
kaylaBot v1 01:L arm wrist IK elbOri CTRL	off	0	0	0	0	0	0	0	0	0	yzx	1
kaylaBot v1 01:L arm wrist IK palmRoll CTRL	off	0	0	0	0	0	0	0	0	0	yzx	1
kaylaBot v1 01:L arm wrist IK sub CTRL	off	0	0	0	0	0	0	0	0	0	yzx	1
kaylaBot v1 01:L brow 01 CTRL	off	0	0	0	0	0	0	0	0	0	xyz	1
kaylaBot v1 01:L brow 01 int CTRL	off	0	0	0	0	0	0	0	0	0	xyz	1
kaylaBot v1 01:L brow 02 CTRL	off	0	0	0	0	0	0	0	0	0	xyz	1
kaylaBot v1 01:L brow 02 int CTRL	off	0	0	0	0	0	0	0	0	0	xyz	1
kaylaBot v1 01:L brow 03 CTRL	off	0	0	0	0	0	0	0	0	0	xyz	1

The Attribute Spread Sheet has multiple tabs to organize attributes.

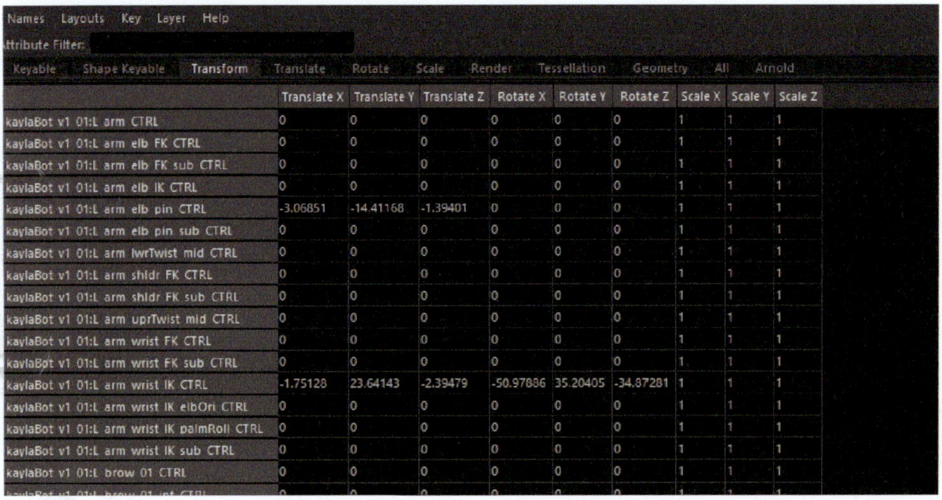

	Translate X	Translate Y	Translate Z	Rotate X	Rotate Y	Rotate Z	Scale X	Scale Y	Scale Z
kaylaBot v1 01:L arm CTRL	0	0	0	0	0	0	1	1	1
kaylaBot v1 01:L arm elb FK CTRL	0	0	0	0	0	0	1	1	1
kaylaBot v1 01:L arm elb FK sub CTRL	0	0	0	0	0	0	1	1	1
kaylaBot v1 01:L arm elb IK CTRL	0	0	0	0	0	0	1	1	1
kaylaBot v1 01:L arm elb pin CTRL	-3.06851	-14.41168	-1.39401	0	0	0	1	1	1
kaylaBot v1 01:L arm elb pin sub CTRL	0	0	0	0	0	0	1	1	1
kaylaBot v1 01:L arm lwrTwist mid CTRL	0	0	0	0	0	0	1	1	1
kaylaBot v1 01:L arm shldr FK CTRL	0	0	0	0	0	0	1	1	1
kaylaBot v1 01:L arm shldr FK sub CTRL	0	0	0	0	0	0	1	1	1
kaylaBot v1 01:L arm uprTwist mid CTRL	0	0	0	0	0	0	1	1	1
kaylaBot v1 01:L arm wrist FK CTRL	0	0	0	0	0	0	1	1	1
kaylaBot v1 01:L arm wrist FK sub CTRL	0	0	0	0	0	0	1	1	1
kaylaBot v1 01:L arm wrist IK CTRL	-1.75128	23.64143	-2.39479	-50.97886	35.20405	-34.87281	1	1	1
kaylaBot v1 01:L arm wrist IK elbOri CTRL	0	0	0	0	0	0	1	1	1
kaylaBot v1 01:L arm wrist IK palmRoll CTRL	0	0	0	0	0	0	1	1	1
kaylaBot v1 01:L arm wrist IK sub CTRL	0	0	0	0	0	0	1	1	1
kaylaBot v1 01:L brow 01 CTRL	0	0	0	0	0	0	1	1	1

Go to the Transform tab to limit the sheet to Translate, Rotate, or Scale.

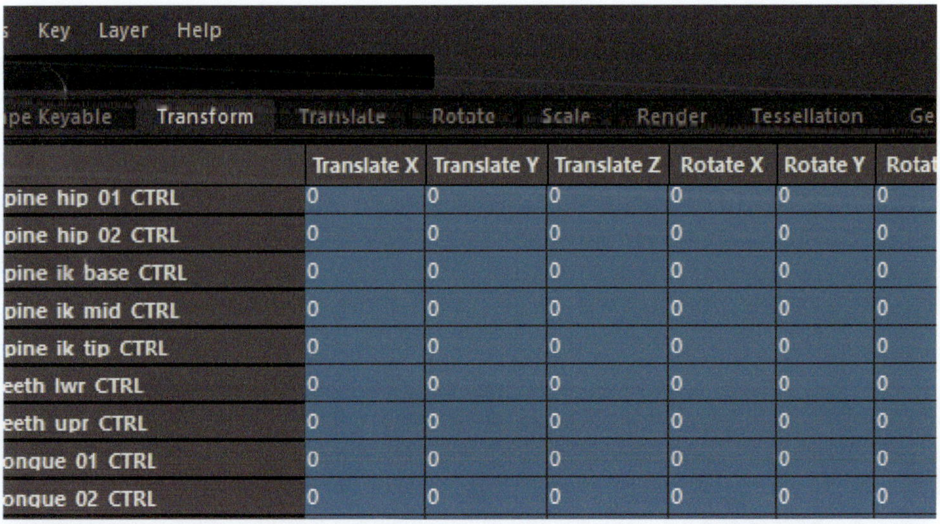

	Translate X	Translate Y	Translate Z	Rotate X	Rotate Y	Rotat
pine hip 01 CTRL	0	0	0	0	0	0
pine hip 02 CTRL	0	0	0	0	0	0
pine ik base CTRL	0	0	0	0	0	0
pine ik mid CTRL	0	0	0	0	0	0
pine ik tip CTRL	0	0	0	0	0	0
eeth lwr CTRL	0	0	0	0	0	0
eeth upr CTRL	0	0	0	0	0	0
onque 01 CTRL	0	0	0	0	0	0
onque 02 CTRL	0	0	0	0	0	0

Shift select all translation boxes. Holding Shift, type 0 in the lower right box. This will set every selected Translate and Rotate channel to zero as long as it is not locked. Repeat the process for Scale with 1 if needed.

PICKERS, SHELVES, AND BUTTONS

Part of testing the rig may include installing any extras that come with the rig. The rig may come with a picker or shelves that need to be loaded into Maya. You may need to access the plug-in directory or shelves directory.

To install plug-ins, first consult any instructions that came with the rig. Some plug-ins will have an installation program, some need to run a script, and some simply need to be copied into the correct location. To load the plug-ins, go to Windows > Settings/Preferences > Plug-in Manager. There is an option to check Loaded for a single session, or Auto Load to make the plug-in activate every time you launch Maya.

To run a script in Maya, copy the script and paste it into the Command Line or the Script Editor. You need to know if the script is MEL or Python before running it. Both the Command Line and Script Editor can be set to MEL or Python, so make sure it matches.

To install a shelf, go to Documents > maya > 2026 > prefs. Inside, you will find a shelves folder. Consult with the instructions that came with your rig, but often it is as easy as copying the character shelf into the shelves folder. Next, go to the shelf modify, the gray gear, and click Load Shelf.

Creating Shelves and Buttons

To make your own shelf, go to the shelf modify, the gray gear, and choose New Shelf. This will open a dialogue box to name the shelf.

Let's make a button. It will be time-consuming to have to select multiple controls. For example, we can make one button to select all the FK spine controls on the KaylaBot rig.

CHEAT

Help! I deleted a shelf I made! Your shelf still exists. Go to Documents/maya/2026/prefs/shelves. You will see the shelf file is grayed out, and the name has been changed to shelf_name.mel.deleted. Just highlight and remove: [.deleted] from the end of the file name. The shelf file will be restored and can be reloaded.

First, clear all selections, just click out into space.

Then we will select the spine controls, select the first one and then hold down the shift key to add to the selection.

Once all the spine controls are selected, go to the Script Editor, the button on the lower-left corner with the semicolon in parentheses.

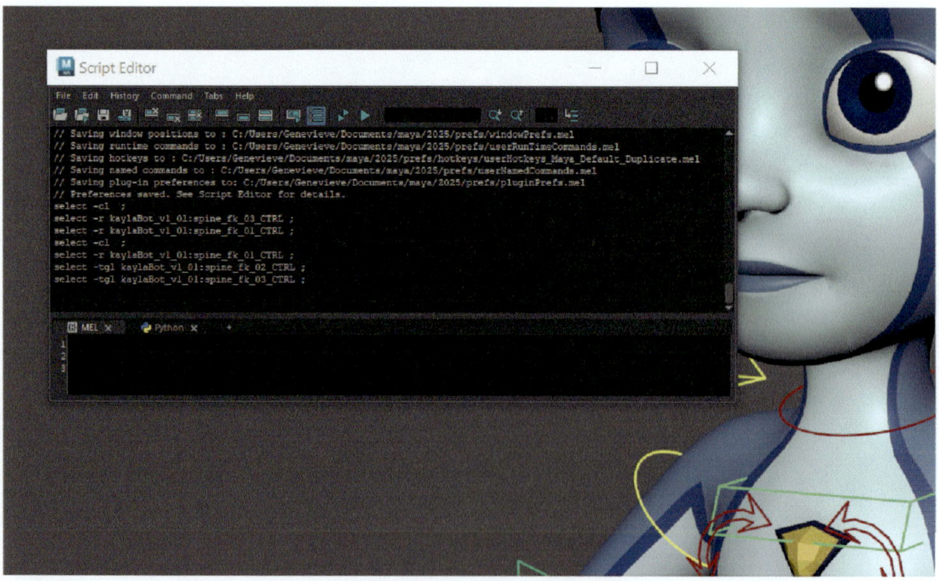

Every action in Maya has been recorded as a line of code. Look for the line: select -cl; this is the code where we cleared the selection.

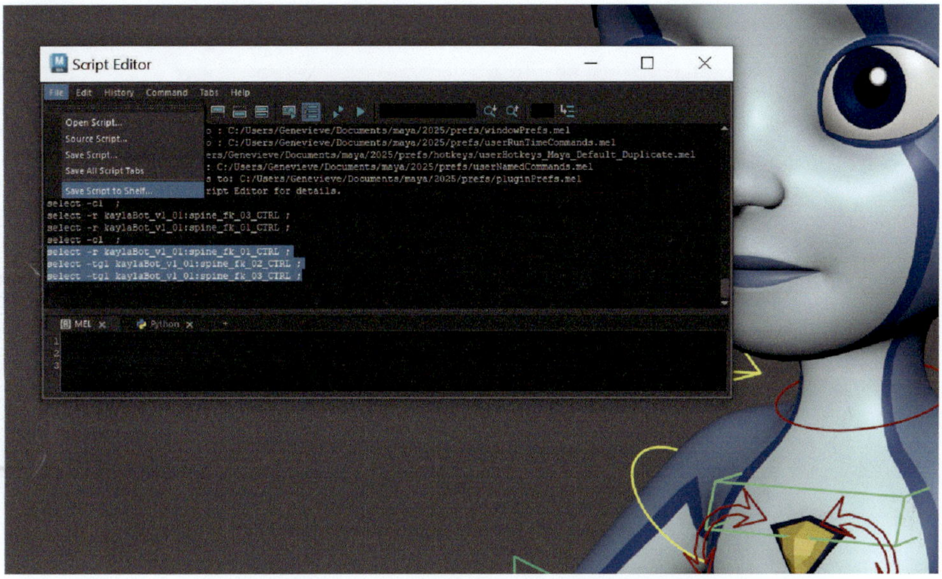

The next lines of code will be: select -r kaylaBot_v1_01:spine_fk_01_CTRL ; select -r kaylaBot_v1_01:spine_fk_02_CTRL ; select -r kaylaBot_v1_01:spine_fk_03_CTRL;. Highlight the lines of code that selected all the spine controls. Next go to File > Save Script to Shelf.

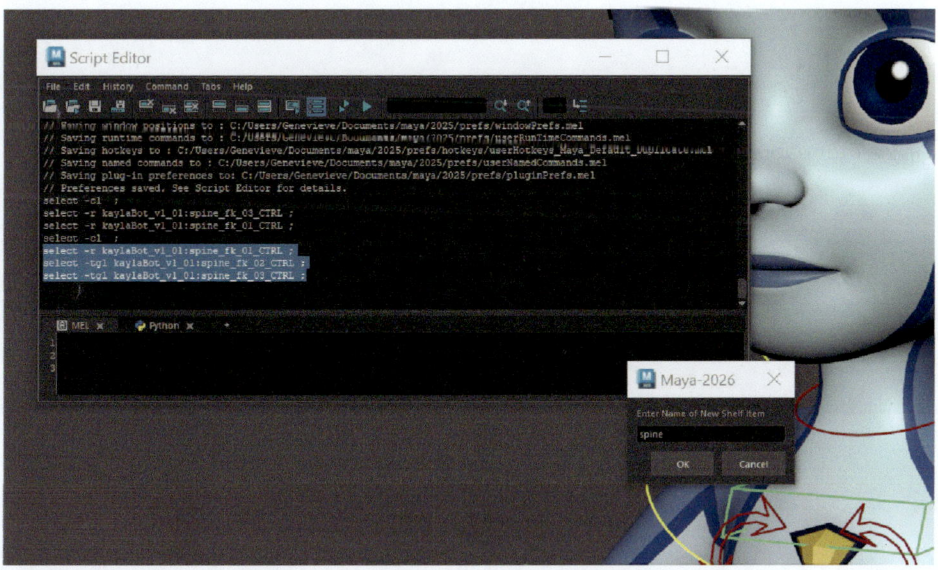

The dialogue box to name the button will pop open.

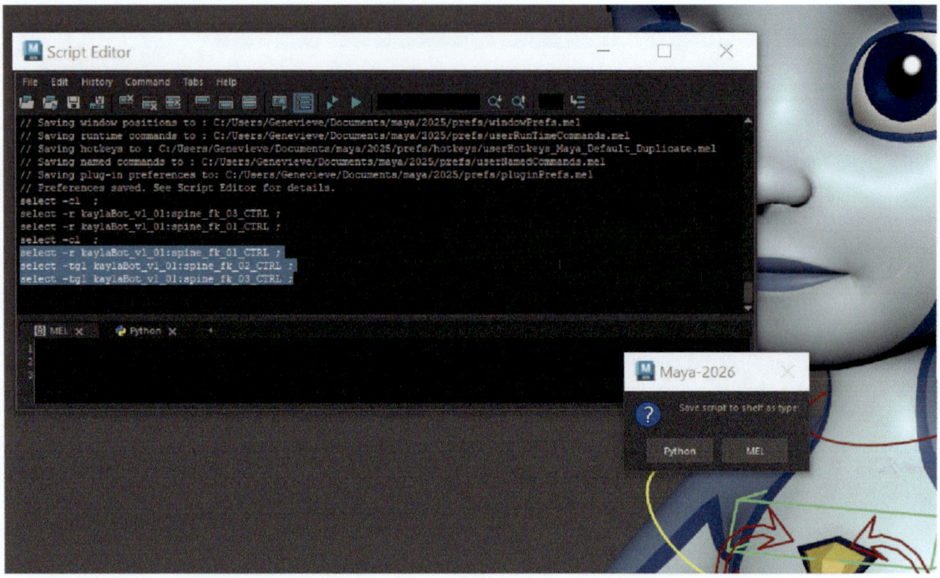

Next, choose if the script should be MEL or Python. The selected text is MEL, so we will choose MEL in this dialogue.

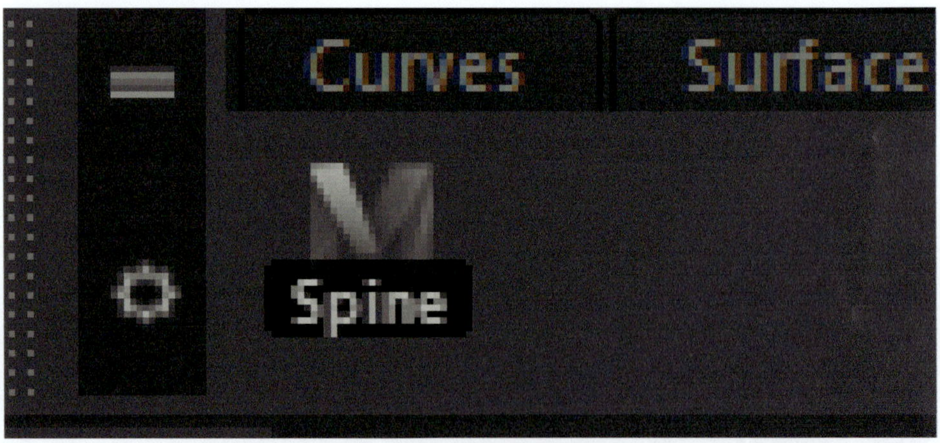

WATCH OUT!

Do not include the line: select -cl; to the button script, or it will keep selecting the controls and then immediately clearing the selection.

To edit or delete any button, just RMB on the button. Click Edit to open the Shelf Editor for adjusting the label, icon, and placement of any button. Go to the Command tab to edit the script. Go to the Shelves tab and click Save All Shelves to save changes. MMB to move the button around the shelf.

To add an existing Maya menu item to any shelf, navigate to the menu item and hold your cursor over it, press Ctrl + Shift + RMB. It will make a button at the end of the active shelf. RMB to edit or remove it or MMB to move it.

Edit the shelf button you just made. RMB the button, click Edit. In the script, replace each instance of [-tgl] with [-add]. This will make sure the selection does not unintentionally toggle any preselected items off.

COMMON TOOLS AND MENUS

Quick Select Set vs. Character Set

Quick Select Sets group controls into sets as an easy way to put keys on all the controls and their attributes.

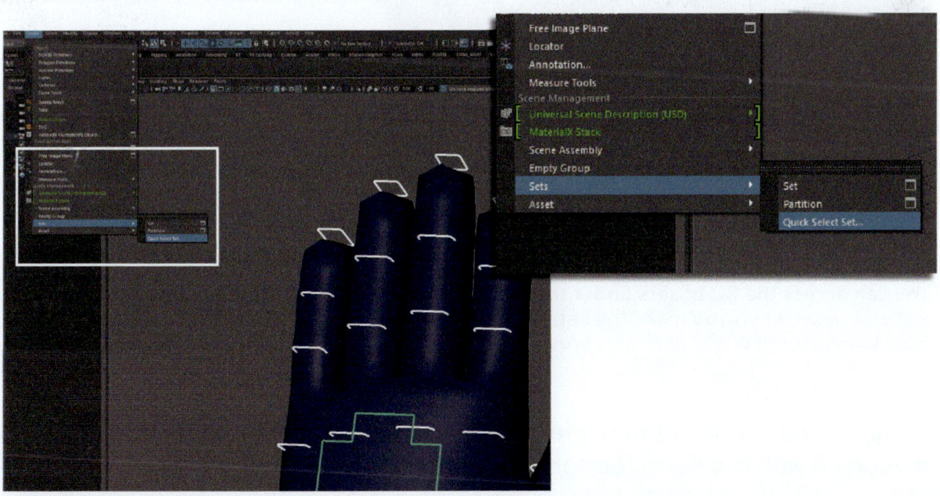

Let's make a Quick Select Set for KaylaBot's left hand including all finger controls. To make a Quick Select Set, create the set first. Select the controls to be in a set and go to Create > Sets > Quick Select Set.

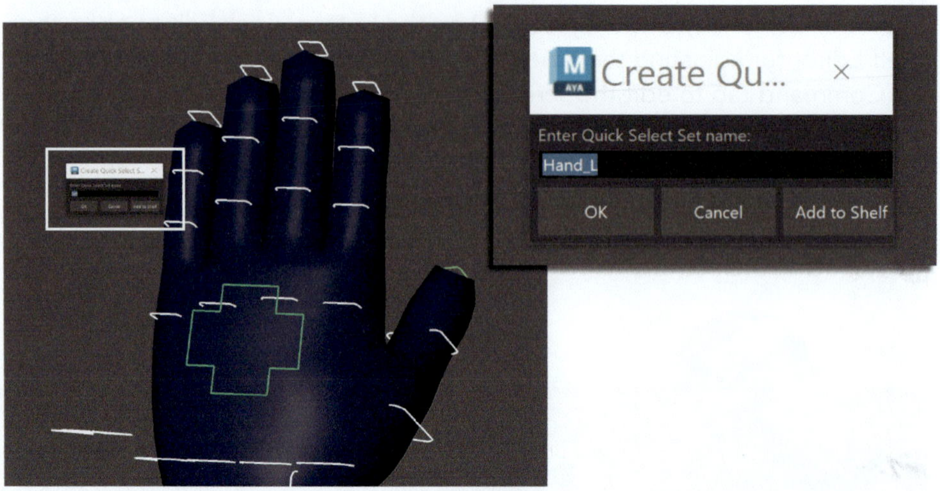

Open the options box, name the set, and add the set as a shelf button.

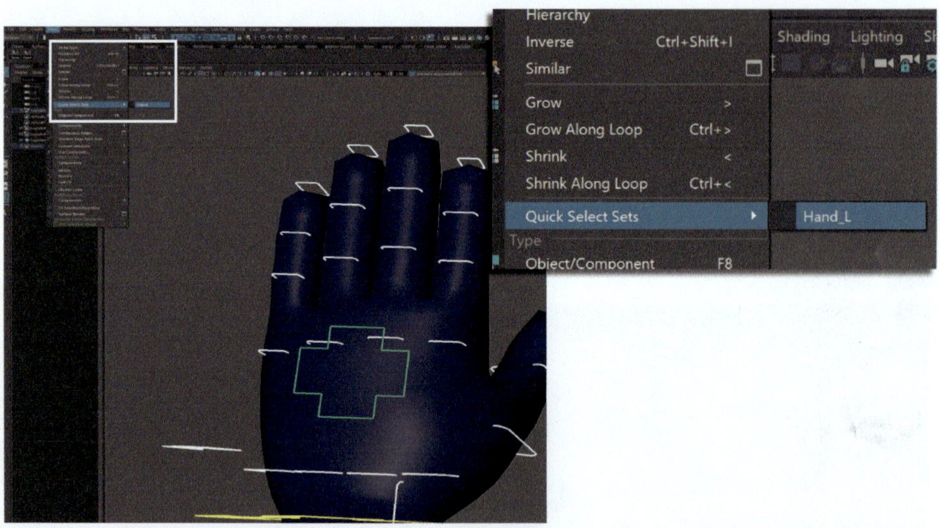

You can access the list of sets under the Select menu, Quick Select Sets. Forget to add a shelf button when you make the set, go to the list of sets under Select > Quick Select Sets, hold the cursor over the item and press Ctrl + Shift + RMB.

For a fast way to select multiple controls and a handy shelf button, make it yourself with the Script Editor or create a Quick Selection Set. The only difference is the Quick Selection is saved in a list, so if you lose the shelf, you can go back to the list and make a new shelf. Character Sets make sets out of any selected attributes linked to the controls.

Let's make a Character Set for kaylaBot's right hand including all finger controls. To make a Character Set, select the controls. Go to the Key menu > Create Character Set option box.

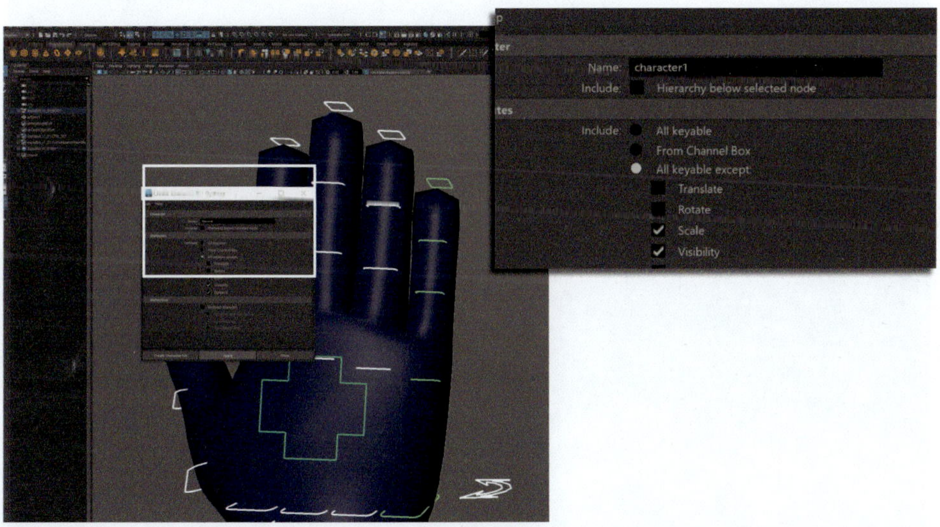

When setting up the character set, choose to have every attribute available in the channels keyed or choose what to exclude. Instead of the shelf button, you get a Character Set menu below the Time Slider.

Use the pull-down menu below the Time Slider to switch between Character Sets or None.

DON'T FORGET

Character Sets are required if using the Trax Editor. They are needed to create clips and store poses.

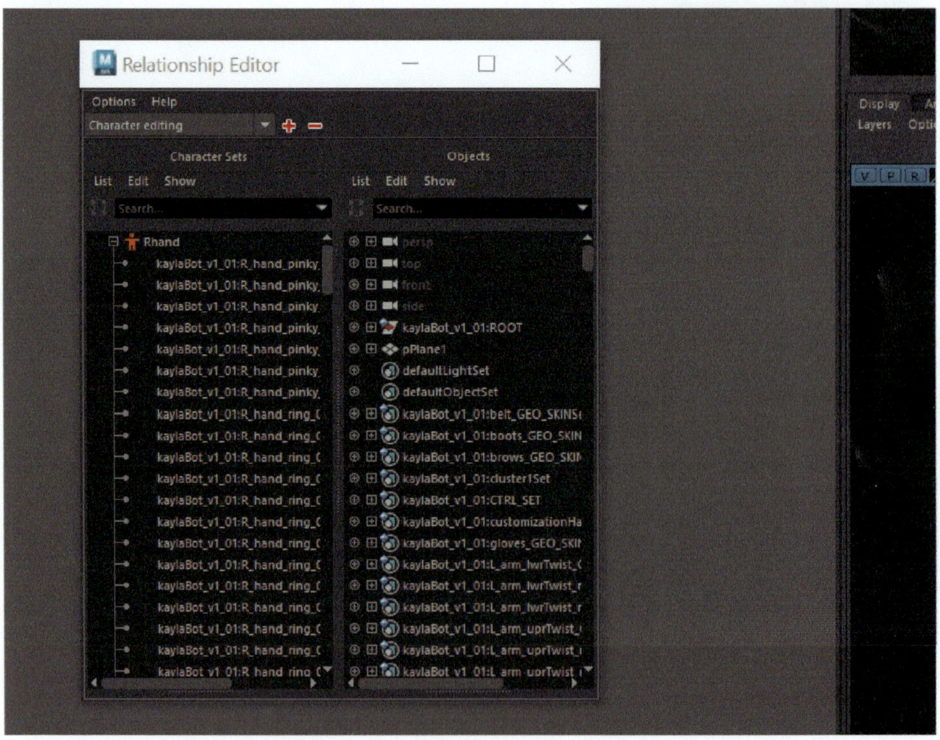

Go to Windows > Relationship Editors > Character Sets to add or subtract objects to an existing Character Set.

If a rig has scale and translate options on the FK controls, make a Character Set that only keys the rotation channels. The drawback is that there are no options to make shelf buttons and you need to keep an eye on which Character Set is active. Of course, instead of making Character Sets, there is the option of locking the Scale and Translate channels to avoid keying them.

It is recommended to spend the time to make selection buttons, Quick Select Sets or Character Sets before you start animating. It is much easier to make selections when the rig is in its default bind pose.

Quick Select Sets group controls into sets as an easy way to put keys on all the controls and their attribute.

Display Layers

A rig may come with Display Layers already made. Find them in the Channel Box/ Display Editor tab. Layers have three modes:

Box 1: V – Visibility, toggles on and off.

Box 2: P – Playback, when set to P, objects in layer will be visible during playback.

Box 3: T or R – T is for Template; objects are displayed as wireframe and not selectable. R is for Reference; objects are displayed as normal and not selectable.

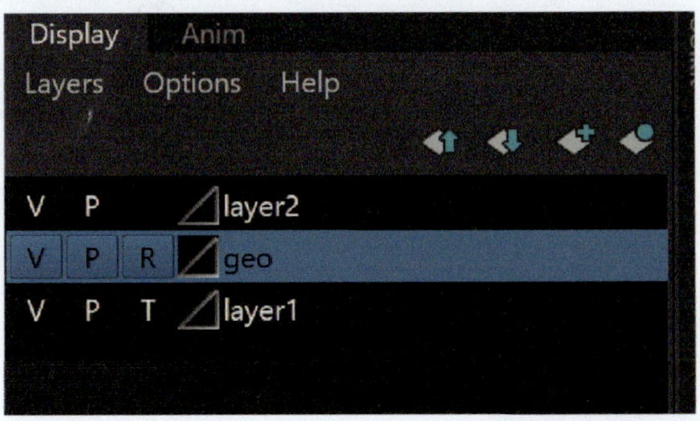

The easiest way to add something to its own layer is to select it; go to the Display tab > Layers > Create Layer from Selected. Or go to the Display tab > Layers > Create Empty Layer. Then add objects by selecting them and RMB the layer or going to Options > Add New Objects to the Current Layer.

The Show menu only affects one Viewport panel at a time. If toggling on/off in the Show menu, and an item is still not visible, then check if it is on a Display Layer with visibility turned off. Display Layers do affect every Viewport panel, but only the objects placed in that layer. If the Display Layer is set to visible, and most of the objects are visible but one or two are missing, look in the Outliner to see if the individual items have been hidden. Select items in Outliner and press hotkey Shift + H to Show and Ctrl + H to Hide.

CHEAT

Rig geometry should be set to unselectable. If the rig has layers, make sure the geo layers are set to R.

Outliner

The Outliner can be useful for accessing controls and to see the hierarchy of the rig. To expand the entire hierarchy of a rig, go to the top node and Shift click the plus sign. Toggle to collapse. This method works on any branch of the hierarchy. Shift click any plus sign to expand or collapse everything underneath.

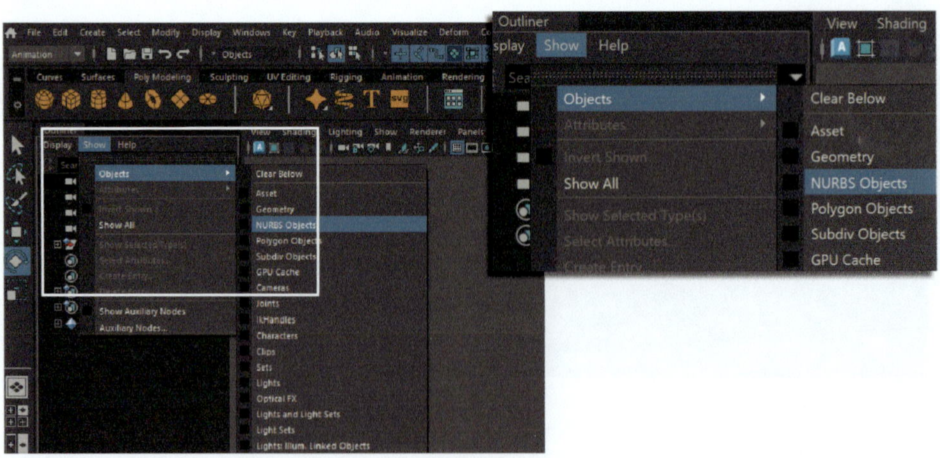

Use the Show menu and Display menu in the Outliner to select the type of objects you wish to list.

Select a control on the rig. Move your cursor over the Outliner and click F to frame selection. This will open expand the nodes and highlight your selection. Shift click the plus to collapse.

RIG CHEATS

Having Trouble Selecting Controls?

Most rig controls are NURBS curves or surfaces. Set Selection mode for NURBS only.

Go to the Status Line toolbar, RMB on Selection Mask, and set it to Objects.
Expanding the section may be necessary to see the Selection Mask buttons.
Set all the Selection Mask buttons off except NURBS Selection Mask Button (blue curve).

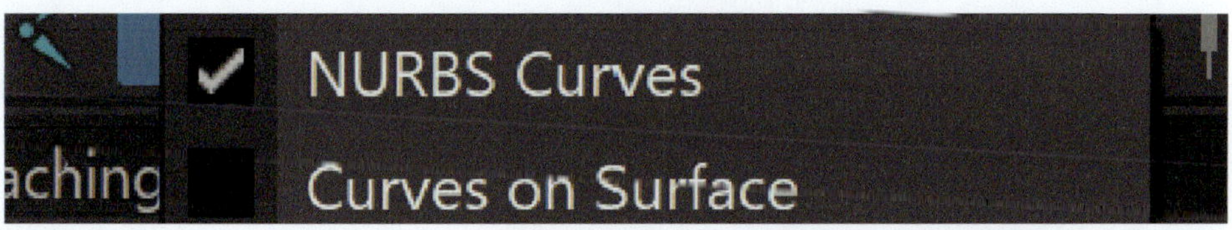

Optional to narrow the selection mask even more, RMB on the NURBS Selection Mask button and set it to NURBS Curves only.

Make the controls stand out. To make a single control curve thicker:

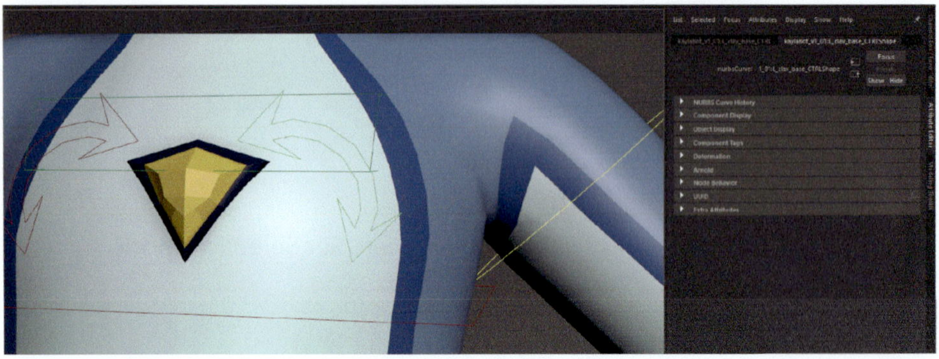

Select kaylaBot's shoulder rotation control, the red arched arrows.

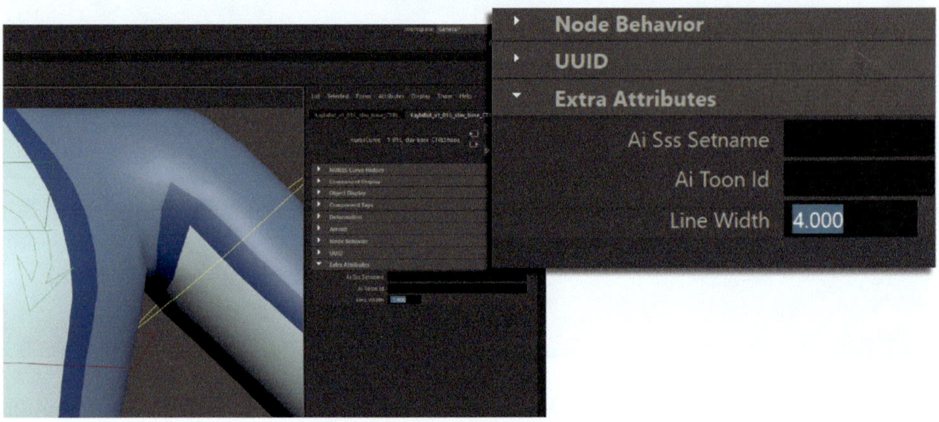

Go to the Attribute Editor, second tab (shape tab).

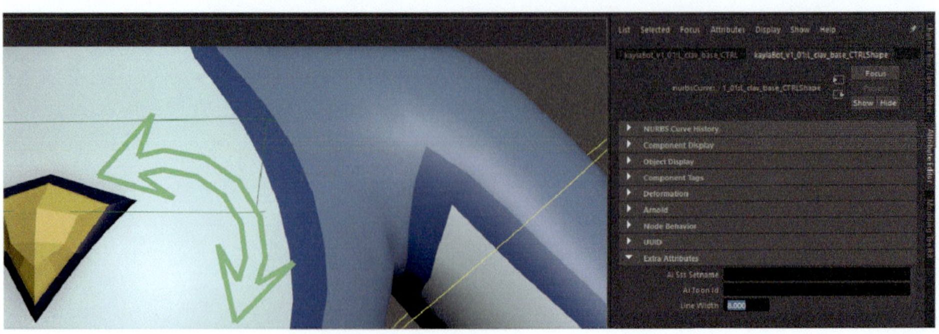

Go down and expand the Extra Attributes section and increase the Line Width value.

To increase the Line Width on all curves and wireframes in your Maya scene:

Go to Windows > Settings / Preferences > Preferences. Click on Display. Under View, go to Line Width.

DON'T FORGET

Changing individual control curves may not be available if the rigger has locked off the attributes.

Make a control curve bigger:

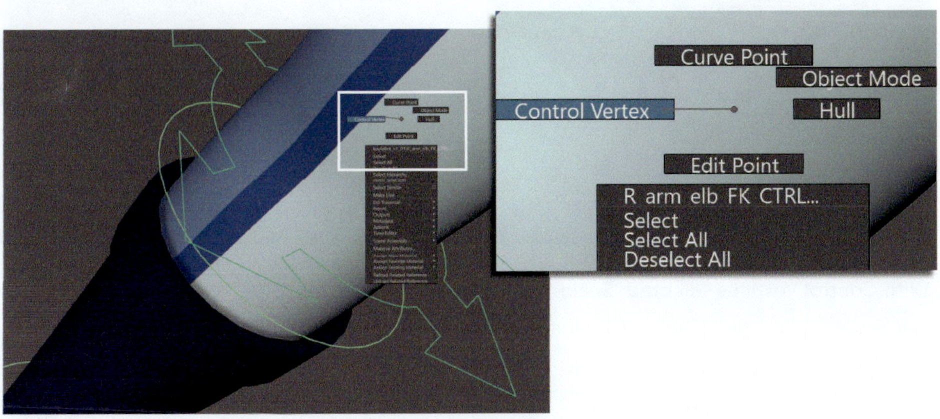

Select the control and RMB to the side to select the NURBS component.

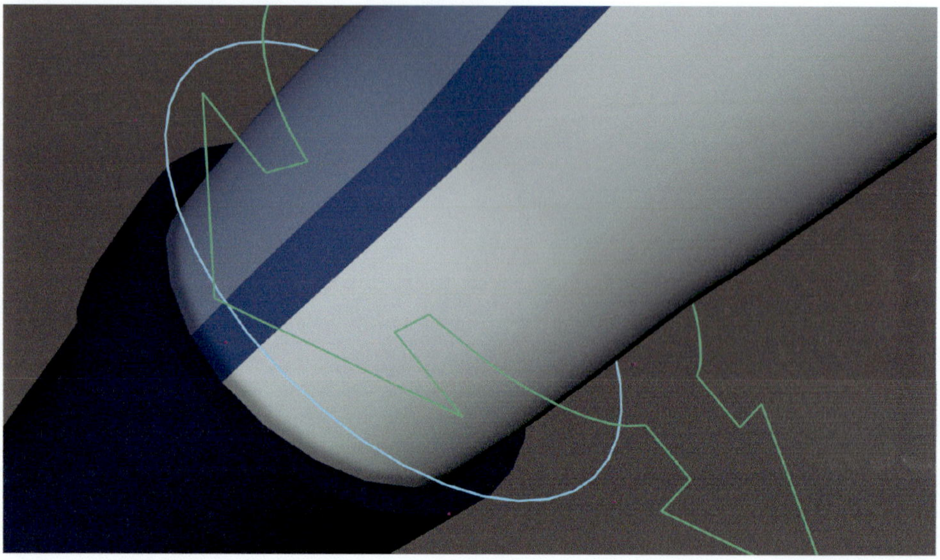

Choose Control Vertices and select all vertices.

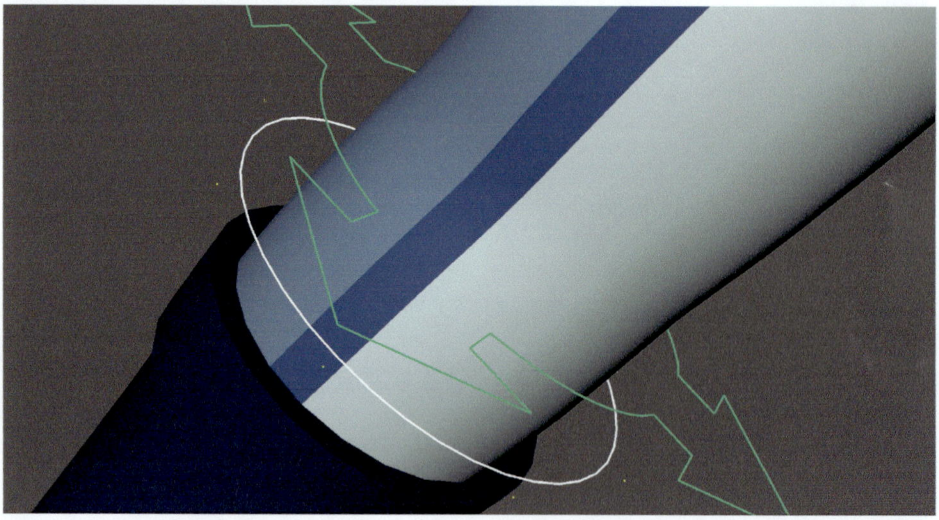

With Control Vertices selected, Scale (hotkey R) out the points.

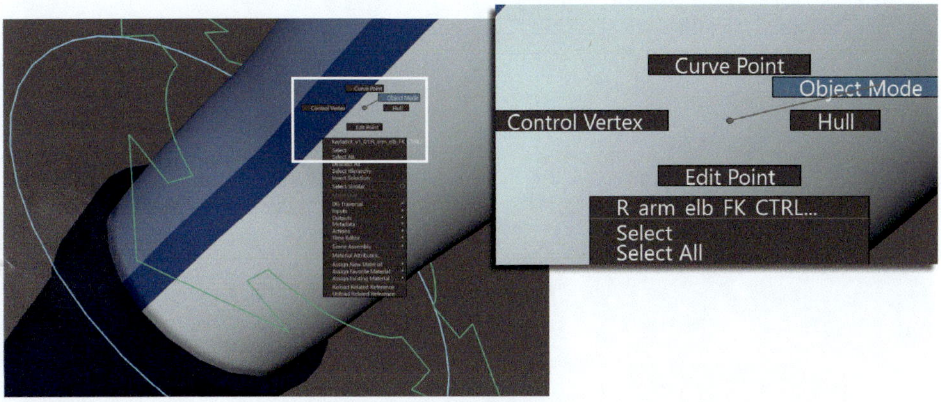

When done, RMB off to the side and select Object Mode.

CHEAT

Selecting more controls than desired or selecting controls through the back side of the geometry? Set the selection mode to only select what is visible to the camera.

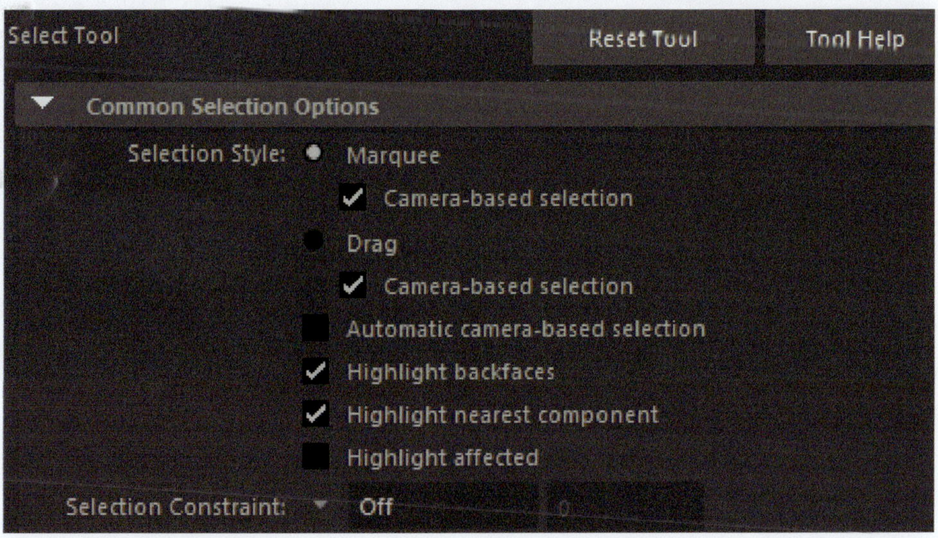

Double-click the Selection icon in the Toolbox. Check Camera-based selection to only select what is visible in the viewport.

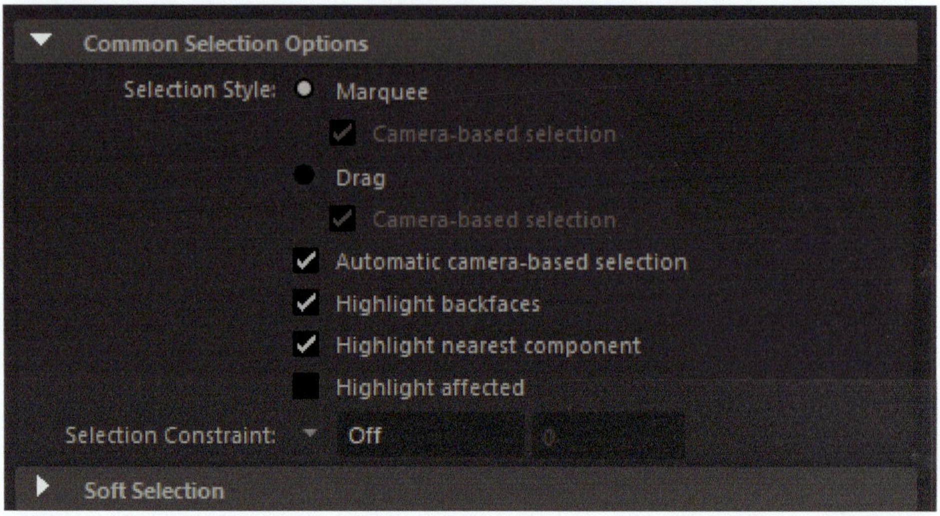

Automatic camera-based selection will turn on when selecting in shaded mode and turn off when selecting in wireframe and x-ray modes.

If geometry is in the way, then hide everything but the rig controls so they are easier to select.

Use Display Layers: If the geometry is on a layer, toggle off visibility, V.

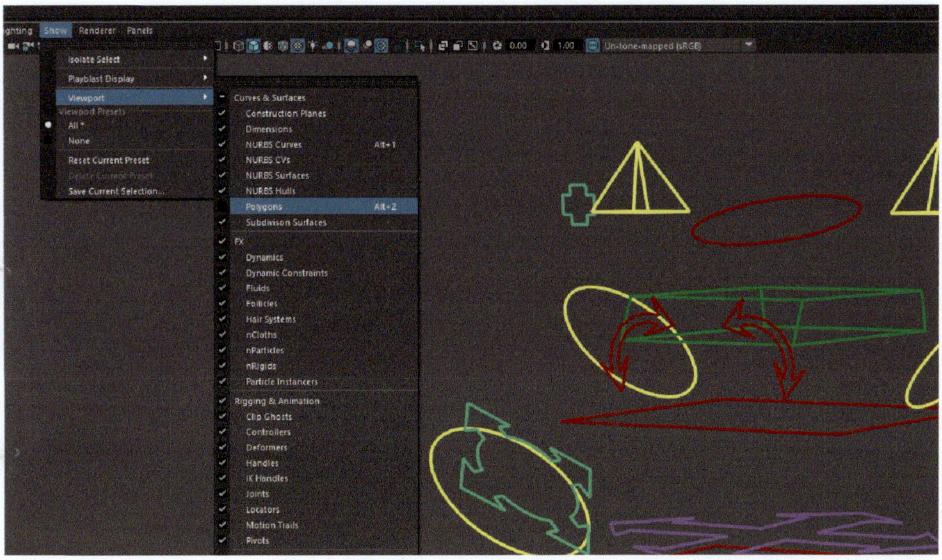

No layers? Go to the Show menu and uncheck polygons. Or, go to the Show menu and hide everything else: Show > None and then check on the NURBS Curves, or hotkey Alt + 1

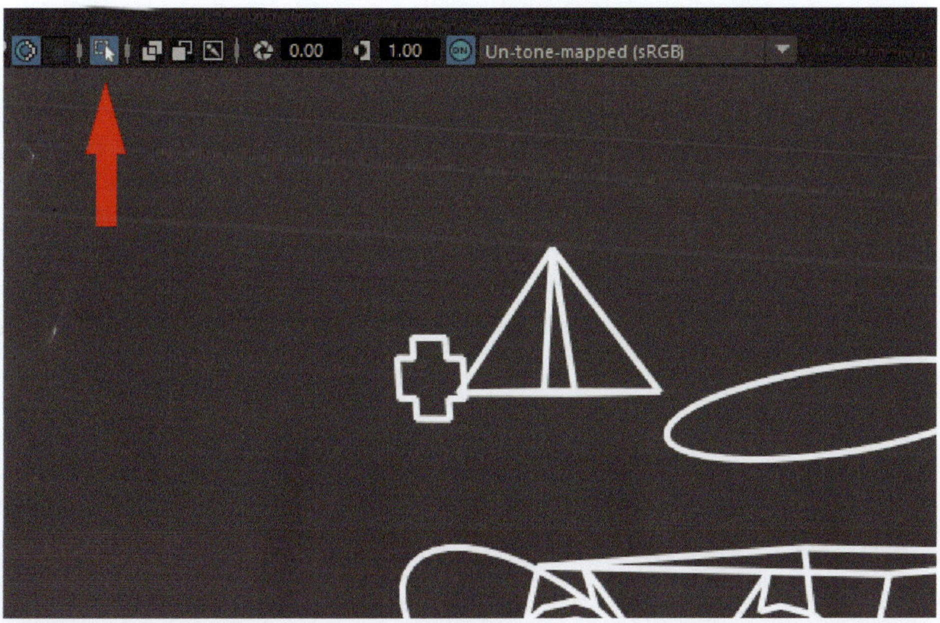

Use isolate: Locators and other non-poly objects in the way? Go to Select > Select all by Type > NURBS Curves. Then use Isolate. This will hide everything but the controls. Isolate can be found on the Viewport toolbar, it's a blue dash rectangle with a white arrow. The Isolate hotkey is Shift + i. To toggle off, deselect isolated object and press Shift + I.

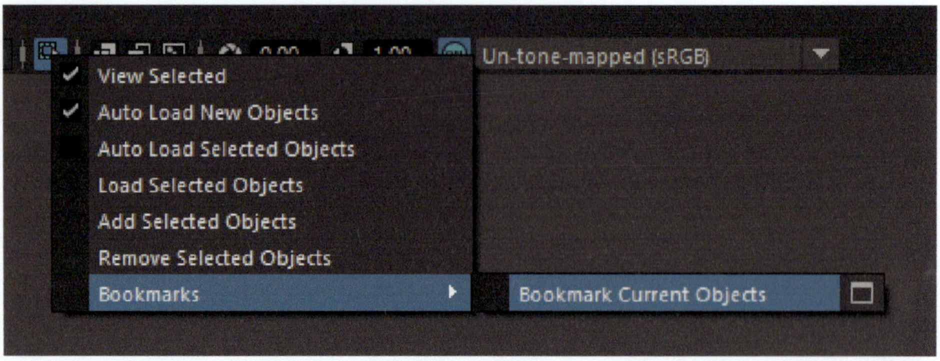

RMB the Isolate icon to bring up options like adding or subtracting objects, or create bookmarks. Go to Bookmarks > Bookmark Current Objects.

Heavy Rigs

The rig is heavy, the geometry is dense, and it is slowing down Maya.

In professional studios, there will be several levels of geometry on the rig, so a real-time performance is always available to the animators. The rig will often have a super-lightweight mesh called a proxy. Instead of a body, the character will be divided into simple cylinders or boxes. Next, there will be a low-res, or unsmoothed mesh. It will look like the final character but the polygon count is greatly reduced. Then the default mesh, which may have an option to increase the geometry to higher resolution or a smoothing option which can be toggled on and off. After animation is complete, it is baked, exported, and applied to a very high-res, sub-d mesh which is not animatable for the final render.

If the rig does not come with any options built in, we will have to approach it in another way.

CHEAT

If the rig is heavy, check the Main control on the rig for a proxy or low-res option first. If there is a smoothing option, put it on the lowest setting.

Smooth Preview applied: hotkey 3

Smooth Preview removed: hotkey 1

Select the geometry, and press hotkey 1 to set preview smoothness to none. This will stop Maya from calculating smoothness and speed up the Viewport interaction.

Go to viewport toolbar > Shading and select Flat Shade All or Selected Items. This will make every poly face flat and shaded in one color. The computer is no longer calculating a gradient of light and dark to make the appearance of a smooth curve, speeding up interaction more.

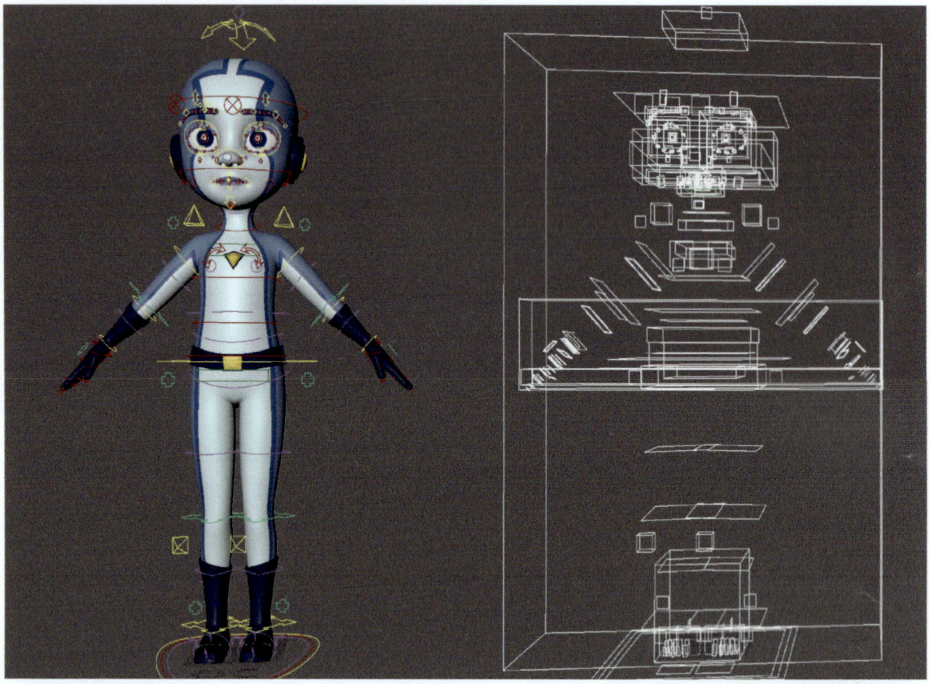

For extreme cases, geometry can be hidden and represented by wireframe boxes or Bounding Boxes. Select all geometry. Go to Display > Object Display > Bounding Box. This method is not very helpful if the rig body is one continuous mesh object. It works best on rigs with proxy bodies that are already divided into many pieces of geometry.

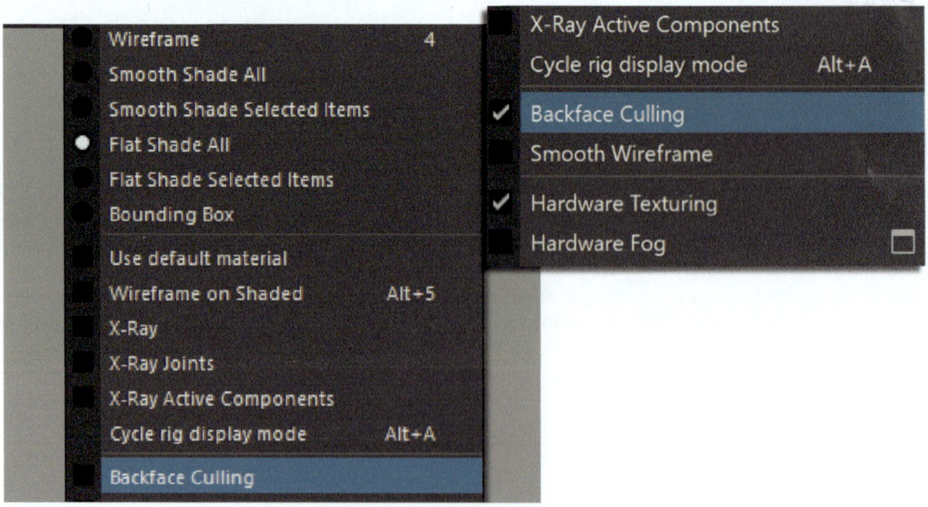

Go to viewport toolbar > Shading and check Backface Culling. This will stop Maya from drawing the back side of shaded objects that are not visible to the camera.

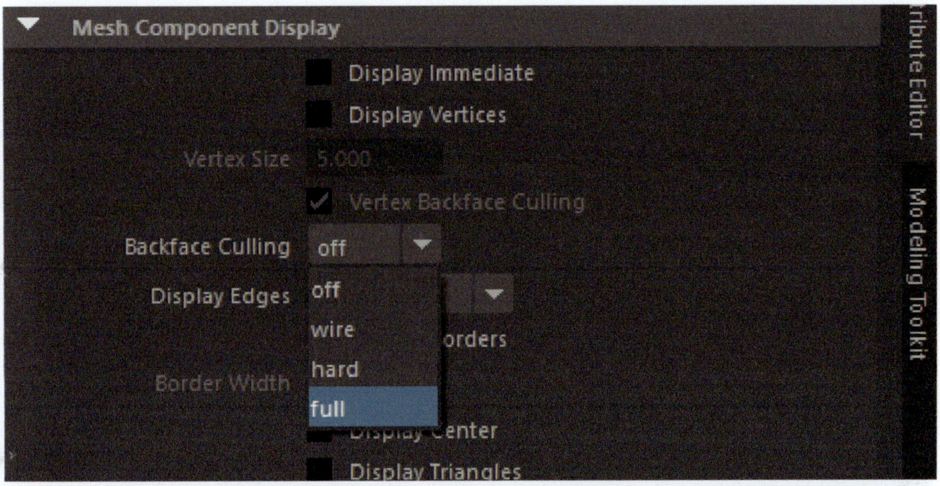

To apply Backface Culling to objects in shaded, wireframe or x-ray modes, select all the geometry. Go to the Attribute Editor, second tab (shape tab), Mesh Component Display, and set Backface Culling to Hard or Full.

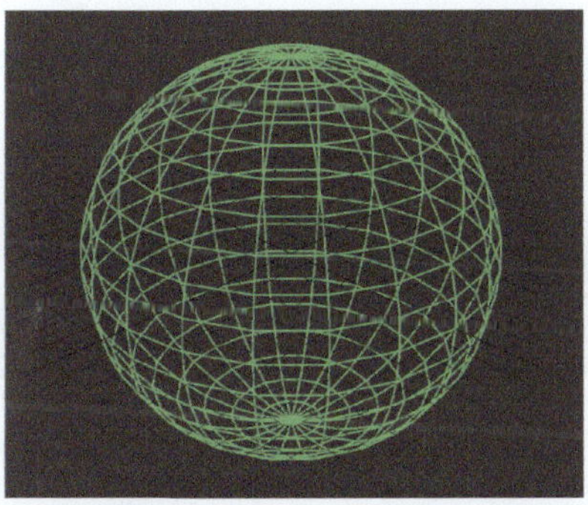

Wireframe Shaded

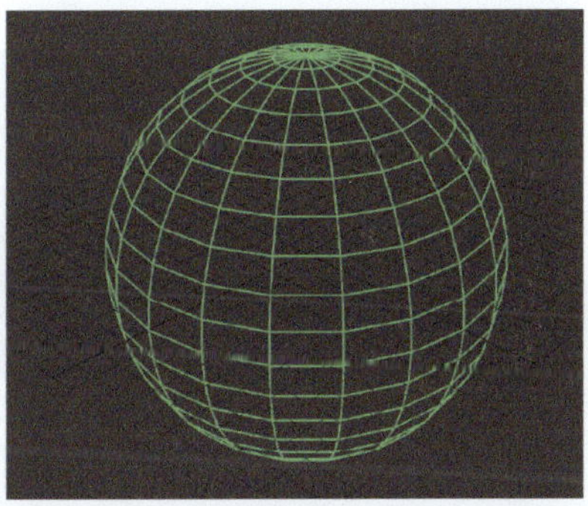

Backface Culling applied to sphere

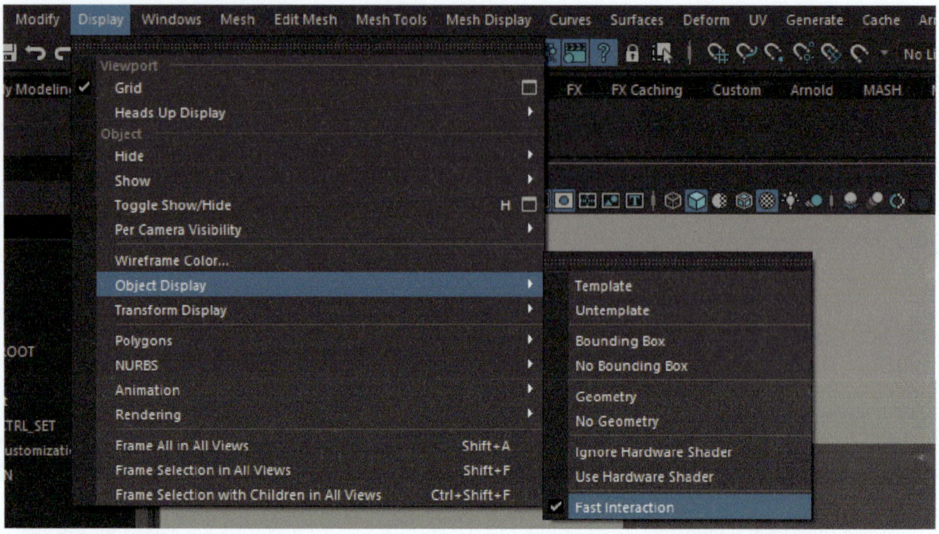

Go to Display menu > Object Display and check on Fast Interaction. This will make Maya draw objects at a lower resolution when they are farther from the camera.

By default, Maya should be set to redraw the active viewport only. Click the Time Slider Preference (orange man with gear), go to Playback and make sure Update View is set to Active. Setting the Update to View to All will make the animation play in every viewport but may slow the playback speed.

ANIMAL RIGS

This book concentrates on mainly human animation, but let's talk a little bit about animals. First, use reference videos! There is a wealth of animal locomotion reference available online. Use it. Here are some suggestions on what to look for when selecting and testing animal rigs:

Mammals

All mammal skeletons are very similar to our own. You see the same finger bones in a bear, a bat, and a dolphin fin.

For quadruped animation, most mammals walk on their toes or hooves (modified toenails). Bears and apes do occasionally walk with heels on the ground. But most mammals never lower their heels to walk. What causes much confusion for beginning animators is: quadrupeds are walking on tip toe. The knee and elbow joints are way up on the side of the body, and the legs that are visible are actually elongated lower legs, ankles, and mid-feet in the back and elongated forearms, wrists, and 'hand' bones in the front. No, horses do not have backward knees and elbows! We are looking at their ankles and wrist equivalents.

Treat a quadruped's shoulders much like another pair of hips. The rig will be constructed like two pairs of hips and legs connected with an IK spine. The foot roll is heavily modified because the animal is up on its toes. Depending on the type of animal, the front foot can have very different poses from the back feet.

Consider the animals' flexibility. Are they rigid like an elephant or liquid like a cat? Do they have a trunk or prehensile tail? Prehensile tails can grab branches. To animate a prehensile tail or trunk, IK controls will be needed

Birds

Much like mammals, birds also stand on their toes. An ostrich does not have backward knees; you are looking at the ankle. The wing consists of a very thin upper arm, elbow, forearm, wrist, and fingers. Feathers project out, and the bird can use them to direct the airflow around the wing.

Flight has an upstroke and a downstroke. For a downstroke, the wings go down and forward. Upstroke birds bend their elbows and drag the tips of the wings. The wings go slightly back on the upstroke. The arms lift first and the wrist and fingers drag still pointing down. Finally, the entire wing flips up.

Bats are mammals. Instead of feathers, they have shorter wings consisting of a skin membrane down the arms and between their fingers. The downstroke is the same as a bird, but the upstroke is different. Bats do not drag their wings. They flick their wings up and back with a twist. Bats are faster and more maneuverable fliers than most birds.

Insects

The insect kingdom is incredibly diverse. Do your research to animate species properly. Depending on the insect, they can crawl, walk, run, jump, fly, or swim. For many types of insects, their walking gait includes 2 or 3 feet on the ground in each step, but it can vary with speed. Some flying insects have muscles that move their wings, others oscillate their thorax to make the wings move. Most fly with a half-stroke in one direction (up and back, down and forward), then twist the wing and do a half-stroke in the opposite (down and back, up and forward). When animating very fast repetitive motions, it's best to create a cycle for wing motions or multiple legs.

Reptiles

Lizards walk with their bodies low to the ground with bent knees and elbows, called sprawling. They also flex their spines and swish their tails side to side to help propel them. You will need a quadruped rig with IK spine and IK tail for prehensile reptile tails.

Snakes are all muscle. To move, they contract the muscles and curve their bodies, then push down where the body is curved to propel themselves forward. Make sure the rig has many IK controls along the body.

Sea Creatures

Fish and sharks move through the water with S-shaped body movements through the tail to push against the water with fins to steer and optimize body shape.

Soft body invertebrates often use some variation of taking in water and pushing it out to create forward momentum. A rig with a deformation system and IK for tentacles will be needed.

Imaginary Creatures

What if it doesn't exist? We need to find similar real-world creatures we can draw from. For example, does a dragon fly like a bat, perch like a falcon, or move like an iguana? Find animals with similar physiology and anatomy to the creature. It will usually be an amalgamation of many animals.

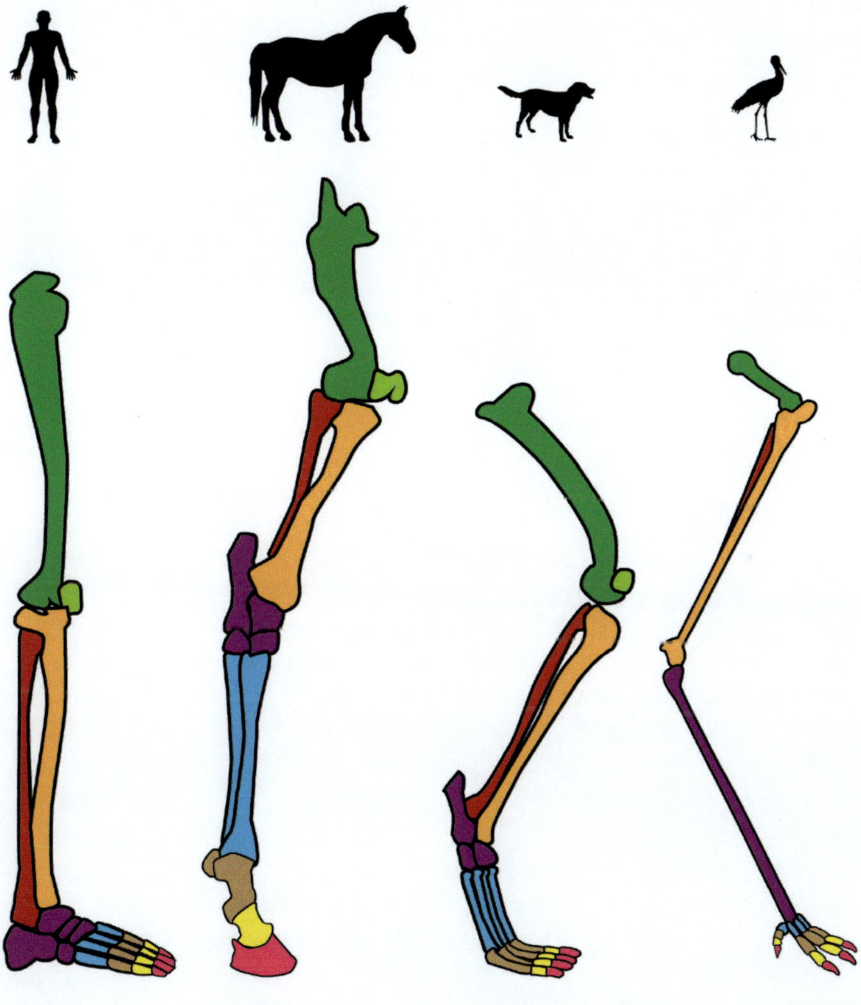

Here are the legs of a human, horse, dog, and bird. They all have the same bones, just in different configurations.

WHY DO WE KEEP SEEING THE SAME FACES?

There is a moment in almost every modern animated feature when a new character appears on screen, and you feel like you've seen them before. The large doe eyes. The soft, rounded features. The slight asymmetry in the face that suggests charm without imperfection. Whether it's a Disney princess, a DreamWorks rogue, or a Pixar sidekick, the aesthetic of CG animation has slowly converged into something eerily familiar.

Looking back at the early days of CG animation, character designs varied much more than today.

This was not always the case. Looking back at the early days of CG animation, character designs varied much more than today. Comparing the appealing, cartoonish faces in *Toy Story* to the stylized grotesqueness of *Shrek*, characters all felt distinct from one another. Today, despite the vast number of studios producing feature animation, there is a creeping sameness to character design across the industry.

Some of this can be attributed to practical considerations. CG models require a massive amount of work to rig, texture, and animate, and certain design choices make that process easier. Large eyes make for more expressive performances. Soft facial geometry deforms better for exaggerated expressions. Simplified hair and clothing reduce simulation time. These are all efficiency-driven decisions, and in a high-stakes industry where a single feature costs hundreds of millions of dollars, risk is something to be minimized.

But efficiency alone does not explain the shift. Part of it comes down to market-tested familiarity. Animated features are expensive, and studios want to ensure broad appeal. Audiences, especially younger ones, are drawn to faces that are inherently appealing: big eyes, symmetrical features, and rounded edges. Decades of research into psychology and likability have reinforced this, and animation studios have leaned into the stats. Especially for non-U.S. based studios, copying what Disney and Pixar have done is the safest path, even if over-done. And, in a world where merchandising can make or break a franchise, characters must be designed to be instantly likable, memeable, and recognizable on a lunchbox from across the cafeteria.

Some of this was intentional; Glen Keane was brought in to direct the animation of *Tangled*, and established the new 3D 'look' for Disney films. The success of *Tangled* and *Frozen* created a cascade of design choices that continue to ripple through the industry. *Moana, Encanto, Wish*, and even non-Disney films like *Ruby Gillman: Teenage Kraken* all share a similar DNA in facial proportions and expressiveness. Meanwhile, DreamWorks shifted from their early, exaggerated caricatures (*Shark Tale, Madagascar*) to the now-familiar soft-featured leads of *Croods, Monsters vs. Aliens, Peabody and Sherman*, etc. Once a visual style proves successful, it is hard to resist using it again.

This phenomenon is not unique to CG. In the golden age of 2D animation, studios borrowed from each other relentlessly. The appeal of the 90s "Disney New Renaissance" influenced films from Don Bluth, Warner Bros, and even anime of the time. The difference now is that CG characters require an enormous investment in infrastructure. The cost of developing entirely new modeling, rigging, and shading pipelines for each film is prohibitive, which leads to studios reusing methodologies and design choices rather than reinventing the wheel.

However, there are signs of change. *Spider-Man: Into the Spider-Verse* shattered expectations by fully embracing stylization, inspiring a wave of films that experimented with breaking the mold (*The Mitchells vs. The Machines, Teenage Mutant Ninja Turtles: Mutant Mayhem*). While these films still rely on appealing character design, they prove that CG does not have to be constrained by realism or safe aesthetics.

So why do we keep seeing the same faces? Because familiarity sells. Because pipelines dictate design. Because audiences subconsciously favor certain shapes. And because, for now, studios are more interested in refining what works than risking what might not. But as technology evolves and filmmakers push boundaries, perhaps we will finally see a new generation of animated characters that feel as fresh and distinct as they once did.

5 GRAPH EDITOR

INTRODUCING THE GRAPH EDITOR

The Graph Editor is a very powerful tool. Evaluating and adjusting animation keys in curve form is industry standard in most animation software. It is very important to become comfortable with curves and working in the Graph Editor.

The Graph Editor can look very messy and complex when there are many curves on the screen. However, once you learn to read it, it is the best tool to examine the animation across the shot. The graph is quite simple, it shows value vs. time. Reading the graph left-to-right is time or frames. Reading the graph up and down is the value. The values are positive above the zero line and negative below. The steeper the slope of the curve, the faster the motion. The flatter the curve is, the slower the motion. A flat line — zero slope or or zero change — means no motion at all.

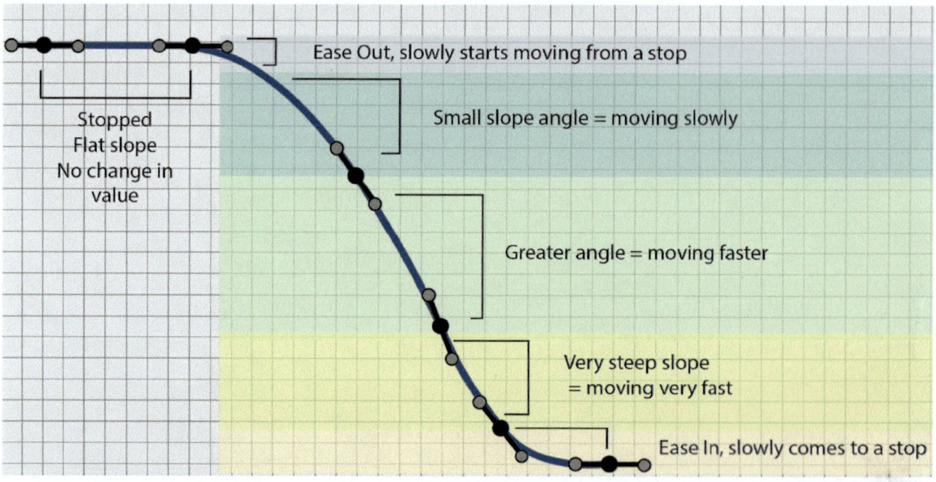

Each animated attribute will have its own curve. Maya automatically plots the keyframes on the graph and interpolates, or draws a curve between the points. The curve shape is initially set by the type of interpolation chosen. The curve can be further shaped with each key's handles, called tangent handles. The tangent handles can be moved in unison or broken and moved individually.

Open the Graph Editor from Windows > Animation Editors > Graph Editor as a floating window. Or open the Graph Editor in any panel by going to the Viewport > Panels > Panel > Graph Editor. If using the Animation preset in Workspaces, the Graph Editor will be fixed in the bottom panel.

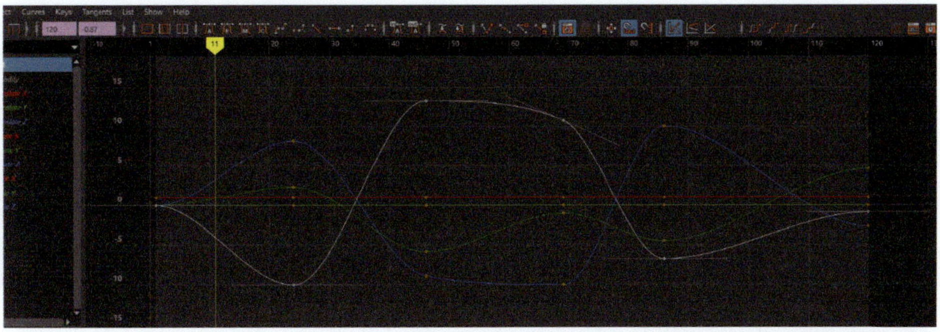

The Graph Editor will display time in frames on the time ruler and have a time indicator just like the workspace Time Slider. In fact, the Graph Editor is connected to the workspace Time Slider. If using the range slider, the animation outside the active range will be shaded dark. To adjust the play range, grab the dark handles on the time ruler and slide them.

The left side of the Graph Editor has its own Outliner. It functions exactly like the workspace Outliner. Shift select for multiple attributes, and Ctrl + LMB to subtract or add to the selection. Next to each attribute listed, there is a pin icon. Click the pin so it is upright, and it will pin that curve to the Graph Editor, so even if the object is de-selected, that curve will remain displayed. The Outliner also displays special icons if you Mute or Lock the curves.

CHEAT

Many pro animators use multiple monitors, with the graph editor permanently open on the second. If you don't have two monitors, at a minimum set a convenient hotkey to open the Graph Editor.

The camera controls work in the graph view area. To see the whole curve use hotkey A to frame all. To frame a selection use hotkey F. Both pan (Alt+MMB) and zoom (Alt+RMB) are available in the graph area. Orbit will not work since the graph is a 2D plane. Use Shift to constrain both the pan and zoom. Hold the Shift key, the cursor turns to a question mark, then slowly move the cursor vertically or horizontally. Shift + Alt + RMB and drag horizontally to zoom time or drag vertically to zoom value.

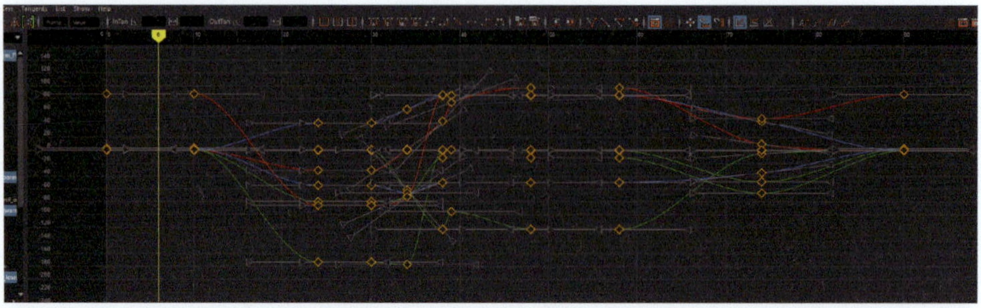

Absolute View (hotkey 1): The Absolute view is the default view. Always work in Absolute view because it displays the true scale of the curves relative to each other. The left side of the graph area will display values in Maya units for translation and scale or degrees for rotation when in default.

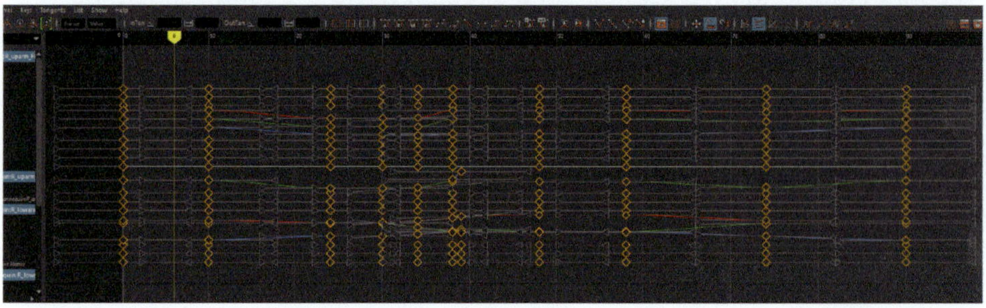

Stacked View (hotkey 2): The Stacked view separates all the curves, and scales them to fit the space stacked one over the other. Curves are distorted.

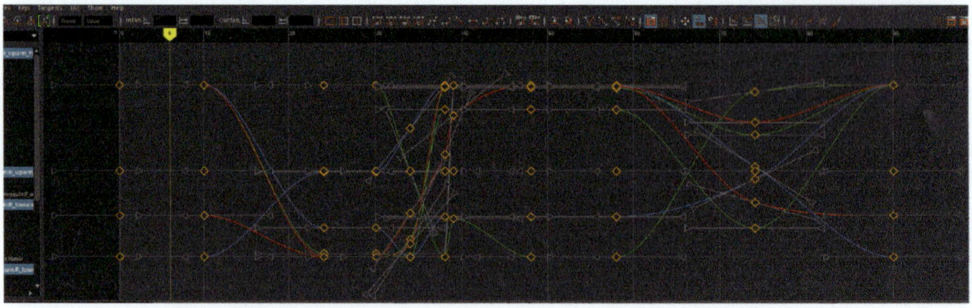

Normalized View (hotkey 3): The Normalized view resizes all curves to display as the same size to take up the display area. Curves are distorted.

The Graph Editor is completely customizable. If you are new to Maya, it may be a good idea to stick with the default settings until you become more familiar. To customize the Graph Editor, go to the View menu. The Frame All option should be left checked on. It frames the attribute curves automatically. It is optional to have keys and handles to only be visible when active, display time ruler to the top or bottom, or display curve names. There are multiple color themes to choose from. Finally on the bottom, there is a check box for Simple Toolbar, the simplified toolbar hides icons that are usually set once, like autoload, snapping, cycling, and view types.

TANGENTS AND WEIGHTS

There are two types of keys: Keys with Weighted Tangent handles and keys with Non-Weighted Tangent handles. You cannot mix the two types of keys on a single curve, so we must set the entire curve under the Curves menu.

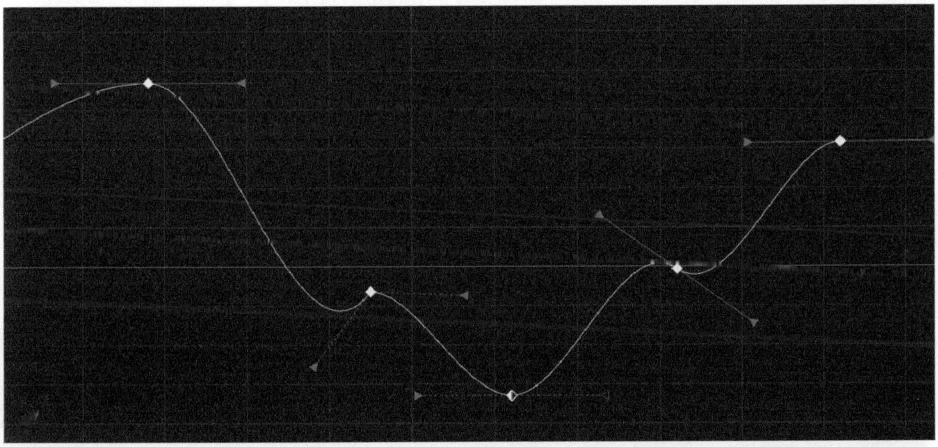

Non-Weighted curves have keys with fixed handle lengths. Take a curve between two keys. The angle of rotation of the handles on the first key has a strong influence on the first half of the curve but then falls off. Likewise, the handle of the second key has the strongest influence on the back half of the curve. If you want to change the shape of the curve beyond what can be done by rotating the handles, you need to add more keys.

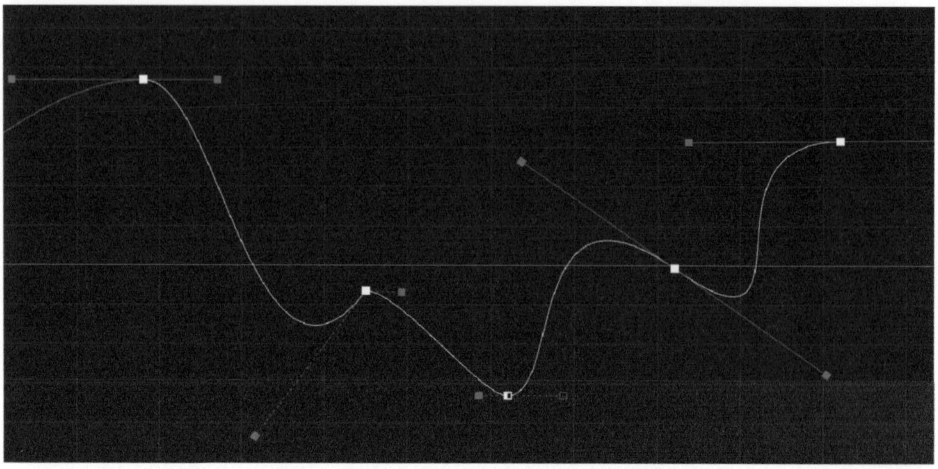

Weighted curves differ because both the angle and length of the tangent handles can be adjusted. The curve is influenced by the angle of rotation and the scale, or weight of the handles. This allows for re-shaping a section of curve between two keys beyond what is possible with non-weighted tangents.

Which one is better? They are both good. A studio may have a preference depending on the pipeline. For example, if working with weighted curves, baking your animation after the shot is approved may be required.

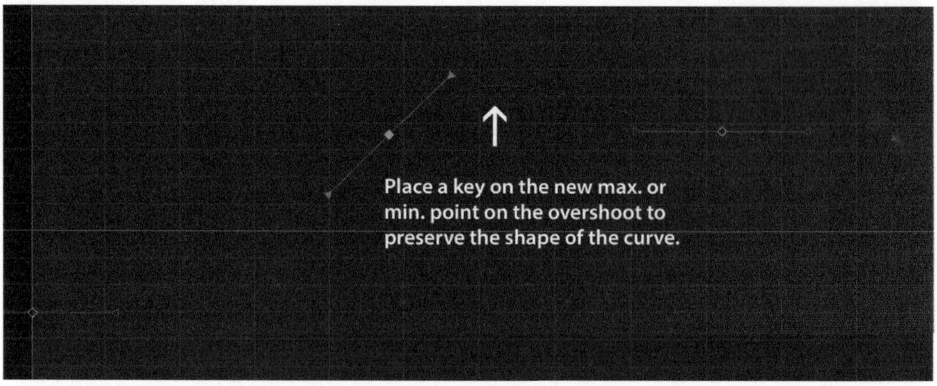

An overshoot is where the tangent handles are turned in such a way that the curve shoots beyond the minimum and maximum keys. Do not allow the shape of your animation curves to be controlled by handle-influence alone. It is very important to add a key to the extreme highs and lows to preserve the shape of the curve. Scaling animation over time will change the shape of the curve between the handles, especially on weighted curves. Lock down the shape of the curve with additional keys or the animation will change.

CHEAT

Pros build in anticipation and overshoot into their blocking, by adding the keys they'll need later to refine these principles. It's common to think to oneself "4 frame anticipation, 12 frame move, 6 frame overshoot, settle in 8". Try to think in terms of timing and the resulting curves in the Graph Editor to improve your workflow.

INTERPOLATION TYPES

The Graph Editor shows the animation curves. The curve represents how Maya is interpolating the motion between keys. Choose what type of interpolation Maya is applying. The interpolation type can be applied to the whole curve, selected keys, or individual handles.

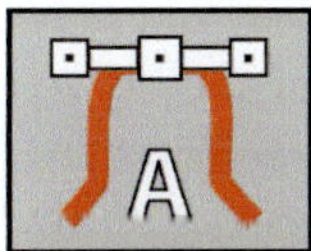	**Auto Span (Legacy):** default setting, the first, last, top, and bottom keys will be a flat tangent. Any keys on slopes will have the handles automatically rotated to match the slope.
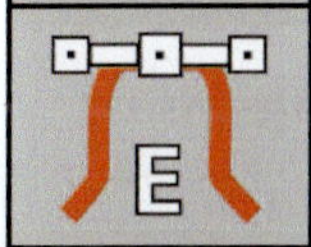	**Auto Ease:** like Auto Span, keys on slope will be calculated slightly differently with more weight placed on neighboring keys.
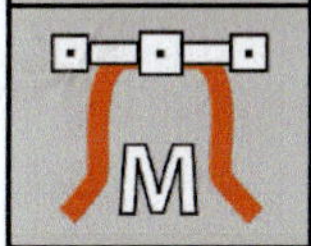	**Auto Mix:** like Auto Span, keys on slope will be calculated slightly differently with linear blend of slopes.
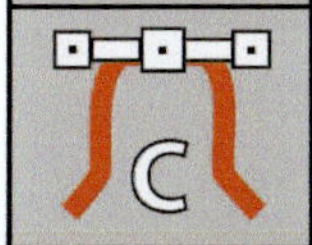	**Auto Custom:** like Auto Span, keys on slope will be calculated by your choice.
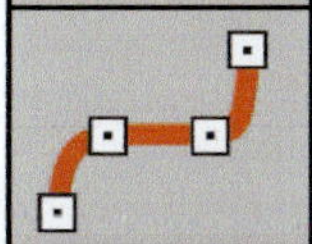	**Spline:** all keys will have slope based on the previous and following key. Keys at the bottom, where the curve changes direction will overshoot and not be flat.
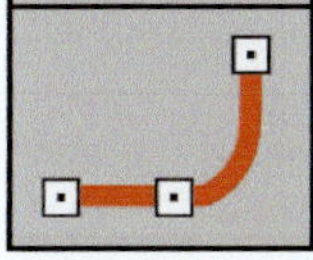	**Plateau:** the first and last keys are flat, keys close in value will be interpolated as flat, keys on slope will be rotated.

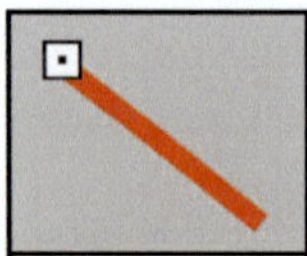	**Linear:** constant speed from one key to another, no eases.
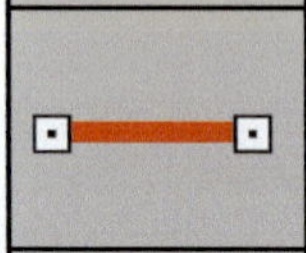	**Flat:** all keys have zero slope; object slows to a stop at every key with a flat tangent.
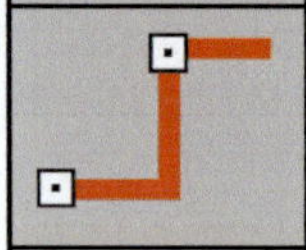	**Step:** no interpolation, object freezes, or is held, until the next key. Movement is instantaneous over one frame.
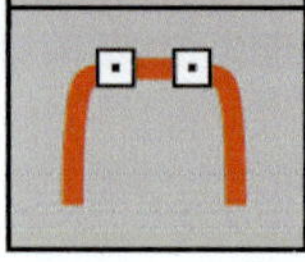	**Clamped:** like spline, first, last, top and bottom keys will be rotated. If any keys are close in value, they will be interpolated as flat, keys on slope will be rotated.

INSERTING OR ADDING KEYS

The hotkey S saves a key on all animatable attributes. To set keys on individual translations, use Shift + W for move, Shift+ E for rotate, and Shift+ R for scale. To set a key on one or more attributes at a time, go to the Channel Box, RMB, and Key Selected. Inserting a new key will place a key directly on the existing curve without changing the shape of the curve. To insert a key, one key must be selected to make the curve active. You can insert keys on multiple curves as long as they are actively selected.

- **Method 1:** Place the time indicator on the chosen frame, RMB and choose Insert Key or use hotkey Alt + I.
- **Method 2:** Go to Keys > Insert Key Tool or click the icon in the toolbar. The cursor will change to a plus sign, click where you want the new key to go. It is not dependent on the time indicator position. To exit the tool, hit Enter or hotkey Q to go back to selection mode.

Add Key allows you to add keys and change the shape of the curve at the same time. LMB above or below the curve and it will add a key in that location and simultaneously re-draw the curve. To add a key, first make the curve active by selecting a key. To add keys on multiple curves, make sure they are all actively selected.

Both the Add Key Tool and Insert Key Tool have two additional settings.

1. **Add or Insert Breakdown Keys.** The breakdown key has a spatial relationship with the surrounding keys, meaning when a breakdown key is moved, it will push and pull the closest keys. Breakdown keys are displayed in green.
2. **Preserve Tangent Type.** The angle of the handles of the added or inserted keys will adjust and change the shape of the curve so that the tangent handles of the key that came before and after are unchanged.

DON'T FORGET

Having the Graph Editor open as you learn these new tools is really helpful for watching the results update in real-time.

DELETING OR REMOVING KEYS

Select keys or curves in the Graph Editor and hit Delete. Shift + LMB to select a range of keys in the Time Slider and RMB and choose Delete. The default setting for Delete is to only affect what is selected.

For more options on how things are being deleted in the Graph Editor, use the Remove Key tool. To remove keys by type, go to Keys > Remove Key and choose an option. Or RMB in the Time Slider and choose Keys > Remove Key > options.

- **Unsnapped:** This will remove any key not on a whole frame. This can be very useful when you have sped up an animation by scaling the time down, causing multiple keys to be squeezed in between two frames.
- **Before Current Frame, After Current Frame, Outside Current Frame:** Place Time Slider on frame or go to the Timeline and Shift select a range of keys.
- **Ripple Delete:** This will move keys up into the space left behind when removing a section of animation.
- **Redundant Keys:** In flat sections of curves, it will keep the first and last key but remove any extra between keys since there is no change in value. You can accomplish similar results with more fine control with the Key Reducer Tool brush, Key Reducer Filter, or the Curve Simplify Filter.

COPYING AND PASTING KEYS

In the Graph Editor, select keys or curves and use the hotkeys Ctrl+C to copy, move the Time Slider, and Ctrl+V to paste. By default, Copy is set to copy all selected and Paste is set to Merge the pasted keys with the original curve. In the Time Slider, RMB and choose to Copy, Paste, or Paste Connect. To adjust the settings, go to the Graph Editor Edit menu.

In the Graph Editor, go to Edit > Copy and go to the option box. The options control how much of the curve to copy.
In the Graph Editor, go to Edit > Paste and go to the option box. Paste options are Insert, Merge, and Replace.

- **Insert** inserts copied keys and shifts the original animation over.
- **Merge** overwrites keys on the same frames and insert other keys on the original curve.
- **Replace** needs a start and end of range and will replace all existing keys in the chosen range. Replace can be set to Region, Time Range, or Entire Curve.

There is the additional setting of Paste Connect. If pasting a range of keys, Paste Connect will adjust the key values at the start and end of the range so that it blends smoothly.

Another way to copy a key is to use the MMB Time Slider scrub method, covered in the next chapter.

To move from key to key, use the hotkey (comma) to move left and hotkey (period) to move right. This works in the Time Slider and the Graph Editor. To move from key to key and select the key at the same time, use hotkey Ctrl + Alt + comma and Ctrl + Alt + period.

CHEAT

Double-clicking any icon will open the Tool Settings for additional options.

GRAPH EDITOR TOOLBAR

Let's look at the first few tools that show up in the Graph Editor Toolbar.

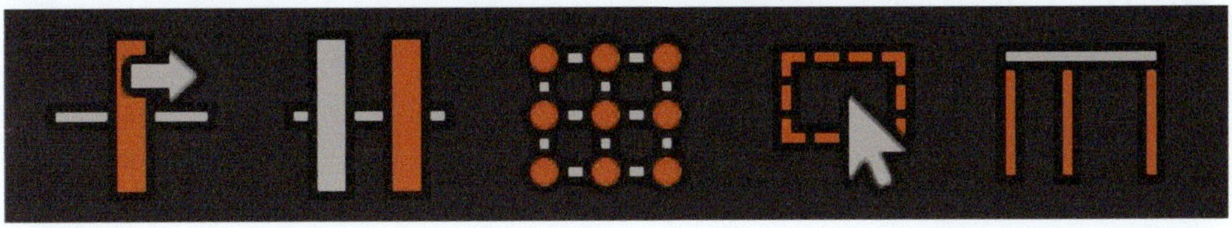

Move Keys is the first tool. By default, it moves selected keys. Use Shift to constrain the movement to horizontal or vertical. Either double-click icon or go to Edit > Transformation Tools > Move Key Tool for options. Move Over is default behavior, you can move a key anywhere. Move Only means you cannot move the selected key past another key. Ripple setting is where moving the selected key will also move all the following keys on the curve.

Insert Key Tool: See "Inserting or Adding Keys" earlier in this chapter.

CHEAT

To nudge keys over one frame at a time, use Shift +9 and Shift + 0.

Lattice Deform Keys puts a cage around the selected keys. Click the points of the lattice to move the keys within. Lattice moves in time and value, so snap the keys to whole frames after use.

Region Tool draws a selection box around selected keys or curves. Grab a side handle to scale keys in time or grab a top or bottom handle to scale in value. Region tool is more precise than a Lattice.

Retime Tool selects the region by making a start and end point. Grab the retime markers to scale the speed of the animation. The tool will ripple the animation before and after the retime tool. Double-click to turn on the option to make markers snap to frames.

DON'T FORGET

It is always a good idea to snap your keys every time you scale your animation over time. Select all curves, and go to Edit > Snap or Shift select all keys in the Timeline and RMB Snap

Next are the Curve Sculpting Tools.

Grab Tool, Smooth Tool, and **Smear Tool** are three brush-based tools that allow you to sculpt the shape of the curve. By default, Grab and Smear change the value by moving keys vertically. If you want to move keys in time and value, double-click to open the tool setting and check the box Affects Time. In the Tool Settings, you will also find a Falloff curve graph for the brush opacity. Use the Shift button to toggle from Grab to Smooth. Smooth gently pushes the keys toward zero. Completely smoothing a curve will result in a flat line.

DON'T FORGET

When using Grab or Smear to change time, keys will need to be snapped on frames afterward.

Sculpting tools can be useful for smoothing out or adding some texture to motion capture. They could be useful for adjusting animation on layers or polish. Too much curve sculpting will make the animation mushy, so we do not recommend them for blocking or the bulk of animating your shot. You want to have control of your poses and how the controls move.

Key Reducer Tool is a brush tool that will delete redundant keys anywhere the brush passes over the curve.

CHEAT

Brushes can be set with hotkey B for size and hotkey M for strength. Adjust with MMB drag horizontally for size and MMB + Ctrl drag vertically for strength. For exact numerical amounts, open the Tool Settings.

The Stats Boxes show time or frame number on the left and value on the right. You can do math in any numerical input box in Maya. If the Stats box is lavender, that means multiple keys are selected and they have different values or frame numbers.

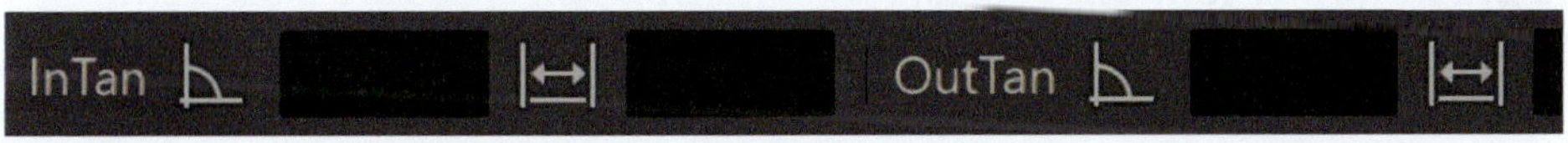

The Tangent Control Input Boxes allow you to set the tangent angle and length numerically. On weighted curves, both the angle and length of the handles are adjustable. For non-weighted curves, only the angle of the handles can be set, as the handle will be fixed at a length of 1. By default, the in and out tangent values will be locked together. Tangent handles must be broken to be adjusted separately.

Next are the view options.

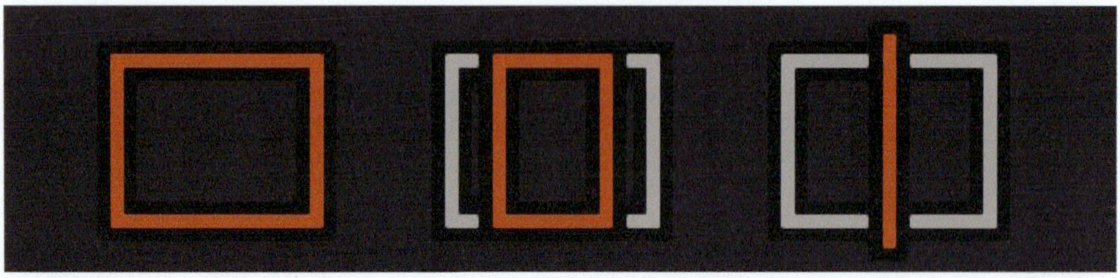

Frame All, Frame Playback Range, and **Center View** on Time Slider.

Followed by curve interpolation types.

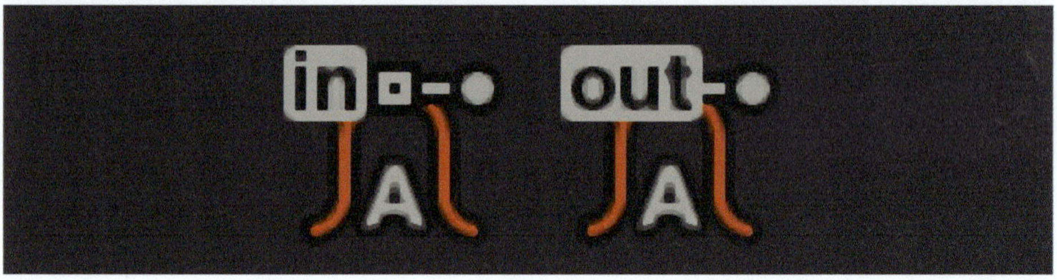

Default In/out Tangent sets tangent interpolation types are also found under Tangents menu.

Buffer Curves are also found under Curves menu.

To use Buffer Curves, first make them visible. Go to View and check the box for Show Buffer Curves. The Snapshot takes a picture of the curve and displays it under the curve while you move keys. The original curve will be displayed as black.

Swap Buffer Curves restores the curve back to the original curve and turns the new curve into a buffer curve.

Tangent Tool is also found under the Tangent menu.

Break Tangents makes each handle independent.

Unify Tangents locks both handles together at their current angle. Use Flat tangent to set the angle to zero on both sides. Or you can set the angle to zero in the tangent control boxes.

Free Tangent Length and **Lock Tangent Length** only work on Weighted tangent curves.

For the most part, professionals prefer to block in either stepped or spline, and only start manipulating weighted tangents, and breaking tangents late in the life of a shot. Think of all the myriad options available for editing keys as mirroring the animation process; start broad and refine later.

Auto Load Graph Editor and Load Graph Editor from Selection displays curves based on what is selected in the Outliner. Options are also found under the List menu. Turn off Auto Load to make multiple Graph Editors and the Dope Sheet display different selections.

Unconstrained Drag, Constrained X Axis Drag, and **Constrained Y Axis Drag.** Click on the icon to toggle between modes. Alternately, hotkey Shift + drag will constrain movement in the same way.

Time Snap moves keys to whole frames automatically. We always want our keys to be on whole frames. It works when moving keys directly, but it is less successful when you are scaling or sculpting a range of keys over time. Therefore, occasional key snapping is recommended. Go to Edit > Snap.

Value Snap will force keys to the nearest whole number. However, you will still have snap keys after scaling or sculpting.

CHEAT

Maya has a handy feature to warn users about keys between frames. The unsnapped keys on the Time Slider are displayed as a dashed red line.

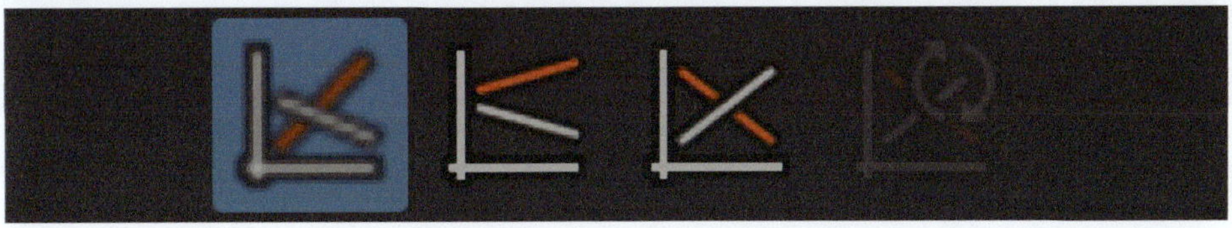

Graph Editor Views: **Absolute, Stacked,** and **Normalized**

CYCLE CURVES

To use Cycle Curves, you first need to make them visible.
Go to View and check Infinity. By default, all curves are set to Constant.

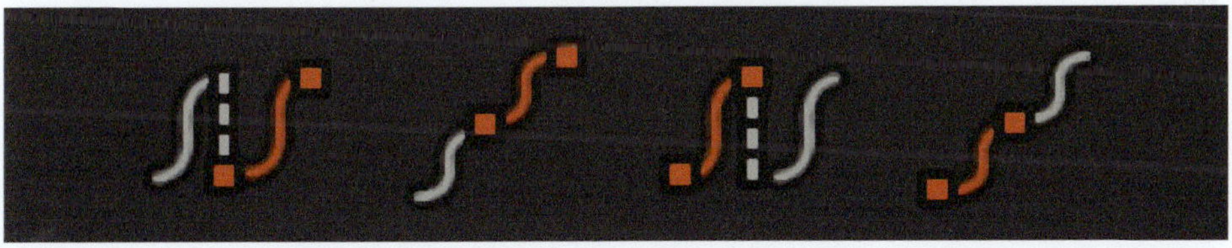

Cycle Before repeats the curve before the first frame or Pre-Infinity.

Cycle Before With Offset repeats the curve but offsets the previous cycle to end where the next cycle begins.

Cycle After repeats the curve after the last frame or Post-Infinity.

Cycle After With Offset repeats the curve but offsets the next cycle to start where the last cycle ends.

For more cycle types, go to Curves > Pre-Infinity and Post-Infinity menus to select Oscillate, Linear, or Constant cycling.

Finally, at the end of the toolbar on the right-hand side, there are buttons to open the Dope Sheet, Trax Editor, and Time Editor.

DON'T FORGET

There is an entire chapter on Cycles! Chapter 11 is where you'll want to look to learn all about these cycle types.

USEFUL CURVE TOOLS

When working with multiple curves, if you only want to display one without changing your selection, go to Curves > and check Isolate Curve.

Bake Channel locks down the animation curve by placing a key on every frame. There are many reasons why you might want to do this when exporting a simulation, moving or copying animation files through a studio pipeline or into a game engine. Bake Channel has an option to **Sparse Curve Bake**, this repeats only the selected keyframes on a chosen frame range.

Create a tail swinging back and forth with cycling curves. Then convert the generated cycles into keyframes for further adjusting the animation.

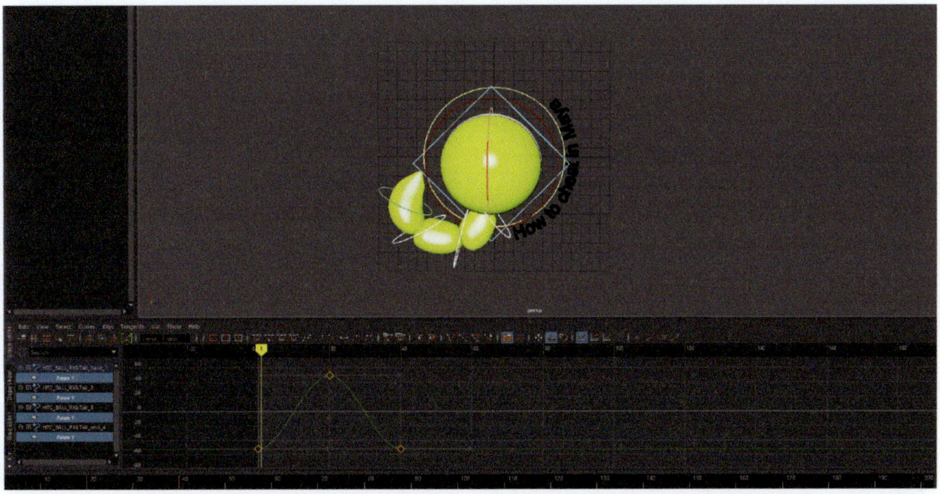

Go to the Graph Editor > View and check on Infinity. Animate one loop of the tail swinging. Swing the tail left on f0 and key and key again on f40, swing right on f20 key.

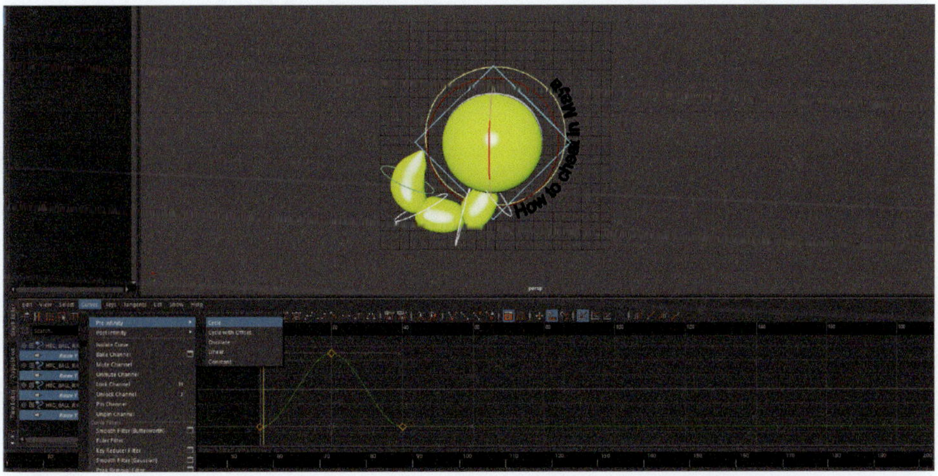

Select the correct rotation channels in the Graph Editor Outliner and go to Curves > Pre-Infinity > Cycle.

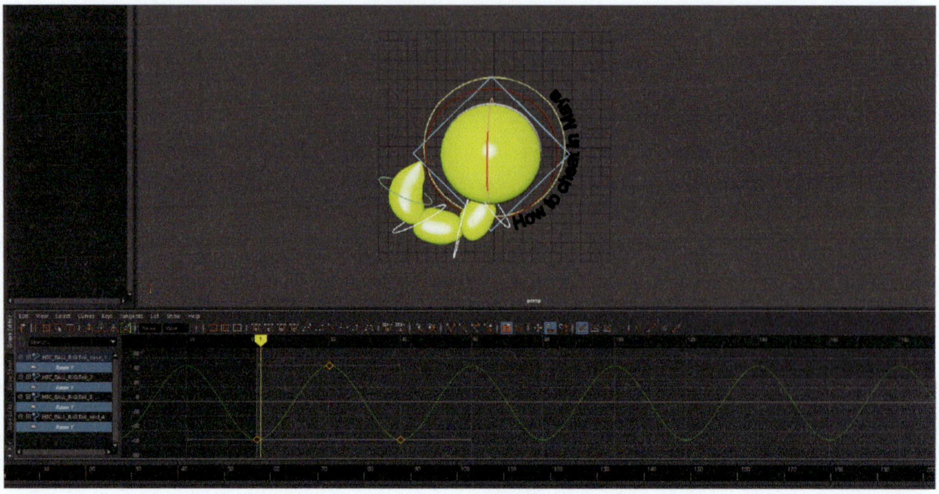

Repeat and go to Curves > Post-Infinity > Cycle. Now, the tail swings back and forth forever.

Go to Curves > Bake Channel Options and select Sparse Curve Bake and set the time range, then Apply.

DON'T FORGET

Bake Channel will make a key on every frame by default. Turn on Sparse Curve Bake to repeat only specific keys.

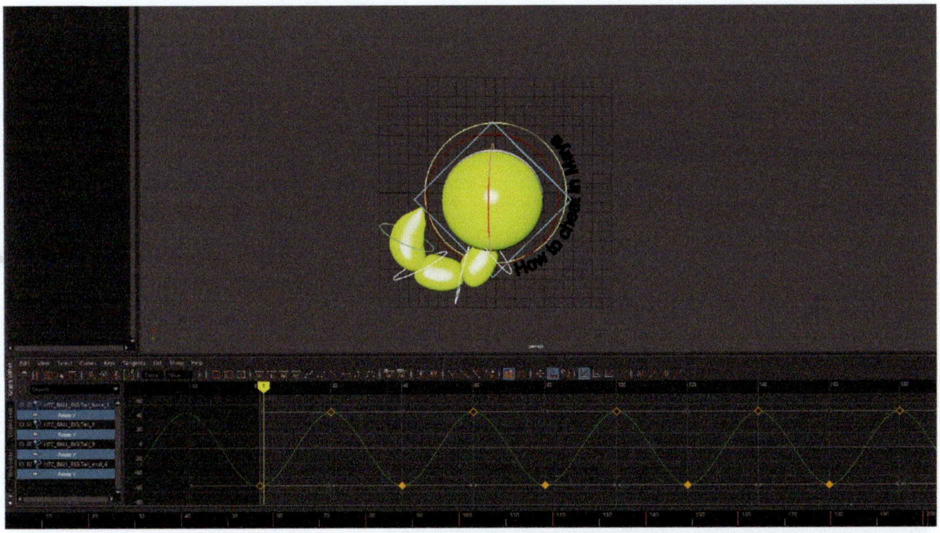

Now the cycled animation will have repeating keyframes that can be used to change the animation's timing and spacing.

Mute and **Unmute Channel**: Mute stops an animation curve from playing. It will display as a dashed line and the object will not move in the muted channel. Unmute to restore. You will have a Mute icon displayed in the Outliner, and the channel will be tan in the Channel Box.

Lock and **Unlock Channel** prevents any edit to curve. Hotkey H locks a channel and hotkey J unlocks. You will have a Lock icon in the Outliner and the curve will turn gray.

Pinning Channels forces Maya to display the pinned curves no matter what is currently selected. Next to each curve name is a push pin icon. Click it once to pin the curve, click it again to unpin the curve. Pin/ Unpin can also be found under the Graph Editor Curves menu.

CURVE FILTERS

In the Graph Editor, go to the Curves menu to find the Curve Filters section. Use the options to set the range of frames affected and additional settings.

The filter that gets the most use is the **Euler Filter**. Named after the Swiss mathematician, it is pronounced (Oy·lr). The Euler filter looks at the rotation curves for gimbal lock. If two rotation axes lock together and increase or decrease by intervals of 180° or 360° degrees, it causes controls to flip around. This filter adjusts the curves to solve the flipping in most cases.

Related to the Euler Filter are the new **Rotation Reorder** tools. These are specialized tools that can predict the likelihood of gimbal lock for each rotation order. This allows you to quickly select an option that should not gimbal lock.

Simplify Curve and Key Reducer Filter work similarly removing keys that are redundant and not necessary for holding the shape of the curve. A common use for these tools is to reduce excess keys after baking the curves.

Key Sync Filter adds keys to curves. It looks for frames where only a few attributes are keyed and adds new keys to every other keyable attribute on that frame.

There are various filters for smoothing the curves. Each filter can be applied to All, Frame, Playback range, or Custom range.

Smooth Filter Butterworth smooths noise, but does not affect minimum and maximum keys.

Smooth Filter Gaussian smooths by averaging keyframes.

Peak Removal Filters smooths down the minimums and maximum values.

Resample Curve rebuilds a new curve. First choose a filter: Closest Sample, Linear Interpolation, Box, Triangle, Gaussian 2 or Gaussian 4 filter, Next choose a Time Step or how many frames between each new key.

Clamp Curves puts limits on the minimum and maximum values. Any keys that go beyond the limits will be clamped down to the new min and max values.

Too much smoothing will make animation mushy or floaty. Smoothing filters should be used sparingly. They are more suited to cleaning up motion capture data.

Offset Curves moves selected keys or curves in time. You must go to the options to input values, so the results can be achieved easier by dragging keys or using math in the stats boxes.

GRAPH EDITOR THEMES

Take a few moments to familiarize yourself with the display option available.

To display labels on your curves, go to View > Curve Name. Name display has the option of Always, Never, or Active Only.

Active only is recommended.

By default, the keys are set to Always, and the tangent handles are set to Active Only.

Key View gives the option of Simple or Detailed. Simple makes every key a dot. Detail displays non-weighted keys as diamonds and weighted keys as squares. If mixing weighted and non-weighted curves, stay with a Detailed view.

Go to View > Themes to change the look of the Graph Editor.

- **Dark and Light** change the background of the view area.
- **TRS Distinct** gives every attribute a different color, instead of repeating red, blue, and green.
- **Color Blind Compatible** adjusts the curve color for better visibility for the most common color blindness (red - green).
- **Classic Theme** is similar to old Maya versions.

Finally **Color Preferences** is a shortcut to color settings where the color for every single element of the Graph Editor can be adjusted. Save your customized theme with the Export Current Theme.

CURVE BOOKMARKS

Pinning a curve to the Graph Editor keeps it visible and available no matter what is selected. However, once unpinned, the control would need to be re-selected and the curve re-pinned. Each curve can only be pinned individually in the Outliner. To pin groups of curves, select and go to Curves > Pin Channels.

This is where bookmarks are superior. Select objects like rig controls or curves and turn them into bookmarks that can be loaded and unloaded at will. The controls do not need to be selected to load the bookmarks.

Objects: To select the object name (top node) in the Graph Editor Outliner, go to List > Bookmarks > Bookmark Current Objects and options. Go directly to the options box to enter a name for the bookmark. Now go to List > Bookmarks and a list will be generated at the bottom of the menu. Check the box to load/ unload the bookmark in the graph. Every new bookmark will have options to rename or delete.

Curves: To make a bookmark for a curve(s), select one key or the entire curve(s), go to List > Bookmarks > Bookmark Selected Curves and options. Name the bookmark right away.

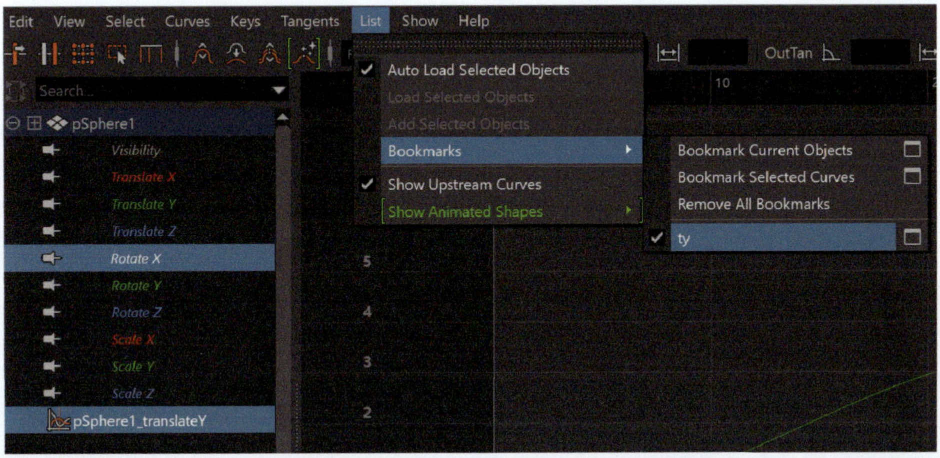

MULTIPLE GRAPH EDITORS

Is the Graph Editor overcrowded and hard to read? Divide the curves into two Graph Editors!

1. In any Panel, click on the Panels menu and choose Panel > Graph Editor.
2. Then, click again on Panels > Tear Off Copy. A new Graph Editor appears.
3. Both Graph Editors will be displaying the same curves. To make them independent, go to List and uncheck Auto Load Selected Objects in both or use the toolbar icon.
4. Select controls in the rig. Go to the second Graph Editor > List > Load Selected Objects or use the toolbar icon. Now both Graph Editors are displaying different objects.
5. Select additional items and go to List > Add Selected Object to add more objects.
6. The Time Indicator will always be synced to the same frame in all Graph Editors, Dope Sheet, Time Editor, Trax Editor, and the Time Slider.

Want More Graph Editors?

You can continue to Tear Off Copy of a Graph Editor loaded as one of your Panels ad nauseum. There does not seem to be a hard limit, but if you load too many, there will surely be a performance cost in your scene. Also, loading and adding objects in independent graphs seems to get a little twitchy after a while.

Manually loading and adding selected objects to separate Graph Editors disconnects what is highlighted as selected in the Viewport from what is going on in the graph. Deselecting objects in the Viewport did not remove them from the Graph Editor.

Instead of removing objects, they can be hidden. RMB objects in graph Outliner and select Hide In Outliner > Hide. To undo RMB in Outliner and select Hide In Outliner > Unhide.

To remove objects, reset everything, and return to normal Graph Editor functionality:

1. Close extra Graph Editors.
2. Go to the remaining Graph Editor > List and check on Auto Load Selected Objects or use the icon in the toolbar.

MOVING KEYS IN THE TIME SLIDER

Hold down Shift + LMB and select the keys in the Time Slider. To make things readable, the selection box is blue and the selected key ticks turn white. To move the entire selection of keys, click in the middle of the box and drag. To scale the selection of keys, click on the arrow handles on the right and left. Hold down Ctrl and drag, and Maya will copy the selected keys on whatever frames they're dragged to.

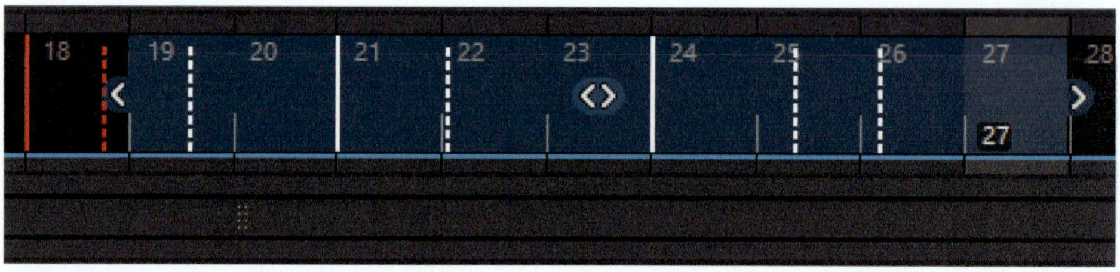

Maya will not automatically snap keys to whole frames every time. Before deselecting by clicking off to the side, RMB and choose Snap. There is an auto snap feature. RMB on the Time Slider and check the box for Auto snap keys; this still doesn't solve every situation. Be especially careful when scaling down keys to speed up animation. Sometimes Maya will stack two keys on one frame. If keys are too dense, sometimes Maya will place a key in between two frames. To solve this, use a combination of snapping the keys and using the Graph Editor tool Keys > Remove Key and choose Unsnapped.

CHEAT

To move the selection box in the Time Slider without selecting or affecting the underlying keys, keep Shift pressed down.

SECURE YOUR KEYS

When moving or deleting large sections of keys, you don't want to mess up the surrounding animation. Whether using the Graph Editor, Dope Sheet, or Time Slider, you want to protect the animation you have worked hard on. This method is generally referred to as 'bookends.' Let's say we want to delete frames 45 to 90. First, save the scene.

Next, select every control with animation and make sure there is a key on the first and last frame of the shot. Next, key all on frames 44 and 91. These four keys will secure everything before and after the range that will be deleted.

The 'bookends' also work for adding time into an animation. If you want to insert 60 frames in the middle of a shot at frame 80, make sure you have all keyed on the first and last frames, then make new keys on frames 79 and 80. Select all keys from frame 80 to the end of the shot and slide the selection over 60 frames.

There are multiple ways to copy keys and paste keys.

- **Time Slider Copy:** Shift select a key or region of keys and use hotkey Ctrl + C or RMB and select Copy.
- **Time Slider Paste:** Go to the options to choose to Insert, Replace or Merge copied keys. Move Current Time Indicator and RMB for paste options. Paste makes exact copies. Paste Connect will adjust the value of the key to flow with the existing curve.
- **Graph Editor Copy:** Select keys and hotkey Ctrl + C or RMB and go to Edit > Copy.
- **Graph Editor Paste:** Select keys and hotkey Ctrl + V or RMB and go to Edit > Paste.

Options for how Maya copies and pastes keys in the Graph Editor and Time Slider can be found under the Edit menu in the Graph Editor.

TIME SLIDER MMB METHOD

Another way to copy a key is to use the Time Slider MMB method. Holding down the middle mouse button and scrub back and forth on the Time Slider, you will see the animation does not update. It is holding on whatever frame you pressed the middle button on.

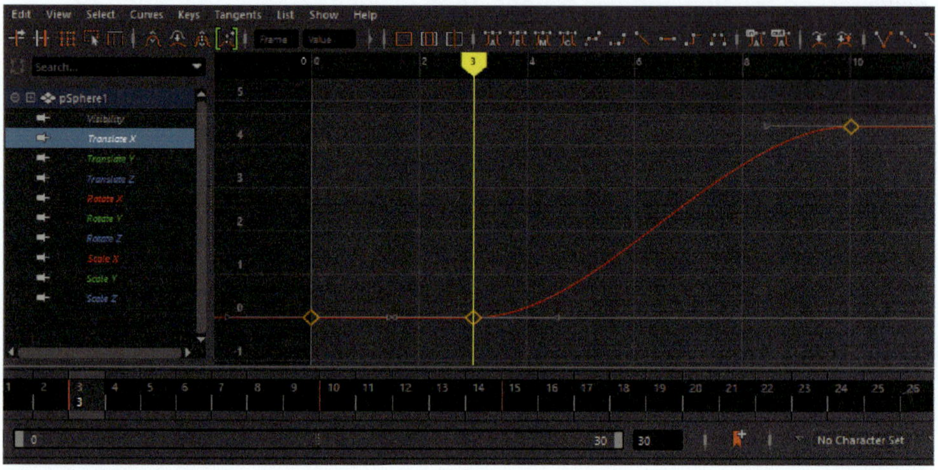

Place the Current Time Indicator on the frame you wish to copy.

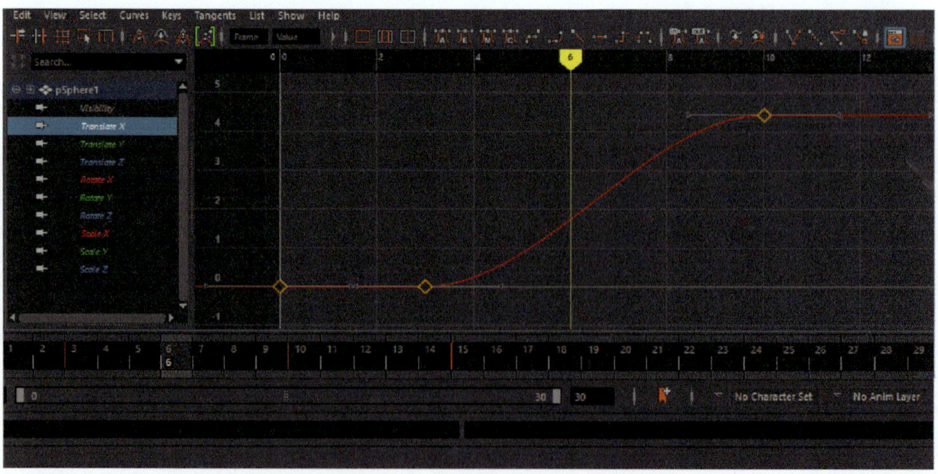

Hold down the MMB and slide over to the frame you want to paste on.

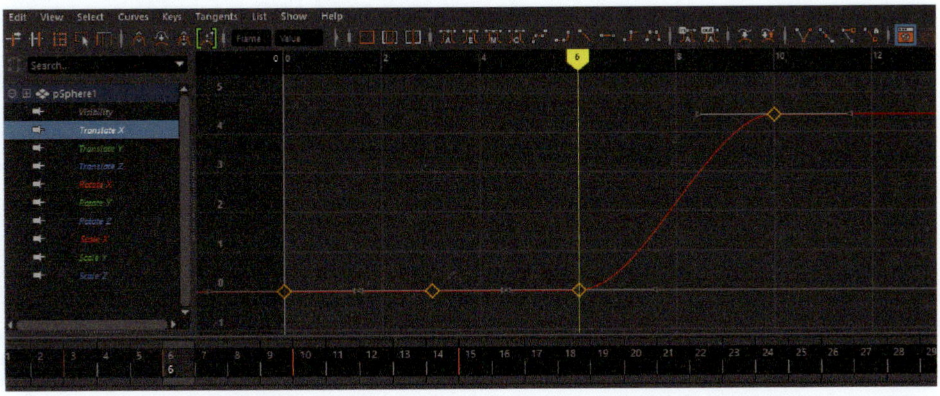

Hit S to copy the values on all keyable attributes or select the channels you want, RMB and choose Key Selected.

COPIED PAIRS

To hold a pose in blocking, we used copied pairs. Basically you copy the first pose and paste the exact same pose a few frames forward. Copied pairs are important if you do Stepped blocking. Don't let the stepped curves hold the pose for you because, when you change the curve to spline, the hold will be gone and the controls will drift to the next pose. The MMB method is the quickest way to make copied pairs in the Time Slider.

Favoring a Pose with the MMB Method

If you have two poses, A and B, and you want to ease-in to pose B, you can use the MMB method.

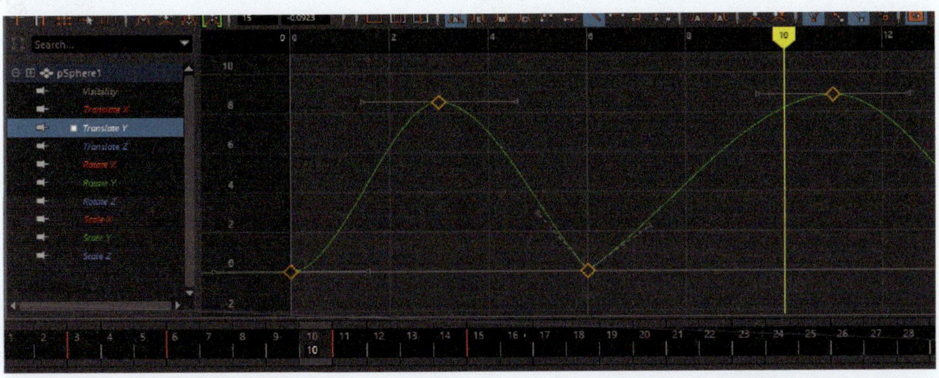

Place your Current Time Indicator near pose B, click MMB on the Time Slider.

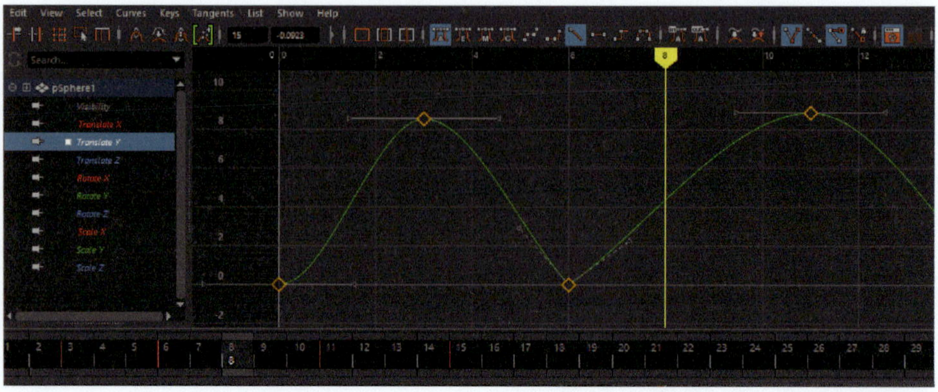

Then drag the indicator towards pose A, stop and then hit hotkey S.

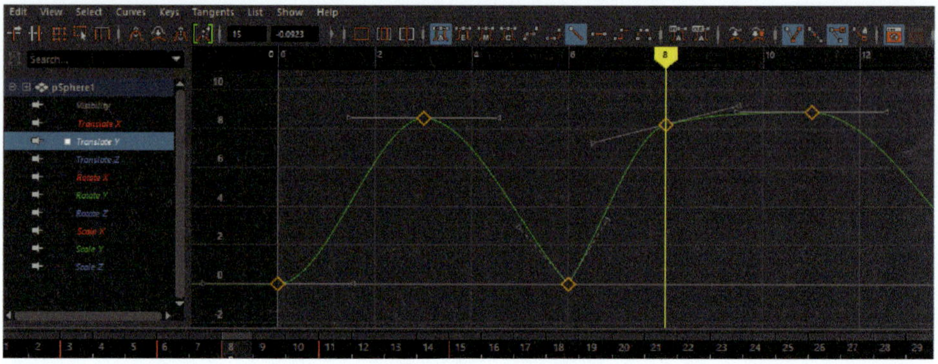

This will cause a fast exit from pose A and a long ease-in to pose B.

TIME SLIDER BOOKMARKS

A relatively new and very useful feature is the Time Slider bookmarks. They allow you to create color-coded and labeled markers and region markers along the length of the Time Slider.

To create a bookmark, use hotkey Alt + T, or RMB in the Time Slider and choose Time Slider Bookmarks > Create. It will open an option box where you can assign a color and a label.

Move the bookmarks by holding down the Ctrl key. Grab and drag in the middle to move the entire bookmark or grab the ends to scale the bookmark range. You can always RMB the bookmark in the Time Slider and choose Time Slider Bookmarks > Edit and change the range.

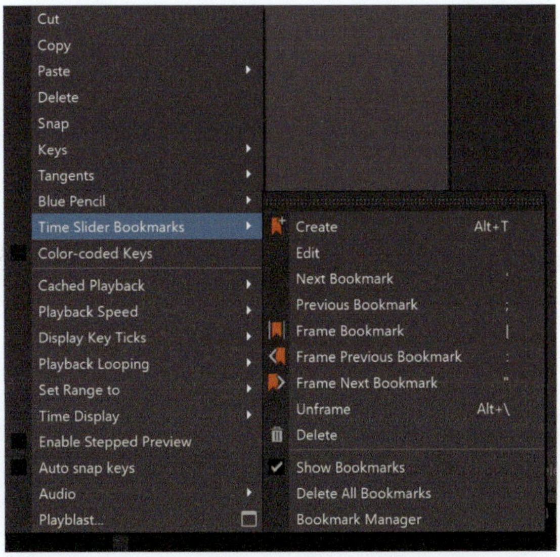

Time Slider bookmark option window.

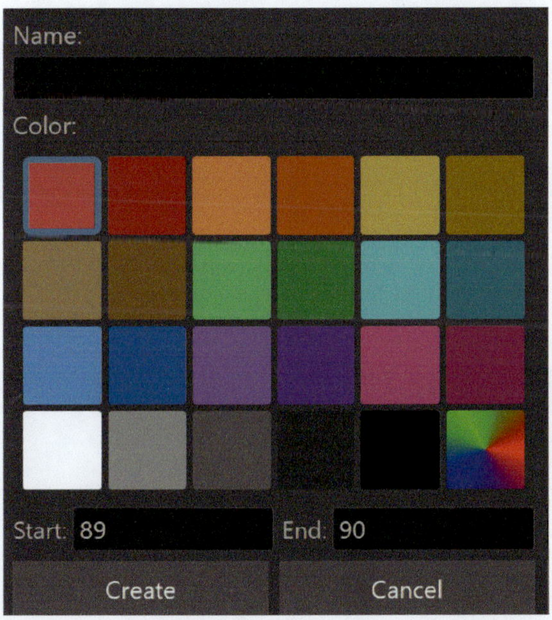

Create Bookmark - name, color picker, and range set.

Let's examine the bouncing ball exercise. A good ball rig will have separate controls for movement, squash and stretch, angling the stretched shape, and rotation. If using pose to pose, the animator will manipulate and key all the controls at each pose. However, if animating in a layered fashion, the translate keys would be placed first. When the Move control is deselected, the keys will disappear from the Time Slider. One would either need to remember the frame numbers for the top of the arc and the hits, or find the frames by scrubbing the Time Slider, or keep re-selecting the Move control to see where the keys are.

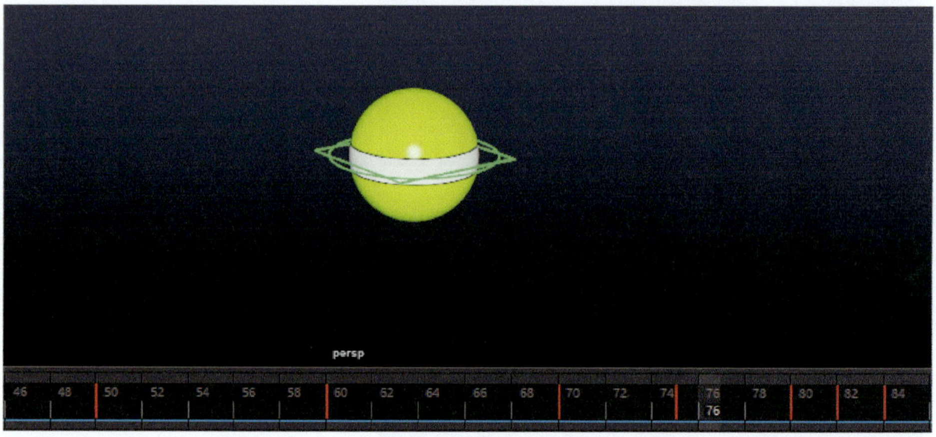

Before, in the layered method, when the Move control was deselected, the keys would not be available in the Time Slider, and it was hard to keep track of frame numbers. Not anymore! Make a colored bookmark for the top of the arc (color A) and the hit (color B).

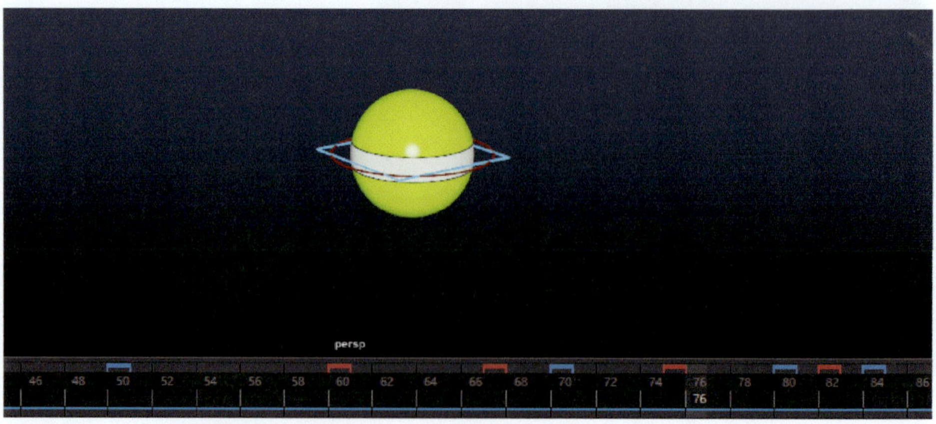

The color-coded bookmarks allow the animator to see the top of the arc frames and the hit frames without searching or toggling the Move control on and off.

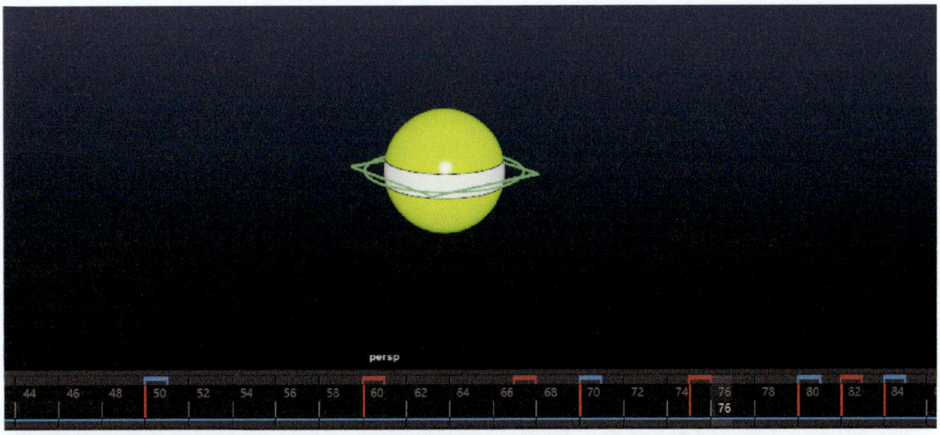

Go to the color A mark (top) and ensure the ball is round and upright. Then go to the color B mark (hit) and make sure the ball is squashed and upright. One frame before and after the squash key, add maximum stretch with appropriate angle to emphasize the motion. This approach significantly speeds up the workflow.

Bookmarked ranges can be overlapped. A layer of bookmarks can be used for actions, with additional layers for emotion or mood. Bookmarks can also be placed for dialogue accents and exclamations, as well as for rhythm in musical pieces. The possibilities are endless.

Bookmark Manager

Bookmark Manager is a convenient way to organize and edit the bookmarks. Bookmarks are displayed with the name, color, and frame range. Select a different range of frames in the Time Slider and click the first icon, Update Bookmark with Selection, to edit the range. The second icon frames the bookmark and the third deletes it.

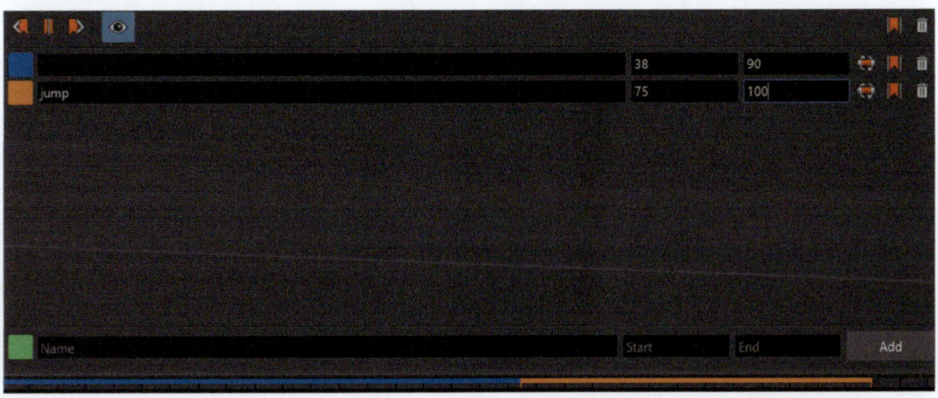

TIME SLIDER COLOR-CODE

Save a key and it shows up as a red tick mark on the Time Slider. The red tick does not tell you if there is one attribute keyed on the frame or ten. Maya allows for color code the tick marks in the Time Slider. RMB the Time Slider and check the box for Color-Coded Keys. If you wish to change the color of the beads, go to Windows > Settings/ Preferences > Color Settings. Go to the Time Slider section.

At this time, there is only one color for move, rotate, and scale attributes.

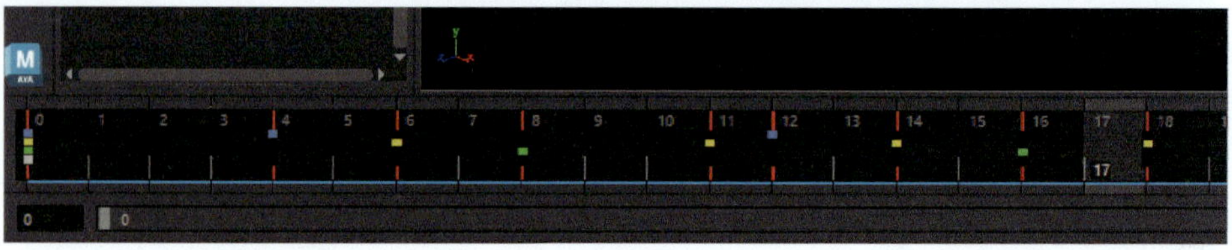

REGION TOOL

The Region tool does not have any options; it just does one thing. The region has handles on the top, bottom, and sides. Everything inside the region will be affected. It is often a better strategy to select all the points over the zero line or under the zero line when scaling vertically. Otherwise, you will push keys off zero. Deselect individual keys from a region by holding down the Ctrl key and draw a selection from outside the region. It's recommended to make the selection, de-selecting certain keys, then activating the Region Tool. This tool does not ripple keys.

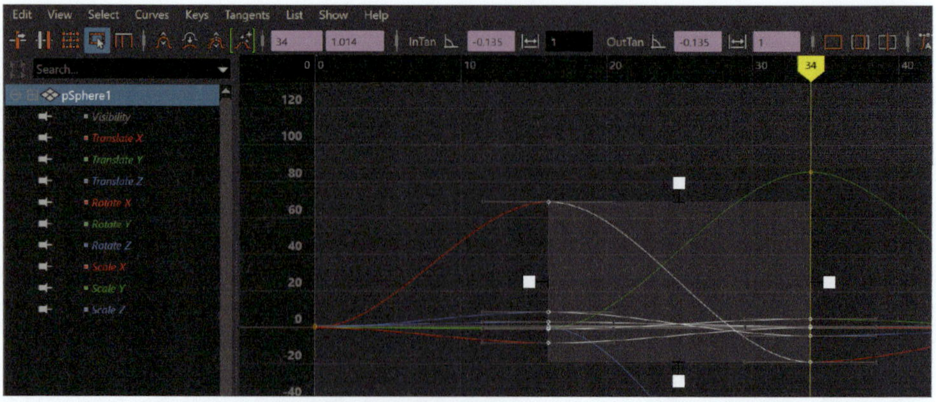

RETIME TOOL

To use the Retime tool, you do not need to select keys. Set the start and end of the region by double-clicking in the Graph Editor. To scale the keys inside of the region, grab the thick area on the yellow handles. The small x on the bottom of the vertical handle will delete that handle and let you make another one by double-clicking again. Grabbing the top of the tool will move the entire curve. The Retime tool ripples keys, meaning everything outside the Retime range will get pushed or pulled as you scale the selection. The only option on the Retime tool is to check on the option to make markers snap to frames. This turns the key marks on Time Slider into dashed lines if the keys are off whole frames. Remember to select all the keys and Snap.

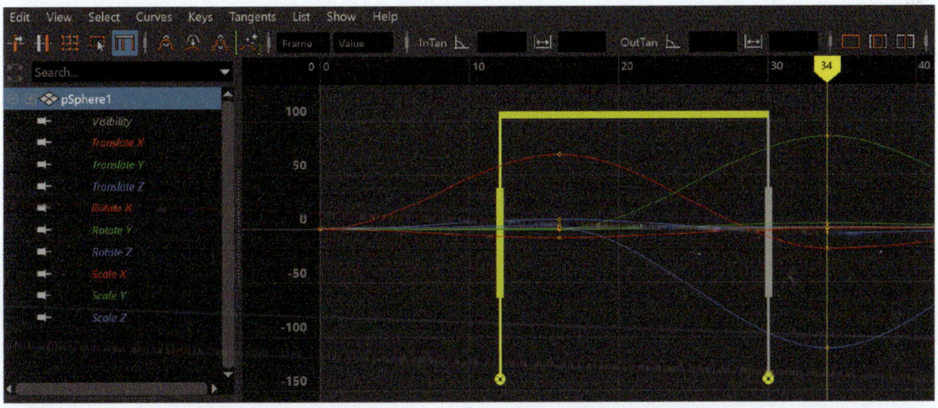

CHEAT

Quickly exit the Region, Retime of Lattice Deform Tools by using hotkey Q to enter selection mode or press Enter.

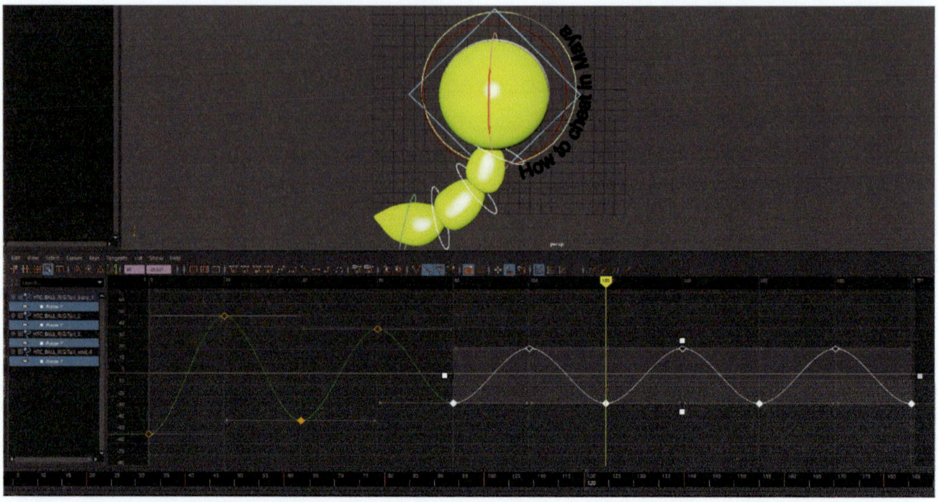

Go to Curves > Post-Infinity and Pre-Infinity and set the cycle to Constant. Select rotation curves and click on the Region tool icon. Skip the first swing and select the rest. Use the top and bottom Region tool handles to scale the rotations.

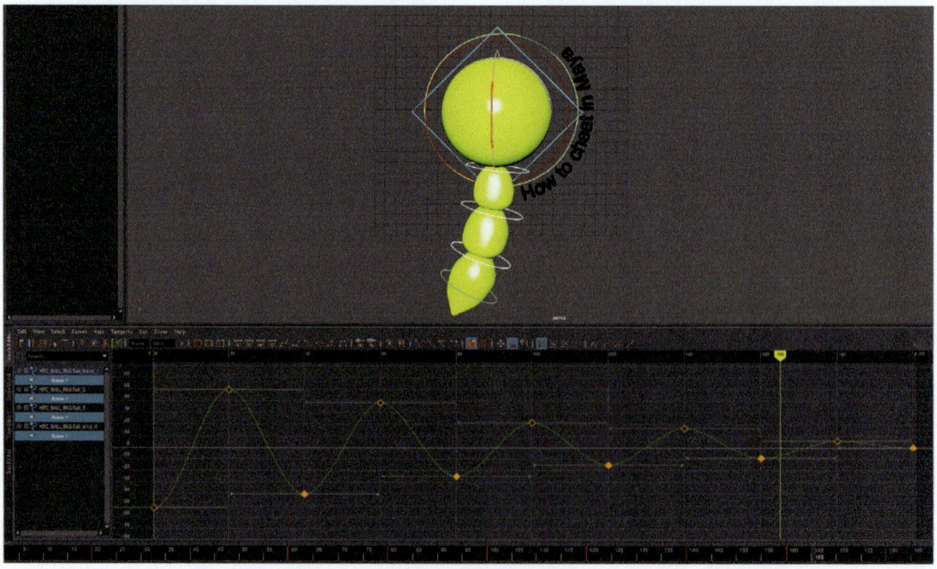

Deselect the second swing and scale down the rest. Repeat on each consecutive swing until the rotation is a zero, and the tail has stopped swinging.

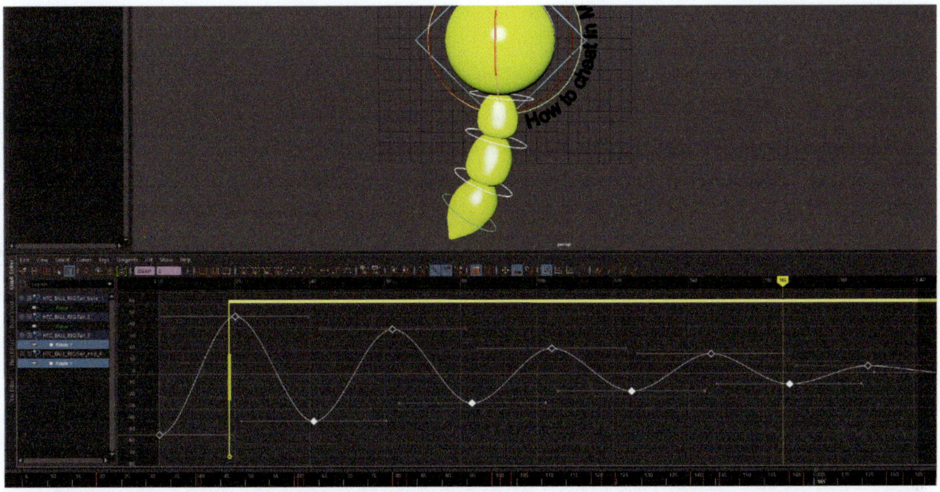

We are now going to offset the tail controls with the Retime Tool. Deselect the base of the tail, control 1. Apply the Retime tool to tail controls 2, 3, and 4. Double-click in the first swing and at the end, grab the right-side bar and stretch out the curves over time so they take longer than the base of the tail.

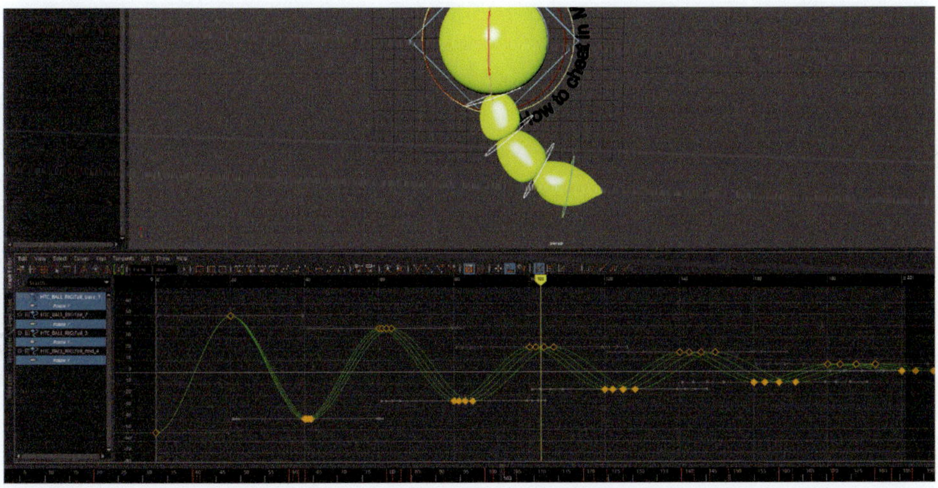

Deselect control 2. Retime controls 3 and 4 to lag further behind. Finally, deselect 3 and Retime just control 4 to be last to finish the swing motion. Now all your tail rotations are offset from another for a more realistic tail swing with offset.

6 MASTERING TIME

DOPE SHEET

The Dope Sheet comes from traditional 2D animation and functions like a spreadsheet for planning the animation. Maya's Dope Sheet is an editable spreadsheet of animation keys. For a very long time, the ability to manipulate the timing of keys in the Time Slider and Dope Sheet was evenly matched. For years, animators ignored the Dope Sheet's existence, opting for the conveniently positioned Time Slider. However, Autodesk has added some new features to the Dope Sheet making it a more powerful tool.

The main difference between the Graph Editor and the Dope Sheet is, in the Graph Editor, you can see interpolation of the motion when editing the keys, curves, and handles. The Graph Editor is where we go when we want to do changes to individual keys. The Dope Sheet is primarily for editing the time and value of the keys. The Dope Sheet is a better tool for when you want to do timing changes for large groups of keys. Additionally, we also have a scene summary, where we can play multiple audio tracks. You also have more power in displaying, sorting, and grouping attributes.

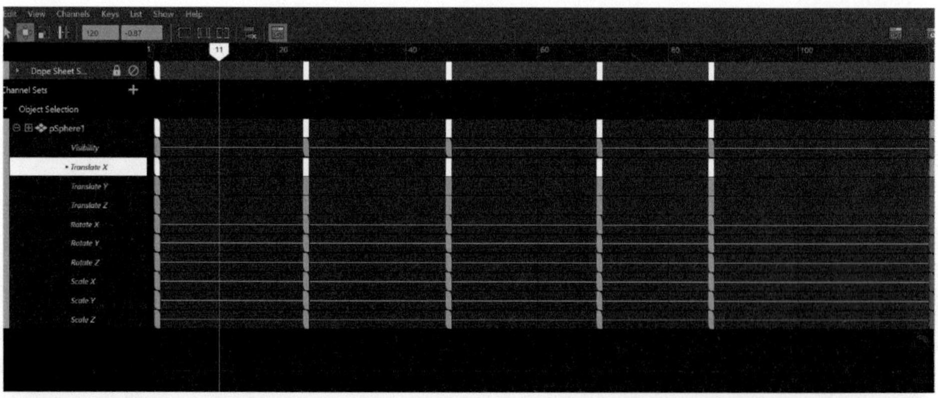

Go to Windows > Animation Editors > Dope Sheet or you can access from the Graph Editor toolbar.

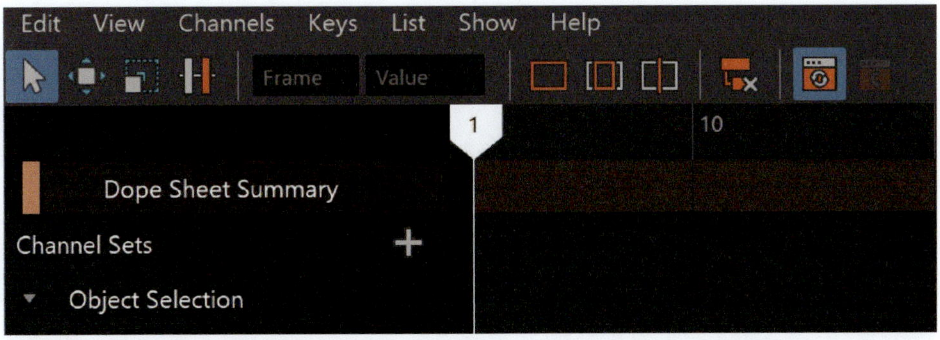

The top of the View Area is the Scene Summary, followed by the Dope Sheet Summary, any audio, any Channel Sets, and finally the current selection. If you want to change the timing of everything all at once, select the key ticks in the Dope Sheet Summary. For individual selections, open the summary and select the attributes you want.

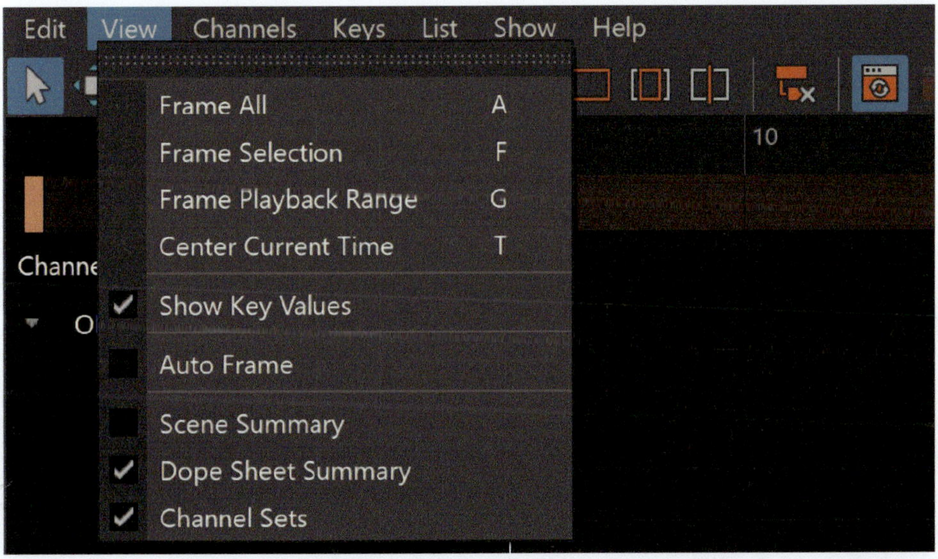

Navigate the Dope Sheet View Area with the same hotkeys as the Graph Editor.

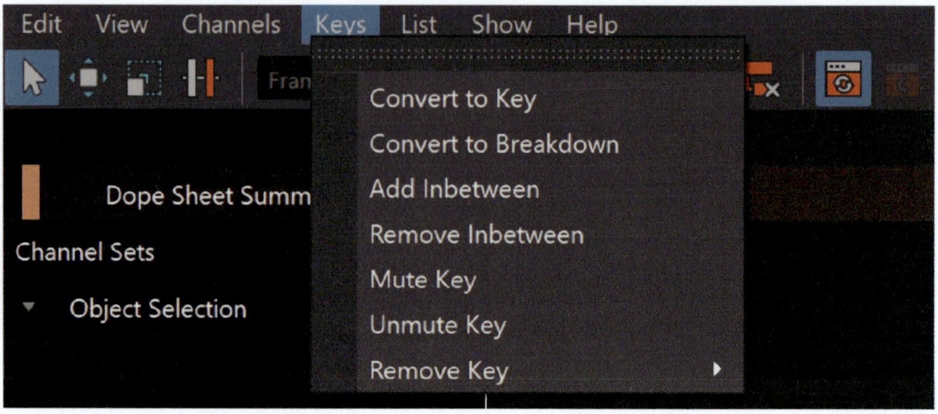

Many of the tools inside the Dope Sheet are the same as the Graph Editor.
You can move, scale, insert, snap, copy, cut, paste, lock, mute, and bake keys.

Double-click the key tick box to edit the value of a key. Hold down shift to edit multiple keys. When moving or scaling keys, double-click the icons so you can choose to move the key, move over, or move ripple. Unfortunately, there doesn't seem to be a way to ripple keys in the Time Slider. In older versions of Maya, activating ripple in the Graph Editor or Dope Sheet would affect the behavior in the Time Slider, but it doesn't seem to be the case anymore. Make sure to turn on Time Snap. The time snap in the Dope Sheet is superior to the snap in the Graph Editor or Time Slider.

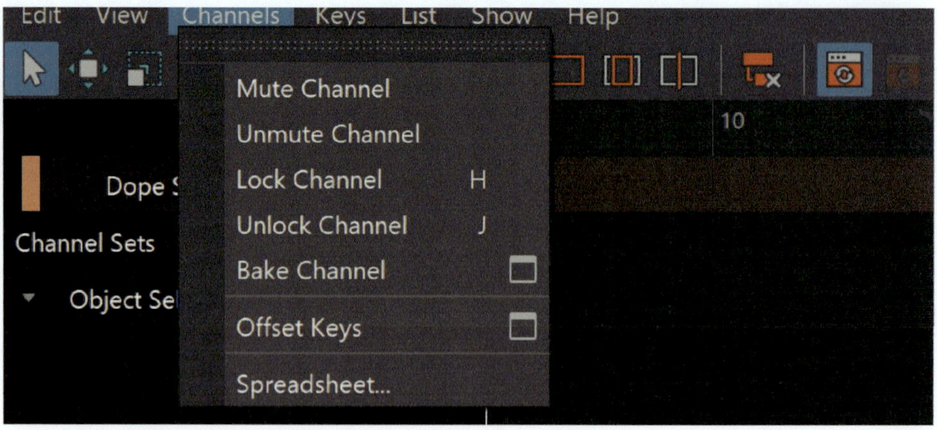

Channel Sets are a way to group channels together so you don't have to select them every time. Click the plus sign to make a new set. Name it. Shift + select multiple attributes and drag and drop into the set. Double-click the color tab to the left to change the color.
The sets can be exported and imported into different scenes, so you don't need to do the setup again.

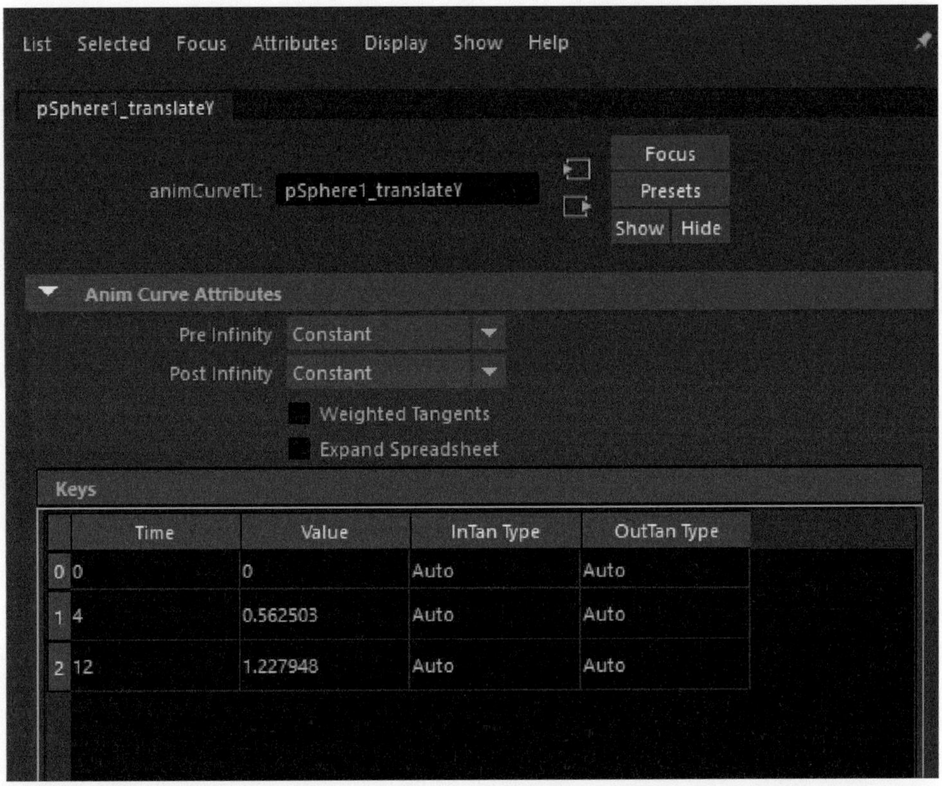

The Spreadsheet inside the Dope Sheet is different from the Attribute Spread Sheet in Chapter 3. In the Dope Sheet select a channel and go to Channels > Spreadsheet. This will launch a spreadsheet of keys in the Attribute Editor panel. The spreadsheet will include key and tangent handle values. Technically, one could edit interpolation through the spreadsheet, but that is a difficult way to work unless you are setting multiple keys to a specific interpolation type or everything to flat tangent.

SCHOOLS

Employers hire based on talent, skill, and teamwork, not school names. A great reel or portfolio is what matters. So, do you need school to become an animator? No.

Many successful animators are self-taught, but it takes discipline and focus. Most people benefit from structure, guidance, and deadlines. Since there's no one-size-fits-all advice for animation education, here's how to navigate your options.

First, identify what you want to do. Animation jobs go beyond animating and modeling. Research different roles, watch behind-the-scenes features, and note job titles in artist interviews. Second, study the job market. See which positions are in demand, what skills and software studios want, and where jobs are located. Check company credits on your favorite films and games, then look them up. Use this knowledge to find schools that teach relevant skills.

If you're new to 3D and unsure if it's right for you, start with low-cost options like local community colleges or online introductory courses. These are short-term, affordable ways to gauge your interest before committing to a full program.

Don't rush into choosing a school. Reputations change, so talk to current students and look beyond online reviews. A once-great program can decline under new leadership.

The amazing artists at top companies are not born with superior skills that us mere mortals will never possess.

A student recently shared that they felt trapped in a bad program because an industry professional had recommended it. The professional based his advice on his own positive experience 15 years ago. Schools evolve, so always verify current quality.

Internships

Apply early. Many internships have strict schedules and guidelines, so read their instructions carefully. Unpaid internships must provide educational value and cannot replace employee work. If an internship seems exploitative, it likely is. Even if the work seems minor, internships are a chance to prove reliability and professionalism. Be proactive, ask questions without pestering, and build relationships — contacts from an internship may lead to future jobs.

Being a Good Student

The amazing artists at top companies are not born with superior skills that us mere mortals will never possess. They just have years of practice and experience. They make better decisions, are faster, and more confident because they have a careers' worth of knowledge to draw from. If you stick with it and practice animation, some day you will too.

- Keep projects manageable. A polished short animation is better than an unfinished long one.
- Plan before animating. Act out movements, shoot reference, break down dialogue, and thumbnail key poses.
- Share your work often. Feedback from peers sharpens your skills.
- Observe and study. Watch films, take acting classes, play sports, and analyze movement.
- Take breaks. Staring at a screen all day is bad for your work and health.
- Keep notes. Make "fix" lists when sitting down to your work with fresh eyes, and work on small sections at a time.
- Put a twist on assignments. Instead of aiming for something "never seen before," take something ordinary and make it unique and personal.

What if I Find Out I Hate Being an Animation Student?

Not everyone who loves animation enjoys working in the industry. That's ok. If you start at a community college, you've lost little time and money. A 2-year online school is a slightly bigger commitment but still manageable. A 4-year school allows you to switch majors, though transferring from a certificate program may be harder. Leaving school may trigger loan repayment, so weigh your options carefully. You're never truly trapped; there are always alternatives.

Final Thoughts

School isn't necessary for an animation career, but for many, it provides the best chance at success. Whether you choose formal education or self-teaching, what ultimately matters is consistent practice, a strong portfolio, and the ability to collaborate with others.

SCHOOLS

4-Year Programs: Bachelor of Arts

Pros:

- Well-rounded education, with access to many classes in other supporting subjects.
- You will be eligible for more internships.
- Graduates can pursue higher degrees. More options for jobs that require higher degrees (STEM fields), name recognition of the school.
- Easier to get a visa if you wish to work overseas right away.
- You have more financial aid and grant options.

Cons:

- More expensive: more debt, and it takes longer to complete your degree.
- Not focused: you will need to balance your degree concentration with required general ed. classes. Less time devoted to your reel/portfolio pieces. Harder work/ school/ life balance when you have a full load of classes.
- Instructors can be removed or out-of-date with current software, technology, teaching practices and industry practices.
- Classes may not be available in a timely manner, class offerings change, equipment and software may be out-of-date.
- You need to advocate for yourself. Advisors may not be familiar with your field, so you need to be proactive in getting the classes you need.

2 Year Programs: Certificates

Pros:

- Significantly cheaper, and you will finish in less time.
- Very focused, you usually take one class at a time.
- Mentors are accomplished professionals currently working in industry.
- Courses are current and follow industry trends.
- You can work part-time or full-time because of the light class load.
- Online, you can attend from anywhere in the world.
- Not locked into a degree program so you can take classes à la carte and take additional classes outside of your concentration.

Cons:

- Online schools are very focused, so you may need to pick up courses on additional subjects at other schools.
- You may not be eligible for some internships that compensate with school credit.
- It will be harder to apply for a visa to work overseas without a B.A., until you have several years of industry experience.
- Technical art for STEM field jobs like medicine, sciences, and law may require a 4-year degree.
- If you wish to teach, you will need a B.A. and an M.A. to become a professor.
- Schools are accredited as trade schools, so not all financial aid applies to online schools.
- You will be provided licenses for free software, but you need to have your own computer and good internet connection.

BLUE PENCIL

Blue Pencil, formerly known as Grease Pencil, is a tool that allows drawing in the Maya viewport. It mimics drawing directly on the camera lens. Blue Pencil can be used to draw thumbnails on frames and play through them like an animatic. This can be useful for planning out animation. It can also be used to do draw-overs on animation to improve posing.

Access the Blue Pencil in the Viewport toolbar or in the Animation menu set (F4) go to Visualize > Blue Pencil. Once activated, it will open the Blue Pencil toolbar over the Viewport toolbar.

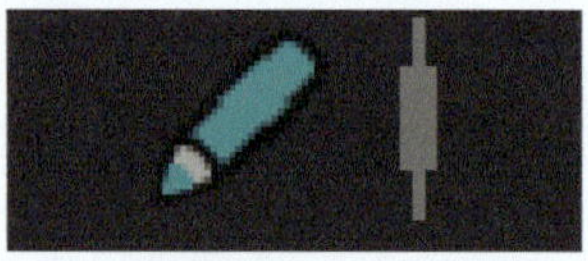

The blue pencil as it appears at the top of the Viewport.

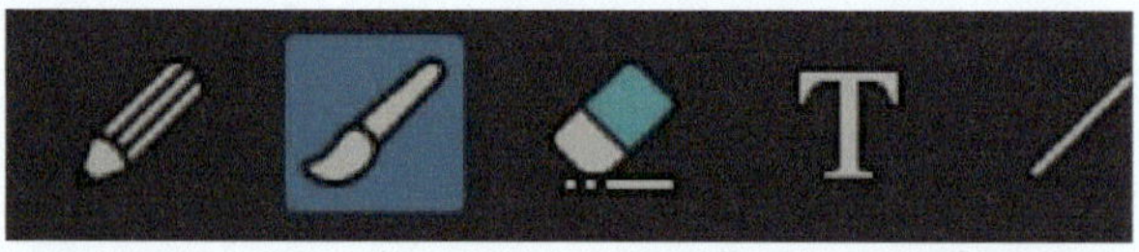

The Blue Pencil Toolbar that appears when the tool is active.

Right-click anywhere to open the Marking Menu for access to all the Blue Pencil options. Blue Pencil options are also accessible by RMB clicking the Time Slider and going to the Blue Pencil menu.

Go to a frame on the Time Slider and start drawing; it will make a Blue Pencil frame. The frame can be moved, copied, and pasted just like an animation key. Use the Blue Pencil Ghosting to see the previous frame morph to the next frame as you play through.

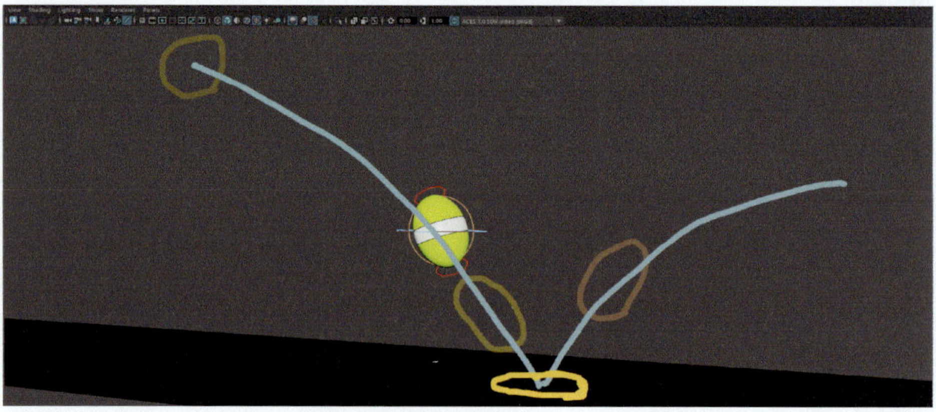

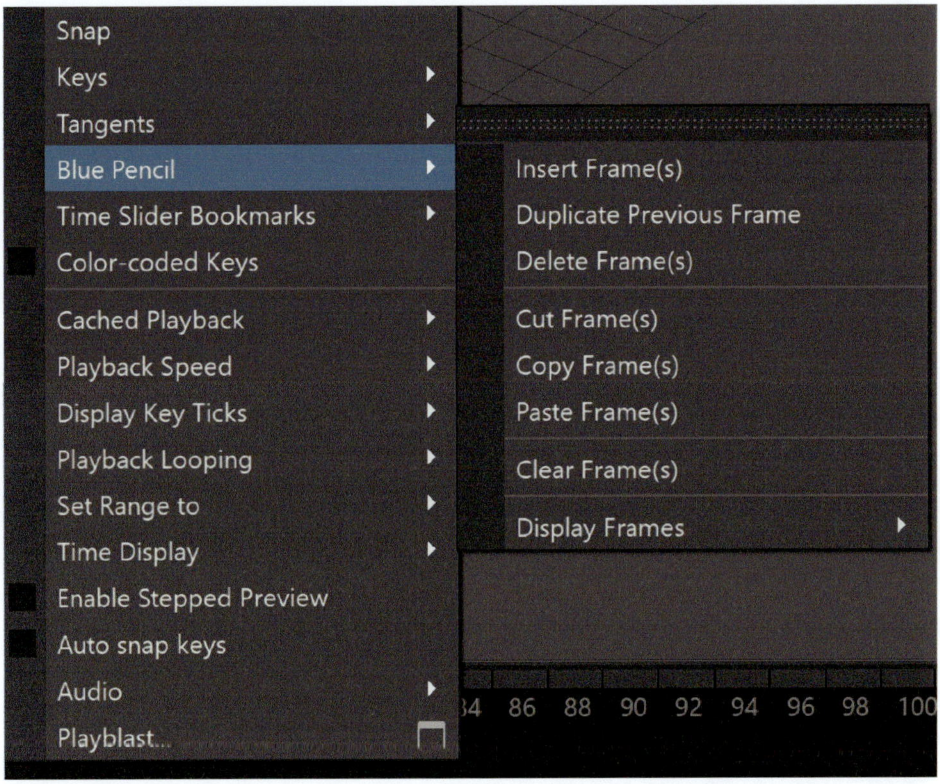

Like all Maya brush tools, the hotkey B adjusts the brush size, and M adjusts the magnitude/ strength (or in this case, opacity). For even more options to adjust the Blue Pencil, open the Tool Settings (the icon in the upper right-hand corner). Or, double-click the Blue Pencil icon in the Last Tool Used area.

To manipulate the Blue Pencil drawings, use the Transform Mode tool. Activate the tool and draw a region around the drawing, press Enter, then move, scale, or rotate the selection. Press Enter to commit, or Esc / Backspace to quit.

To move the Blue Pencil frames in the Time Slider, Shift-click one or more and drag them to a different frame. Toggle the Blue Pencil off by clicking the icon in the Viewport toolbar. This will also hide the Blue Pencil toolbar.

GHOSTING EDITOR

Ghosting displays the frames before and/or after the current frame. It enables the animator to see how the rig moves from pose to pose over a range of frames. The Ghost Editor is located under the Visualize menu or on the Animation shelf.

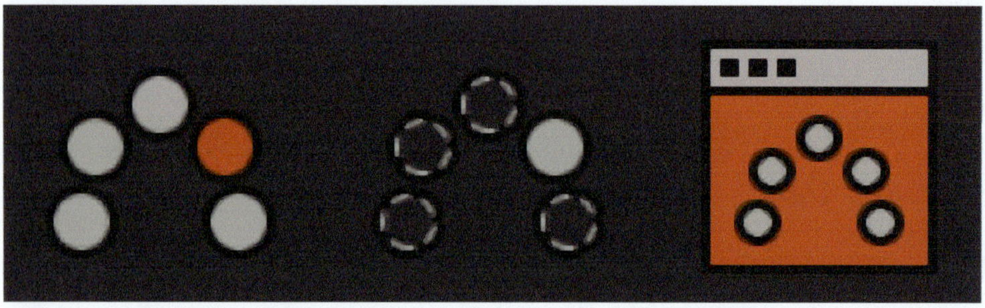

Ghosting is completely customizable through the Ghosting Editor. It can be applied to preceding, current, or following frames, and custom frames or keyframes. It can even use custom frame intervals. By interacting with the list of selected objects, items can be unghosted one at a time. The eyeball icon toggles the visibility of the ghosting on and off. Use the options to choose object types to apply ghosting to. Keeping organized is made even easier through customizing ghosting colors and opacity. Unlike the editable Motion Trail, the ghosts are not selectable or editable. But while a Motion Trail shows only the trajectory of an object, ghosting applies to the mesh itself, showing the entirety of the pose or silhouette change as well as the location of an object over time.

CHEAT

Get better Grease Pencil drawings with tablet and stylus. RMB the Pencil or Brush Icons in the tool bar and Enable tablet pressure for opacity and size.

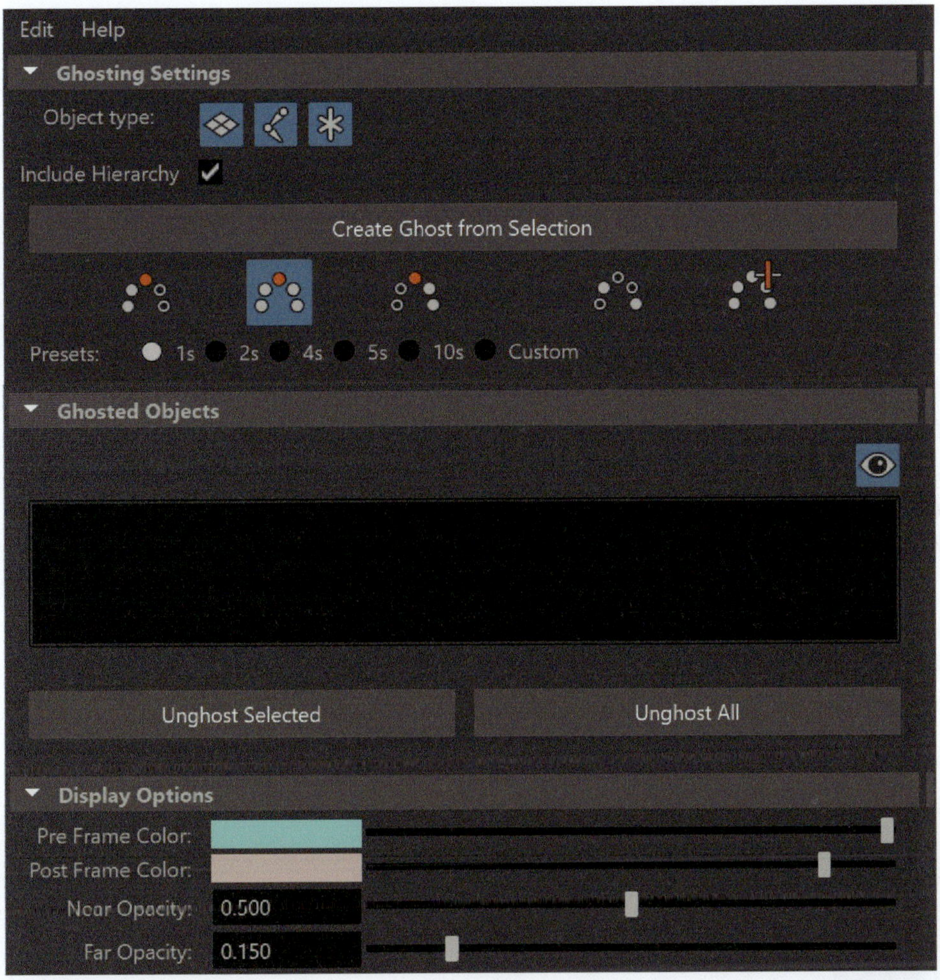
Edit Help
Ghosting Settings
Object type:
Include Hierarchy
Create Ghost from Selection
Presets: 1s 2s 4s 5s 10s Custom
Ghosted Objects
Unghost Selected
Unghost All
Display Options
Pre Frame Color:
Post Frame Color:
Near Opacity: 0.500
Far Opacity: 0.150

7 PROFESSIONAL TECHNIQUES

CHANNELS

The Channel Box shows all the attributes that are keyable. The hotkey S sets a key on all unlocked channels of the selected object. Channels are extremely useful for making isolated changes to values in the scene. Select an object, then one of its attributes, by clicking on the attribute name in the Channel Box, for example Translate Z. The corresponding manipulator and axis will appear in the viewport. MMB drag left and right and observe that only that selected channel's values change. This is really helpful for doing isolated work on a scene with a complex rig and many objects moving, since isolating one channel prevents anything else from changing accidentally.
To key attributes separately, select them individually by Ctrl+LMB on channel names and selecting Key Selected.

Channel Slider Setting

Clicking on the attribute name enables a cursor to scroll right and left. RMB and drag to increase or decrease the value. If the object is moving too fast using this isolation mode, control the speed with the Channel Slider Setting. Remember, the bluer the speedometer, the faster the channel changes.

	Show the manipulator on selected items and allow MMB dragging. Toggle for invisible manipulators or no manipulators.
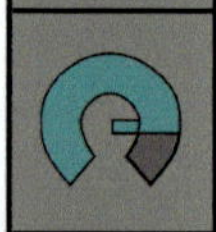	Channel Slider Setting: slowest/slow/medium/fast Press Ctrl,Shift + Ctrl, or Shift to slow down or speed up dragging speeds.
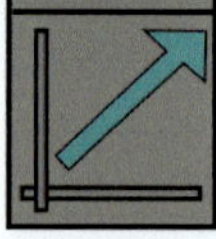	Toggle for linear or hyperbolic Channel Slider Settings.

The fastest method of adjusting the speed of scrolling in the Channel Box, however, is to scroll by using Shift+LMB for faster scrolling, and Ctrl+LMB for slower scrolling. These multiply and divide the speed by 10, respectively. Next to each attribute is a value box, where numbers or equations can be typed and applied by pressing Enter. This is the most precise way to change a key value. Values can be changed with math, just like the stats boxes in the Graph Editor. Math is done with the formula [operator = number]. Operator math symbols are [+ - * /] followed by the = sign and the value desired.

+	Write add 2 as	**+=2**
-	Write subtract 2 as	**-=2**
*	Write multiply 2 as	***=2**
/	Write divide 2 as	**/=2**
%	Write percent as decimals	**50% *=0.5 or 120% *=1.2**

Unlike the Graph Editor, writing numbers as fractions does not work, but decimals do. To make an attribute value 50% smaller or ½, divide using: /=2 or, multiply by ½ as a decimal: *=0.5.

Lock Channel

Riggers will commonly lock attributes on well-made rigs so that they are not accidentally keyed. Sometimes, it can be a good idea to lock other attributes yourself. In the Channel Box, RMB an attribute and choose Lock selected. The channel will be marked dark gray and will no longer be keyed while using the hotkey S (or by manipulating the object with Auto-key turned on).

Sync Channels to Graph Editor/ Time Slider

Sync Selection in Graph Editor displays the selected channels in the Graph Editor. It functions in the same way as selecting attributes in the Graph Editor Outliner. RMB + Ctrl the channel names and check the box to activate.

Sync Timeline Display will display the key ticks of only selected channels. To activate it, RMB + Ctrl the channel names and check the box for Sync Timeline Display.

You can copy and paste animation by RMB the channel name and choosing Copy Selected and Paste Selected. Be aware that the animation will paste on the frame that the Time Slider Indicator is on. Also, the pasted animation will be inserted, meaning any previous keys will be shifted over, not overwritten.

Channel Box Color Guide			
	locked		expression
	nonkeyable		constrained
	muted		connected
	blended		animation layer
	keyed on frame		driven key
	keyed off frame		animation clip
	key altered		

The value boxes are color-coded to signify the state of the channels. The most common are Locked, Keyed On to show there is a key on that frame and Keyed Off to show that the attribute does have animation but not on that frame. If the item is constrained but not animated, the channel will be light blue. Once the constrained item is animated, the channel will be light green for Blended.

IK/ FK TRANSITIONS

In character animation, smooth natural-looking arcs are generally created by using FK controls. Since IK has parent objects solving for child positions and rotations, it is used any time there is a need for a body part to make solid contact with a surface. When a shot has combination of needs, often animators will switch body parts between IK and FK for the best results. A well-made rig will have IK/FK matching (where the two different skeletons will snap to align with each other perfectly to make the transitions seamless), but not every rig has it.

Making a smooth manual FK/IK transition takes some practice. A good strategy is to disguise the switch in motion, for example switch on the frames just as a hand contacts a counter. It is best to make the FK/IK switch over one frame, but making the switch over a range of frames can be another way to create a softer transition.
FK and IK are two completely separate skeletons within the rig. For example, if a shot has been animated with the arms in FK for the entire shot, the first time the arm controls are switched to IK, the hand will snap back to the bind pose position.

How to Manually Match FK/IK Position

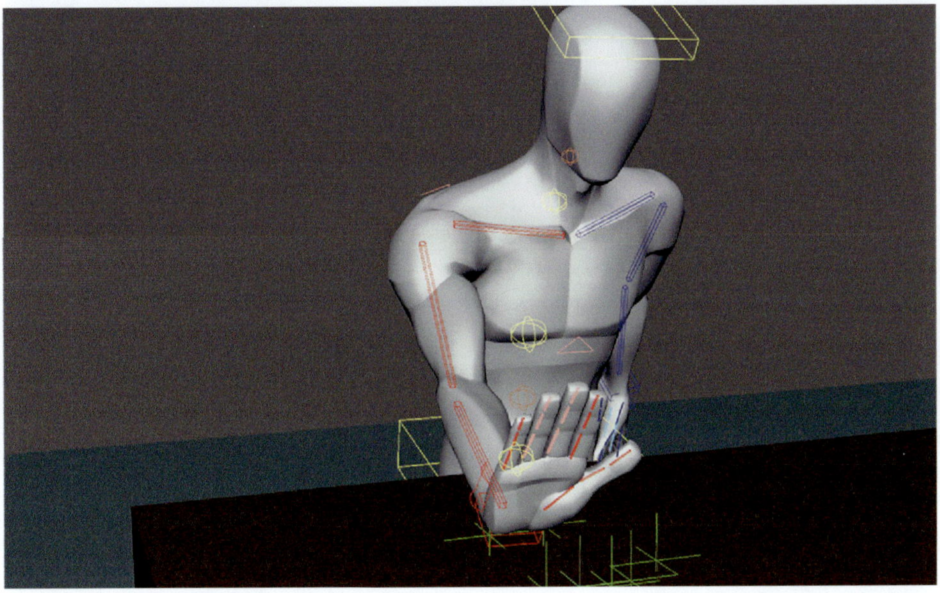

First, the blocking was done with an FK arm. The hand intersected the counter as the body moved forward, so we will have to switch to IK. If the rig does not have IK/FK matching, it is important to mark the location of the FK hand for easier alignment of the IK. It is recommended to mark the location of the FK hand on the frame before switching to IK. Mark the location with blue pencil on a locked camera or use locators to mark hand location and still be able to move the camera.

CHEAT

Before you key the elbow pole vector control, try setting the space to wrist or shoulder. Choose the setting that gives you the best results. You may want to lower the elbow pole vector control because people's elbows usually point downward.

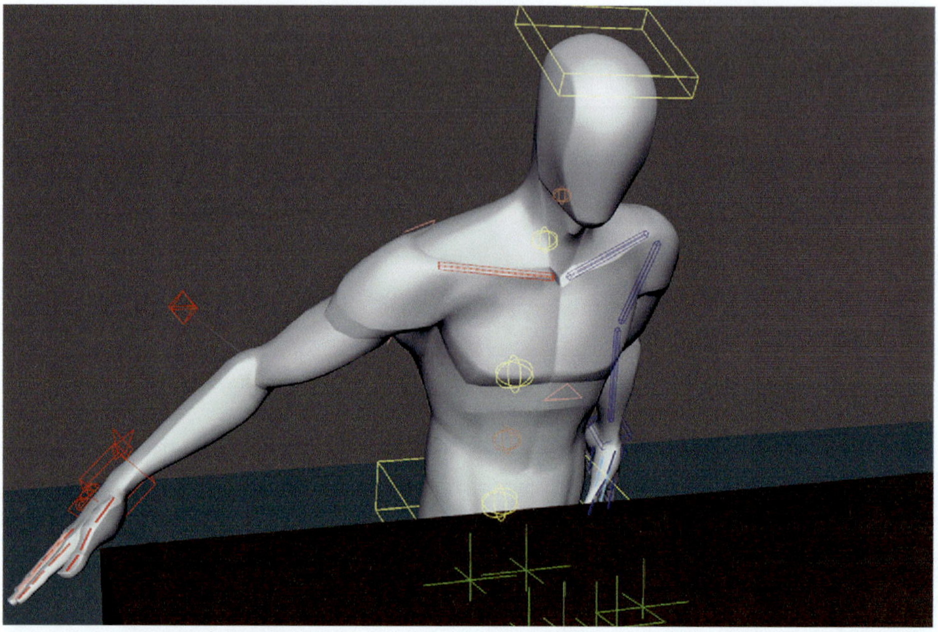

Switch the arm to IK. The arm will snap back because the IK joints have not been positioned yet and are still in their bind pose position over the Master control.

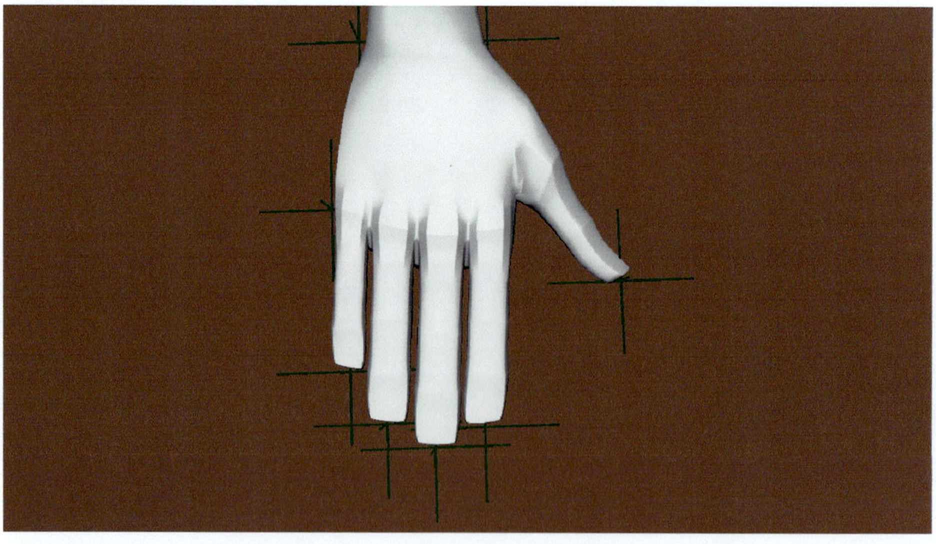

Line up the IK arm to match our locators. We are attempting to hide the IK/FK transition in the moment the hand slaps the counter. Remember to key the IK/FK switch at the beginning and end of the duration; otherwise, the limb will slowly drift between.

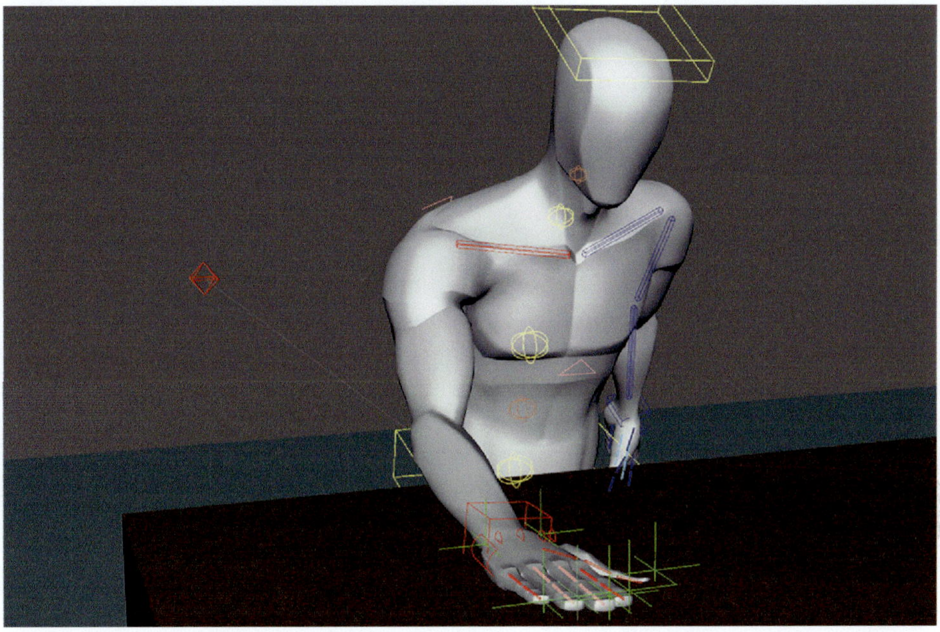

Make sure to keep IK controls in world space so they stay put, if they are set to another body space they will keep moving with the body. If the character straightens up, and the shoulder moves too far away from the IK arm control, the chain may 'pop.' If that happens, either drag the hand back on the counter until the elbow can bend again, or take the hand off the counter and switch back to FK.

A common misconception is that if one avoids FK altogether, and animates everything in IK, it will be easier to work with than to deal with switching. While it's true that IK in general is the easier posing method (certainly there's no IK-like behavior in human spines, and yet it is highly favored for posing), the results from novice animators is animation where the body parts all look highly disconnected. The time gained in avoiding switching is more than lost when having to be extra vigilant using motion trails and checking arc paths with IK. One more drawback to IK is, if the IK control gets too far away from the body, the chain snaps straight causing an 'IK pop.'

CHEAT

Instead of an 'IK pop' the rig's limbs keep getting longer. The rig probably has Stretching enabled. If you are not doing cartoony style, either turn off stretching or set the Max Length to 1, or 100% of normal size.

MOTION TRAILS

Motion Trails are visual representations of the path of an object in 3D space. The trail is built with the position data of the object at each frame, connected with a spline in the viewport.

Editable Motion Trail

The Translate (X,Y,Z) keys will appear as editable points on the trail. Selecting the editable point and moving it will update the keyframes of the object itself. This is ultra powerful, since the editable trails show the object's arcs and path and display not just the current keyframe, but all of its keyframes and positions. Making a simple change to an object is easy and intuitive. In a more complex scene, moving the editable points directly on the motion trail can sometimes be slow. If that is the case, select the rig control, move it and re-key it, and the motion trail should update. If the motion trail stops updating, just delete it and make a new one.

Non-editable Motion Trail

Motion trails can be generated on objects, controls, and components with or without animation. However, without translate (X,Y,Z) keys, no editable points will be generated. Sometimes, it can be extremely valuable to have a motion trail on an object that has no keys at all. An example would be wanting to make sure the tip of a sword is in a perfect arc as it swings around a character's body. This object might be parented to the character's hand and have no keyframes, and additionally, since the motion trail generates at the object's pivot, the sword would be a bad choice for this with its pivot at the handle. To check the arcs on this sword, the best method would be to put a Motion Trail on the vertex at the tip of the sword. Maya has made this newly available; simply select the sword object, RMB-drag on the geometry and select Vertex, select the tip vertex and then in the Motion Trail Editor select Create Motion Trail. Now, any changes to the character pose and hand animation (which is holding the sword) will update the Motion Trail of that sword. Remember if for any reason the motion trail stops updating, simply delete it and make a new one.

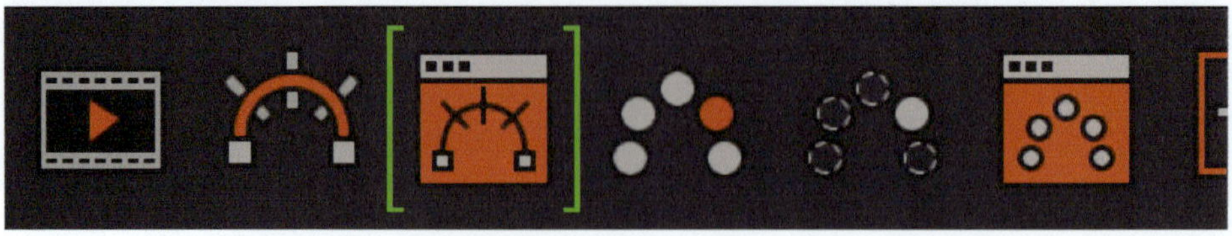

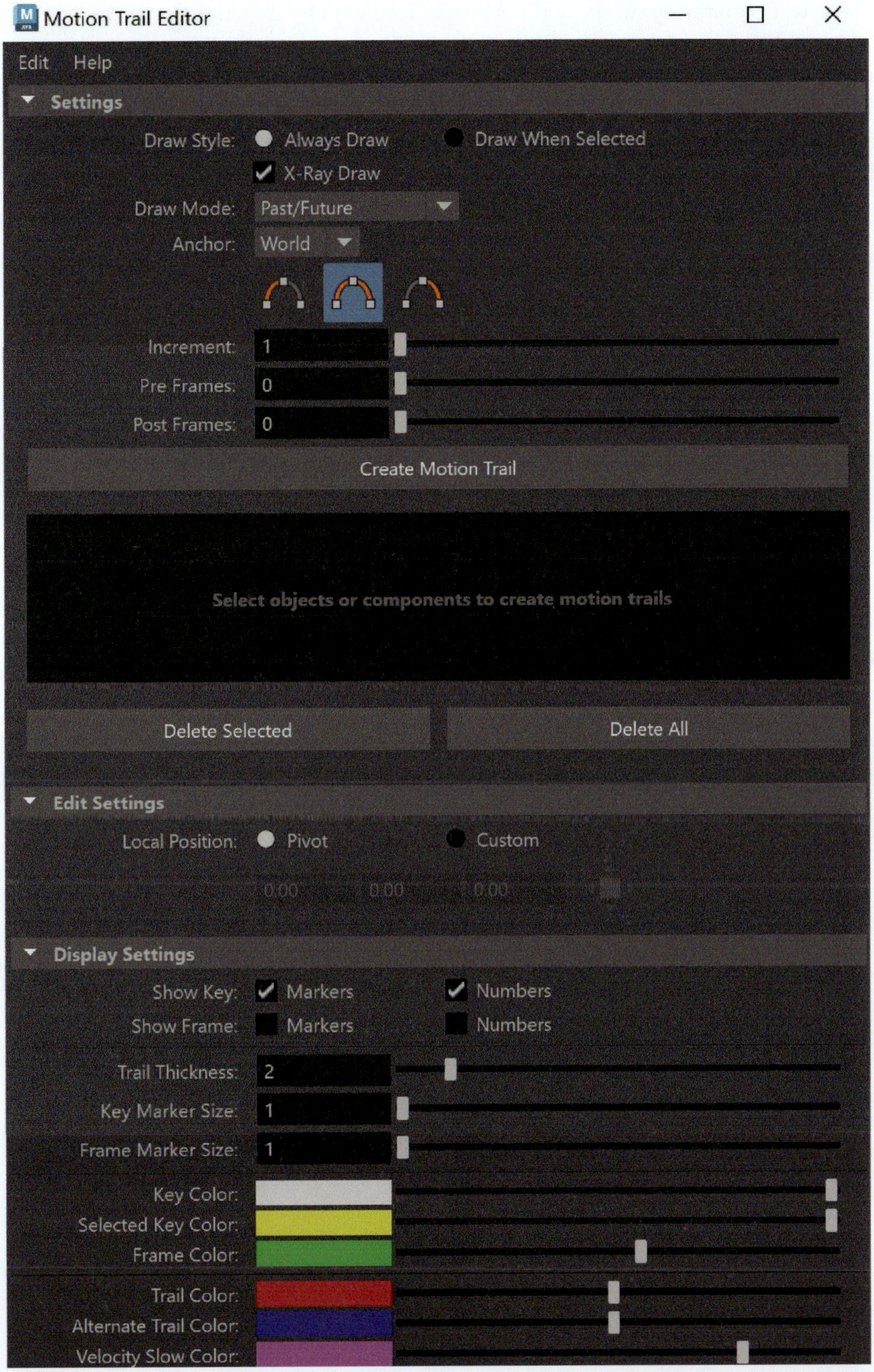
Motion Trail Editor
Edit
Help
Settings
Draw Style:
Always Draw
Draw When Selected
X-Ray Draw
Draw Mode:
Past/Future
Anchor:
World
Increment:
1
Pre Frames:
0
Post Frames:
0
Create Motion Trail
Select objects or components to create motion trails
Delete Selected
Delete All
Edit Settings
Local Position:
Pivot
Custom
Display Settings
Show Key:
Markers
Numbers
Show Frame:
Markers
Numbers
Trail Thickness:
2
Key Marker Size:
1
Frame Marker Size:
1
Key Color:
Selected Key Color:
Frame Color:
Trail Color:
Alternate Trail Color:
Velocity Slow Color:

Maya will constantly re-draw the Motion Trail which can slow down the Viewport. Besides deleting the trail, hide it by going to the Viewport Show menu and un-checking Motion Trails. Motion Trails can also be put into Display Layers. If the trails were made to be simple visual arc checkers, then setting their Display layer to Template (T) or Reference (R), will stay visible but become unselectable and any editable points will be hidden.

IK POP CLEANING

An IK pop is where the beginning and end of the joint chain move too far away from each other and snap straight. This often gives the appearance of knees or elbows going backward. To solve an IK pop on a leg, lowering the body, rotating the hips, or rolling the foot upward might solve it. An IK pop on an arm could be solved by moving the hand closer to the body or bringing the shoulder or torso closer to the hand. It should be mentioned that IK pops are endemic to the system and a large factor in the trade-off of choosing a method of animating when starting a shot. Careful consideration should be given to this trade-off of speed and editability.

Cleaning IK Knee Pops in a Walk

Cleaning IK pops in a walk can be more challenging because the body, hips, and feet are constantly in motion. Trying to balance root movement and hip rotation with the foot roll can be very frustrating. If a rig has a control that overrides the knee position, we can use that control with motion trails to help smooth out the knees.

CHEAT

When fixing an arc on a hand, do not try to fix it with just the wrist control. The path of the hand is influenced by the Root, spine, shoulder, and arm. When trouble-shooting, start at the Root and work your way out.

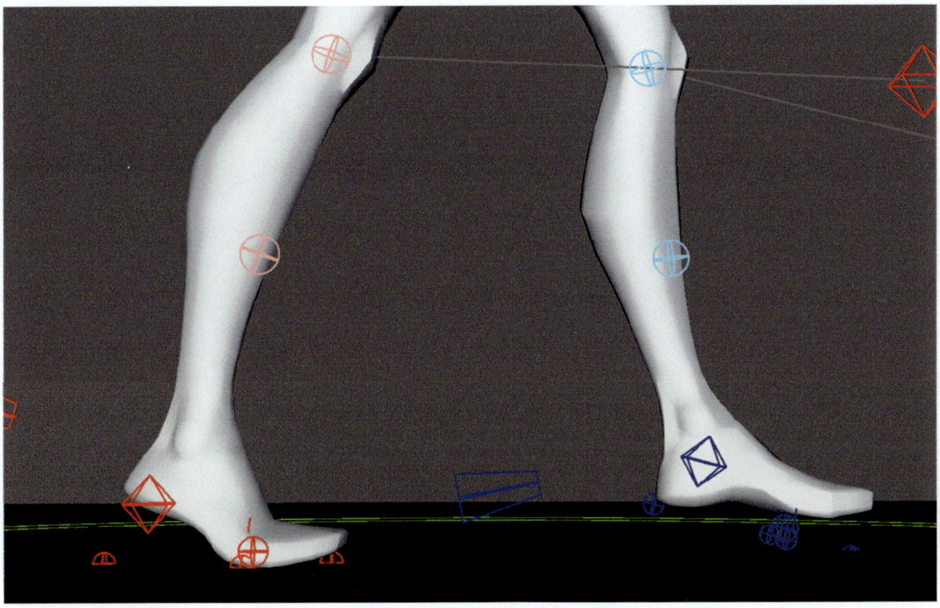

We need a control that overrides the position of the knee by stretching or shortening the length of the upper and lower legs. If a rig has bend controls, turn them on. Find the knee-bend control.

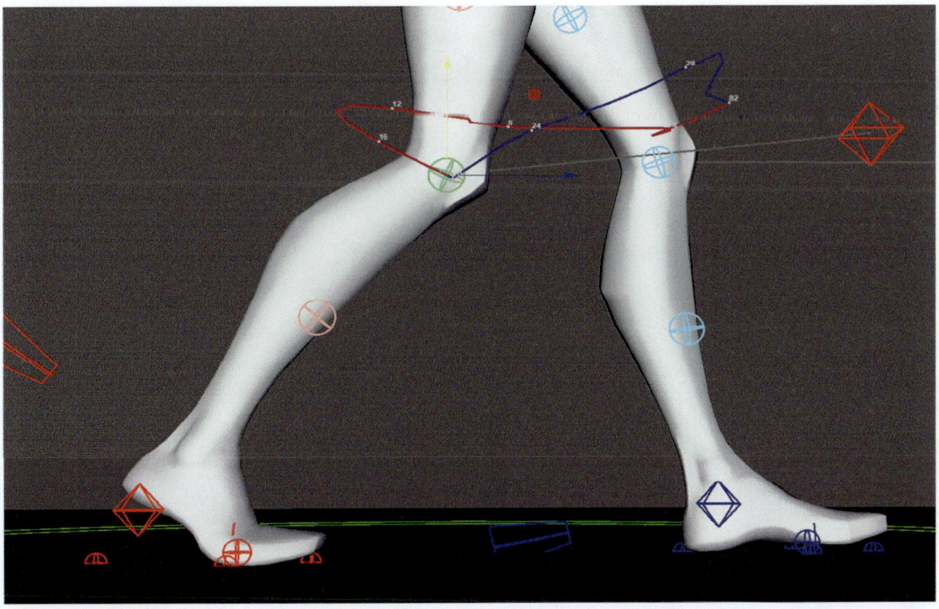

To select the knee-bend control, go to the Animation shelf and select Motion Trails. Look at the trail for any sharp jags, kinks, or backward motion. We need editable points, so we have to put animation on the knee-bend control.

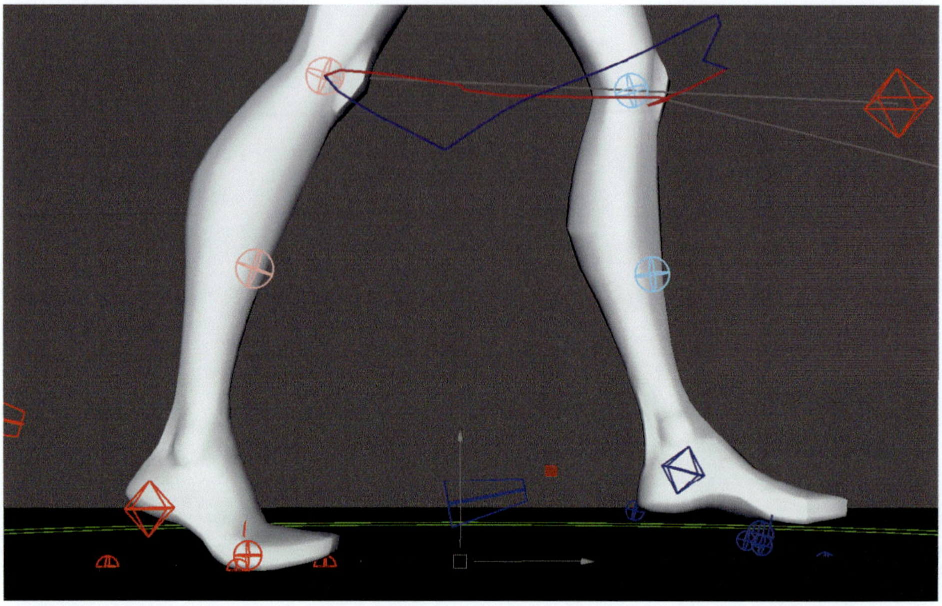

Select the knee-bend control and key it on 3s or 4s or whatever pace the walk is keyframed on. The Motion Trail should automatically update; if not, simply delete it and make a new one. Now we can see the sections of the path that need cleaning.

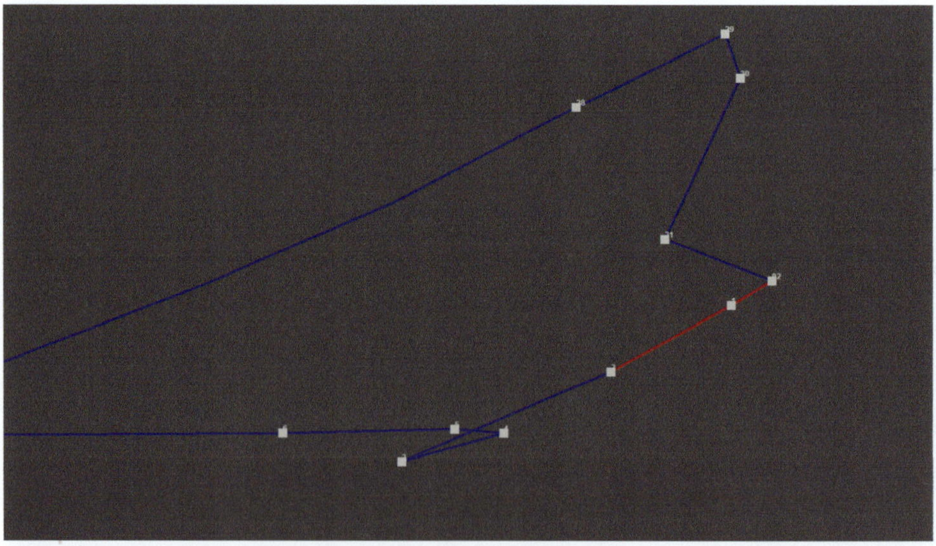

Look for sections of the Motion Trail that are jagged, where the knee stops or moves backward. These sudden changes in direction are what causes the knee shake during the walk.

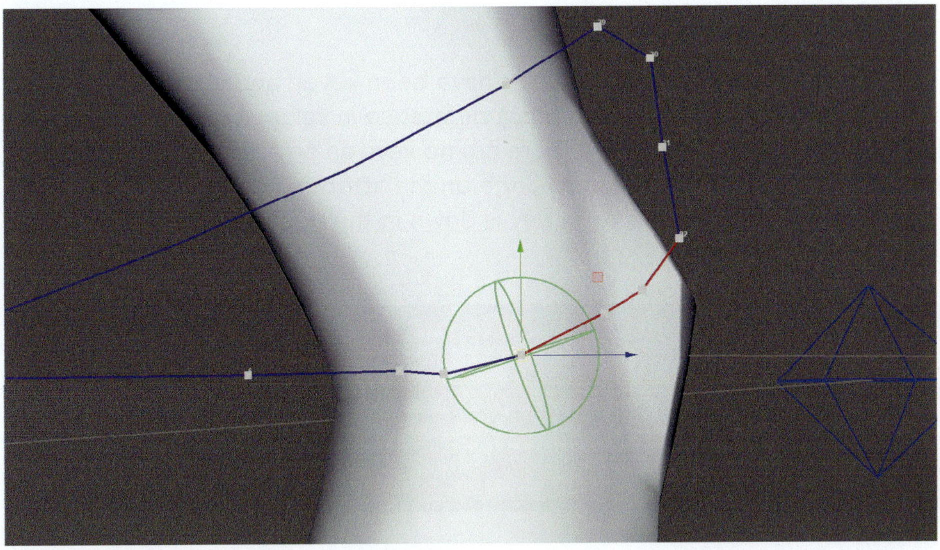

Move the knee-bend control gently and key it on every frame necessary to smooth out the trail. You can also select the editable points directly on the Motion Trail and move them, but it is sometimes slow to update because Maya is constantly trying to redraw the trail.

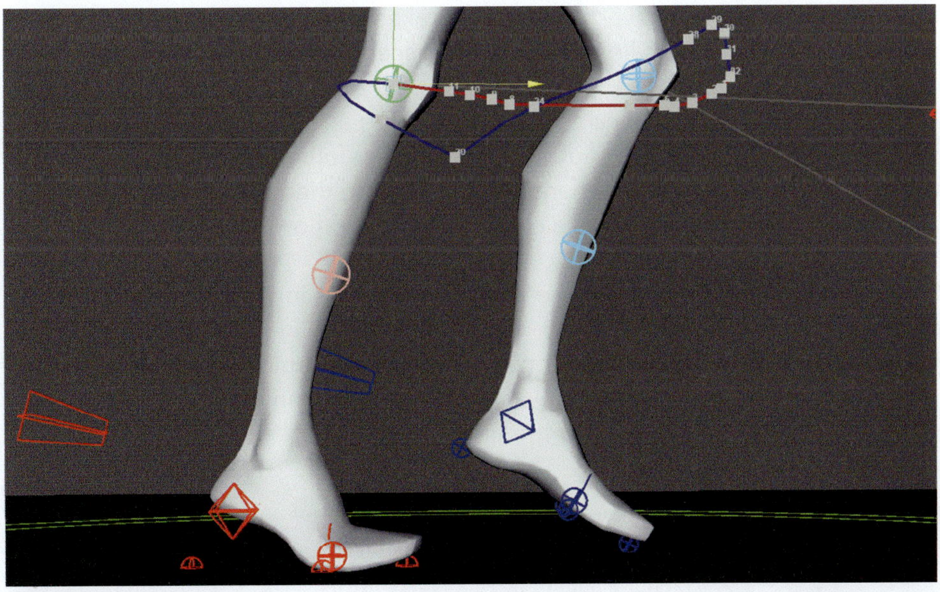

For a stationary walk cycle, the knee should move in a 'figure 8' path. In a progressive forward walk, a cleaned path should look like a gentle wave pattern. This method works really well; but be careful, we are smoothing the path of the knee by stretching the thigh or the lower leg. If too aggressively applied, the audience can see the leg changing sizes.

AUTO KEY FOR POLISH

The Auto Key looks at attributes that have been keyed and checks for differences in value. If it detects a difference in value, it will place a new key only on those attributes. If there are no keys on an attribute, then Auto Key will not work. If there is no change on the attribute, no key will be saved. The button to activate the Auto Key is down in the right corner.

Auto Key is an invaluable tool for experienced animators. However, beginner animators are recommended to turn Auto Key off for the blocking passes of the shot. The reasoning is it's common for this method to produce controls drifting around because the animator didn't realize channels were unintentionally left not keyed long ago. It takes some practice to maintain awareness of where keys lie in an animated scene, and on what controls.

Manual keying is recommended during blocking and initial refinement; turn on Auto Key for polish. Auto Key is quite useful for moving holds though; selecting the entire character and keying, then simply making small adjustments during the hold is a common pro workflow.

For Character Sets only, go to the Auto Key settings in Preferences > Settings > Animation > Auto Key and set it to Key All Attributes. This will force Auto Key to key all. Again, novice animators should not use Auto Key until reaching the refining and polishing stages of an animation, where there will not be any large changes to the timing of the shot.

CHEAT

Check if rig controls are prone to Gimbal Lock before starting animation. Select a control. Click E to bring up the rotation manipulator. Open Tool Settings or double-click the rotation icon. Under Axis Orientation, set to Gimbal. If two axes are lining up together, then there is a very high risk of Gimbal Lock.

NEW INSERT KEY OPTIONS

When using the hotkey S, Maya places a key on all available attributes. The new key will affect the curve depending on the Tangent Type set in Preferences. If you have been working heavily in the Graph Editor, these curve changes may cause extra work.

These hotkeys for inserting keys preserve the shape of the curve:

- **Alt + I** inserts a key on available attributes without any changes to the existing curves.
- **Ctrl + Shift + W** inserts a new key on Translate X, Y, and Z without any changes to the existing curves.
- **Ctrl + Shift + E** inserts a new key on Rotation X, Y, and Z without any changes to the existing curves.
- **Ctrl + Shift + R** inserts a new key on Scale X, Y, and Z without any changes to the existing curves.

NEW REORDER ROTATIONS OPTIONS (GIMBAL LOCK)

Gimbal Lock is where two axes lock together. It manifests itself with FK joints flipping around, often in 360° increments. Avoid this by rotating FK controls one axis at a time instead of the free rotation. Another tool we have is the Euler Curve filter. This looks for differences of 180° and 360° and adjusts the curves to remove the Gimbal Lock.

Some rigs come with multiple rotation order settings. In general, the Rotation Order should always be the most common axis of rotation first, and in descending order of importance. A spine, for example, bends the most in X, then Y, then Z.

New in Maya is the Reorder Rotations options. To use, select the joint/control, and go to Modify > Reorder Rotations. It will generate a list of Desired Rotation Orders with calculation of how likely Gimbal Lock is with each option. Choose the option as close to 0% as possible. This allows a change of rotation order without affecting existing animation.

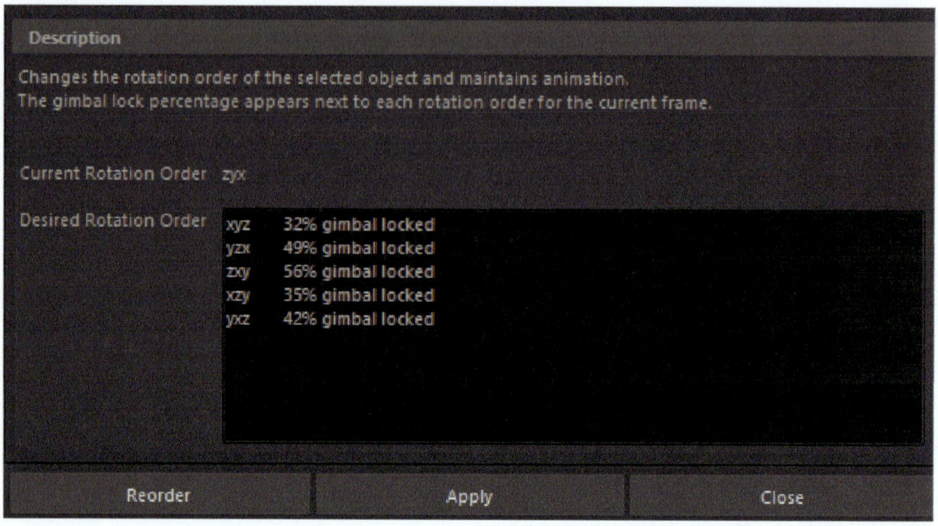

PIVOT POINTS

To change a pivot, use the hotkey Insert or hold down the D key.
It is possible to key the pivot point changing position. To do this, we need to add keyable pivot attributes to the Channel box. Go to Window > General Editors > Channel Control. The Channel Control has three panels: Keyable, Nonkeyable Hidden and Nonkeyable Displayed. We need to move the Rotate Pivot attributes into the Keyable list. Look in the Nonkeyable Hidden list and select: Rotate Pivot X, Y, and Z, and Rotate Pivot Translate X, Y, and Z. The new attributes will show up as channels that can now be keyed.

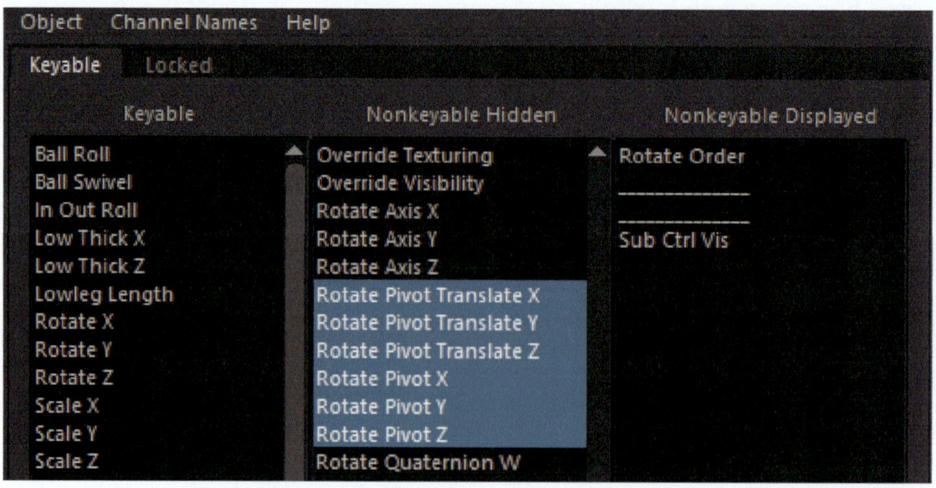

To get more predictable results, key the pivot change over one frame. The movement of the object over a long transition from pivot location A to location B may not be desirable.

It may not be possible to access the Rotate Pivot and Rotate Pivot Translate attributes on rig controls if it was locked by the rigger. In this case, the same result is achievable by constraining the rig controls to locators and key the pivot movement on the locators.

Redirect Tool

Character redirection is often used on background characters to convert a stationary cycle to travel forward, but if you also want the character to change the direction. It is useful for animation that is going to be imported into a game engine. Usually, Redirect is applied to the main control, so it affects the entire rig, but it can be applied to any control. Go to the Animation menu set > Key > Redirect. There are options of: Rotate and Translate, Rotate Only, and Translate Only.

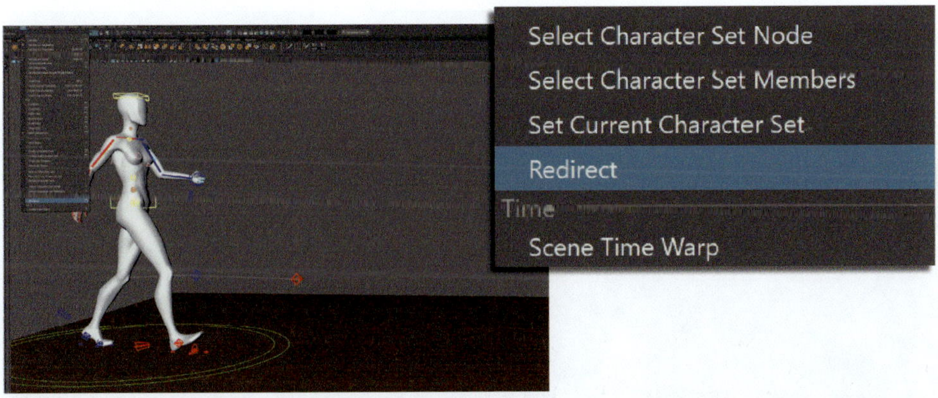

The Redirect Tool can be used on a forward progressive walk or a stationary cycle. To make a stationary walk cycle move forward, measure and add the stride length to the forward translation of the feet and root, and change the Translate Z curves to Cycle With Offset.

Applying many small Redirects, like one on each step, will give a smoother result than a few very large, staggered Redirects.

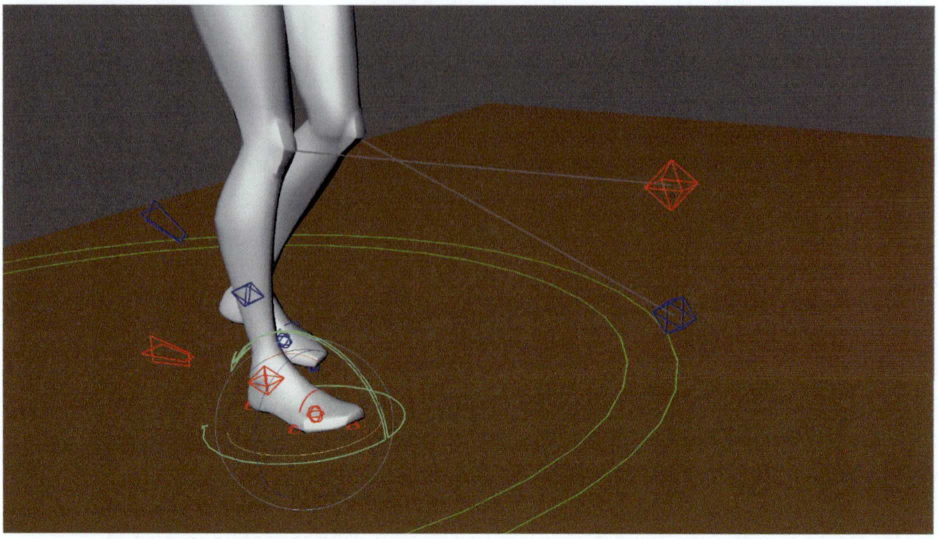

At the passing poses, select the Main Control and go to Key > Redirect > Rotation Only and place the icon at the ball of the foot on the ground and set a key.

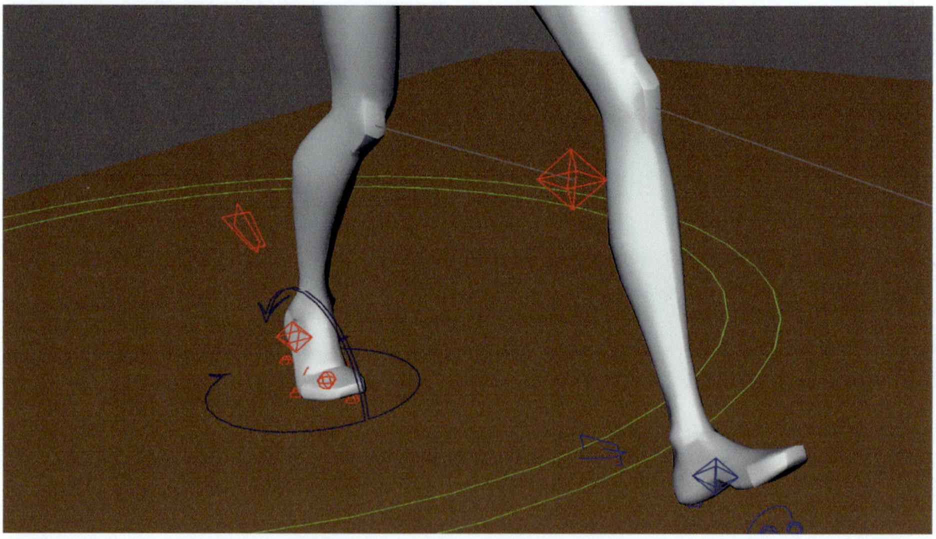

Just before the back foot lifts off the ground, rotate the Redirect icon and set a key again. The character now appears to be pivoting on the ball of the foot.

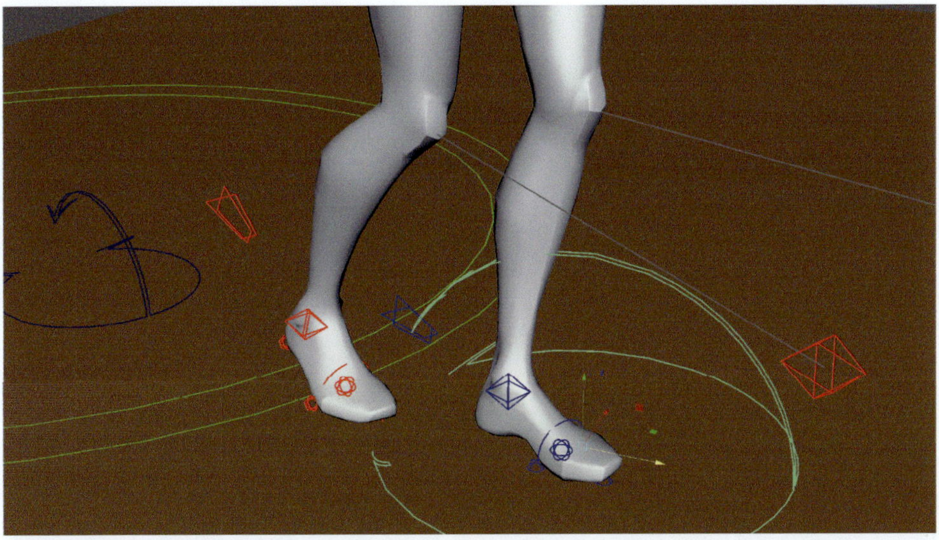

Repeat the process at the next passing pose. Select the Main Control and go to Key > Redirect > Rotation Only and place the icon at the ball of the foot on the ground and key.

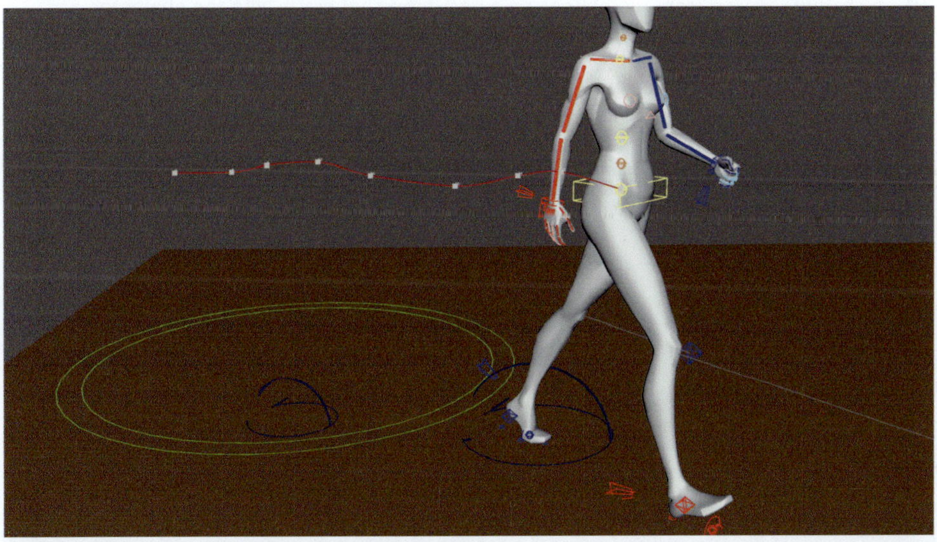

Each Redirect icon will be larger than the last. You can scale the icons, and it will not affect the tool. Smaller rotations on every step will give smoother results than 1 or 2 random large redirects.

Swing with Redirect Tool

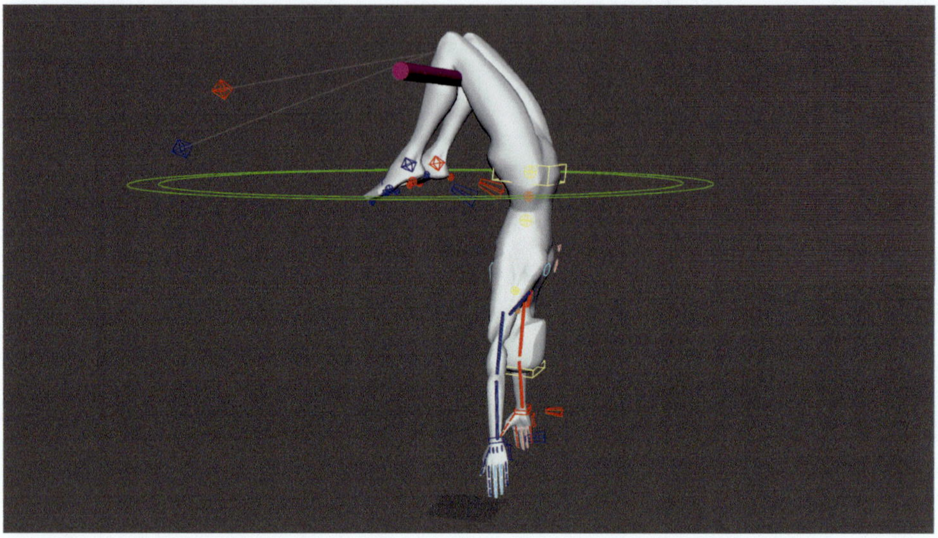

Make a character swing from their knees on a bar. If the shot starts with the character hanging on the bar, use the Main control to position the character up on the bar. Otherwise, keep the Main control on the floor and animate the character getting into position with root and IK feet and IK arms. Switch the arms and legs to FK.

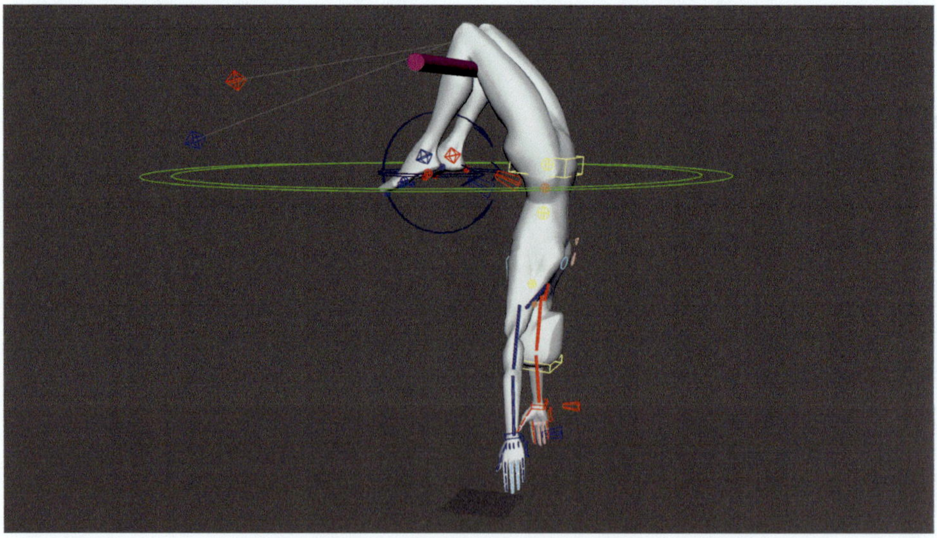

Now select the main control. Go to Key > Redirect > Rotate Only.

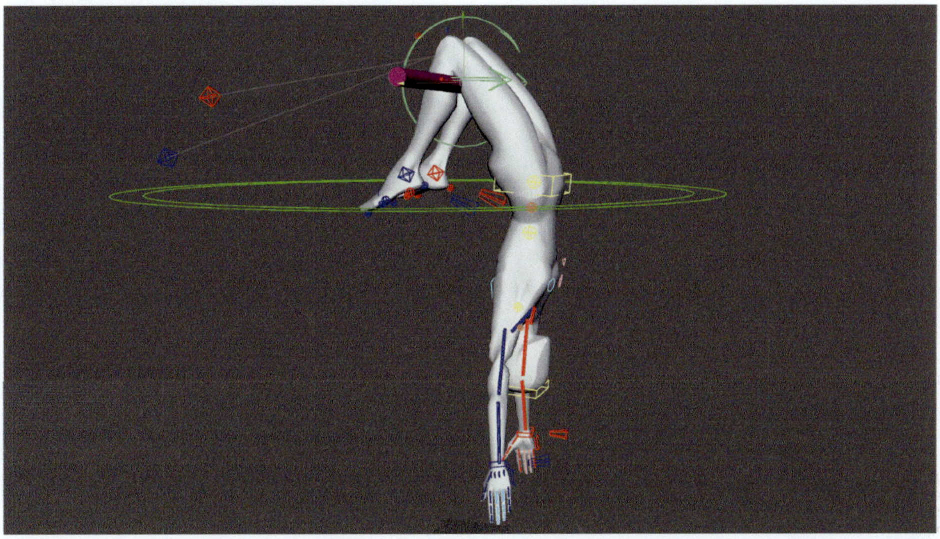

Move to the frame right before the character swings and place the icon at the point of rotation under the back of the knees, centered in the bar and key.

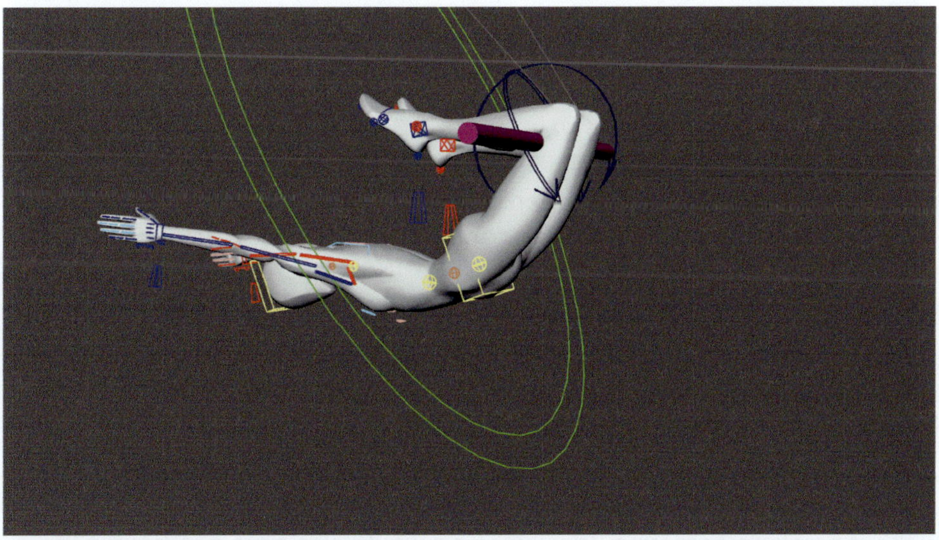

Rotate the Redirect icon and key. The character will swing and all the body FK controls will be free to put additional animation on.

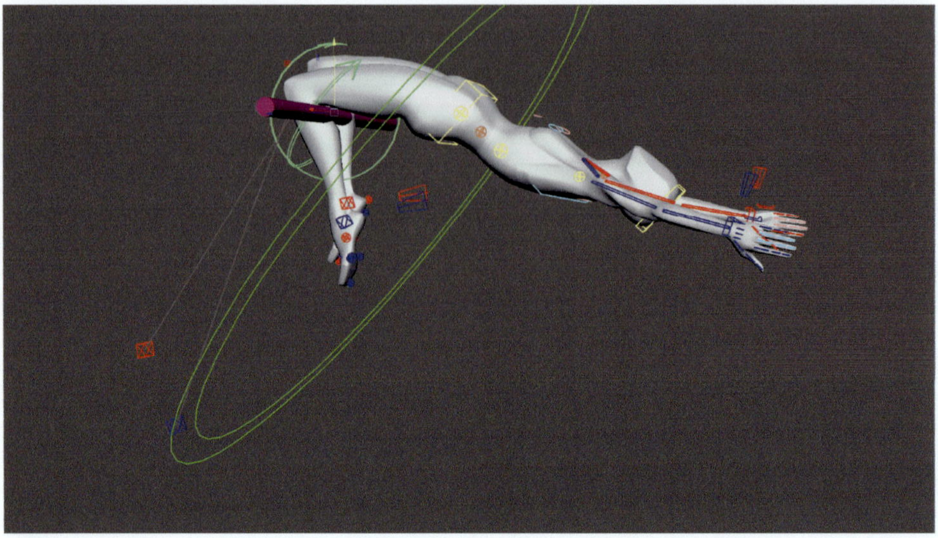

When the character is done swinging or about to dismount, copy the first Redirect key to reset the main control back to the original position and continue animating the character.

CARTOONY ANIMATION

If the animation is always dialed up to 11, then there is nowhere to go. Having a frantic piece of animation where the action never stops, and the character has no consistent solid form, can be just as unwatchable as a piece of animation where nothing happens. The audience needs a place to rest and catch up. We strive for a balance of contrasts: fast and slow, frantic and calm, exaggerated and understated. If you use cartoony animation tricks all the time, they lose their impact. They should be used with deliberate purpose to emphasize actions that are important to our story.

Stretch, Volume, Bendy Controls

A character must be set up properly for cartoony animation. The rig needs a combination of stretch, bend/ bow, and volume controls in order to deform without breaking or tearing. Ideally the rig would also have a reversible IK spine, and additional IK controls, like the fingers and head. Some rigs will use exclusively IK controls for the cartoony poses. Other rigs will have FK controls with translate and scale attributes available.

To find the stretch, bend, and volume controls, check the main control first. They may be located in channels that need to be made visible. The controls are sometimes placed on the IK limbs.

Stretch controls will usually be set to 1 by default: 1 being 100% of normal length. Depending on the rig, there may be stretch max and min limits that can be set. There may also be squash and stretch deformers, or lattice cage deformers, around regions of the body. There will be a volume or volume preservation attribute(s). The bend/bow controls will be along the limbs of the character and allow bending body parts in multiple locations.

Blurs: Smears and Multiples

In traditional 2D animation, blurs can be made with smears or multiple drawings. They function like motion blur on fast movements in live action films. Blurs emphasize the motion and help the audience follow the action. Similar to favoring a pose, a blur pose can affect the spacing by favoring one pose more than the other. The frame will be very distorted and often break the weight, balance, anatomy, and volume preservation. The audience should feel the distorted blur shape, but not see it.

This head whip feels even faster with the blurred middle frames.

A smear is a shape that is part pose A and part pose B with a smeared blending in between the two sides. One of the benefits of 2D animation is the ability to draw any pose. It can be more difficult to manipulate a 3D character into a distorted pose like a smear.

To make a smear pose, we need to see the path of the motion. A smear shape should emphasize the path of the motion. Let's take an example of a smear on a fast head turn. The smear should be 1 to 2 frames. Place a Motion Trail on the head control or nose to get the path from pose A to B. In order to see both A and B poses, go to Visualize > Ghost Editor. Create Ghost from selection on 1s. We want to distort the head and some facial features to accentuate the path. We can squish, elongate, rotate, and scale features to follow along the path. In addition to the available cartoony controls on a rig, one can try distorting the geometry with a lattice. Select the geometry and go to Deform > Lattice options. Set the division numbers to create points on the lattice cage. RMB off to the side, and choose Lattice

Points. First, set keys on the beginning and end of the frame range where the deformation will happen. Then set keys on the changes to the lattice points positions, and everything inside the cage deforms. More points means more complex shapes.

Multiples refers to creating a blur pose out of multiple drawings on top of each other. Let's take the example of a head turn again. We have pose A and pose B. We want to have a Motion Trail to see the path of the motion. We are going to pose the head favoring A or B, and then make 3 to 5 more copies of the head. Rotate each copy to fill in the path of the arc between pose A and B. Distorting the shapes and playing with transparency are both common practices.

To get multiple parts of a rig will greatly depend on how a rig is made. Can geometry be isolated and copied? Are there options to hide body parts? These options will make creating multiples much easier.
One technique is to reference more copies of the rig and hide everything but the body part that is needed, or copy the mesh at keyframes, then edit that copied geometry. This would be done only at the very end of working on a shot, as this geometry would be very cumbersome to edit.

Another option is to make new geometry. Using the same colored materials and textures to match the rig will help it blend together in the scene, and this stand-in geometry can be duplicated, distorted, and scaled.

When is the right time to use a smear or a multiple? Like everything in 3D, it depends on the situation. Smears are usually visually simpler and read better. Multiples can turn into more detailed complex shapes. If the rig is already visually complex, making multiples can create a very distracting frame that can confuse the audience.

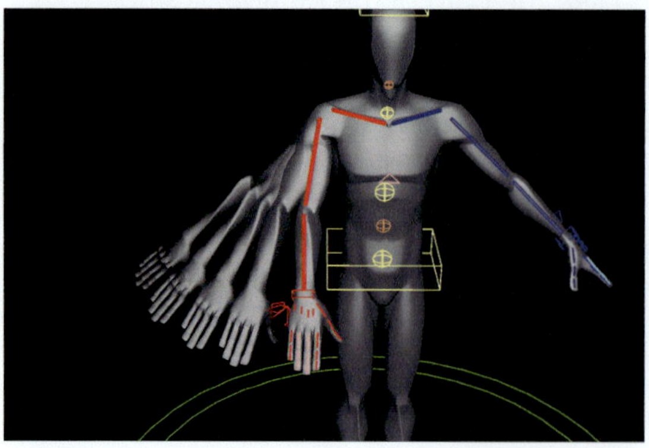

Multiples haven't seen a lot of action in CG animation, but recent cartoony films have explored this age-old trick to great effect!

Lines

Another way to simulate motion blur in cartoony animation is speed lines, wiggle lines, or swish lines. The concept is the same as multiples except gestural lines are used instead of duplicate geometry. Layering the 2D lines over 3D animation was used to great effect in the Spider-Verse movies and the TMNT Mutant Mayhem movie. In the past, this effect was added in 2D post-effects software. However, there are more options and control in Maya for this effect than ever before. A 2D vector drawing can be converted to a 3D object and animated. SVG stands for Scalable Vector Graphics. The Create menu contains the option to create a SVG or import vector art from an Adobe Illustrator file. Once imported, in the Attribute Editor > SVG tab, the object can be controlled by paths and has editable mesh, textures, and animations. This is not the only option. VFX is beyond the scope of this book, but Maya 2026 has motion graphics effects, dynamics, and MASH procedural effects that could also be used to simulate swish lines.

Don't forget transparency for smear, multiples, and swish line methods. We are simulating motion blur that would have various levels of transparency in the blur. Experiment with applying transparency to any object that catches your eye or distracts from the motion or overall animation.

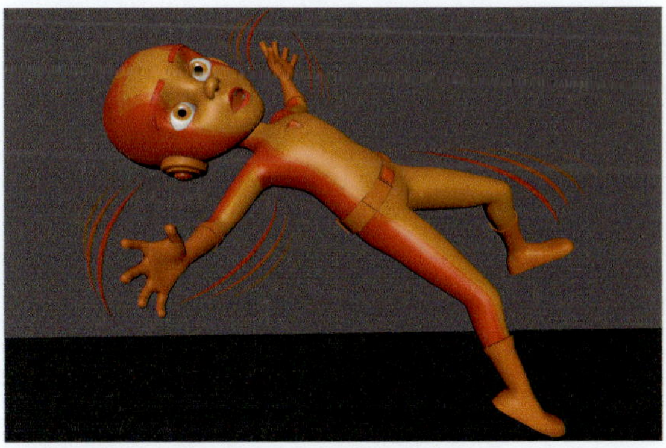

These lines really do well to emphasize the shaking of the limbs. Even in a still image, the viewer gets an exaggerated effect of the wobbly motion.

3RD PARTY PLUG-INS

It is the very strongly held opinion of both authors of this book that plug-ins should absolutely be avoided until an animator has a total grasp of the Maya software and is at least at an intermediate state of work.

Combating a lack of understanding with plug-ins is just going to make the matter worse; especially if later on, the plug-in can't solve the situation or is not available (it is highly regular for large studios to allow no plug-ins in their pipeline!). Nearly everything these plug-ins do can be done within Maya alone, although maybe not as elegantly. The plug-in just bundles everything together into a user-friendly one-click option or a convenient interface. Again, it is highly recommended to work without plug-ins for beginning animators in their first introductory courses.

People have been writing scripts and tools for Maya since it was released. During that time, there have been changes in the Python syntax that may break old tools. If an old plug-in was written in MEL, it may be easier to edit to be compatible with newer versions of Maya. When acquiring plug-ins, look for the most recent version. Please read the descriptions and make sure it is compatible with the current version of Maya. Some plug-in installation is drag-and-drop, and some will come with an installation program. Always follow the provided instructions.

Animbot

Animbot is currently the most robust tool set for animators. Alan Camilo is not only a skilled animator but also a talented developer. At the time, large animation studios that used Maya would develop their own in-house tools to speed up production. Camilo saw a need to make these tools available to the animating public and created Animbot. The list of tools is too long to include in this book, but the features page on the Animbot website has a comprehensive list with descriptions. A few of the best include: temporary controls and pivots, space switching, mirroring, and Xform relationships. It really is a large suite of tools, so there is a bit of a learning curve.

It's true, over the years, Maya has started to integrate some of these features into the software, and this will most likely continue. Animbot turns multi-step processes into a single tool, and that is where it really saves time. They do a good job of updating and refining the tools and staying current. Animbot has several pricing options that are worth the money.

Studio Library

Studio Library is a free plug-in that makes a library of stored poses and animations. The plug-in was created by Kurt Rathjen. The library can be organized by character, and create subfolders for body parts like brows, mouth, hands, etc. Make sets of controls, pose, and save the pose. The saved poses can be applied back to the rig and mirrored.

It even allows for blending between poses. Setup the Studio Library before starting a shot. It will be much easier!

This is a wonderful, tool but dropping stored poses across the Time Slider is not animating. The library is a tool. The prepared poses can get a shot 50 to 75% of the way, but it will be necessary to go in and adjust the poses adding overshoots, overlap, follow-through, asymmetry, contrasts, and texture. Make sure the pose works to the camera and serves the story.

MG Picker

MG Picker has been around for a while, so make sure to get the most current version. It was created by Miguel Gao. Many popular online rigs already come with pre-made MG picker files. There is a free version for students that installs in Maya. Inside is a custom shelf with a load button for pre-made pickers, and a studio button to create a picker. This picker is constantly being updated with new features and has become quite versatile. If creating your own pickers, it is much easier to set up before animation begins! If using MG Picker with multiple rigs with the exact same controls, the same picker can be used by changing the namespace.

Dreamwall Picker

Dreamwall picker is a newer free picker created by Lionel Brouyère and Olivier Ever. It is Maya 2026 compatible. It docks into the Maya workspace and functions like any other Maya panel. One handy feature is the ability to zoom in and out, and the text stays legible. It can import older Animschool pickers which are no longer free to use. The picker is intuitive and has lots of features.

Universal IK/FK Matching

Universal IK/FK Switch and Match 3.1.0 plug-in was created by Monika Gelbmann. This plug-in will match the position of the FK and IK joint chains exactly. No need to line up body parts or attempt to hide the transition in a movement. It can match FK to IK or IK to FK. There is a free version and a paid Pro version available. This plug-in has been around for awhile, so make sure to get the most current version.

8 CONSTRAINTS AND CONTACT

In animation, constraints are the unsung heroes of efficiency. They allow you to create complex, dynamic interactions between objects without the hassle of manually keying every frame. Whether it is a character picking up a prop, a camera tracking an object, or even the very controls that drive every character rig, constraints provide a way to automate motion while maintaining control.

Before constraints were simple and easy, CG animation was plagued by hand keying frame-by-frame almost like stop-motion. When that was impossible, we used tricks like breaking the rig and altering the hierarchy to create shot-specific hierarchical relationships. Tasks like parenting objects mid-animation or synchronizing motion between objects for only a section of the animation were exercises in patience. Constraints eliminate that hassle by letting animators define relationships between objects, controlling how one influences another. They are the ultimate cheat, in essence.

Why have we paired Constraints with Contact? It's simple; the most common reason to constrain an object when animating is because your character is touching it. Now, perhaps the character was always holding the bat, or the pencil, or hanging from a parachute in your shot, and the constraints can be set up beforehand. More likely though is that you are working on a dynamic shot in which the character interacts with an object, and the constraint is animated "on" or "off."

This moment of contact is worth examining in this chapter because novice animators tend to animate these moments the same way. We'll first examine constraints and then move onto animating them at the moment of contact to make it much more natural and fluid.

WHAT ARE CONSTRAINTS?

The different types of constraints all do the same thing: create a relationship between objects, where one object controls channels or attributes in the other. The most common constraints are:

- **Parent:** A Parent Constraint mimics the relationship of a traditional parent-child hierarchy but allows for more flexibility. The constrained object follows the position and rotation of the target object, but without actually being parented in the Outliner. This is useful when an object needs to switch between different parents over time, such as a character picking up and dropping a prop.

- **Point:** A Point Constraint locks an object's position to one or more targets but does not affect its rotation or scale. This is useful when you need an object to follow another's position while maintaining independent rotation—such as a floating balloon tethered to a moving hand, or an eye being locked to the head, but being able to rotate independently.
- **Orient:** An Orient Constraint controls an object's rotation without affecting its position or scale. This is useful when you need an object to align its rotation to another without physically moving—such as a character's head tracking an object while keeping its position locked. It is also used frequently in rigging for keeping joints oriented properly during animation.
- **Scale:** A Scale Constraint makes an object match the scale of one or more target objects. This is useful when dealing with objects that need to grow or shrink in proportion to another, such as mechanical parts that expand or contract in sync, or characters holding stretchable objects that need to remain consistent in scale with their hands.

The most common constraint you will use when animating is the Parent Constraint. To fully understand constraining, it is first essential to understand that when a constraint is made, it sets certain attributes on creation that do not change. Attributes like the offset in position and rotation are set when you create the constraint. You will not animate these attributes; you will only animate the strength of this connection when animating with constraints. So, for the purposes of understanding constraints, they should ***not*** be thought of as a normal parent/child relationship, where the child rides around in a "box" the parent controls. Rather, it is a locked connection. Parent constraint is a very misleading name. It should be called something like a Transform constraint.

WATCH OUT!

This cannot be emphasized enough. Beginners think of constraints as being sort of a 'temporary parent.' It is only temporary in that the connection can be turned off and on, but it is not a hierarchical connection in any way. Instead, think of a constraint as fully locking target attributes together.

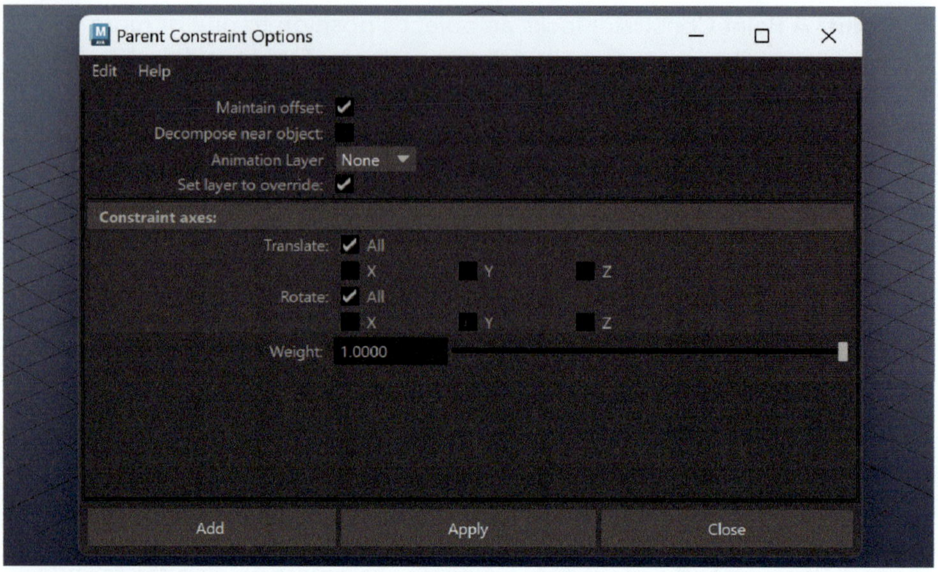

Parent Constraint Tool

Maintain Offset: This determines whether the child channels are going to be locked to the exact values of the target. For almost all use cases, this should remain checked.

Decompose Near Object: This can remain unchecked — it controls how rotation is handled when the objects are near matching, which can be a problem in CG due to Quaternion rotations and gimbal issues.

Animation Layer: This allows you to conveniently apply a constraint to only a certain layer, which is handy if you want to animate constraints on and off using animation layers instead. Use at will once you understand its purpose.

Set Layer to Override: In general, leave this checked, because you will want one constraint node and its effect to override animation, instead of additively moving constrained objects.

Constraint Axes: This controls which transforms and which axes are constrained; you may have a specific need that dictates what you choose here. In general, animators use Parent Constraint to mimic a parent/child relationship, and therefore both Translate and Rotate, and all of their respective axes are constrained. However, if you are animating a rain cloud constrained to a character, following it all around, but you don't want it to move up or down when they jump, you would choose only X and Z Translate channels for your constraint.

Think of it this way: if you create a constraint when a hand catches a ball, the position and rotation of the ball relative to the hand is saved into that constraint on creation. You can turn off the constraint, and the ball will return to the unconstrained position. Whenever a constraint is active, the constrained object will go right back to where that constraint was made, relative to the parent. If it seems like we are repeating this point a lot, we are; the 'locked' characteristic of a constraint is quite confusing to beginners and this all bears repeating!

Open 08 -Ball.ma. As you scan the timeline, you see a ball falling through the hand.

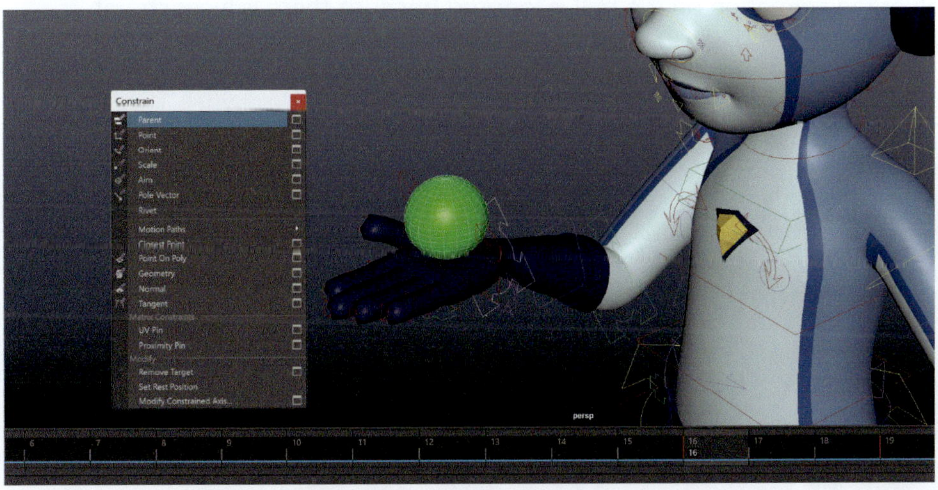

When the ball reaches the hand on frame 16, we create a parent constraint. Select the wrist IK control (R_arm_wrist_IK_CTRL), then the ball, and in the Animation menu set (F4), click Constrain > Parent.

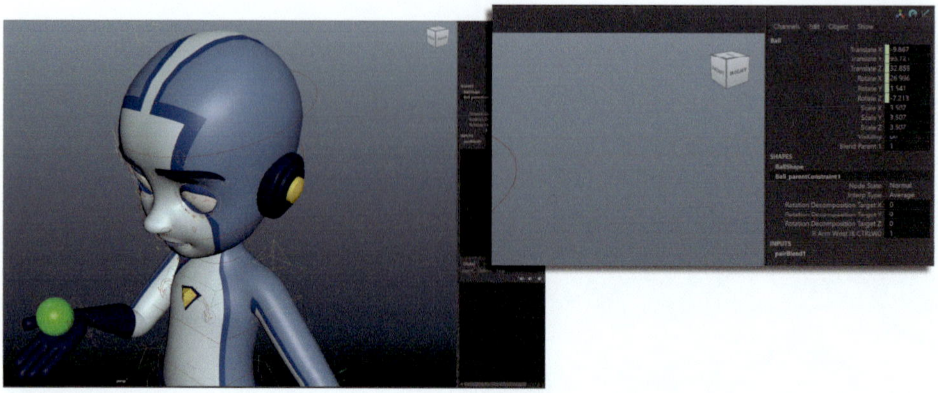

The constraint is created, and whenever its strength is set to 1, the ball will go back to this position relative to the hand. Scroll in the Time Slider, and select the wrist IK control and move it around and you'll see. Undo any movement or set keys before continuing.

This is not nearly complete, as we are only demonstrating the constraint being active. In other words, if you go back a few frames in the Time Slider, all of the animation on the ball is ignored because there is a constraint in the scene, and it is active.

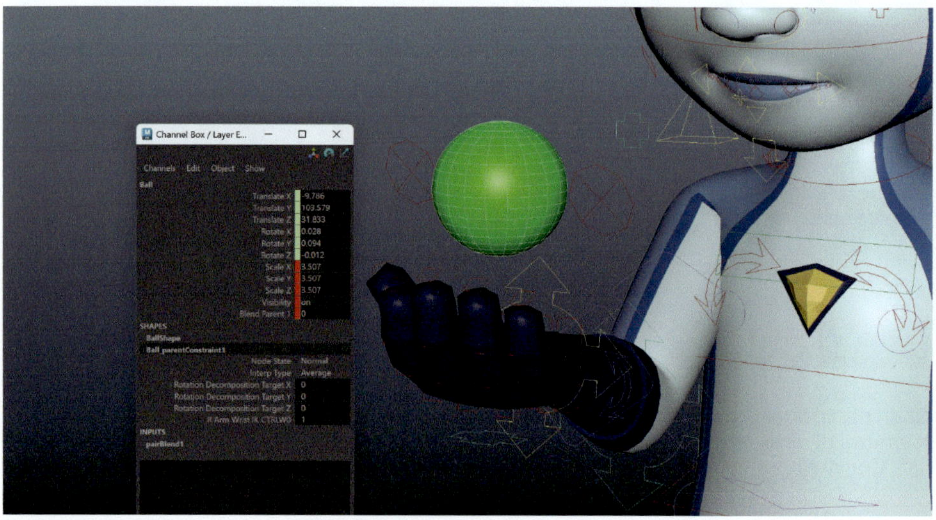

Go to frame 15 and hit S with the ball selected. You will see a key set on the channel called Blend Parent 1. Set that to 0 and hit S again. Then frame forward to frame 16 and key the Blend Parent to a value of 1.

Now that we've animated the constraint "turning on," the keyframes originally on the ball are affecting the ball again in frames 1–15 (before the constraint is active). This is the very basic workflow for creating an animated constraint, but it has major limitations. Quite often, students will become very frustrated because they cannot adjust the position or rotation of a constrained object. It is why we have repeated a few times that constraints have a locking behavior. To achieve flexibility and to move constrained objects, we need to do a little more work.

CHEAT

The G key repeats the last command. When making multiple constraints, it only works between two objects, so you may have to select a control, a target object, and constrain over and over. This is made much faster by just selecting the control, then new target, and pressing G, repeat.

MULTI-LAYERED CONSTRAINTS

It is quite common for an animator to need to make adjustments to a constrained object. But as was mentioned in the previous section, animation is negated on constrained channels while the constraint's weight is set to 1, and the constraint is active. So how do professionals achieve control over constrained objects? We use multi-layered constraints.

Here is the simple workflow. We create a simple "rig" that involves a locator that will receive the constraint from the hand control, and a locator parented beneath the first locator that will constrain the prop. Since the locator that constrains the prop is parented under the locator that is constrained by the hand, it is free to move. It moves by simple hierarchical parenting and is thus free to have keyframes on it. This layer of separation is key to gaining full control over the constraint and motion in professional animation.

8 CONSTRAINTS AND CONTACT

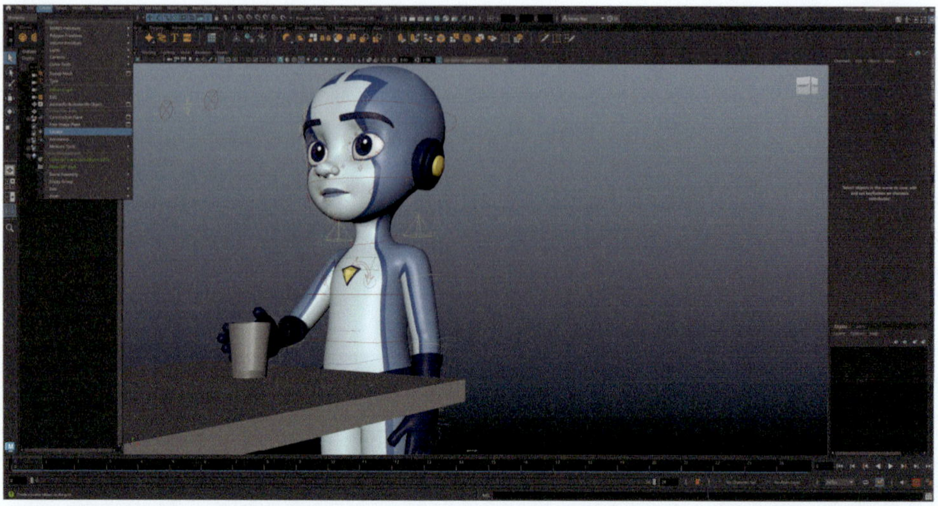

Open 08 - Multi.ma. Create a locator by clicking Create > Locator, or an empty group by pressing Ctrl + G. For the purposes of this demonstration, we'll use a locator. Name it Hand_Loc.

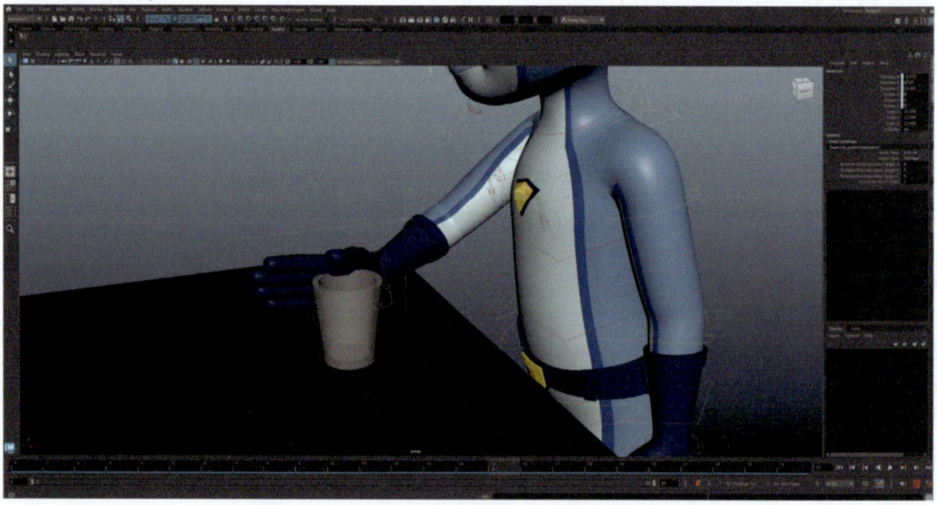

Move the locator to the general position where the constraint happens.

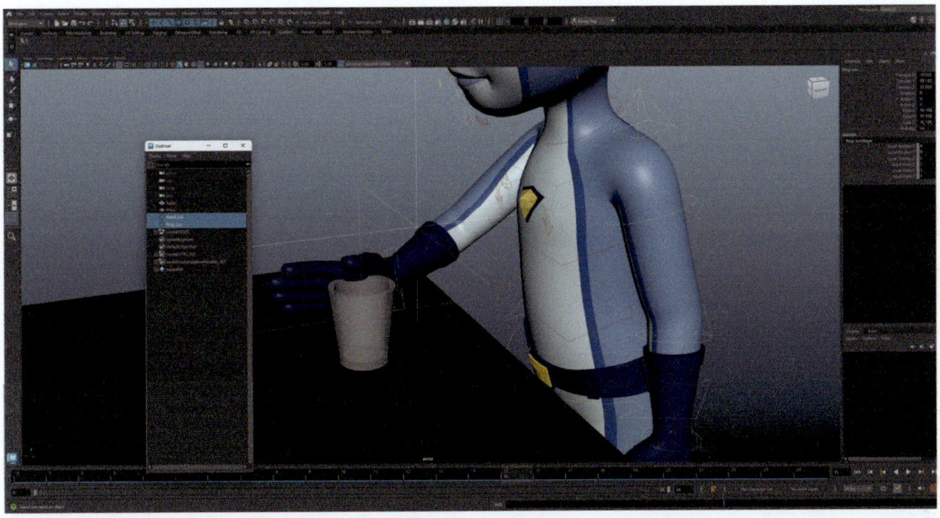

Duplicate the locator and move it to the center of the prop you want to constrain (in this case, the glass). Name it Prop_Loc.

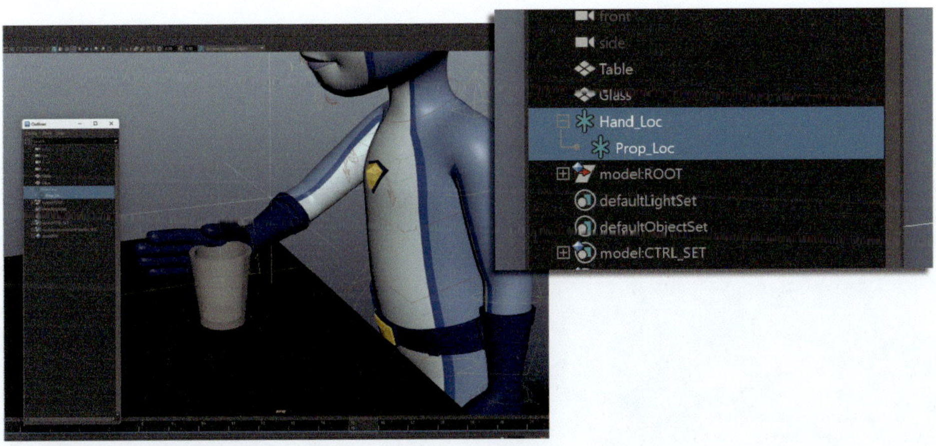

Now we parent the Prop locator under the Hand locator. Select Prop_Loc, then Hand_Loc, and press P.

At the frame of contact, we constrain the Hand_Loc to the Hand, and the Prop_Loc to the glass. In the Outliner, you will see the constraints have been added to their respective objects.

Once we hit S to Set Key on this frame, a channel to control the weight of the parent constraint appears on the constrained objects. This is called Blend Parent 1, and it has a default weight of 0.

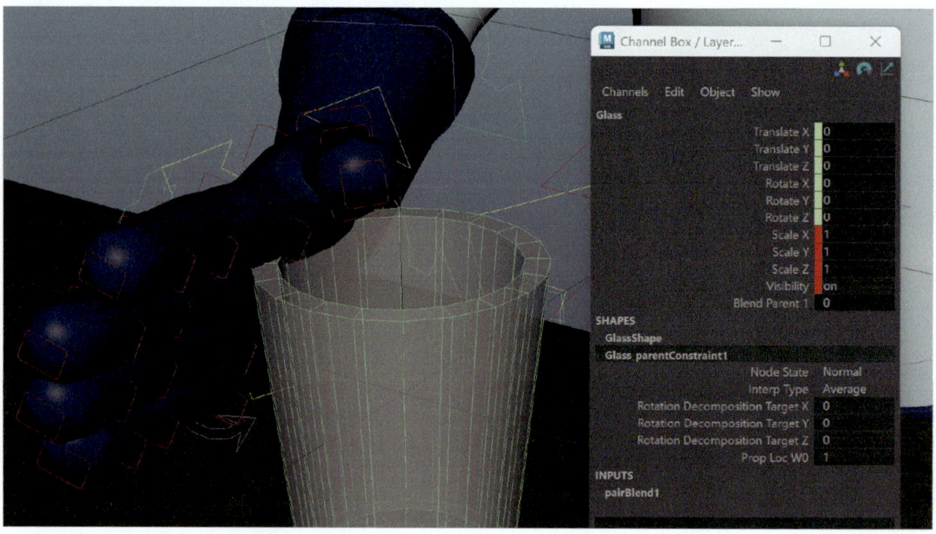

Keying all channels of an object that is constrained will expose the constraint's keyable attributes in the Channel Box.

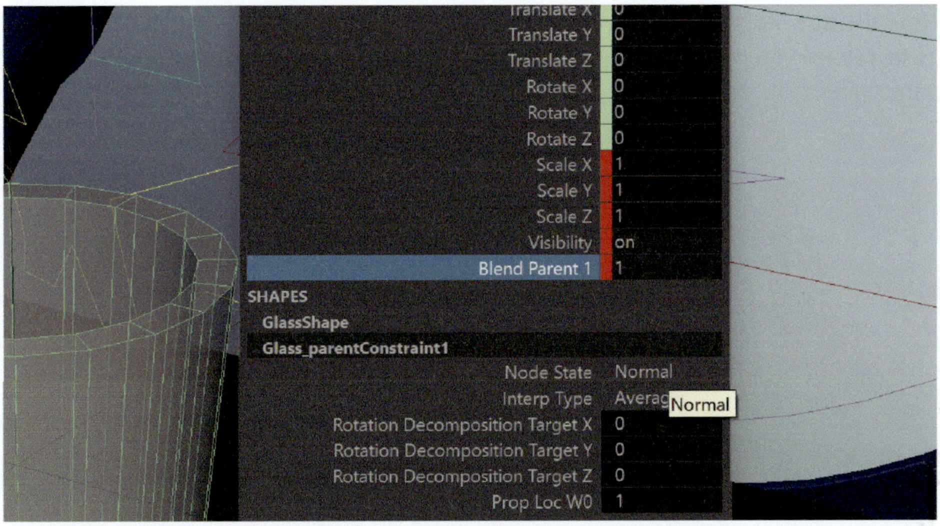

Set a key on the Blend Parent channel and the value to 1.

The constraint on the prop is created and set, and now we must key it "off" on the frame before contact. "Off" is in quotes because technically, we are not actually turning off the constraint, we are just lowering the weight of the constraint to 0.

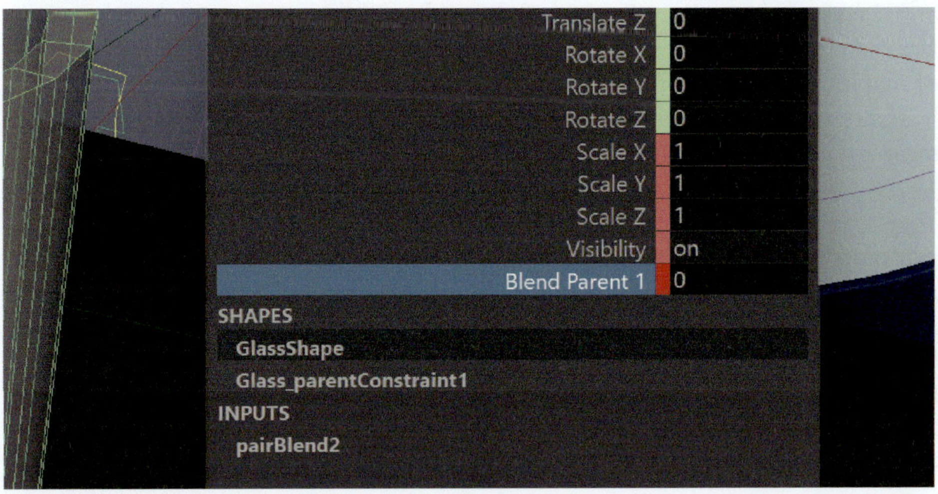

Go one frame earlier and key the weight of the Blend Parent channel on the prop to 0.

Now the simple multi-layered setup is complete. This dynamic setup allows us to create the constraint but still have control over the parents and their constrained objects.

DON'T FORGET

When constraining objects, you need to select the PARENT object first (unlike hierarchical parenting which is selecting the parent last).

Contact

Contact is a particularly sticky subject in animation (pun intended!). Animating contact brings with it particular hallmarks. Novice animators will tend to key the entire body on the point of contact, which makes the animation feel like it is slowing-in to the contact. It is almost as if the animation can be felt all leading up to a moment, when in reality moments of contact happen frequently and fluidly.

Try this; place something soft and not fragile (like a napkin or sock) on a table. Record yourself picking it up. Try a few times picking it up slowly, and a few times picking it up quickly. What you will notice is that your arm, hand, and fingers move fairly fluidly through the motion, the hand pose adjusts even in the midst of the object being picked up, and a lot of manipulation happens throughout. If you cover the object in the video, it is hard to see from watching just the wrist or elbow what frame the moment of contact occurs.

This is because we judge an item's weight and characteristics that affect gripping it, and our arm, wrist, hand, and fingers work together to seamlessly pick it up without having to come to a complete stop. Oftentimes, beginner animators will go so far as to draw a thumbnail in their planning of the full body pose that occurs on the moment of contact, deeper emphasizing the body 'hitch' that is a dead-giveaway for beginner work. Great contact work attends to the fluidity and dexterity that characters have, and brilliant use of constraints is employed to make these transitions invisible.

Here is a simple breakdown of a good approach to contact. We'll use a hand picking up a glass again.

Key the motion as if the contact never happens, all the way up to before the contact.

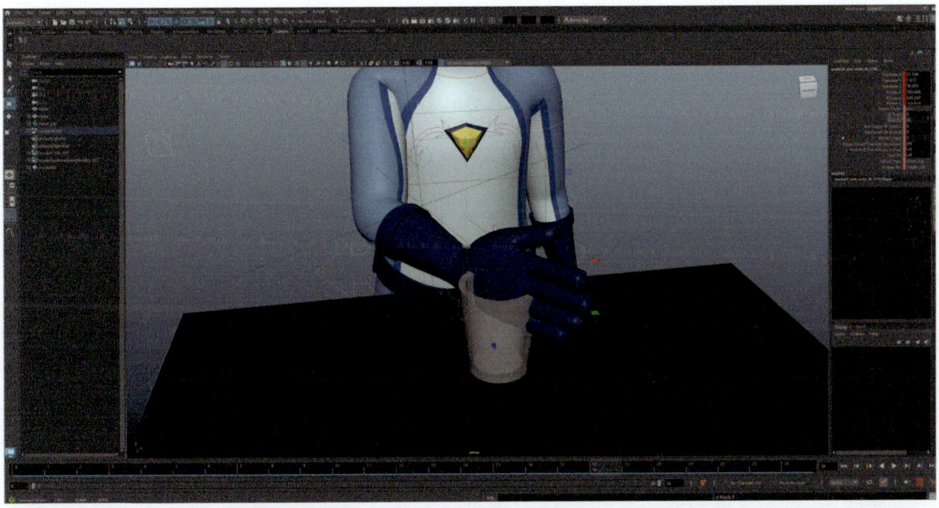

Key the hand going "through" the point of contact. This is a few frames after the contact would have taken place, and notice the hand is past the position when it would have intersected.

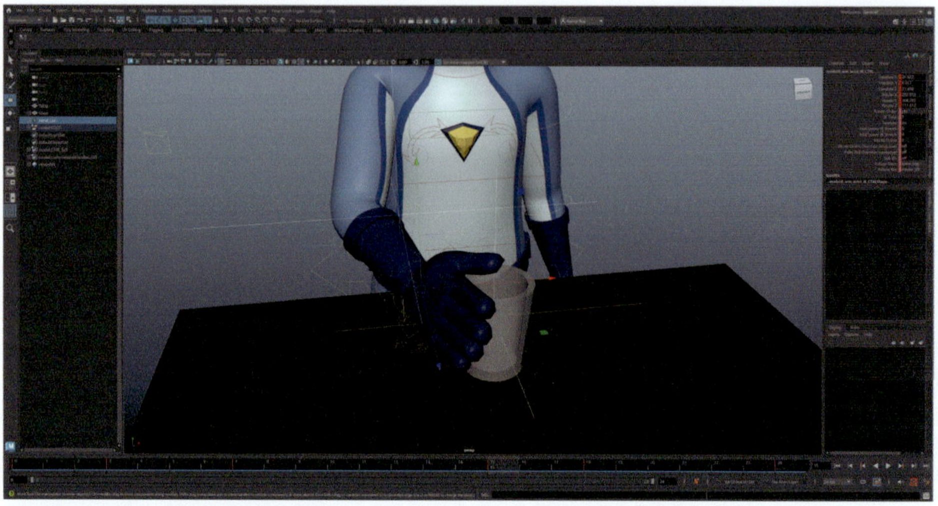

Reverse a few frames and create your constraint rig, keying it on the frame that the hand intersects.

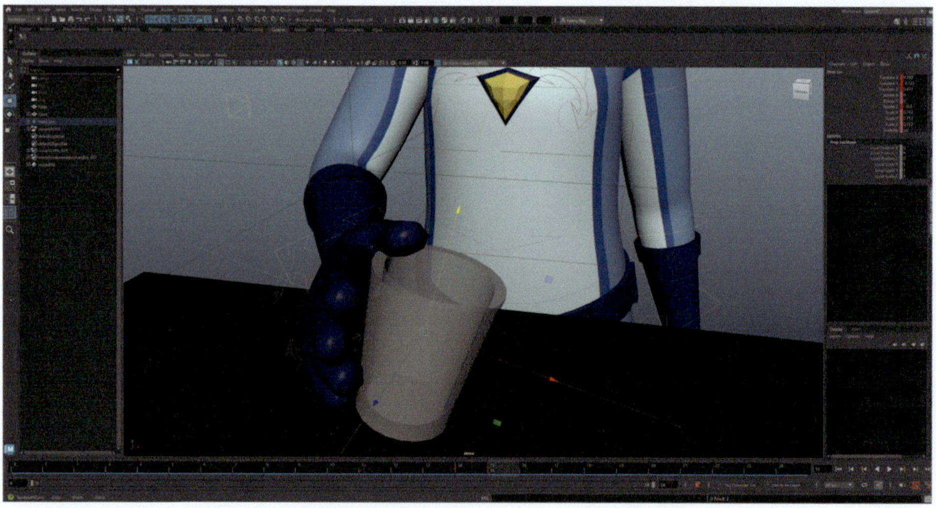

Use the new rig to key the locators such that the prop reacts properly to being touched. Notice how we are using the locator to rotate the cup on the contact frame, and the fingers are beginning to close around it — we don't fully close our hand until we've touched the object!

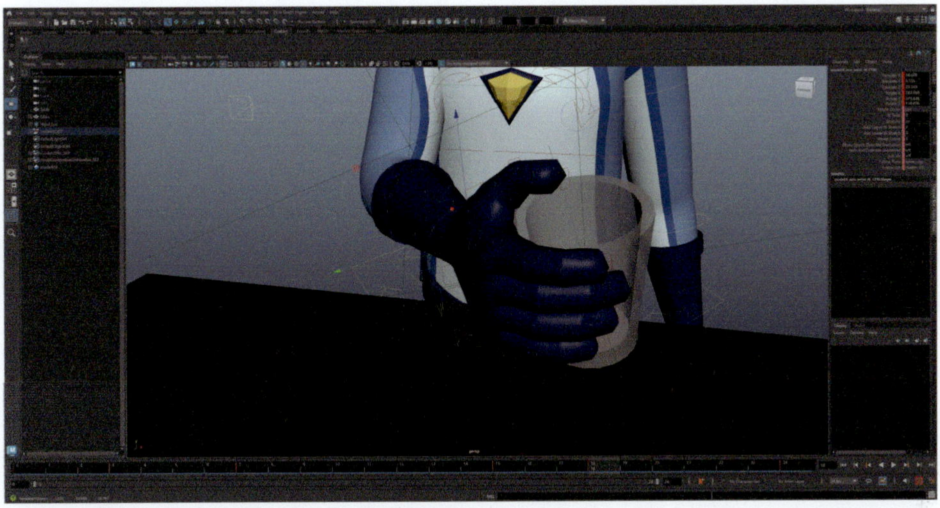

Over the next few frames, key the fingers and prop to show the natural settling and manipulation of the prop that happens as an object is grabbed. It takes a few frames for our hands to fully grasp an object we are picking up!

If this seems a little counter-intuitive, think of contact from another perspective: walking and running. When keying either of these motions, the full body lifts and falls, and rarely does it look correct if the body is keyed to begin to rise or fall on the same frame that the feet touch the ground. On the contrary, the overlapping action (see Chapter 1!) of the body smoothly happens on its own cadence. Though the feet contacting the ground is the only thing keeping the body from collapsing to the ground, the body smoothly rises and falls separately from the moments of contact.

As you progress, constraints become less of a hassle and more of a helpful tool to enable all sorts of great motion. From an acrobat swinging from a trapeze (how would you constrain the body to the handle bar?), to a character running across a collapsing bridge, constraints quite literally enable some of the most exciting and dynamic motion seen on screen.

FUN FACT

On some feature animations and VFX-heavy feature films, it is not uncommon for the rigging department to create a rig specifically for characters that are riding others (like an ape on a horse, or a human on a dinosaur), if there are many shots that require this relationship. Better the riggers do it right, once, than a dozen animators doing it 100 times over and over again!

INDUSTRY BREAKDOWN

Across all sectors, animation grows year after year, opening doors for juniors and new entrants in ways that previous generations could only dream of. As with any career, it is important to understand the industry you are stepping into, its challenges, and where the real opportunities lie.

If you are picturing yourself working at Pixar, Disney, or Illumination, it is worth taking a step back and looking at the total industry landscape. The reality is that only about 10% of animators work in film, and an even smaller percentage (just 2%) are employed on animated feature films. This means competition for these jobs is fierce, and getting there requires not just skill, but perseverance, networking, and often personal sacrifices in order to stand out.

Most animators will not work on the next big Hollywood animated film. But that does not mean there is no future in animation! Far from it; the animation industry is vast, diverse, and constantly evolving.

Where Animators Actually Work

50% Games
30% Television (including streaming and advertising)
10% Other (medical animation, courtroom reconstructions, AR/VR, corporate training, web content, and more)
10% Film (of which just 2% is animated features)

While feature film jobs are the most competitive, other parts of the industry are booming. The video game industry alone makes up half of all animation jobs, and with studios constantly expanding their cinematic teams, high-quality storytelling in games is more in demand than ever. Meanwhile, the explosion of streaming services has ushered in a golden age of television animation, ranging from high-end adult animation like *Arcane* and *Blue-Eye Samurai* to an endless stream of kids' content that still requires skilled animators.

The Remote Work Revolution

For decades, animators moved from city to city, following the work. If a studio shut down or a project wrapped, you packed your bags and went where the next job was. For those fresh out of school, this digital-nomadic lifestyle was exciting; a chance to see the world, work with new people, and gain experience. But for those with families, mortgages, and real-life responsibilities, the constant relocation could be exhausting. Then, in 2020, everything changed. The COVID-19 pandemic forced the entire industry into remote work overnight. The results were surprising; especially to studio heads who had resisted work-from-home models for years. Studies showed that productivity in many industries, including animation, actually increased with remote work. And in cases where productivity dropped, forcing workers back into the office often decreased it even further.

Animation proved that it could be done from home, and for many companies (especially in games and television) remote work has become the norm. While the biggest studios have largely returned to in-person work, many new jobs, especially in games and advertising, remain 100% remote. For the first time, junior animators are getting hired into high-quality jobs without having to move across the world to do it!

Breaking into the Industry

Knowing where the jobs are is one thing, but getting one is another. The good news is that animation is almost entirely a skill-based career. A great demo reel and a strong understanding of industry tools will get you much farther in animation than almost any high-tech industry. However, the type of work you want to do determines what you need to focus on:

Feature Film and TV
Expect high competition. You will need exceptional acting skills, expressive body mechanics, and an outstanding demo reel. If your current job does not give you the work you need for a strong reel, you must be prepared to do personal animation projects in your free time to fill in the gaps.

Games
One of the best areas for growth but requires technical knowledge. Understanding how to implement animations into an engine like Unreal or Unity is just as important as strong motion work. Cinematic animation in games is the closest to film work, while gameplay animation has different constraints, requiring responsiveness and seamlessly looping cycles.

Advertising and Corporate
A solid entry point with reliable work. While it may not be as glamorous as film or games, this sector pays well and offers more stability than many other sectors.

Medical, Courtroom, and Industrial
High-paying but often less creative, this work involves animating scientific, legal, or industrial processes. It is a niche field but one where skilled animators can carve out long-term careers.

Is It Worth It?

Animation is an incredible career, but it is not for everyone. There will always be crunch time, job instability, and high competition in certain fields. But, it is also one of the few creative careers where hard work and skill actually make you rise to the top. If you love bringing characters to life and are willing to put in the time to refine your craft, there is a place for you in this industry.
The bottom line? Animation is bigger than it has ever been. Your dream job might not look exactly like you imagined, but if you are adaptable, are willing to keep learning, and stay open to new opportunities, you can absolutely build a fulfilling and successful career.

9 CAMERA

In video games, the animation needs to look good from all angles because the user may be able to move the camera anywhere. In TV and film, the camera is set, and we animate to the camera. In large studios, Layout Artists are responsible for setting up the camera in the scene files. At a small company or as a student, cameras may be set up by the animators.

CHEAT

A good working knowledge of photography, filmmaking, and cinematography is invaluable as an animator. Pick up classes or study books and videos on these subjects. As an animator, you want to become a student of all things cinema.

Maya cameras are set up to function like real-world cameras with lenses, F stops, and shutter angles. If not matching live-action film plates, an animator may never have to go too deep into all the camera settings. However, you should familiarize yourself with some of the common settings.

FILMMAKING

Shot Types

Establishing Shot
Shows the character(s) and their positions relative to each other and the environment.

Extreme Wide Shot
Characters are tiny in the frame, and this shot can include large landscapes.

Wide/ Long Shot
Characters are small in the frame, introducing location, and the camera may be far from subjects.

Full Shot
The entire character is in the frame, head to toe. Good for showing the character doing a whole-body action.

Medium Shot
Shows character from the waist up.

Cowboy Shot
A medium shot from hip up to show gun holsters.

Medium Close-Up Shot
Shoulder up, to show some body language through shoulders with a complete view of facial expressions.

Close-Up Shot
Shows the character's head and neck, and can also be a close-up of an object or body part.

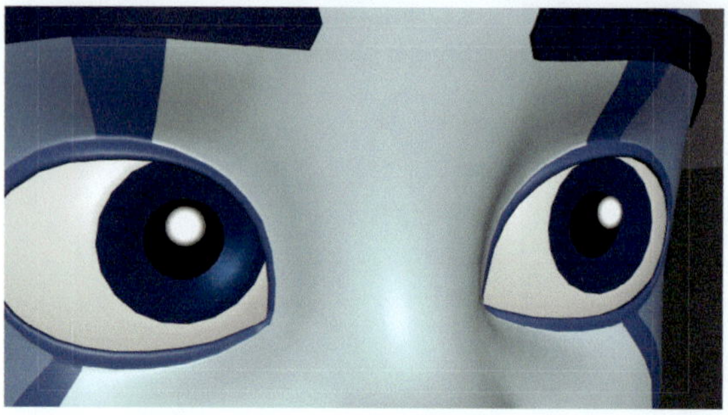

Extreme Close Up
Very close to a single detail of the face, body, or object.

WATCH OUT!

For close-ups of the character's face, it is acceptable to cut off the top of head at the forehead, but do not cut off the bottom of the head at the chin.

Shot Angles

Dutch Angle/ Tilt
Camera is tilted and rotated on its side, to make the audience uneasy. Shows tension, confusion, suspense, or fear.

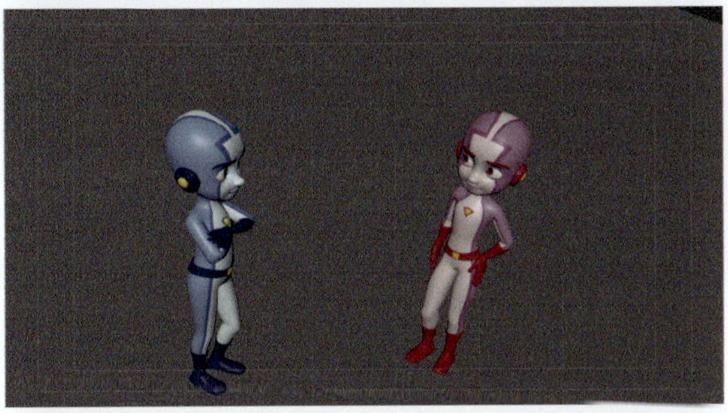

Bird's Eye, Aerial, or High Angle
Camera is high up looking down on the character. Can make the character feel small, lost, or powerless.

Worm's Eye or Low Angle
Camera is low down looking up at the character. Can make the character look large, powerful, heroic or threatening.

Over the Shoulder
Place the camera just over one character's shoulder to see the person or people the character is looking at, often used for conversations.

Cut Away/ Neutral Shot
Cuts away from the action, characters, or objects of interest to something else. Useful for changing the 180° line or as a reset.

POV
Point of view, to turn the camera in the direction that the character is facing, to show what the character sees.

Focal Length

Focal length is not the size of the lens but the distance from the lens to the plane where the image is in focus.

- **14 to 35 mm:** Wide-angle lens, objects appear smaller/further away, objects are in focus, good for landscapes. Wide-angle lens will cause distortion if the subject is too close to the camera.
- **50 to 60 mm:** Standard lens, closest to the human eye, good for a wide variety of shots, with very little distortion. Standard lenses have a shallow depth of field, meaning the subject is in focus but the background is out of focus.
- **70 to 200+ mm:** Telephoto lens, the camera can be very far away from the subject but still gets a clear close-up. It tends to flatten distance or make objects look closer together than they are.

Maya cameras have a default focal length of 35 mm. Zooming in too close to your subject will cause some distortion. To change the focal length, select the camera and open the Attribute Editor > Camera Attributes.

Framing

Don't place the subject dead center in every shot. It's boring and doesn't give us much information.

Rule of Thirds: Divide the image into thirds with two evenly placed vertical lines and two horizontal lines. The four points where the lines intersect are where to place the subject or line up the background. This makes for more dynamic shots using the space around the characters for storytelling. Leaving space in front of the character (lead room) can make them feel free, whereas leaving space behind the character can make them feel trapped.

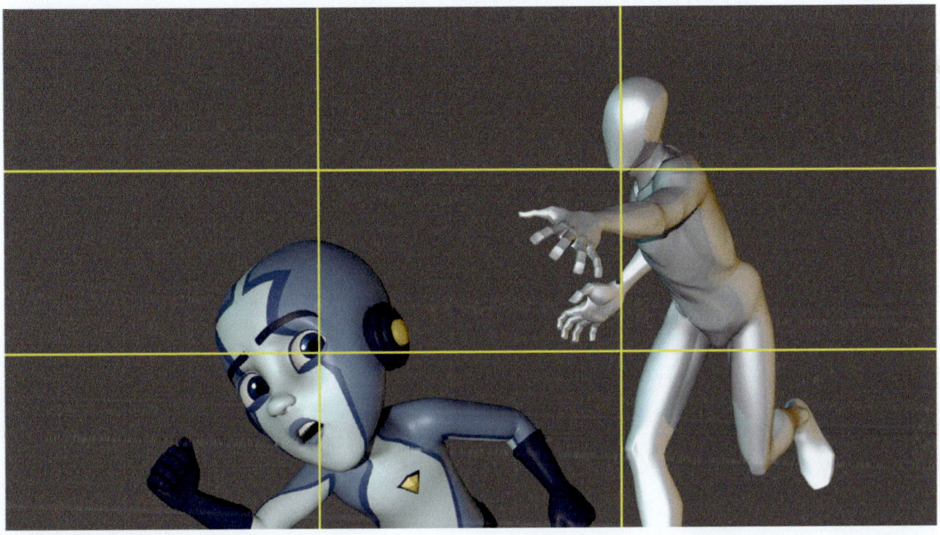

CAMERA MOVEMENTS

Camera moves need time! The average animated shot is quite short. If animating a series of shots in a sequence, then you can set up camera moves with surrounding shots. For a single stand-alone shot as an animation test, avoid complex camera moves. Never move the camera without a reason. Animators should be leading the audience's eye to make sure the story point and action is understood. If the story can be told with a single shot or a few cuts, choose that. Keep it simple and clear. It is advisable to cushion camera movements with ease-ins and ease-outs. When presenting your audience with a single shot without context, it takes about eight frames for the audience to take in the entire shot and understand the relation of the character to their environment. Starting a single stand-alone shot with a camera move could be confusing to the audience unless the move is small and slow. The term tracking comes from early filmmaking where the heavy cameras were placed on tracks so they could be moved.

- **Truck:** A tracking shot where the camera travels left or right.
- **Dolly:** A tracking shot where the camera travels forward or backward.
- **Pedestal:** Camera is moved up and down on a pedestal.
- **Pan:** Camera stays put but pivots side to side.
- **Tilt:** Camera stays put but pivots up and down.
- **Zoom:** Camera stays put, focal length is changed; can distort at the extremes.
- **Dolly Zoom:** Adjusts focal length and moves the camera forward or backward.
- **Crane:** Camera is attached to a crane arm; the crane can be placed on a track, so the camera is free to Track, Dolly, Pan, and Tilt.
- **Handheld:** The bump and shake of the person moving around is the desired effect, can go anywhere the operator can.
- **Gimbal:** Moved by an operator, but movement is smoothed out by a gyroscope, can go anywhere the operator can.

Beware! A camera move could work against the movement of the character if you are not careful. For example, if the character is going right and the camera is going left at the same rate. It could cause an optical illusion where it looks like the character's motion is frozen. First, use a stationary camera and make sure the motion of the character is correct. Then a decision needs to be made whether to drop the camera move or change the camera angle and speed so that it accentuates the character's actions.

180° RULE

This rule establishes clarity when moving the camera between two characters. Draw a straight line between two characters and keep the camera on one side of the line, hence 180°. That way, character A will always be on one side of the frame and character B on the other, whether the camera is facing them or over their shoulders. Include an establishing shot that shows the position of the two people in the environment. To reset the line, cut away to a neutral shot of something else and then cut back to establish a new line.

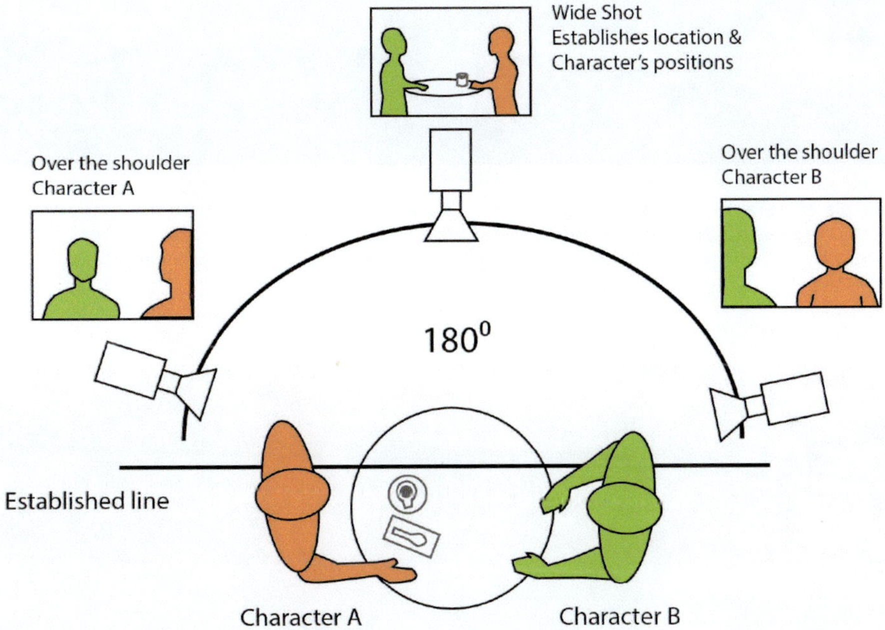

JUMP CUT

Two consecutive shots must differ by a certain amount. If they are too similar across the cut, it will look unintentional like someone bumped the camera. In general, two similar shots should differ by 30° or have a change in framing.

9 CAMERA

MAYA CAMERA

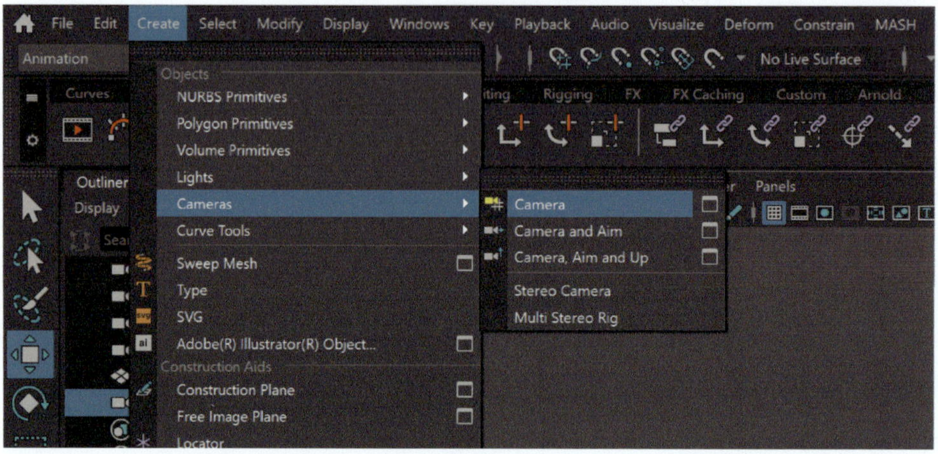

To make a camera, go to Create > Cameras > Camera. The camera will be a perspective camera unless using the options to choose another type. You can also make a camera by going to the Viewport menu and right-clicking the camera icon, and choosing New Perspective.

CHEAT

Camera and Aim, and Camera and Aim Up, are used for complex moving shots where the camera may be following something on a path. They are not normally used for common student animation tests where we want to see the character animation clearly.

To select the camera, use the plain camera icon. Once the camera is selected, access the camera attributes in the Attribute Editor.

To lock your camera, go to the Viewport menu and click on the camera icon with the padlock, or select the attribute channels and right-click and Lock Selected.

Save your favorite camera angles with camera bookmarks. To make the bookmark, click on the icon that looks like a white flag bookmark. This makes a bookmark attached to the current camera.

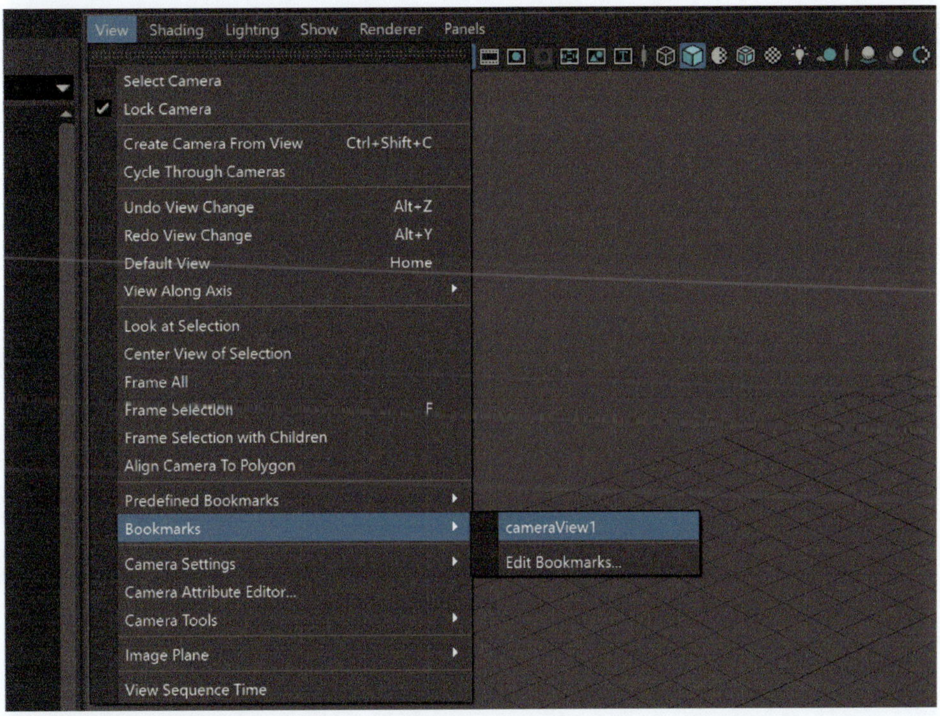

Access your bookmarks by RMB the bookmark icon or through the viewport View menu > Bookmarks. They will show as a list cameraView1 and so on.

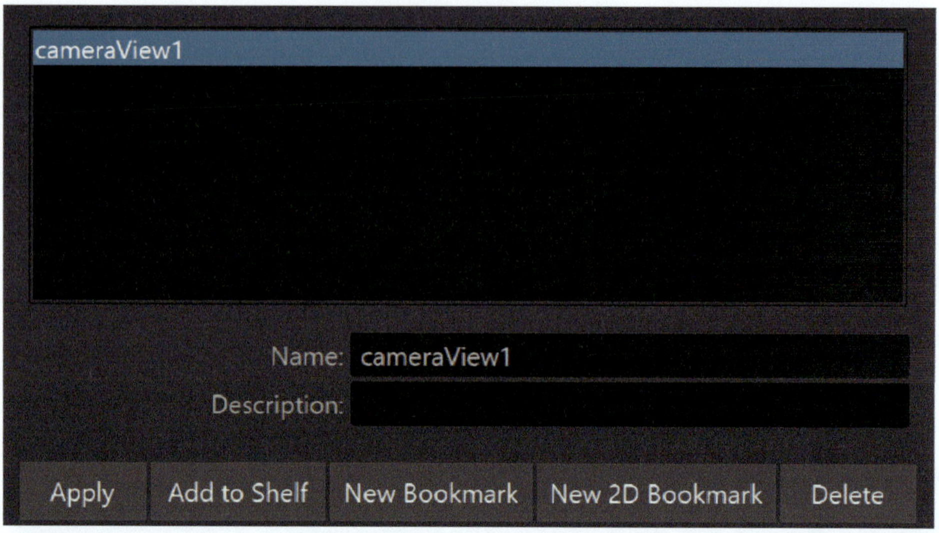

To rename your bookmarks, RMB the bookmark icon, or go to View > Bookmarks > Edit Bookmarks. In the Bookmark Editor, select the bookmark and go to the Name field. Type a new name + Enter. There is also a button to add the bookmark to the current Shelf.

Maya Camera Guides

- **Film Gate** shows the camera aperture, by default it is a larger area than the render resolution.
- **Resolution Gate** is the size of the rendered image as set in the Render Settings.
- **Gate Mask** grays out the area outside of the Resolution Gate.
- **Field Chart** overlays a grid on the Resolution Gate.
- **Action Safe and Text Safe** show the outer limits of where subjects or text can be placed on the screen without distortion or being cut-off.

FUN FACT

Since curved TV screens are no longer common, the distortion is less of a problem. To make sure important information is not cut off or out of the shot, keep it within the Action Safe.

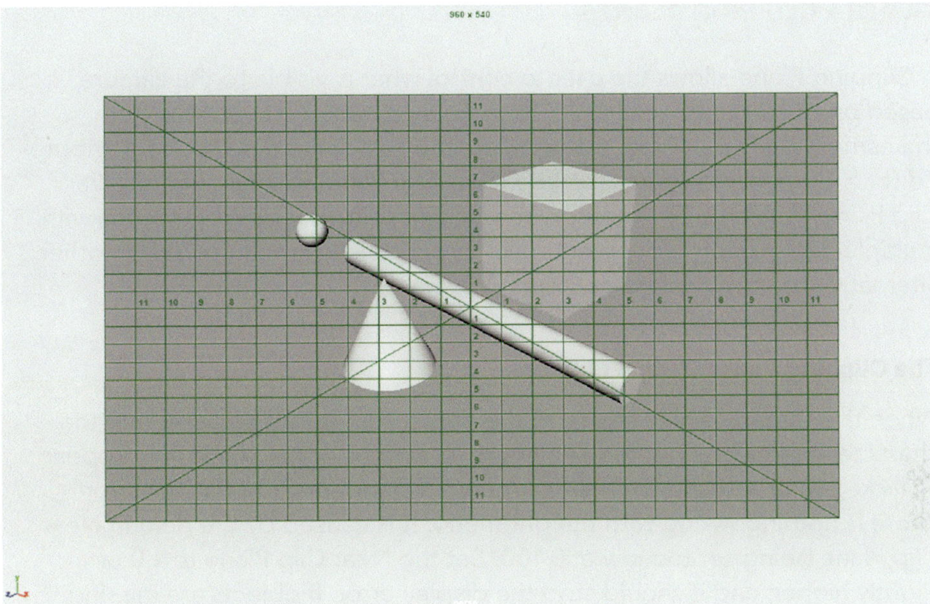
960 x 540

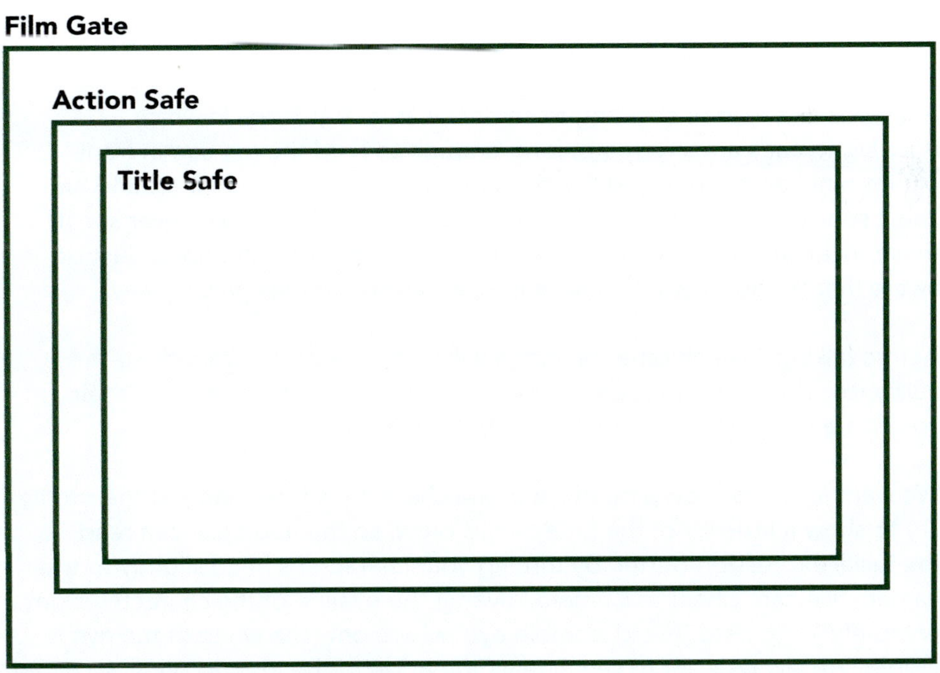
Film Gate
Action Safe
Title Safe

9 CAMERA

CAMERA CLIPPING PLANES

A Clipping Plane allows the user to control what is visible to the camera based on distance. For example, to make a character 5 feet away from the camera the only visible thing, select the camera and go to the Attribute Editor > Camera Attributes, set the Near Clip Plane to 3 feet and the Far Clip Plane to 7 feet. This method can be useful in speeding up scenes with multiple heavy geometry objects, like a complex environment. It is another alternative to using Isolate or Display Layers.

The Clipping Plane Optical Illusions

When the camera is far away from the rigs, it sometimes appears that the character's skin/ body is intersecting their clothes or hair. Or it may appear as flickering or artifacts on the environment geometry. This is an illusion. There is nothing wrong with the geometry. It is caused by the default Near Clip Plane being set too low at 0.100. Set the Near Clip Plane to 1.0 or slightly higher, and it should stop the display error. If objects are missing in the distance, increase the Far Clip Plane.

CHEATING TO CAMERA

A famous example of cheating to camera was in *Toy Story*, in which Buzz Lightyear's arms were not long enough to hold the tea cup in front of him. Animators detached the background arm and moved it around his chest so the shot could work. If you are sure the audience will never see it, these tricks do work and can occasionally solve difficult situations. Just be aware that shadows or reflective surfaces can sometimes give it away.

Actors talking to each other on stage will turn their bodies slightly to the audience. This is so the audience can still see the actors' faces, and their voices are projected forward. We do the same thing in 3D.

We want to try to show a bit more of the character's face than just the profile. Try to show a little bit of the far eye and brow, so the audience can read the facial expression better. By turning your character's head slightly to the camera, we can 'Cheat to Camera,' even if the eyeline of the character is not completely accurate. Avoid 'zombie eye' where only the white of the eye is visible. We always want to see at least the edge of the iris and pupil, so move them over if needed.

WATCH OUT!

If your character moves out of the shot, do not stop animating them on the frame where they are no longer visible. If they freeze just out of sight, shadows and reflections can ruin the shot. Put some animation on the character until the shot is over or they are full out of view, shadows included.

PLAYBLAST

Playblasting is a convenient way to preview your animation. There will be times when your scene is so heavy, the computer will not be able to play it back at 24 frames per second accurately. In that case, you want to make a playblast. A playblast is just a series of screen captures from the viewport put together as a movie. Playblast often to see your animation running at the proper speed.

To Playblast, go to the Playback menu in the Animation menu set or LMB the first icon on the Animation shelf. However, the easiest way to make a playblast is to RMB in the Time Slider. You need to set the format or type of file produced. The encoding is the type of compression. This will make the size of the file smaller, so the move is easy to upload or email.

Maya will make a playblast of the frames within your Time Slider Range.

Formatting

PC native formatting is an avi movie file. The .avi format is not ideal, the encoding/compression options are limited, and the movie files are often large. If this is your only option, choose the IYUV encoding.

Mac users, the native formatting will be AVFoundation or HEVC movie files. Beware sending HEVC movies to PC users, as they are not natively compatible with Windows.

Quicktime movie player H.264 encoding is our best option as animators. Yes, Quicktime is older and no longer supported, but it still works great on PCs and Macs. Quicktime comes with many encoding and compression formats. Download it directly from the Apple site. Just close Maya, install Quicktime, and re-launch Maya. Quicktime will be available as qt file format in the Playblast panel. If you are worried about security risks, you do not need to install the complete movie player. During the install, choose Custom Installation and choose Quicktime Essentials to install only the codecs.

Display Size

From Window will give you exactly what you see. If your viewport is tall and narrow, it will make a tall and narrow playblast. On a low-resolution laptop screen, the size of the move image will be small. High-resolution displays will result in larger image sizes.

From Render Settings or Custom will cover most use cases. From Render Settings will set the size to rendered image size. By default, Maya is set to the HD 540 preset. This makes a 960 x 540 playblast which is a good size for previewing your animation.

Next is Scale; this setting will override the Display size. Scale = 1 is 100% of the set Display Size. By default, scale is set to 0.5 which will make it 50% smaller, so adjust accordingly to what is needed.

Make sure to check the Save to File box. If you do not check the box, the playblast will be a temporary file that will disappear once closed. Playblasts will save in the Projects > Default > Movies folder unless another location is selected.

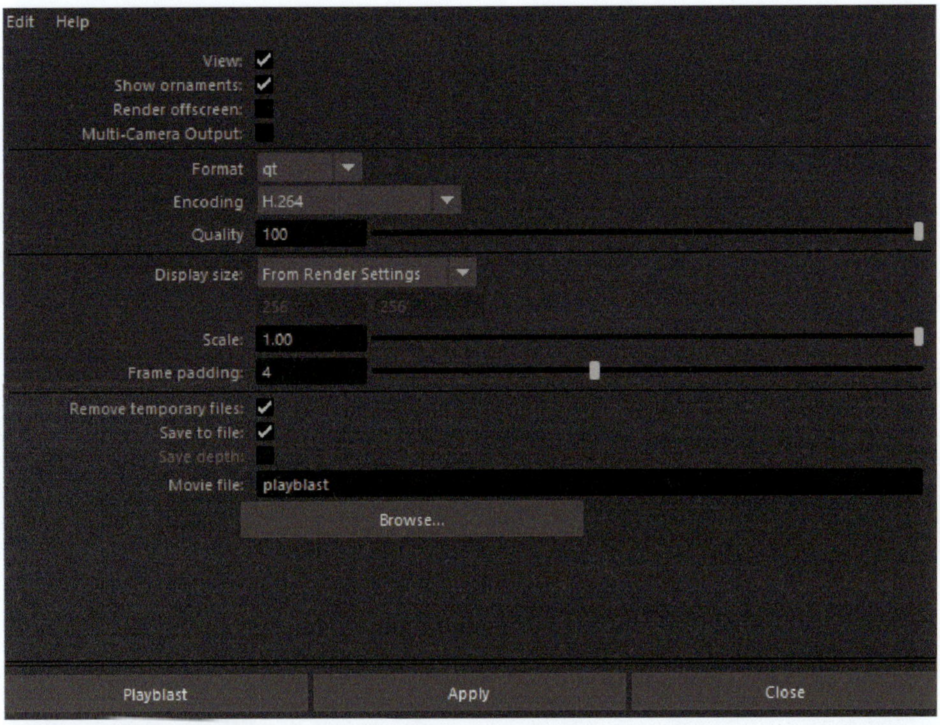

Settings for a Work-in-Progress Playblasting

What you see is what you get. Please deselect everything before playblasting, or selected items will be highlighted. To control what is visible in the playblast, use the Show menu at the top of the viewport. There is an extensive list of types of objects that can be shown or hidden in the viewport or during the playblast compiling. Show > Viewport is what is currently visible. Show > Playblast Display needs to be activated by checking the Override Viewport box. Playblast Display is useful because it doesn't matter what is left visible in the viewport; it will automatically be overwritten when the playblast is made.

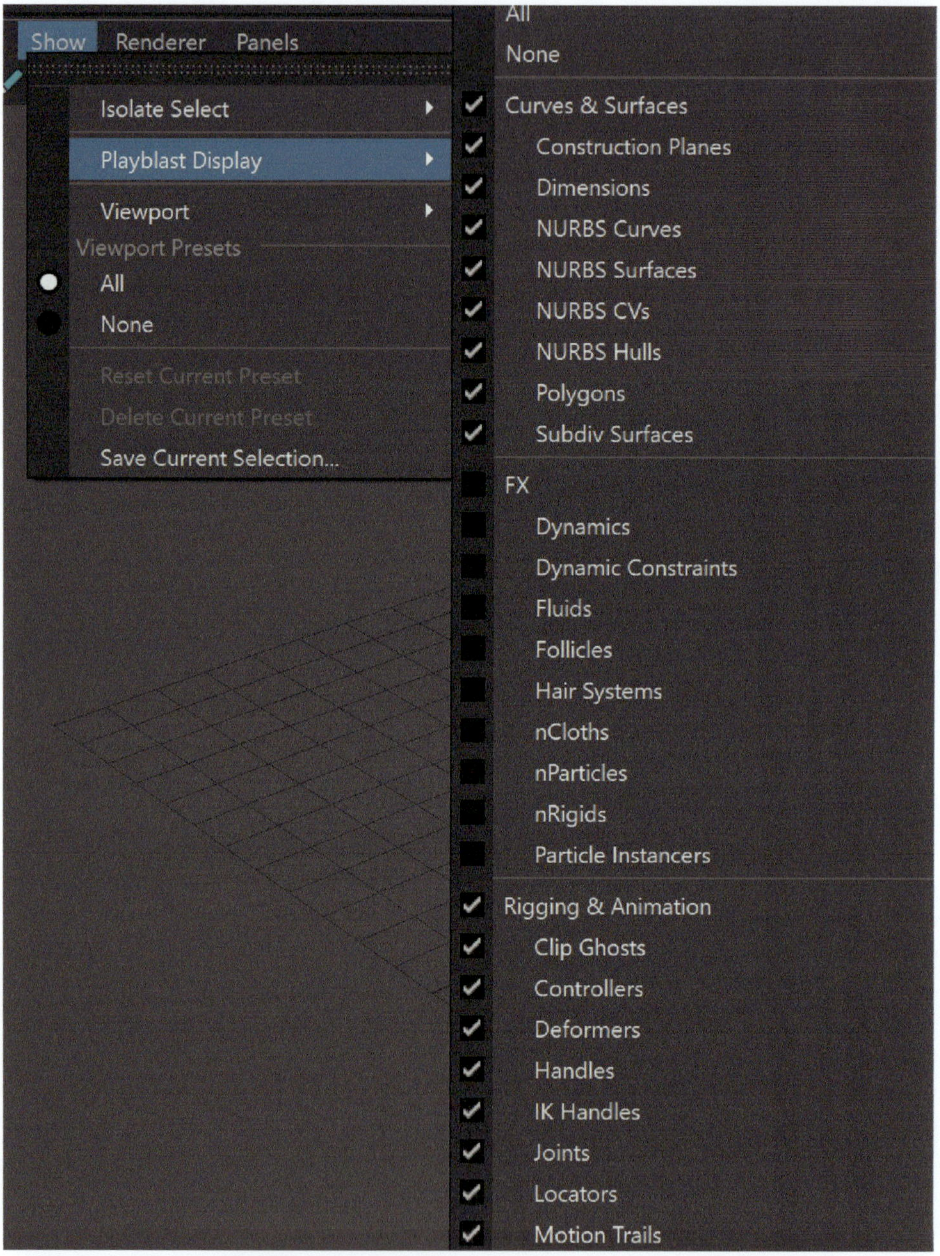

The Playblast Display menu shows an extensive list of object types that will display when you playblast. Check or uncheck ones that you want to include or exclude.

Hide the HUD

HUD is an acronym for Heads Up Display. Any extra information displayed on the viewport falls into this category. Items like the camera name, view axis, timecode, view cube, memory stats, evaluation, polygon count, or various tool modes are part of the HUD. To select items, go up to the top Display menu item and go to Heads Up Display, there is a list of items that can be checked on and off. To show or hide all active items as a group, go to the viewport Show > Viewport > HUD and uncheck.

Fastest Playblast Setup: Show None, then turn on Polygons, and maybe NURBS Surfaces, so everything is hidden except for the geometry.

DON'T FORGET

Do not include lights or shadows in your playblast if you are seeking feedback on your animation. It is better to wait until your animation is done to add back lighting and shadows because they slow the playblast down.

MAKING YOUR PLAYBLAST LOOK GREAT

This section is for those who may not have time to render but need to make their finished animation tests look as polished as possible.

While it is possible to set your viewport to Arnold and playblast with Arnold materials and lights visible, this is not recommended unless you have a high-end system, as it's very resource intensive. The Arnold lights, shadows, and textures will not be 100% accurate. Also, keeping the sampling low is necessary, or creating an Arnold playblast will run very slowly and possibly crash.

Instead, use the default viewport settings, with Maya materials and Maya lights found on the Rendering shelf. Reflections or special effects like glows or raytraced effects will not be visible in a playblast. Your rig will most likely be textured, so press 6 or the checkered sphere icon to make textures visible. Bump, displacement, or normal maps may not display correctly.

	To see textures, press hotkey 6, or the checkered sphere icon on the top of the Viewport.
	To turn on the lights, press hotkey 7, or the light bulb icon on top of the Viewport.
	To turn on the shadows, click the icon to the right of the lightbulb, the blue sphere with a gray shadow.

Texture, Lights and Shadows icons can be found on every Viewport toolbar.

LIGHTING FOR PLAYBLAST

There are six types of Maya lights. They all render well, but for playblasting use Directional Light, Point Light, and Spot Lights. These three lights look the best previewed in the viewport. In the viewport, the brightest setting for a light is an intensity of 1. Any brighter, and the playblast will be over-lit and the details will be washed out. Each additional light should be set with an intensity of less than 1.

	Directional Light: position of light does not matter. Rotate the light and it will shine infinite rays of light in that direction.
	Point Light: functions like a floating light bulb.
	Spot Light: aim the light and scale up the cone to control how far the light spreads to the sides. Penumbra Angle blurs the edge of the cone.

Maya Lights can be found on the Rendering Shelf or under the Create > Lights menu.

CHEAT

Every light attribute can be animated. For example, you can animate the color of the light changing. Set color and go to Channel Box and key channels Color R, G, and B.

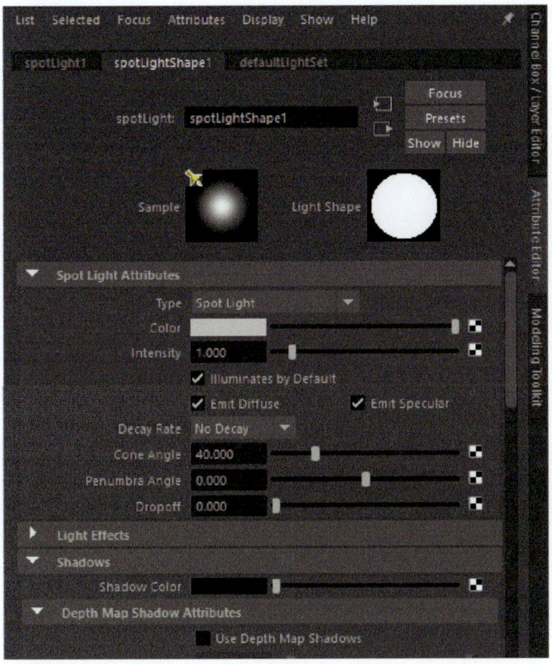

Select the Light and go to the Attribute Editor. Here you will find all the light settings including Intensity, Color, and Shadow Settings.

Three-Point Lighting

A Three-Light Setup is a simple standard light setup used in film and photography.

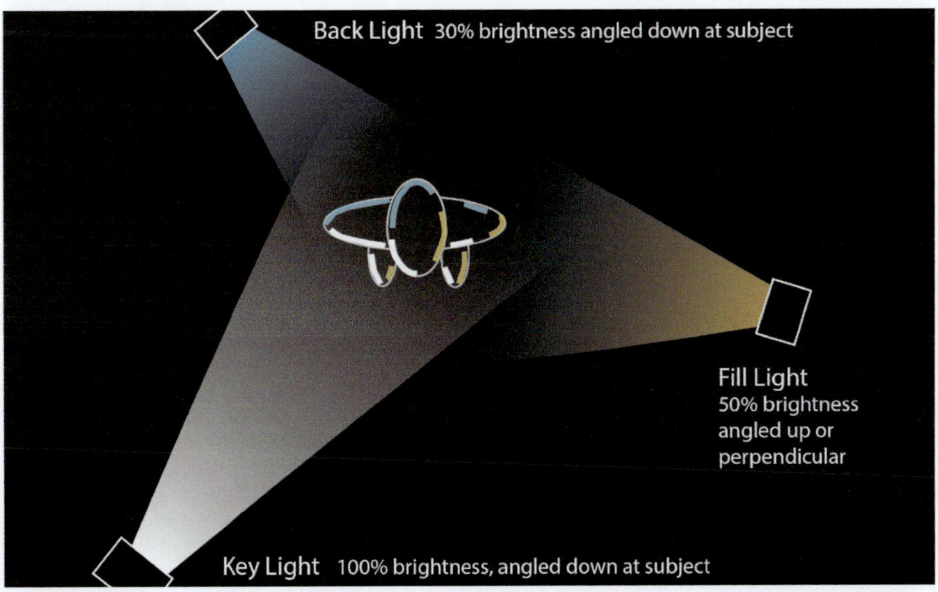

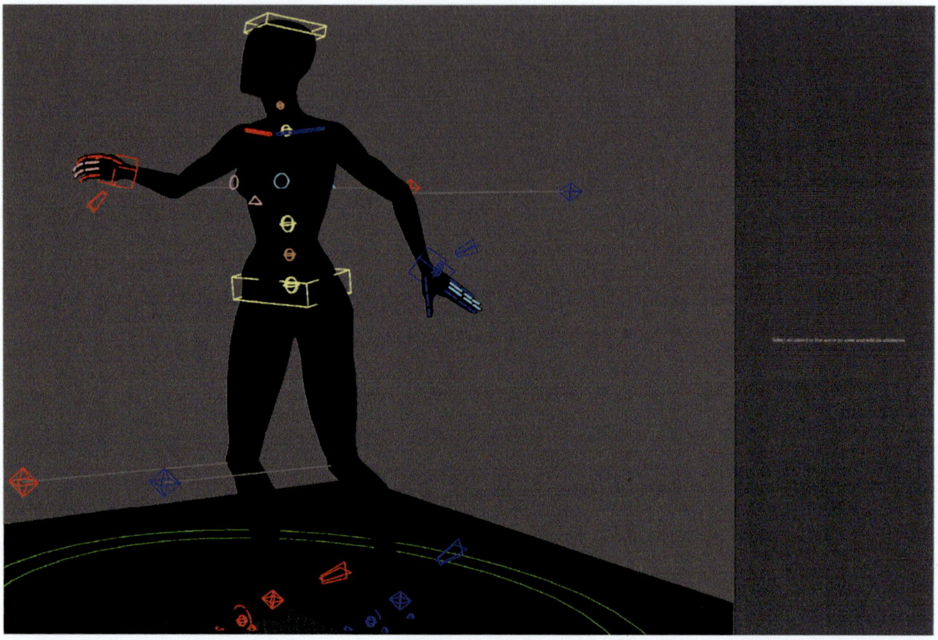

Use hotkey 7 to turn on lights. If you have not added any lights yet, everything will go black when the default global lighting is switched off. Next to the Light icon, you will find the Shadow icon, turn that on as well.

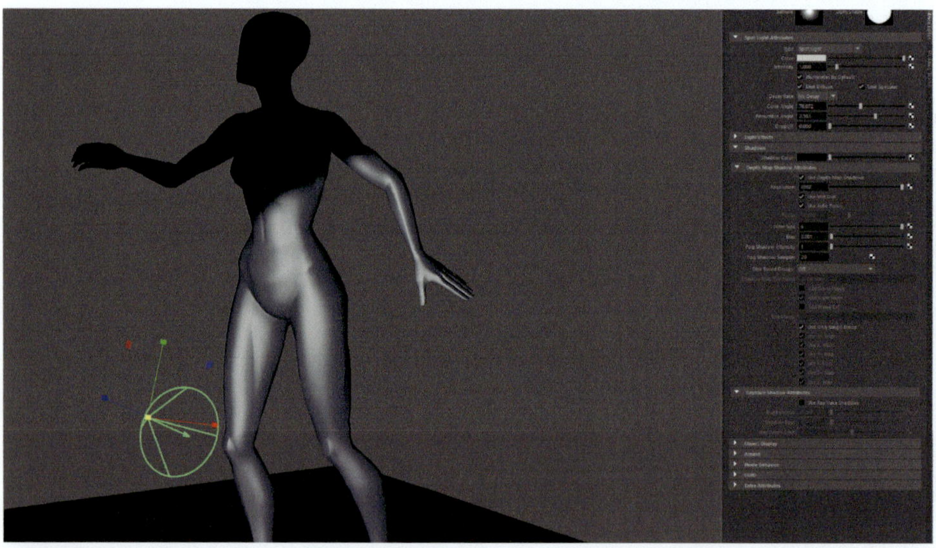

Key/ Main Light: This is the main light which illuminates the subject(s) and the scene. This light should light up the action to make it clear to the audience. In an outdoor shot, the main light would be the sun. The Spot Light produces the best shadows with minimal adjustments. You can scale the Spot Light icon for easier adjusting; it will not affect the light.

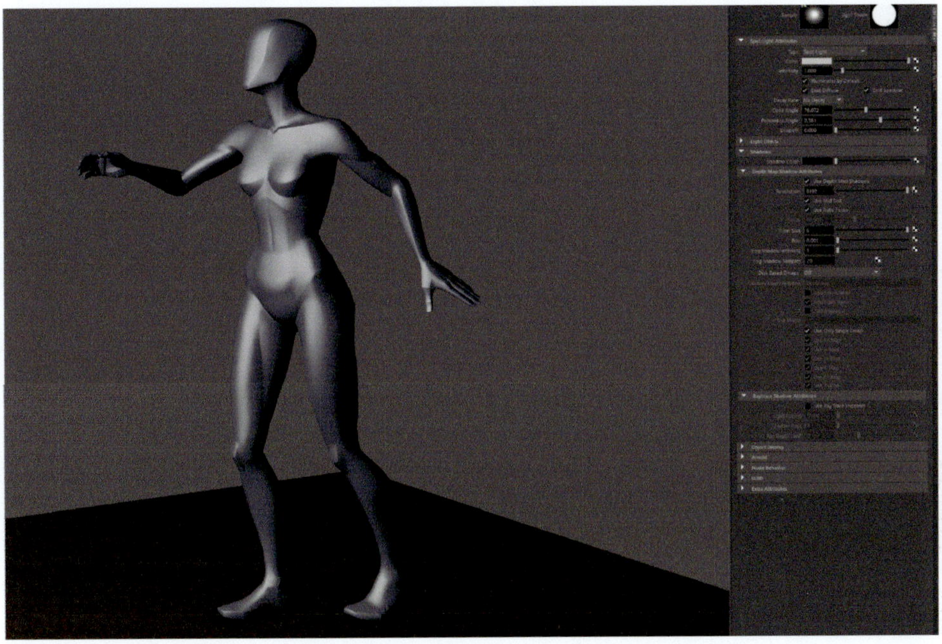

This will be the brightest Maya light with Intensity set to 1.000. This is also the light you want to cast shadows from. The Main Light will often be slightly higher than the subject and angled down.

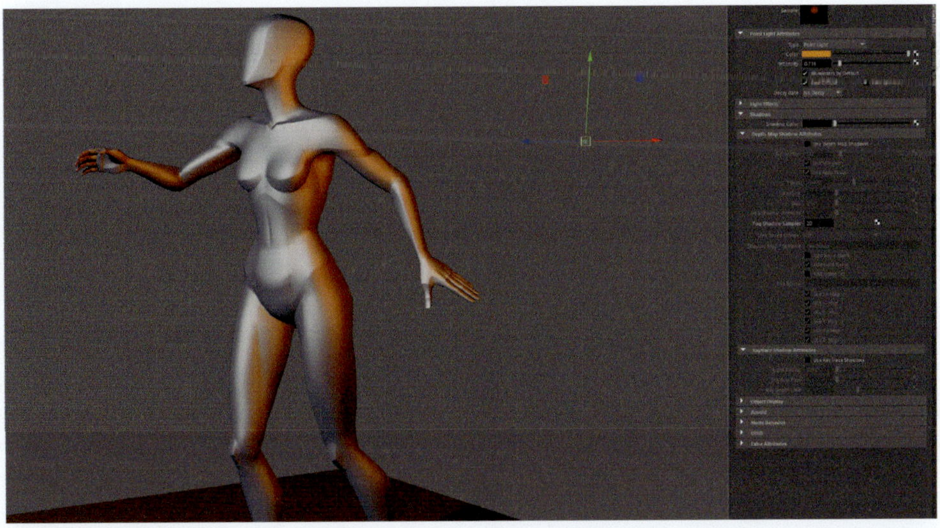

Fill/ Bounce Light: This light is placed lower and off to the side of the subject. This light will not be as bright as the main light. With only one light, there will be very harsh black shadows around your character's face and body. The Fill light will cast a little light into those shadows and make them softer and make more details of the characters visible. Here, a Point Light was used, with shadows off so there are not multiple moving shadows.

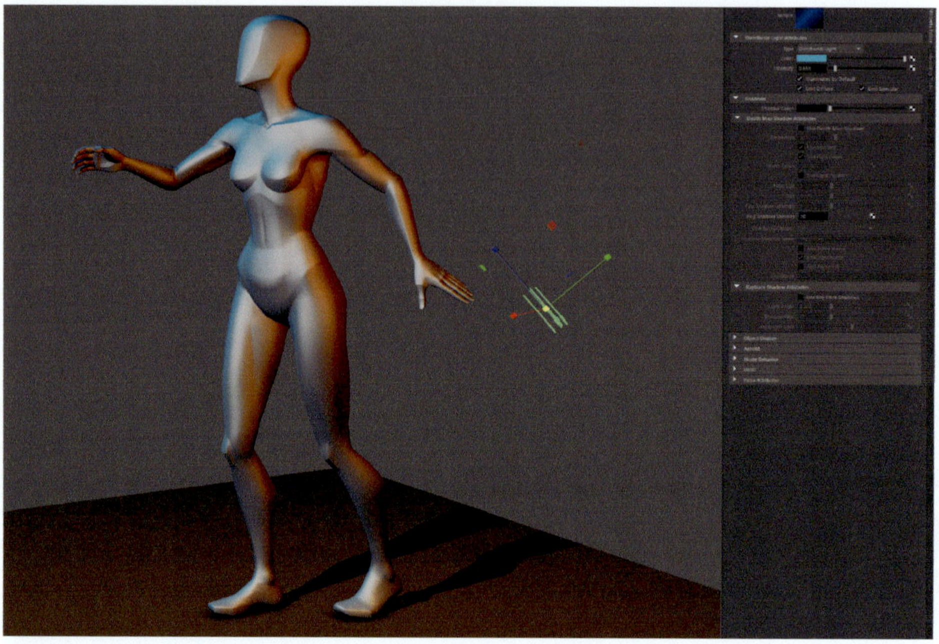

Rim/ Hair/ Back Light: This light is usually placed behind the subjects, higher, and on the opposite side as the Fill light. It casts highlights on the subject's head/hair and shoulders separating the subjects from the background. Here, a Directional Light is used. You can scale the icon up for easier adjustments; it will not affect the light. The position of the Directional light is not important, instead rotate to aim the light rays.

More than three lights may be needed to light your scene. It will vary greatly depending on how many characters, how much they move around, and what type of environment they are in. For multiple lights, keep the intensity set lower than the Main light in a playblast, and only have shadows enabled on the Main light as well. It may not be the most realistic effect, but a moving character with multiple moving shadows becomes very distracting.

Natural light falls in a blue-white spectrum. If your shot takes place outdoors, keep your key light white/blue and make your shadows lighter with a blue tint. Indoor lighting has traditionally been incandescent, which has a warm orange tint. This works well because blue and orange are complementary colors. It is rare to have pitch-black shadows, as there is usually bounced light, moon light, or even light pollution at night.

Having trouble aiming a light? Scaling the light object up will not affect the light, but it does make it easier to see the light's orientation. Select the light and go to Panels, Look Through Selected. This creates a camera shape at the center of the light that will allow you to see where the light is aimed.

Orbit, pan, and zoom will reposition the light. In the Light Editor, click on the Look Through Selected icon to open a panel to see the light's POV.

If making a piece of geometry a light emitter, use the Look Through Selected option. There is a Near Clipping Plane and Far Clipping Plane setting in the options. The camera shape will be created at the center of the geometry. If you find yourself inside the geometry and can't see, slowly increase the Near Clipping Plane until you can see outside. Orbit, pan, or zoom will reposition the geometry.

SHADOWS FOR PLAYBLAST

Maya lights have two types of shadows: Raytrace Shadows and Depth Map Shadows. Both render very well, but we are focusing on how they perform in playblasting. Select the light and open the Attribute Editor, go to the Shadows section. By default, the light will be set to Raytraced. Raytracing is done in rendering, so preview of Raytraced shadows in the viewport is not adjustable — what you see is what you get. If you do not like the appearance of the Raytrace shadows, then turn them off. Uncheck Use Raytrace Shadows and check Use Depth Map Shadows to activate.

Depth Map Shadows are adjustable. When first turning it on, the resolution will be very low. Go to the Attribute Editor, go to Resolution, and push the slider over all the way to 8192. This will create pretty good-looking shadows in the viewport. To soften the edges of the Shadows, go to the Filter Size and push the slider to 5. This will usually result in the best-looking shadows possible without actually rendering your shot. Both the Resolution and Filter can be set higher by typing in the input boxes. Be careful increasing the values too much will slow the computer.

CHEAT

For playblasting, Spot Lights tend to make the cleanest shadows. However, keep the cone angle less than 160° or shadow distortion may occur.

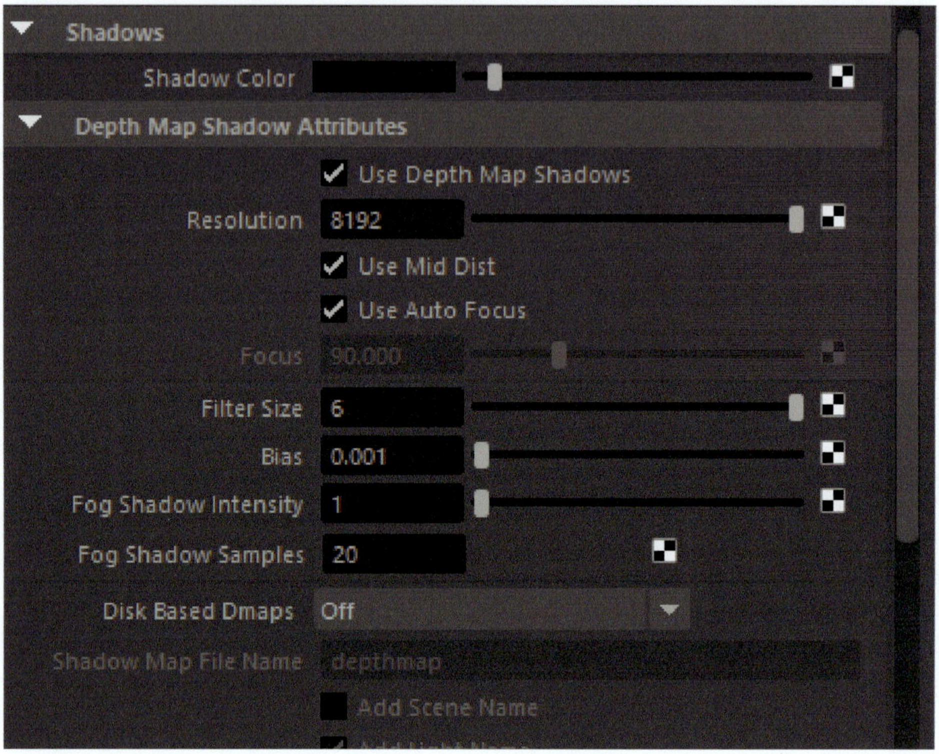

Common settings for nice-looking shadows using Depth Map Shadows.

CHEAT

When changing the color of the shadow, if it does not update on screen, toggle the shadow icon off and on. It will then force an update in the view panel.

Light Editor is a helpful tool for managing multiple lights in your scene. The Light Editor lists all the lights in the scene, and their color, intensity, exposure, sampling, and the ability to mute or solo individual lights. Selecting the light will open a small attribute panel that also includes the translation values. Add lights with the toolbar, group lights together, and import and export the light setup into other scenes. Go to Windows > Rendering Editors > Light Editor or use icon on Status Line.

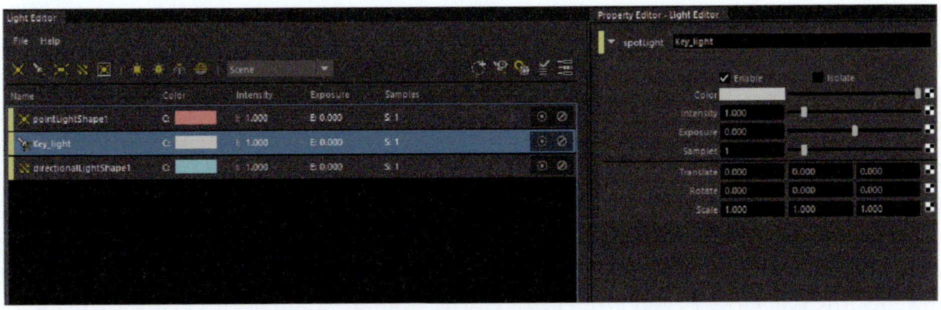

The Light Editor is handy to adjust all the lights in your scene.

FINAL TOUCHES FOR A CLEAN PLAYBLAST

Turn on Screen Space Ambient Occlusion and Anti-Aliasing in your Viewport. The Ambient Occlusion icon looks like a white ball with a blue shadow. It makes a shadow based on where the computer calculates a shadow would be. It can add a little more contrast and can pop out details. The Anti-Aliasing icon looks like a blue 'C' and white triangle. Anti-Aliasing smooths hard edges as much as possible in a Viewport preview.

The icons for Ambient Occlusion and Anti-Aliasing. These two settings greatly improve visual fidelity.

WATCH OUT!

It can be tempting to enable motion blur in your playblasts, but try to resist! It can make it extremely difficult to critique the animation, and even worse can be seen as an animator trying to hide their mistakes from a professional.

Viewport 2.0

By design, the Viewport quality is set low for faster performance. However, the quality can be adjusted further in the Hardware Renderer 2.0 Settings. For example, to increase the Anti-Aliasing or Ambient Occlusion, go to the Viewport > Renderer > Viewport 2.0 options. Scroll Down and open the tabs. Increase the Sample size for both to get the smoothest results. Ambient Occlusion can also be adjusted to control the amount and how far it spreads. Pushing the hardware Rendering Globals to their maximums will slow down computer performance. Save your settings under Presets and only use them for making high quality Playblasts. While working, go to Presets > Set Preferred Preset > Default Settings.

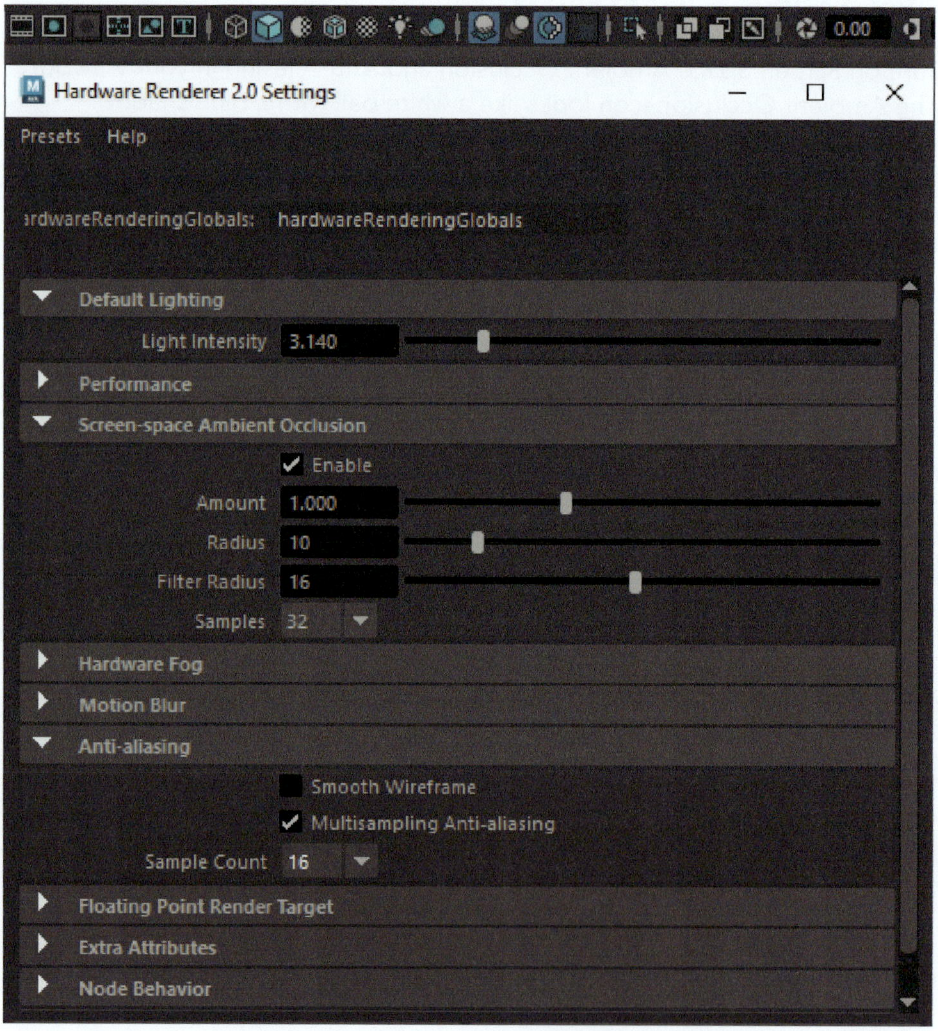

PLAYBLAST A SEQUENCE OF SHOTS

What are the options for playblasting a sequence of shots?

- **Multiple-Scene Method:** Create a sequence by playblasting several Maya scene files separately, then assemble the playblasts into a movie file in another software. Making every shot its own individual scene file offers the most control. We want the ability to shoot, light, and texture every shot for best results. Multiple cameras in a single scene make it hard to optimize the lighting for every angle. Having every shot be its own file is the preferred method in professional settings. It is also a safer way to work in case a single scene file gets corrupted.
- **The One-Camera Method:** Animate a single camera which changes shot angles over the shot duration. Camera moves will happen over one frame, so that the audience will not see the camera moving. Create a camera. Key the camera location at frame 1 and frame 50. At frame 51, reposition the camera and key location at frame 80. At frame 81, reposition camera and key location. The playblast will now contain a sequence of three shots. The downside to this method is creating one light setup that looks good in all camera angles can be difficult.
- **Camera Sequencer:** The Camera Sequencer allows the user to switch between multiple cameras within one scene and add one audio track to a sequence. Go to Windows > Animation Editors > Camera Sequencer. Create the cameras needed and position them. Next, go to the desired frame, then go to Create > Shot options. Choose which camera to use and the start and end frames. Repeat for all the cameras. Inside the Camera Sequencer, go to the Playblast menu. Go to Playblast Sequence options. This is a separate set of options from the usual Playblast tools, so you must reset the resolution and size of the playblast. You must have the Camera Sequencer open, clicking in the viewport will just select one camera at a time.

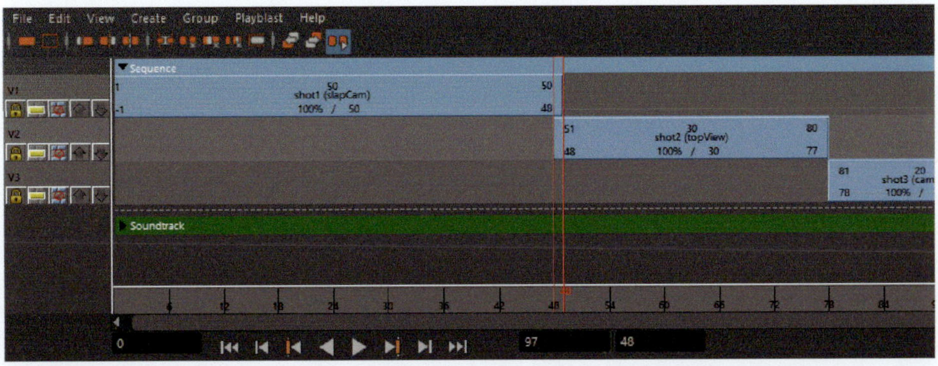

Ubercam

Once your cameras are loaded into the Camera Sequencer and you have set the time for each, they can be combined with the UberCam. The benefit to the Ubercam is it gives you one new camera with all your shots. Ubercam uses the regular playblast and render methods. If you want to change the sequence, select the Ubercam and go to the Graph Editor and adjust. Some users report better results playblasting audio with the Ubercam than the Sequencer. Ubercam is best for longer sequences with lots of edits.

Again, keeping everything in one scene may make it more difficult for the lighting to work from every angle.

10 CYCLES

In the years since the last edition of this book, animation cycles have only become more important to the production process across TV, film, and games.

Understanding the basics of creating looping animation is fundamental to success as an animator. To go beyond, animators must develop tricks for quickly iterating on cycles. These cheats will ensure you can arrive at appealing results in less time. Perhaps more important, these workflow shortcuts make sure the generated cycles stay technically within the parameters required for the job.

We'll look at Infinity extrapolation types and also use a cheat called "offsetting" to lay down keys quickly and iterate fast.

CYCLE BASICS

When dealing with cycling in animation, there are a few technical terms and workflow practices one must be aware of. We'll cover the most important ones in this chapter.

To start, the "forward" direction of a cycle is the Z axis. This pairs with the way that rigs are most commonly created.

FUN FACT

The depth channel (forward and backward) in computer graphics and rendering is called the "Z-buffer". Don't listen to those crazy folks who use other 3D programs who insist that Z is up!

When cycling, animators will work extensively with Maya's Pre-Infinity and Post-Infinity curve types. It is vitally important to understand what these different curve types do. In basic terms, these choose the method Maya uses to determine how to extrapolate motion after the last key, and before the first key. We'll test out all of the different types here.

Open Cycle_Infinity.ma. This is the start of a cycle that we'll use to talk about common concepts.

INFINITY CURVE TYPES

First of all, what does Pre Infinity and Post-Infinity mean? When channels are keyed, Maya needs to decide what those channels are going to do before the first keyframe, and after the last. Imagine you keyed a controller from f15 to f21 in a 24-frame cycle. What happens between f1-f15, and from f22 to the end? If you are imagining this, then you are probably imagining that, well, nothing happens. That is correct, but it is also Maya interpolating the curves using "constant" interpolation, for infinite time before (Pre) and infinite time after (Post) the keyframes on that controller. So, one could say that "constant" is the default. To change the interpolation for Pre-Infinity and Post-Infinity, go the Graph Editor, and choose Curves > Pre Infinity or Curves > Post Infinity and with a curve or channel selected, choose the appropriate one.

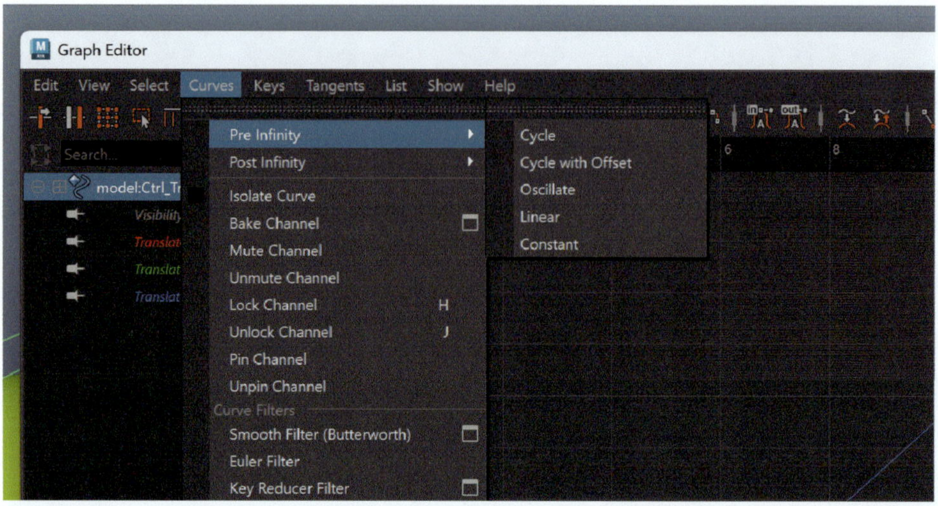

Here are the different types of infinity curves:

- **Cycle:** This type applies to most controls in a cycle. This means that the first and last keyframes are assumed to be the same, and that the motion is meant to repeat the same, forever.
- **Cycle with Offset:** This type applies to channels on controls that are meant to have world-space progress over the course of a cycle. That means typically ONLY the Translate Z channel on IK controls like feet (and hands if you are using them) and the body Translate controller.
- **Oscillate:** Curves set to oscillate will 'bounce' back and forth from the first key to the last key and back again. It's an uncommon type.
- **Linear:** Linear interpolation means that whatever angle the curve is evaluated at will be extended linearly into infinity. Typically, this only applies to channels used to offset or treadmill a cycle, or things like propellers that must just spin constantly.
- **Constant:** The default interpolation type "constant" simply means that the value will remain static before the first keyframe, and after the last.

CHEAT

Tear off the Pre-Infinity and Post-Infinity menus any time you work on a scene with cycles. It saves mere seconds over finding those menus each time; but over the course of working on a cycle, you'll do this hundreds of times!

In general, all world-space progress is on Translate controllers, and as we said before, typically the Z axis is forward. For this one channel, (Translate Z) on the character's main translation controller, we will always use the Pre-Infinity and Post-Infinity curve types of "Cycle with Offset."

This knowledge actually gives us a pretty easy way to check if a cycle has been properly created. Knowing that the rotations of the rig and most of the other translations (Translate Y on the feet, all of the Translation on the knee and elbow pole vectors, for example) are going to be "Cycle" types, and that only Translate Z will be "Cycle with Offset," a normal cycle Graph Editor should look something like the following:

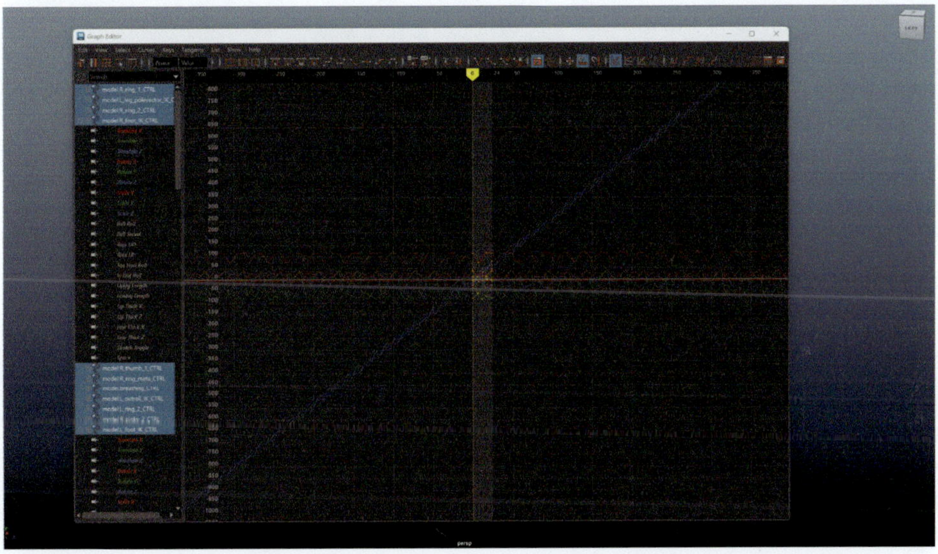

Notice how there is animation on many channels, but the interpolation is set to Cycle, and hence stays repeating in the same value range. However, the Translate Z curves of the body and feet stair-step off into infinity.

At a glance, an animator can tell that this scene is at least set up properly, because the animation all takes place in the proper range, the Pre-Infinity and Post-Infinity types have been set, and the rig has no problems that are affecting the cycle negatively.

Take a look at the below graph and see if it is obvious what is wrong with the animation, or the rig:

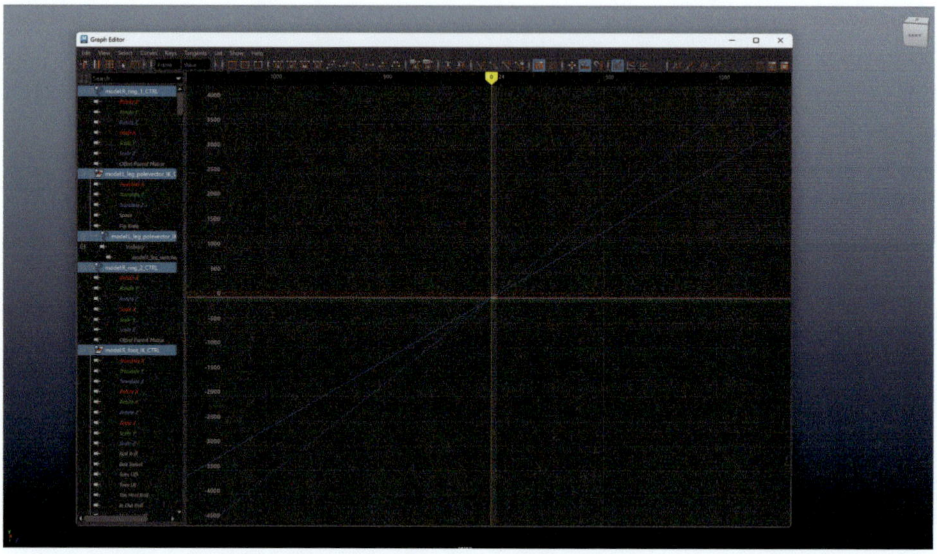

Uh oh, looks like there is something awry with the curves in this scene. Can you guess what is going wrong?

This kind of graph is a tell-tale that something is wrong with the animation, the rig, or both. If the controls are set up properly, there should be no divergence in the values of Translate Z. Or, the animator might have set keys that are off of the stride length. When we talk about stride length, it will be obvious that small amounts of inaccuracy can introduce major flaws to the animation.

FUN FACT

When working on AAA games or feature films, animators sometimes work so long on an animation that they can identify it just by looking at the Graph Editor!

TIMING AND DURATION

All of the keyed controls of your animation need to have the same duration of frames between their first and last keyframe. The controls don't necessarily have to be keyed on the same frames, but all of their animation needs to have the same duration. For instance, if you have correctly applied Pre-Infinity and Post-Infinity types, one control in your rig could be animated between f01 and f24, and another could have keys between frames f19 to f42.

This starts to get a bit complicated! How are animators supposed to keep track of timing when different controllers are keyed on different segments of the Time Slider? Cycling is a lot more manageable when you are familiar with the idea of "offsetting" your keyframes in the Graph Editor. The basic idea is to create all your keyframes within your set frame range (0–24 for example), then move the keyframes backward or forward in time (therefore offsetting them) to get overlapping movement. These now-offset keys maintain the same total duration of the cycle, but you don't have to worry about overlapping animation being difficult to match at the beginning and end of your cycle. An example of this is if there is an extremely wobbly antenna on your character; it's hard to imagine exactly at what point in the overall motion that antenna should be started at on f01, whereas it's easy to key the entire flopping motion and then offset it. We'll cover offsets in a bit.

CHEAT

To figure out the timing and rhythm of a cycle, click Create > Polygon > Sphere. Set a key on frame 0. Then hit play and tap the S key (set key) to the rhythm you are imagining. When you hit stop, keys will appear on the Time Slider! Look at the average tempo and use that going forward.

10 CYCLES

STRIDE LENGTH

Of the utmost importance to make really technically solid cycles is to understand stride length. We define this as the total distance in the forward axis that the character traverses in a single cycle. What is sometimes surprising to most is that the stride length is the same for every single controller that is in world space. Imagine a zombie dragging one broken foot on the ground, another arm dangling by his side, and taking a swipe with his good arm on every step. The total distance covered in the Z axis during a cycle by both feet, both arms, and the main body Translate controller will be identical! Finding this stride length is so important for saving time.

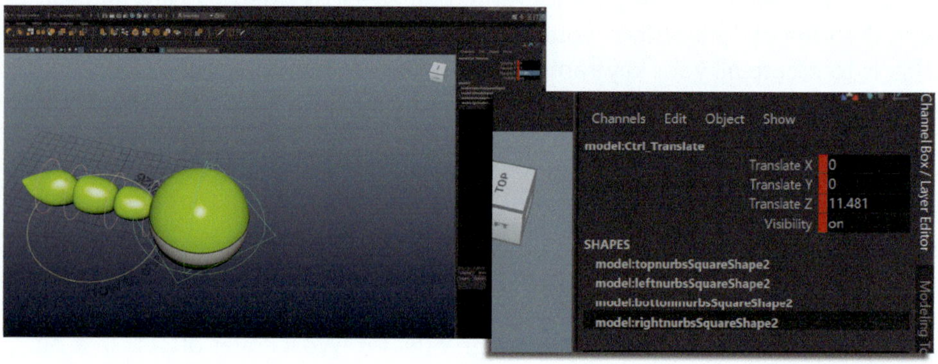

Open Cycle_Mid.ma. Notice how the Translate Z channel is at 11.481 on frame 14.

This scene was timed to be almost two hops per second and to cover roughly one-body length of distance over a cycle. My stride length is 11.481, or is it?

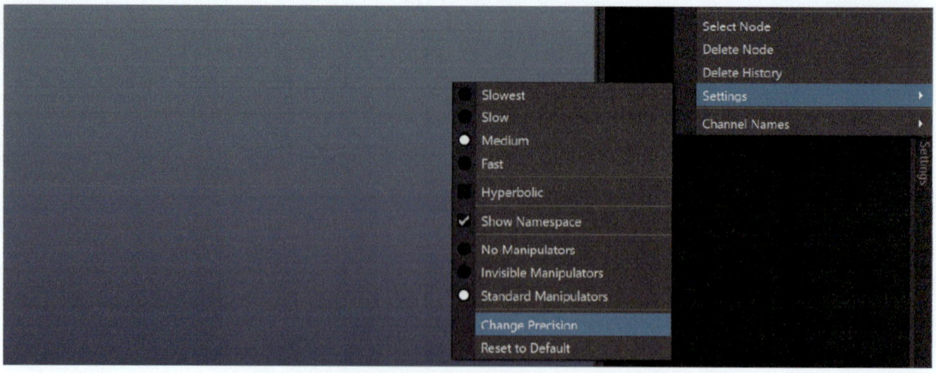

In the Channel Box, click Edit > Settings > Change Precision. Choose 6 digits of precision.

Well, would you look at that? Changing the precision of the display of the Channel Box reveals that the cycle is actually not exactly what was showing before. The 11.481 was a rounded value; changing the precision reveals that.

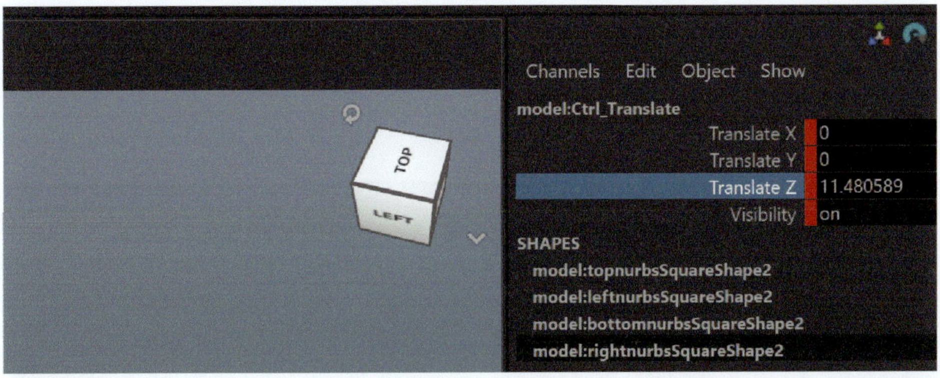

This is a different value than was first shown! It comes down to floating point math in Maya.

What is happening is Maya shows approximate values because normally the user doesn't need to know the values to within a millionth of a unit. This may seem trivial, but, especially in games, having a lack of precision in your stride length can lead to some bad effects in the long run. Even in film, if the stride length has not been properly determined and set, the character's arms and legs can start to drift away from the body and feet. It only takes 10 cycles for a difference of 0.1 in stride length to mean a control drifts a full unit. So, whenever you find your stride length at 3 digits of precision, type it back into the channel box on your last key. This sets the value at *exactly* the value you typed in, and there is no longer any worry about a lack of precision or approximate value. Having 2 digits of precision when you are typing it back in is quite enough.

DON'T FORGET

Once the stride length has been determined, write it down! This number will come up over and over when working on this cycle.

When working on cycles that cover a lot of ground, it is typical to counter-animate (key a control in the opposite direction of movement) a master control against the body's Translate Z channels. This makes it so that the character stays centered over the world origin, as if it's on a treadmill. This is extremely handy for adding details to a cycle that covers a lot of distance, like a run cycle. It is easy to create this treadmill: simply animate the master controller to move backward the same stride length and frame range as the character cycle.

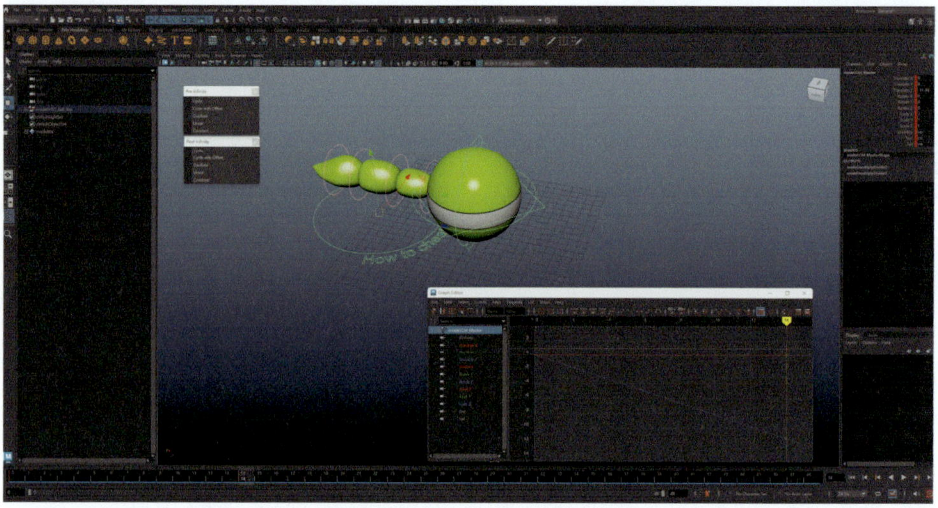

Open Cycle_Treadmill.ma. Select the Master controller and open the Graph Editor. Notice how this controller is animated backward in Translate Z at -11.48?

Now that we have a treadmill effect, it's much easier to see the results of the cycle without accounting for the character gaining or losing ground on screen. This is the basic setup for the way a professional would start a cycle.

CHEAT

Almost all rotations will use the Pre-Infinity and Post-Infinity interpolation of Cycle. When in doubt, choose "Cycle" on all your curves besides Translate Z.

STRIDE LENGTH OF WALK CYCLES

Finding the stride length of a walk cycle is incredibly simple.

Simply start by posing your character in a natural walk pose at the moment of foot placement. However, instead of moving one foot forward and one backward, create the pose with one foot at Translate Z of 0. For this demonstration, the left foot is left at 0.

Here is the character posed with one foot with a Translate Z of 0.

We're actually almost done. Now select the forward foot, and see what the value is. Remember, we're going to type the number back in again to avoid floating point errors.

We've selected the front foot. Notice the value is an approximate value of 32.054. Let's just type in 32 and hit Enter.

Now, imagine over the course of the walk cycle, the back foot will lift off, travel past the front foot, and land the same distance ahead as the other foot was before. That's it! The stride length of a walk cycle is ***twice the distance between the feet at the start, assuming the starting pose is the moment of foot placement.***

One last thing to do. Walk cycles should be centered on the master control to start; it's cleaner and it makes for better technical compliance if you work in games. Let's now move *all* of the world-space IK controls which are just the feet and body (in this case, I'm using FK arms) back to center. What distance do we move it backward? A quarter of the stride length, because the feet are half a stride apart at the start, and half of that is a quarter.

To do this very quickly, select those controls, and in the channel box, in the Translate Z channel, type in "-=16". Replace this value with your stride length of course.

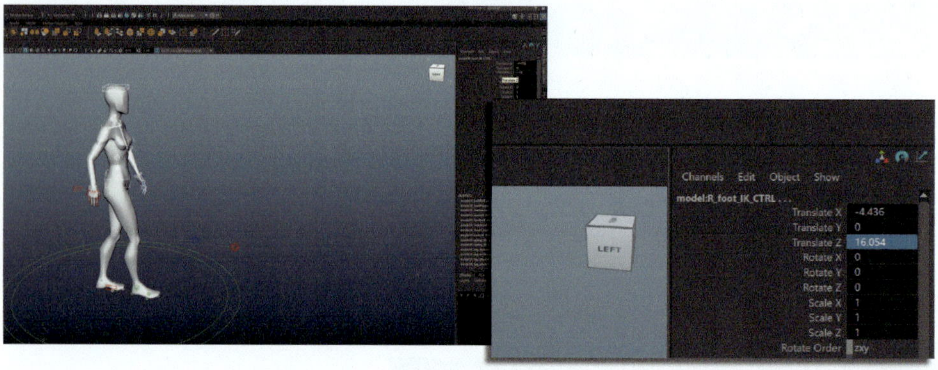

Now the walk cycle is beautifully centered on the master control.

This workflow is a quick and simple way to make sure a walk cycle starts off on the right foot. Or left foot. It's up to you.

WATCH OUT!

It is very important to properly test your rigs! Even the smallest issue like the Hips and Feet translating different distances, or a fraction of rotation built into the foot controls can mess up your entire workflow.

Continuing Setting up the Rest of the Cycle

Now that the first pose is set, the quickest workflow is to find the duration, and apply the stride length to the rest of the cycle. Funny enough, a 24-frame walk cycle is a comfortable pace for a relaxed walk, and you can even get away with up to 30 frames without it looking too slow. Let's go with 24 frames for ease.

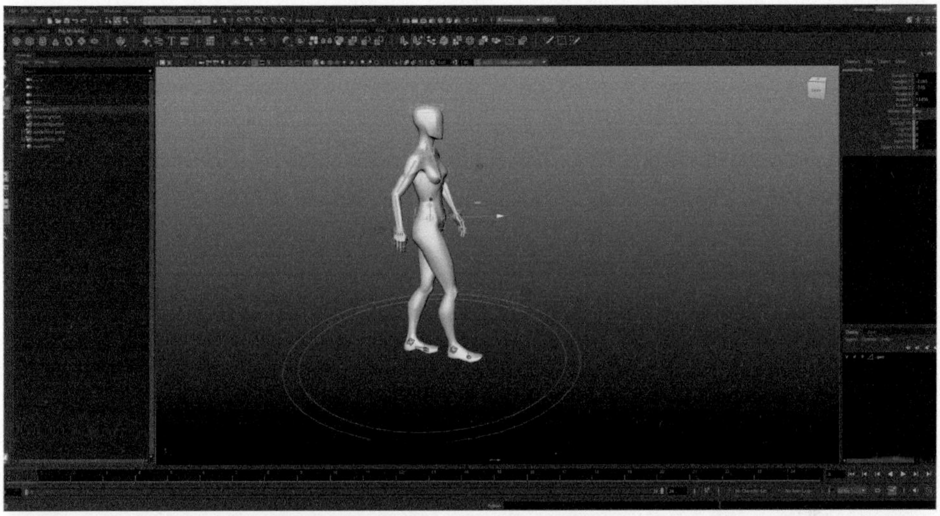

Open Cycle_Walk_Start.ma. You'll see a few keys have been set here.

What have we done so far? Essentially, it only takes three keyframes on each foot, and two keyframes on the body to fully establish the timing and stride in a walk cycle. Our walk cycle is 24 frames, so starting with the body_CTRL, a key is set on frame 0, and on frame 24. It's fastest to set the keys, then move to the frame on the Time Slider and in the Channel Box, type in +=64 on the Translate Z channel and press Enter.

For the feet, it's nearly as quick. Starting with the back foot, we set a key on frame 0, and frame 12. At frame 12, we once again type in +=64 in the Translate Z channel in the Channel Box. Then, move ahead to frame 24, and hit S again to set a key here. For the right foot that started in front, it needs to stay put while the other moves. Select it, move the Time Slider to frame 12, and hit S. Now, move the Time Slider to frame 24, and in the Channel Box, type "+=64" into the Translate Z channel and press Enter.

DON'T FORGET

MMB + Drag from a key on the Time Slider to the frame you want to copy it to, and pressing S is still by far the fastest way to set the same value on all channels, just be sure you want to set a key on all channels when you do this!

Open the Graph Editor in this scene, and it should look like the below:

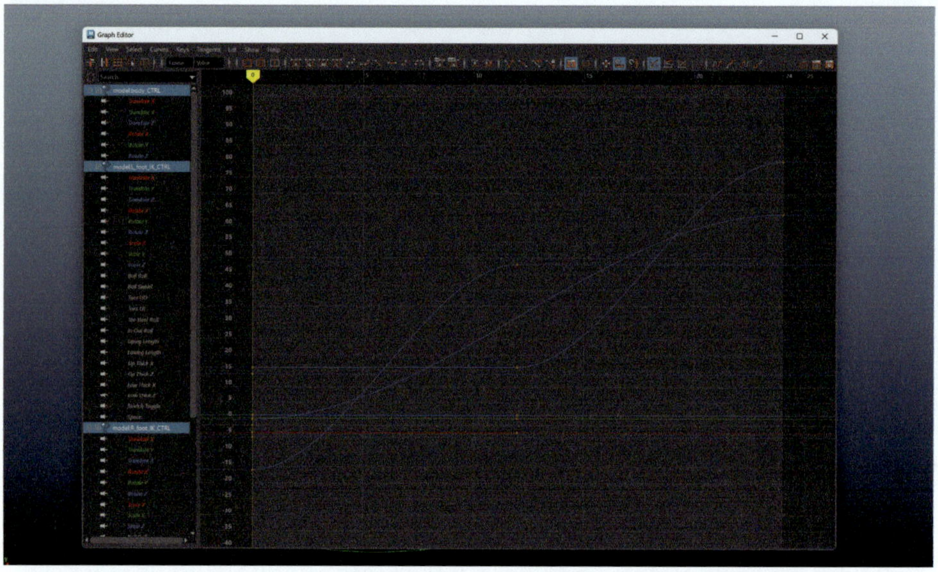

The stair-step pattern of Translate Z channels will become very familiar to you as you animate more and more cycles.

One last thing to do, let's set the Infinity curve types. For the Translate Z channels, they should always be Cycle with Offset.

OFFSETS

Whether it be the coattails of a character in a walk cycle in a film, or the braid of a huntress riding a tiger in an attack cycle for a game, cycles often have many small details. The trouble is, we don't ever want these details to come to a dead halt at the beginning and end of the cycle. Keying secondary motion and smaller details within the same frame duration as the rest of the cycle can lead to a result that looks too repetitive.

So, how do we get these details to look correct, when their motion is determined by other elements moving throughout the cycle, and across the 'seam' of the cycle? This is when we use offsets.

Open Cycle_Offsets.ma. Select the four tail controls and open the Graph Editor. Look how they are keyed in the same 14-frame duration as the rest of the cycle.

It would be very challenging to determine the correct starting position of the tail, seeing as the rest of the animation was keyed to 'frame' the main action of the ball, which is the jump. Where should the tail be in its overlapping animation on frame 0? Is it rising or falling? Like many details, the tail is best animated and then offset to make it look right.

Whenever you are primarily working with a single channel, like Rotate X in this case, select one of the channels on the left side of the Graph Editor and choose Show > Show Selected Types. When you're done, choose Show > All.

Let's get this looking better. First, let's offset the tail parts. Select the three lower parts of the tail (controls, 2, 3, and 4) in the Graph Editor on the left.

With only Rotate X showing, the Graph Editor is nice and clean. I have the three channels selected and am ready to offset.

Select the three curves and Shift + MMB drag them two frames to the right. This is "offsetting" the animation within the tail shape, and we'll offset the entire tail in a bit.

Deselect the Tail 2 curve, and repeat. Deselect the Tail 3 curve, and offset two more frames.

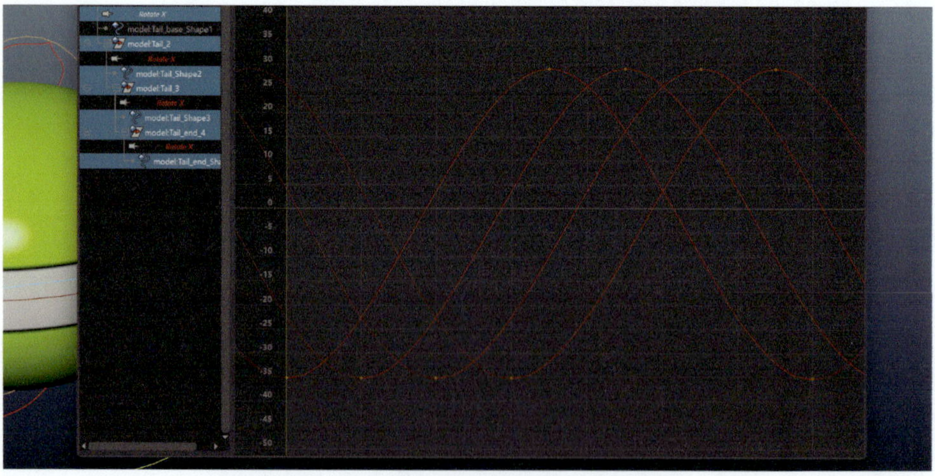

When you are done, the Graph Editor should look like this.

Playing back the animation, it doesn't look great! That's because the tail is not moving at the right overall time compared to the rest of the animation. That is ok, because we'll offset the entire tail animation again.

Select all four tail controls, and in the Graph Editor, select all four Rotate X curves. Shift + MMB drag them to the left three frames.

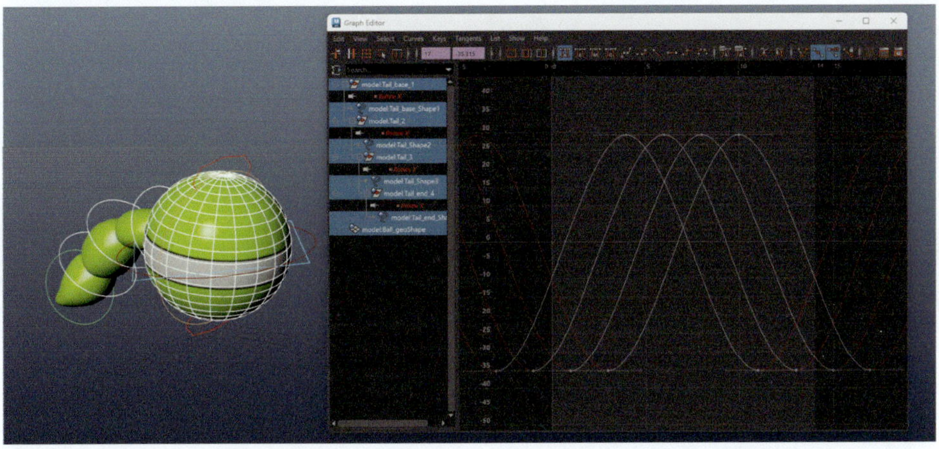

Notice how the tail's animation is not all keyed within the frame range of the main ball motion (f0 to f14); however, the duration is the same.

With the Pre-Infinity and Post-Infinity curves set to Cycle, and with proper duration applied to the tail, it can be keyed on frames f0-f14 and then offset to where it needs to go in the overall cycle. This method is employed endlessly in professional work and makes life so much simpler for animators.

Go ahead and open Cycle_Offsets_Finish.ma to check the results. This cycle needs polish, but it's a great start and is highly editable because we have a set stride-length and sparse keys taking full advantage of Pre-Infinity and Post-Infinity curve interpolation.

REAL-TIME FILMMAKING

For decades, animation production followed a rigid pipeline: pre-production, production, and post-production. Pre-production includes storyboarding, animatics, and character and environment design. Production involves voiceover, layout, animation, and rendering. Post-production refined everything with sound, compositing, editing, and final visual effects. Each phase is a separate, linear step, with minimal room for backtracking. Once a shot reached rendering, it was for the most part locked in (though many crunch times on films are the result of that rule being broken)!

Real-time filmmaking has changed it all.

With the rise of game engines like Unreal Engine and Unity, filmmakers no longer need to wait for final renders to see their shots in near-finished quality. Lighting, animation, and effects can all be adjusted on the fly, allowing for an iterative workflow that blurs the traditional boundaries of CG production. What used to be set in stone is now fluid; cameras can be adjusted in real-time, feedback can be implemented instantly, and entire sequences can be reworked without the bottleneck of waiting for final renders.

This shift has already upended animation pipelines in major studios. *The Mandalorian* is a recent example of pioneering virtual production for live-action filmmaking, using real-time environments rendered in Unreal Engine to replace traditional green screens. But animation studios are also adopting these techniques. In the 2019 *Lion King*, director Jon Favreau and team used Unity to set up all the cameras and preview animation in real-time in VR. Adjustments could be made on the fly by animators and seen seconds later in the virtual environment. In Disney's *Baymax Dreams*, artists experimented with real-time workflows in Unity to speed up episodic animation. Even traditional animation-heavy productions like "Spider-Man: Across the Spider-Verse" have started incorporating real-time tools to preview complex scenes before committing to final animation.

The biggest advantage of real-time workflows for animators is the ability to see their work in near-final quality without waiting for renders. Traditionally, animators relied on low-resolution playblasts, making movement decisions without the benefit of shading and lighting. The final rendered shot could sometimes reveal unforeseen issues; poses that looked great in a playblast are unreadable under production lighting, or silhouettes that worked in isolation getting lost against a busy background. With real-time rendering, animators can see how their movement interacts with the actual scene, ensuring clearer silhouettes, stronger compositions, and more confident animation choices without excessive back-and-forth.

However, the real-time revolution is not without its challenges. While game engines offer instant feedback, they are not always optimized for high-quality animation workflows. Many real-time rigs sacrifice deformation fidelity for speed, and some do not support the nuanced facial and muscle simulations animators rely on for expressive performances.

The biggest advantage of real-time workflows for animators is the ability to see their work in near-final quality without waiting for renders.

This may mean a version of a scene is needed for real-time preview, and another refinement pass completed after the live-action plate is shot. Additionally, real-time workflows often shift more responsibility onto the animator, requiring them to be mindful of how their work interacts with lighting, shading, and camera settings; all factors that were traditionally handled in later stages of production. Some studios mitigate this by maintaining hybrid pipelines, using real-time engines for layout, blocking, and animation previews while still relying on offline rendering for final polish.

There is also a shift in skill sets. Animators trained in Maya must now learn game engine workflows to contribute to a virtual production. Lighting artists accustomed to ray tracing must adapt to the constraints of real-time global illumination. The need for technical artists who can bridge the gap between creative intent and engine limitations has skyrocketed. The line between animator, technical director, and cinematographer is increasingly blurred.

Despite these hurdles, the benefits of real-time production are undeniable. Faster iteration times, more creative flexibility, and the ability to see near-final results at any stage of production are reshaping the industry. The days of waiting hours or even days for a single frame to render have disappeared.

The traditional animation pipeline is not dead, but it is evolving. Real-time tools will not replace every aspect of animation production, but they will continue to shape its future. We are entering an era where animation is no longer locked into a rigid sequence of steps, but rather an ongoing, dynamic process where the line between pre-production, production, and post-production no longer exists.

11 FACIAL ANIMATION

FACE

The character's face is the first place the audience looks. We are social creatures, and we scan each other's faces to gather information about who the person is, their emotional state, if they are communicating directly to us, or what else has their attention.

Have you ever heard the old saying, "the eyes are the windows to the soul"? The audience will focus most of their attention directly on the character's eyes. The attention shifts from the character's eyes, to the face, the hands, and the body, but will keep coming back to the eyes.

The eyes reflect the true emotional state of the character, whereas the mouth may or may not. In a false smile, a character can force a grin on their mouth, but the eyes will not have the correct muscle tension on the eyelids and cheek raise found on a true happy smile.

In 3D animation we want to treat the eyes as the entire area from the lower forehead, brows, eyes, down to the cheekbones. This area is often referred to as the mask. It is very important that the eyes and brows look like they are connected and working together.

HOW TO SHOW A CHARACTER THINKING

Every decision we make in facial animation should have a purpose. It should serve the story and work to tell us who the character is and what they are thinking. Equal attention should be paid to showing the character thinking before, during, and after they speak. Likewise, it is very important to show what the 'listening' character is thinking to show the audience how they are receiving and processing the information. How do we show the character is thinking about something other than the cliché 'thinker' pose? Eye direction. Humans tend to have eye movements linked to searching certain parts of the brain for information. This is not a precise science, it's just an easily observable behavior. People glance off into the distance without focusing their eyes while they remember information or construct (imagine) information.

- **Visual Information:** upper-right to remember and upper-left to construct.
- **Auditory Information (sound):** directly right to remember and left.

- **Sensory Information:** (touch, taste, smell) lower-left for remembering and constructing.
- **Internal Dialogue:** talking to yourself or the voice in your head, is lower-right.

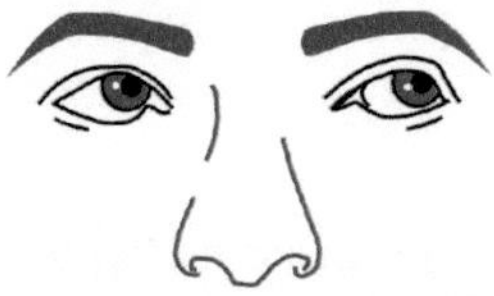	Visual Memory Remembering Images
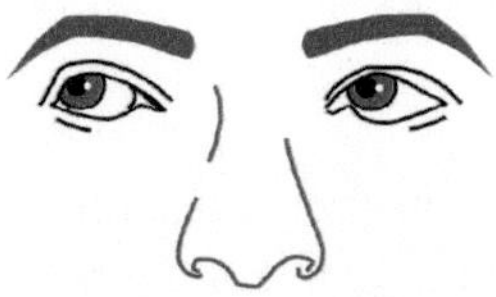	Visual Construction Imagining Images
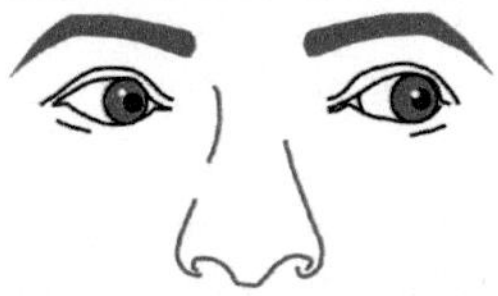	Auditory Memory Remembering Sounds
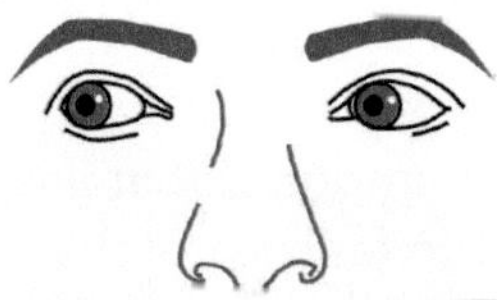	Auditory Construct Imagining Sounds
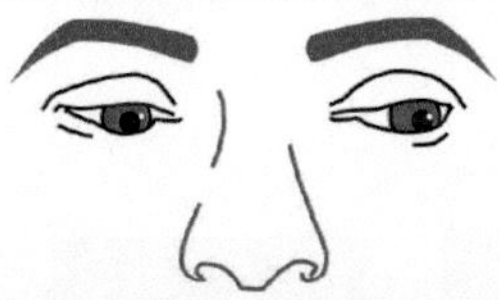	Internal Dialogue Talking to ourself in your head
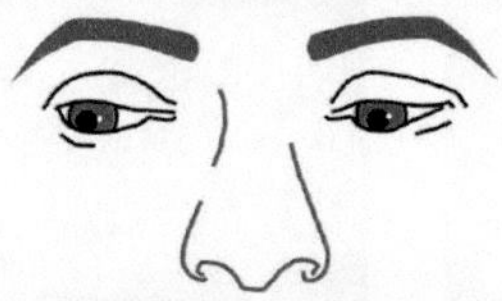	Sensory Memory and Construct Remembering and Imagining touch, taste, smell
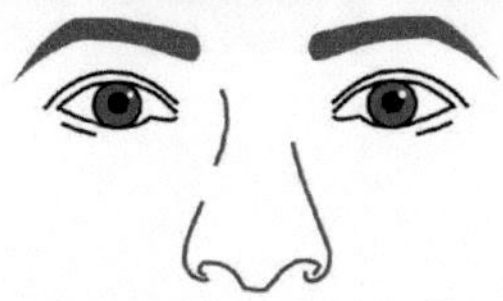	Visual Construct Eyes not focused Day-dreaming, zoned-out

These are not set in stone rules. For example left-handed people may look in the opposite directions. Some people think looking left to construct images or sounds is a sign of dishonesty. It is not. Eye direction is not an accurate way to detect dishonesty. Despite these ambiguities, incorporating eye direction combined with the character's facial expressions creates a rich layered performance.

MICRO-EXPRESSIONS

People do not experience a single emotion at a time, but a complex mixture of overlapping emotions. However, we need a way to simplify our approach to animating emotions.

We can use the research of Dr. Paul Ekman to simplify the basic emotions. Dr. Ekman finds there are seven universal emotions: sadness, anger, happiness, fear, disgust, surprise, and contempt. These emotions and their corresponding facial expressions can be found across all cultures.

Macro-expressions are conscious expressions of emotions that are displayed on the face for seconds, minutes, or longer. These overlapping emotions often match the tone of what is being said.

Micro-expressions are unconscious expressions of emotions that flash across the face in less than a second. They expose the true feelings of the character despite what is being said. These expressions are subconscious and cannot be controlled.

Anger

Contempt

Disgust

Fear

Happiness

Sadness

Surprise

BROWS

Brows frame the eyes and magnify the subtler shapes of the upper eyelids. They can be very useful in exaggerating emotions, accenting dialogue, indicating changes of thought, showing eye direction, and enhancing the asymmetry or squash and stretch of the facial pose. The brow is divided into three sections, the inner (at the nose), the mid, and the outer. The brows move up and out, or they move down and in following the curvature of the skull. To understand why the motion is up and out and down and in, we need to know a little about the muscles underneath.

This set of muscles affects both brows at the same time:

- **Frontalis** is a band of muscle across the entire forehead. When it contracts, it lifts both brows up. For some people, the frontalis has more influence at the mids, for others, it lifts the mids and inners.
- **Procerus** is a muscle at the top of the nose that pulls the inner brows down and toward the center (makes the line/wrinkle over the nose or glabella).

Both muscles influence the left and right inner brow region at the same time. Therefore, no matter what the individual brow poses are, the inner brows are connected, and they need to point at each other. Treat every character like they have a unibrow, and you can't go wrong.

This set of muscles comes in pairs on the left and right and can affect each brow individually:

- **Corrugator** goes from the mids to the inner and pulls each brow down and into the center, and it wrinkles the brows.
- **Depressor Supercilii** is a small muscle on each side of the nose that squeezes the inner brows down and to the center.

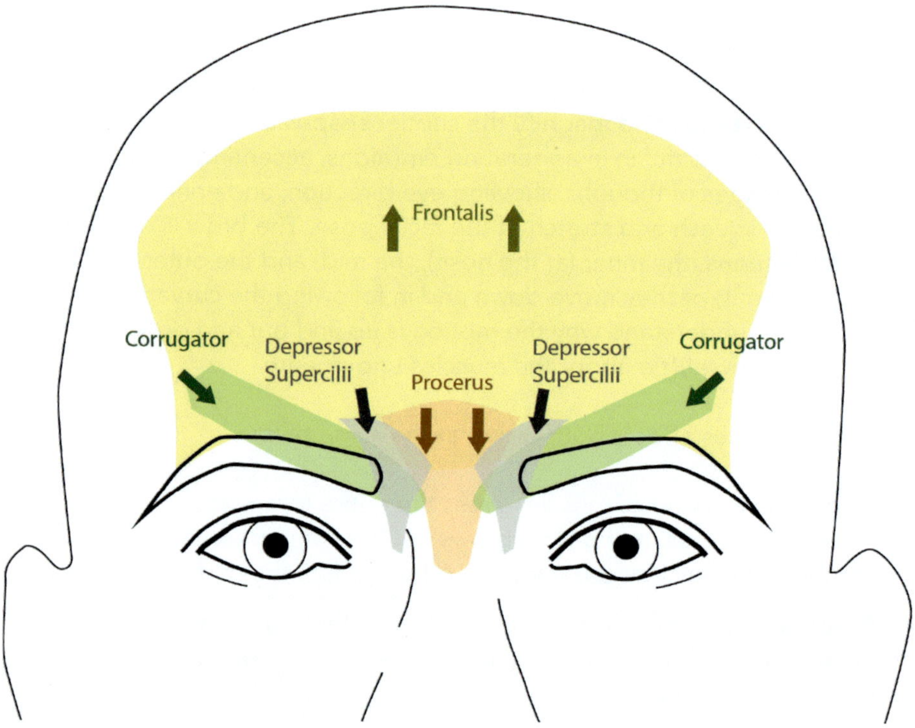

Notice the four muscles listed primarily affect the middle and inner brows. The outer brows are mostly outside any direct muscle influence and just get pulled along. Adding excessive movement on the outer brows will not only cause them to look disconnected from the face, but it may make them look like living things crawling on the face.

Some people naturally have a lot of control over each eyebrow. It's mostly genetics. Although thanks to the wisdom of the internet, there are exercises one can do to improve their range of motion.

FUN FACT

People who can raise only one eyebrow at a time are not using half of the frontalis; they just have really strong independent control of each corrugator muscle to resist the lift of the frontalis.

EYES AND EYELIDS

Eyelids are moved by two muscles:

- **Levator Palpebrae** is a small muscle in the upper eyelid. It lifts the upper lids in a blink.
- **Orbicularis Oculi** is a ring of muscle that goes around the entire eye. Squeeze it lightly to narrow the eyelids, blink, and squint. Squeeze it hard to shut your eyes tightly.

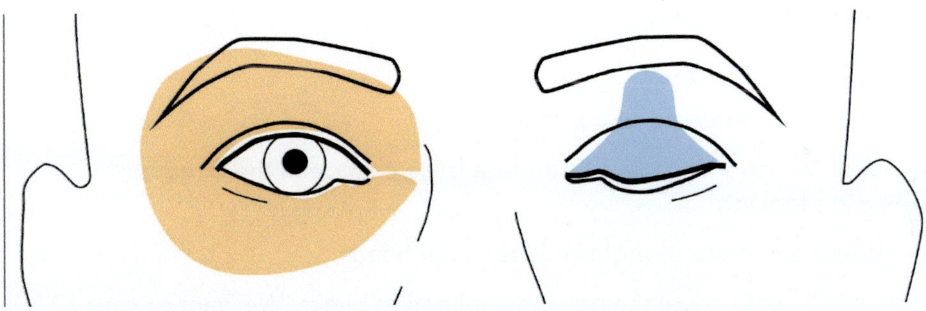

Orbicularis Oculi: The ring of muscle squeezes the lids closed and pulls the lower lid up and in.

Levator Palpebrae Superioris: This muscle lifts the upper eyelid.

Like the brows, the upper eyelids have three regions: the inner, the mids, and the outer. The shape of the eyeball is not a perfect sphere. The cornea of the eye covers the pupil, iris, and lens. It projects forward from the eyeball, and eyelids rest on top of it. When you look to the side, the cornea pushes the eyelid up and over the iris and pupil. The result is the upper eyelids will have a more complex shape than the lower ones.

Rigs come with their eyes wide open. It's easier for the modelers and riggers to work with a wide open eye. However, as animators, we don't want this. We want to reserve a wide open eye for surprise, or fear.

When you start to pose the face of a realistic character, close the eyelids a bit so they are resting on the iris.

The upper eyelid shapes should mirror the brow shapes.

WATCH OUT!

Zombie Eyes! This is the phenomenon where the character's head is turned and all we see is the whites of the eye. Avoid this. We always want to see a bit of the iris at minimum or iris and pupil. Cheat to the camera. Turn the character's body or head, or move the eyeball over, or a combination of all three.

BLINKS

When do we blink?

- To keep the eyes from drying out.
- To protect the eyes.
- When we are scared or nervous.
- When we do a large head turn or a large change in the direction we are looking.
- After a complete thought or idea in our heads.

We want to avoid equal timing when animating blinks. We want to vary the speeds within the blink, sometimes closing faster and opening slower or vice versa.

In a realistic human blink, the upper eyelid closes most of the way, and the lower eyelid barely raises. For stylized or cartoony human characters, you can bend the rules and have the lids meet in the middle. There is a lot of variety in the animal kingdom, so do your research for non-humans.

In longer blinks, close the lids together lightly, and then cushion the close by squeezing the lids together, then open. Faster blinks can be done with half-blinks. The lid blinks quickly and does not close completely. When doing a double blink or rapid succession of blinks, you may not have time to completely close the lids.

FUN FACT

Adults blink more than babies and toddlers.

OFFSET BLINKS

In *Toy Story* (1995) the characters had an offset blink. The style was chosen for toys but dropped for later movies. When do we have offset blinks in the real world?

- Old-fashioned doll eyes with rotating parts.
- Popular trope in old 2D animation to show a sleepy or bashful character.
- Babies can have offset blinks because their motor skills and vision are still developing.
- Someone wearing mascara can get their eyelashes stuck together.
- Someone extremely impaired, either intoxicated or with a very serious head injury.

EYELINE

Eyeline is just that, it's the direction the character is looking. It sounds simple but can be tricky. In live action, there is often a stand-in, so actors have someone to look at while performing in front of the camera. We want to use this same technique in 3D. Use a second rig or just use a sphere to mark where a head would be. This gives you a tangible object to direct the main character's line of sight at to make a perfect eyeline with a rig or sphere, but sometimes it still doesn't look good on camera. The shot camera is more important. Cheat the eyeline. Maybe look past the stand-in or slightly off to the side; whatever it takes to make it look good in camera.

CHEAT

Does the rig look slightly cross-eyed? If the rig has an aim control in front of the face, move it out farther and see if that fixes it.

LINE OF ACTION: HEAD

Line of action is the direction of force, or movement, through the body or body parts. The line of action in a face is most often a variation of a C curve. The line of action on the head may follow the same direction as the body, or it may differ. It also creates a foundation that we can build upon to exaggerate the facial pose. We want some asymmetry in the facial pose. How do we apply a C curve to a face? Slightly squash one side of the face and stretch the other. The stretched side of the face, the eyebrow pose is a little higher, the mouth corner is a little lower, the pose is slightly easier to read. It can help clarify where the character is looking. Much of the asymmetry can be built with the facial controls, but don't forget to look for head-deforming controls on the rig to help squash and stretch the entire face.

EMOTIONAL ASYMMETRY

We want the parts of the face to be connected and work together for a believable performance. But there are times when we want to break from that. When characters are not being truthful, we may want to display one emotion across the eyes (top) and another on the mouth (bottom). Or we may wish to display more tension around the eye area than the mouth. Displaying a different emotional state in the eyes and mouth not only works, but it can also make very complex and layered performances.

Splitting the face down the middle and making the left and right sides of the face exhibit different emotional states is a very different matter. It is not normal human behavior and will make the audience very uneasy. This phenomenon has been labeled 'Chirality' by Joe Navarro, a former FBI agent. Like a split personality, the differences from left and right can be seen on photos of psychopaths. Unless you are animating a character like that and are trying to upset the audience, please make sure to keep the emotional state consistent across the top and the bottom of the face. We do want left and right asymmetry in our facial poses, but not in the emotions.

LIP SYNC

Often, what is not said is more important than the actual words heard. Creating a convincing performance of a character delivering a line of dialogue is not just dependent on perfect mouth shapes. We don't watch someone's mouth closely when they speak to us. We look at them. We look at their eyes, the whole face, the body language, and the hand gestures. The most important thing is: what is our character thinking? All your acting choices will be guided by that information. Everything should support the story.

To tell a story, we work with text, context, and subtext. Text is the exact words that are said. Context is the available information that makes the story point clear. Subtext is the unspoken meaning behind the words.

When you receive a line of dialogue to animate, spend some time studying it before jumping into animation. Beginning animators need to learn to let go of spelling and punctuation. Focus on what is the character thinking, the emotion, what is being emphasized, what is not, the breath, and the sounds you hear. We want to break the line of dialogue into ideas or complete thoughts.

11 FACIAL ANIMATION

"I know what's going on but, uh, maybe you should explain it to the others."

There are two complete ideas in the line of dialogue.

"I know what's going on. + You should explain it to others."

What does the character really mean? Since we have no audio or visual cues from words on a page, let's imagine two very different interpretations of the line.

- Stating a fact (confident) + Making a suggestion (thoughtful). Our character is a good person delegating a task because of time constraints.
- A boast (lying/ fearful) + Making a suggestion to manipulate (contempt). Our character is dodgy, trying to trick others into answering the question so they don't look dumb.

We created two completely different performances based on the same words by changing the subtext. Our knowledge of who the character is, what they are thinking, where we are in the story, combined with the voice actor's performance will guide our animation choices.

SPEECH

How do humans talk? We fill our lungs up with air and then push the air out through our vocal tract. The air passes up our throats, then larynx, moving the jaw, into the mouth, over the tongue and teeth, and out the lips, and nose.

- **Visible to the audience:** breath (mouth and chest), jaw rotation, and mouth/lip shapes.
- **Sometimes visible to the audience:** tongue movement and teeth.
- **Rarely visible to the audience:** air moving up the vocal cords / throat, into the back of the mouth, behind the teeth and tongue, or out the nose.

Ever wondered why we divide letters into vowels and consonants?

Vowels are sounds that are made with an open vocal tract or open mouth. A, E, I, O, U, and Y, need your jaw to rotate open with a corresponding open mouth shape. It is important that they can be seen by the audience.

Consonants are sounds made with a partially closed vocal tract.
The mouth can be open or closed. There may be a corresponding mouth shape or not. The consonant sound could be made in the throat, nose, back of mouth, or against the teeth. We can divide consonants into two groups.

Consonants that have mouth shapes the audience can see:

- **M, B, P:** lips are closed for two frames, pop open on the third. For P, add puffed cheeks.
- **F, V:** curl bottom lip in under the top teeth.
- **W:** pucker lips tightly.
- **L and sometimes TH, T, D:** flick tongue up to roof of mouth.
- **SH and sometimes ER, CH, ZH, and J:** lips slightly puckered.

Consonants without specific mouth shapes or unseen in the back of the mouth: C, D, G, H, J, K, N, Q, S, T, X, Z.

Phoneme is defined as, "one of the smallest units of speech that distinguishes one utterance from another." In animation, this is the sound of a single letter or letter combination. We will be breaking up words phonetically and ignoring the proper spellings.

DIALOGUE DIAGRAM EXERCISE

Beginners animating lip-sync for the first time, here is an exercise to help you break down the sounds and concentrate on the most important phonemes.

Let's look at our line of dialogue again.

"I know what's going on but, uh, maybe you should explain it to the others."

Rewrite the line ignoring the spelling completely, but concentrate on the phonemes you hear:

"I nO wats gO ·ng on but, uh, mA ·bE U shud X ·plAn it too the o·thrz"

Re-write again with only the phonemes with specific mouth shapes that can be seen by the audience: (AEIOUY, M,B,P, FV, W, LTh, ShChErZhJ.)

"I O wat O o but, u, mA·bE U shud e·plA it oo the o·ther"

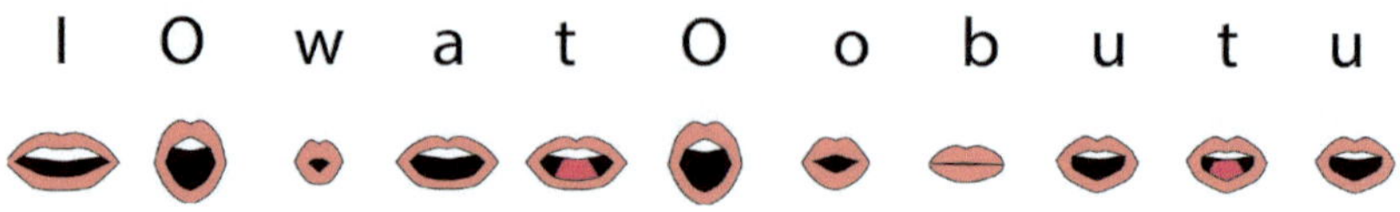

I know what's going on, but, uh

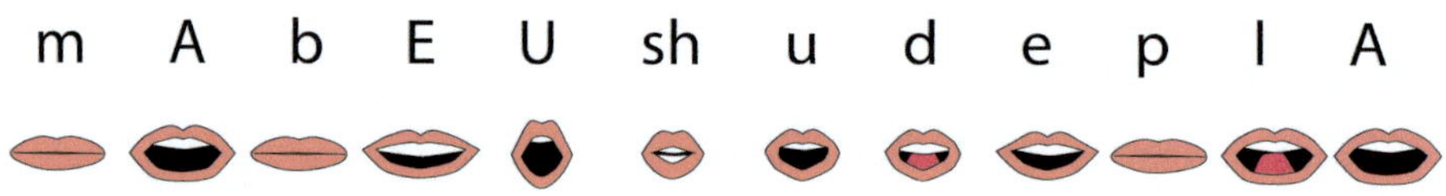

maybe you should explain

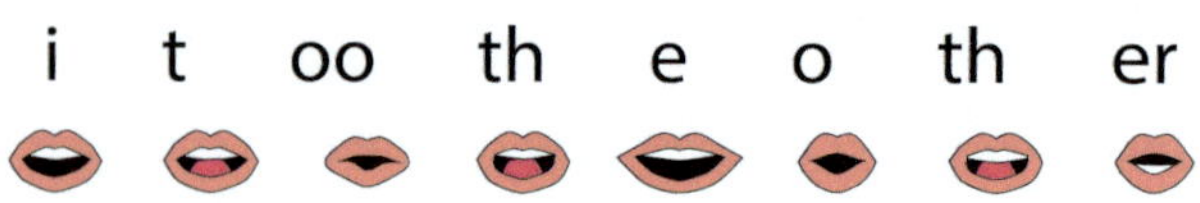

it to the others.

These are the key mouth shapes that the audience should see. The missing consonants g, n, s, t, x, and z are made inside the mouth and will happen while the character's mouth is moving between the visible mouth shapes.

The diagram exercise is useful for planning the mouth shapes, but they are symmetrical and emotionless. We still need to combine the phoneme shapes with the emotional facial pose.

FUN FACT

Linguistics is the study of languages including how sounds are made. Need to animate in a foreign language? Use linguistic research, charts, and texts for help animating unfamiliar phonemes.

ANIMATING LIP SYNC

After studying the line of dialogue and gaining a sense of what the character is thinking, what they are saying, and how it fits into the story and scene, we plan out the shot. In a large studio, storyboards, animatics, director notes, video footage of the voice actor, etc. will be provided. Students doing a dialogue test may have the original footage the audio clip came from and their own imagination. The next step is to act out the shot for reference.

Some people make thumbnails of ideas to act out for reference, some people act it out and turn it into thumbnail sketches, or a combination. Do what works best.

Acting and Lip Sync Reference

A big mistake when creating reference is trying to both act and speak the dialogue in perfect sync with the recording. Why? It's almost impossible. The first 50 tries, you will be off-sync. The acting will be stilted because you are focusing on the timing of the audio, not performance. The results are bad reference videos. At the end of the day, we are not making reference to copy frame-by-frame. We are making reference as a guide and inspiration. Study the line and listen very carefully to it. Make note of the emphasized words, accented syllables, breath, pauses, mood, attitude, body shifts, and any other background sounds like clothing or environment.

Divide your reference session into two parts. First for the body, play the audio on loop and just act out the motions of the body and add in the facial expressions. Do not try to lip sync or keep in perfect time with the audio.

Explore ideas for movements, poses, and gestures of the body. Then, turn off the audio and record a close-up of yourself saying the line. It is ok if you are not saying the line at the exact speed. This is only to observe facial expressions and mouth shapes. Incorporating some performance is ok, but again, we are not copying a performance, we are expanding on it and making it our own.

DON'T FORGET

Act out the line many times and take the best bits and pieces from multiple recordings and combine them together. Don't try to manifest every acting choice in a single take.

11 FACIAL ANIMATION

Keep a mirror at your workspace for reference on the spot. Some students prefer using the webcams instead, so whatever works best.

Visual Library

What are we looking for in our reference? Acting ideas and body mechanics, but also those individual little quirks and gestures that tell the story and make the performance real, personal, and unique.

Where do we get these ideas? Ourselves, the people around us, everyday life, and from actor performances in theater, film, and television. The best animators I know build up a visual library of drawings, pictures, and video clips to pull ideas from. If you're lucky enough to get a job in a big studio, they have libraries where you can pull references from videos, TV, and films. But a good place to start is watching old, new, foreign, and domestic films. Animation is filled with hommage (tributes) to famous scenes, actors, and directors. As a professional, you will be expected to have a fair knowledge of film and animation history.

Creating a Face Camera

Some rigs come with a face camera already set up. Go to the Viewport > Panels > Perspective and choose the face camera. If the rig did not come with a face camera, make one. Go to Create > Cameras > Camera. Name the camera by double-clicking the camera in the Outliner, Channel Box, or Attribute Editor.

In the Outliner, MMB drag any node to change its position in a hierarchy, or drag the node into or out of any hierarchical group.

Attach the camera to the head control, or nose control. Look through the new face camera and frame it for a close view of the face and all the facial controls needed. Next, attach the camera to the control so it travels with the character.

Parent Group (position adjustable): Select the camera (child), then Shift select the head control (parent), and use hotkey P to parent group.

Parent Constraint (position NOT adjustable: Select the head control (parent), then Shift select the camera (child,) and go to Constrain > Parent.

For those who struggle to remember the correct selection order, a reliable method to Parent Group is by dragging directly in the Outliner. Select the head control, then in the Outliner press F to frame the selected control. Middle-mouse drag the new face camera node onto the head control node. The camera becomes a child of the head control and will now move with it.

CHEAT

Hotkey A to frame All and hotkey F to frame selected work in any Maya panel, list, or graph.

For the parent grouping method, lock the camera position so you don't accidentally mess it up. Go to the left side of the Viewport toolbar. The Lock camera icon is a camera with a blue padlock, toggle it on. Or go to the Channel Box, select attributes, and RMB Lock Selected.

11 FACIAL ANIMATION

ANIMATE THE BODY FIRST OR THE FACE FIRST?

Most professional animators start with the body. In the past, some animators did animate the face first and then the body. The argument was it's harder to get a clear view of the face with the body in motion. Attaching a camera to the character's face solves that. A drawback to doing the face first is having to go back and readjust the facial animation to make sure it looks good in the camera. Therefore, it's recommended to do the body first.

Blocking the body may include adding a few key facial expressions. It depends on what is expected by the director or your leads. Approach eye and brow animation with pose to pose, straight ahead, or layered animation. However, lip sync is almost always animated straight ahead as we tend to flow from one mouth shape to another. Which facial expressions should be included in blocking? Take your clues from the subtext in the dialogue and any exclamations or stressed syllables in the line. For example, if the dialogue has three distinct thoughts (subtext)—happy, confused, and sad—those three facial expressions should be reflected in the eyes and brows during blocking. The mouth may also be included, depending on what the director needs to see.

JAW ANIMATION

Usually, people start to open their jaws before they begin to speak. Light moves faster than sound. We see before we hear. Your brain is working faster than your mouth. The thought has already happened and starts to display across the face. Your eyes and brows first, then you take a breath in preparation to speak. Begin to open your mouth and move the lips into position before we hear the first syllable.

We start mouth animation with the Jaw control. The jaw control not only opens the mouth, but it also drives the lower lip, cheek, bottom teeth, tongue, and chin controls. The jaw is a hinge joint that rotates from the pivot points just in front of the ears. If the jaw control has rotations and translations available, we want to rotate. Now on some rigs, the jaw control was created to be translated to make the correct jaw joint rotation, so test the rigs.

What about slacked-jaw characters? While most jaw animation is rotating in one direction: open and shut, there are times where we want to play up side-to-side rotation and even extra translations for exaggeration or cartoony animation. First, check that you are not moving the lower face controls away from the upper face in such a way that the face looks broken or disconnected. If that is the case, instead of using the jaw control, see if the rig has special head deformers that will allow for the jaw to be rotated and moved, but keep all parts of the face connected and working together. Beginners working on a slack-jaw character should start with a straightforward open/close pass on the jaw in blocking, then add a side-to-side rotation pass.

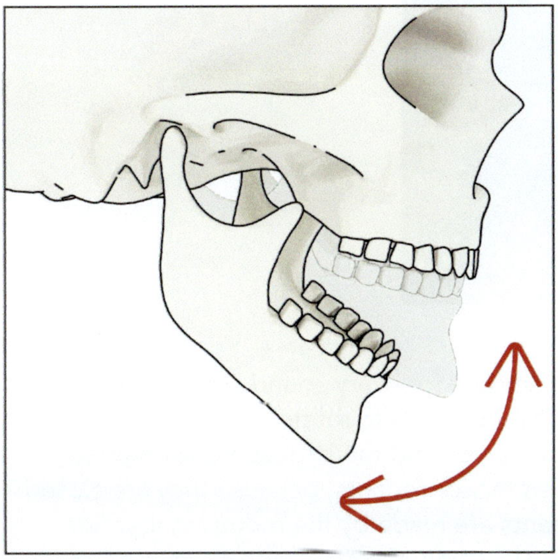

The jaw rotates from a pivot point just in front of the ears. The jaw does not move up and down in realistic animation.

CHEAT

To figure out when and how much to rotate the jaw, try this method. Place the back of your hand under your chin. Feel the jaw rotate open and push your hand down as you say the lines out loud. Use this information to apply rotation to the jaw control.

Place the back of your hand under your chin.

Feel the jaw rotate open and push your hand down as you say each word out loud.

Notice how the amount of open rotation varies on the different phonemes.

Use this information to apply rotation to the jaw control.

The jaw does not move the same amount for every sound. The jaw rotation will vary throughout each word. The jaw tends to rotate open on vowels, because they are open vocal tract sounds and the largest mouth shapes. The jaw doesn't always rotate open for consonants, because they are closed vocal tract sounds. Some consonants are made by the mouth shape/ lips and do not include a change in jaw position. If you put too much motion on the jaw, the character will look jabbery and be distracting for the audience. Do not try to close the jaw between every word or syllable, the more the jaw has to rotate to get to each pose, the faster it will need to go. The slower someone speaks, the more time they have to close the jaw between words and phrases, but that does not mean it is the right choice for the performance. Do not snap the jaw shut after speaking. Often our mouth is partially open before and after we speak because we are drawing in breath. Check the reference and look and see when and if the voice actor closed their mouth completely.

M, B, P are the closed mouth shapes that the audience needs to see. The lips should be closed two frames and pop open on the third. Just because you press the lip together does not mean that the jaw should close all the way. M often has a partially open jaw but lips closed. How much should the jaw rotate closed depends on the phoneme before and after the M, B, P closed lips frame. If they are strong vowels, you may not have time to rotate the jaw closed all the way.

Texture on the jaw animation means there should be a combination of fast sharp moves and softer slower moves. Over-cleaning the jaw animation and making everything too smooth will make the jaw animation mushy like the character is mumbling. What if the character is talking really fast? Don't open and close the jaw for every syllable because it will look jabbery. Instead, keep the jaw rotating in small increments except for the biggest accents.

Jaw animation is the foundation you will build the rest of the lip sync on. Adding mouth shapes over incorrect jaw animation can make it harder for everyone to pinpoint where the problems are coming from.

LIPS

Most rigs will have four macro-controls for the lips: upper lip, lower lip, and two corners. Within the macro-controls, there can be many controls to do fine adjustments to the lip shapes. Start with the larger controls first as they influence many controls. When selecting the macro-controls, take a look in the channels for extra attributes. Many rigs will have attribute controls to roll the lips in and out, curl the lips, compress the lips, pucker the lips, zip lip corners, and more.

Start with the lip corners first. We do not want the face to be symmetric. The positions of the corners of the mouth will be a balance between the shape for the phoneme and the emotional facial expression. The lip corners will move in an arc shape following the curve of the skull. When the jaw opens, it will tend to pull the corners of the mouth in and down. Are the mouth corners wide or narrow on closed lip M, B, P shapes? It depends on the phonemes before and after the M, P, B. For example, the word 'obey': The lip corners are narrowed for the O shape, begin to widen during the closed B, and finish wide for the EY mouth shape.

Next, adjust the top and bottom lip controls to make the connection between the corners. Depending on how the rig is set up, there may be extra lip attributes to roll the lips in or out, to compress or pucker. The rig may have an option for lip zip which helps pinch the corners closed into nice shapes.

Copying Animation on the Face

Once you have the mouth animation, we want to make everything in the lower face feel connected. The area of the face from the cheek bones, ears, nose, and chin is made of loose skin that should stretch and compress while talking and making facial expressions. How many controls the face has will vary by rig. General rule is when rotating the jaw open, it should pull down on the cheeks, bottom of nostrils, and maybe even earlobes. One way to get this is to copy the jaw animation onto the up and down of the lower face controls, and then scale it down. We also want the cheek areas to narrow with an open jaw and widen and lift with a smile. You may not get what you need by just copying the jaw. A better choice may be copying the lip corner animation, and then scaling, adjusting, and offsetting.

Teeth

The audience should never see the character's teeth moving around inside the mouth. However, there are times where we may need to move the teeth. For an F or V, you may need to bring the top teeth a bit forward past the bottom lip. Another situation is a very puckered mouth, we may need to push the teeth back so they don't intersect the cheek. As long as the movement is hidden from the audience, this is fine. A certain amount of teeth needs to be readable to the audience. If only a sliver of teeth is visible, either show more until it is a readable shape or hide them. Do not show too much gum. It's off-putting and it comes from our primitive brain where snarling and flashing teeth and gums is a sign of aggression.

Tongue

There are a few phonemes where it is important to see the tongue flick. On an L phoneme, the tongue should touch the back of the top teeth. More than one frame is needed to read. Try 1–2 frames up, 2 frames hold, and 1–2 frames down. Overlap the tongue moves with other phonemes. Phonemes that are made with tongue on the roof of the mouth include: D, T, and Th. If the inside of the character's mouth is visible, add tongue animation for D, T, and Th.

Final Mouth Polish

The base jaw animation may not require much polish but may make some openings a bit snappier depending on the dialogue. Lip corners should make nice arcs, move down, and narrow when the jaw is wide open. Make sure the face feels connected, where certain parts of the lower face are being pushed and pulled by the mouth shapes. Don't just copy animation, scale it down, and leave it. That is lazy. Adjust everything to work with the facial expressions, adjust for full face squash and stretch, make arcs where possible, and offset where needed. Depending on how sophisticated the rig is, you may need to bring out the second level and third level micro-controls to polish lip shapes, especially if there are no zip lip options. And make sure the face animation complements and is connected to the body animation.

Finally, the mouth animation should not distract from the eyes/ brows. If the mouth animation is so exaggerated it distracts from the face and body, you are going to lose the audience. Unless it's a story point like Sylvester the Cat trying to hide the fact that Tweety is shoved in his mouth.

AUDIO

Students Selecting Audio

Student work and personal projects are one of a few times where one can animate anything they want. That said, there are a few rules students should follow when selecting audio for class projects.

Do *not* choose something offensive! You never know who may see your animation when you're job hunting, and accidentally offending someone is a completely avoidable disaster. Keep it clean. Some dark humor is ok, but if you can't show it to grandma, don't put it on a reel.

Try to use the highest quality audio available. There are lots of sites with free audio, but sometimes the quality is poor. Hunt down a better source or capture the audio yourself.

Choose a complete thought/ idea with a beginning, middle, and end. For example, "I'll be back" is very short, but it is a complete thought. Choosing a fragment out of context could cause the audience to be left hanging or confused.

If it is a two-person clip, try to find two actors that differ from each other in either age, sex, voice, or emotional state.

Pauses are great! It's a place to show off the character's thinking and facial acting.

Be careful with whispering, heavy accents or mumbling.
When a short clip of audio is taken out of context, the audience may have trouble understanding it. Unless you are making a deliberate choice to animate this with visual cues for the audience.

Music is ok as long as it doesn't overpower.

Laugh tracks are always awful, avoid them.

Environmental sounds: if the audience can hear the character jogging and panting in the park, but you animate him sitting in a room, it won't work. Study the environmental sounds and figure out what can be off-screen and what has to be incorporated into the shot.

Go ahead! Edit and change the source audio. With sound editing software, add pauses, cut out pieces, or rearrange the dialogue. Make it your own.

Lastly, do not choose dialogue from podcasts, memes, or 3D animated shows or films.

Podcasters: These are not actors, they don't stay in characte, and their delivery is usually poor. What they said may have been funny in context, but not in the shot.
Memes: What's funny right now probably won't be two minutes from now. What's worse than that, it dates your work, and some people may find it tired, irritating, and in poor taste.
3D animation: It may not be fair, but professional animators can't help but comparing the student's work to the original, especially if the student is animating everything in a similar manner, and we personally know the original animator. Don't put yourself in this position. The only way to make it work is if the visuals and actions are so different and unique from the source material that it breaks the mental connection and becomes its own thing. That's a lot for a student to pull off.

AUDIO EDITING

Maya does many things, but it does not have audio editing capabilities. If you need to edit audio clips, use another software specialized for audio. Audacity is a free, open-source program for PC, Mac, or Linux, and it's easy to use. Despite its small size, it's robust and powerful.

Here is a checklist of things to do in bespoke audio editing software before putting audio in Maya:

1. Record audio.
2. Maya only accepts .wav and .aiff audio files; other audio file types will need to be converted. For PC, I recommend .wav.
3. Check the volume levels and increase and decrease as needed.
4. Do some adding of silence, room noise, and general editing.
5. Do noise reduction, but try to start with the best quality possible since audio can only be cleaned up so much.
6. Layer or mix multiple clips or sound effects into a single track.
7. Do a little fade in and fade out at the ends, so that the clip doesn't pop when looped.

If you drag and drop the audio file into the Viewport, it will add the audio to the Time Slider. The audio will only play if the Playback setting is 24 x 1. The volume control is on the bottom-right corner under the play controls. RMB the Time Slider for Audio options. The only options for the audio is to offset (choose what frame to start the file on) and trim the source start and end to shorten the audio. That is it.

You can drop multiple sound files onto the Time Slider, but only one can be played at a time.

If you want to hear multiple audio tracks, use the Dope Sheet, Time Editor, or Trax Editor. Do not drag and drop. Each tool has an Import Audio option; use that.

11 FACIAL ANIMATION

Time Editor and Trax Editor

Maya will *not* playblast multiple audio tracks. Mixing multiple audio tracks in the proper software is the only way to cross-fade, add effects, and adjust tracks for the best results. However, it is possible to playback multiple overlapping audio files in Maya by using the Trax Editor or the Time Editor, although that is not their primary function.

The Time Editor is the new replacement for the Trax Editor, but both tools are still present in Maya 2026. Both of these tools are best used for mixing multiple animation clips, like mocap clips and cycled animation. The ability to mix and blend animations is quite impressive.

Time Editor is probably the better tool. Go to Windows > Animation Editors > Time Editor or use the button on the top-right of the Graph Editor to open. Drag and drop audio files into the Time Editor. Again the only option is to slide the clips to a different time; no other editing is available. However, one should be able to overlap multiple audio files and play them all at the same time. Go to Preferences > Animation > Time Editor; there you can set the Input Audio Rate to a higher quality like 44.1 kHz.

Go to Windows > Animation Editors > Trax Editor to open. Next go to File > Import Audio. Audio files need to be imported one at a time. Slide the clips to a different time; but no other editing is available. According to official Maya documentation, the Soundtrack arranges the clips in a hierarchy, and clips will be played one at a time in descending order.

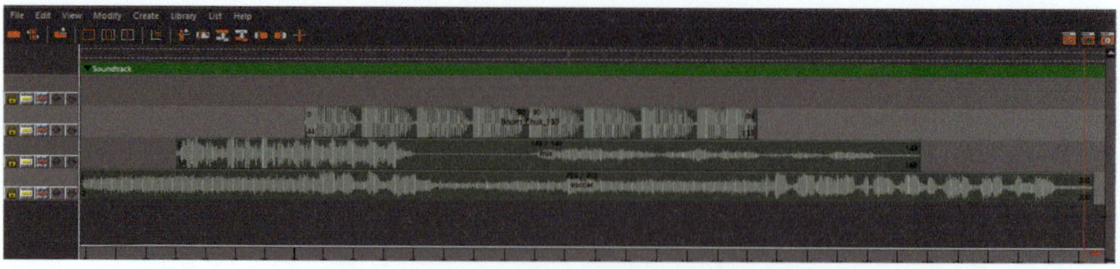

COMMON PROBLEMS

While we've done our best to cover everything in this book we could to set you up for success, there are all of the little things that will give you grief if you accidentally click the wrong box, or hit the wrong hotkey. Here's a non-exhaustive list of the things that we've encountered that have resulted in hair-pulling for decades. Hopefully, reading through this list will plant little reminders for you when you hit these issues later. Your hairline will thank you.

"My geometry is black."

You probably hit the 7 key, which turns on lighting, hit the 5 key to go back to default lighting, shaded mode.

If the rig has random black areas, it may be caused by the playback cache 'baking' shadows on rigs with older shaders. Just turn off the playback cache.

The backside of a polygon is black. Sometimes, older rigs with mirrored geometry display the meshes as inside out. You have two options: Select poly faces, go to Mesh Display, Reverse. For NURBS, go to Surfaces > Reverse Direction. Or go Lighting, Two Sided Lighting to force it to display.

"My animation is playing too fast."

Right-click the Time Slider and set Playback Speed to Real-time. Click the Time Slider Preferences (orange man with gear) in the bottom right of the Maya window, and set playback speed to 24x1 fps.

"My geometry is green."

You may have imported or referenced a rig that is missing its materials. Check to make sure they are there by going into the Hypershade window and that the materials exist.

"My character's body parts are flipping around between keyframes."

That's called Gimbal Lock. For a quick fix, select your keys in the Graph Editor, and in the Graph Editor menu, choose Keys > Euler Filter. To prevent, rotate FK controls use the axis handles by directly clicking and dragging them instead of the free rotate (clicking and dragging anywhere within the circular rotate manipulator).

"My manipulator is tiny / huge."

Use the plus and minus +/- keys to change its size.

"I can't see the rigs controls."

If you put your rigs controls on a display layer, that will override the Show menu. Check Show menu, Viewport, NURBS Curves is checked on, then go to the display layer and toggle the V on.

"I can't select my controls."

If you put your rig's controls on a display layer, Make sure the third box is blank, and not set to T or R locked mode.

Make sure Selection in the Status Line is set to All Objects or NURBS.

"The keys in the Time Slider have disappeared, but the animation still plays."

If you put your rig's controls on a display layer, make sure the third box is blank, and not set to T or R locked mode.

"I suddenly have multiple copies of my rig controls. Or the cursor keeps displaying the words Clone or Extrude?"

Double-click the Translate, Rotate or Scale tool icon to open the Tool Settings. Go to the Shift+Drag Settings and uncheck both boxes; this will disable unwanted cloning on all translation tools.

"I want to move the control straight up, but the manipulator handles are pointing at an angle."

The manipulator is set to local orientation which lines up with the position of the joints. To change orientation, hold the key that represents the transform you are performing, (W,E,R, etc.) while you left-click and drag on the object. A hotbox appears that will allow you to change the gizmo space to World, Object, or others.

"I can't get my audio into Maya."

Maya only accepts .wav or .aiff files. You need to convert your audio in an appropriate audio program.

"I can't hear my audio."

Make sure the volume is not muted.

Make sure the playback is set to 24x1 fps; the audio will not play at any other speed.

"I can't save my Maya scene."

You need to keep saving your scene in the same file format. Check if your scene is a .ma or a .mb. Choose the same file format to save without error.

"The controls are blue with magenta points and don't select like normal."

You have entered a component selection mode. Right-click off to the side and choose Object Mode.

"My selection is yellow/ orange/ red/ purple."

Soft selection is on. Toggle the B key.

"I am pressing the S key, but it is not saving a key."

If your cursor is still in an input box, like a channel, then you have been typing the letter s instead of using the hotkey. Hit Enter or click your mouse anywhere in the screen to get out of the input box, make sure the control is still selected and hit S.

"My menus disappeared."

M + Ctrl is the hotkey to hide menus in whichever panel is active. Repeat M + Ctrl to toggle the menu back on.

COMMON PROBLEMS

"I messed up the camera."

Go to the View menu in your viewport, select Default View or use the hotkey Home to reset the camera position.

Go to the View menu in your viewport, select Undo View Change or use the hotkey Alt + Z.

Choose an object in the Outliner, move your cursor into the viewport and press f to frame the selection.

"I can see the flickering of the character's skin through clothes or hair!"

Nothing is wrong with your rig; this is a bug in the default settings of Maya cameras.

To fix it, select the camera, go to the Attribute Editor, camera Shape tab.

Set the Near Clipping Plane to 1.0 or higher.

"I messed up the workspace. I reset it, but it did not fix everything."

Close Maya. Go to C:Documents/maya/2026/prefs, select the workspaces folder, and delete it. Restart Maya and it will create a new default workspaces folder.

"My IK control moves when the body moves."

Check if the IK controls are set to world or body spaces. Change the controls to world space to keep them stuck in place.

"My IK feet are moving through the floor."

When your IK foot is standing on the floor you can't use rotate. You must use the special built in controls: heel roll, toe roll, pivot, etc., to keep the foot moving relative to the IK control to create the illusion that the foot is standing on solid ground. You can rotate the foot when it is in the air.

"My IK feet are slipping and I can't fix them by putting lots of keys in."

Do not put animation on the master control. Move the character forward with the root/COG and the IK feet. Any motion on the master control will cause the entire rig to move including the IK feet.

"My character's feet/ legs are drifting out of the IK controls during playback. When I select the IK control, the rig snaps back to normal. There's no animation on the mesh and everything looks right, but it keeps doing it."

Maya is having an issue evaluating the IK foot setup or possibly constraints in the rig. Go to Preferences > Settings > Animation > Evaluation, change the Evaluation Mode from Parallel to DG.

You can also try Serial evaluation.

To access deeper Evaluation settings, go to Windows > General Editors > Evaluation Toolkit, and look at 01) Modes and 04) Custom Evaluators.

"My recovered crash scene is crashing too!"

When you open a recovered scene, the first thing it does is execute the last command. If that is what caused the crash originally, then you will most likely be caught in a loop. Unfortunately, you should go back to the last good working copy of the file. Routinely saving named versions of your shot will hopefully keep you from losing too much work.

"I selected the rig and tried to scale it, but it broke/ exploded."

Do not select the controls and scale. Each control will scale at a different rate. A good rig will have locked scale controls or a custom scale channel.

To scale the character, go to the master control and look for a global scaling option; the names can vary. It will make sure the rig scales uniformly and nothing breaks. You can scale up without issue; but if you make the rig too small, it could interfere with some distance-based rig controls.

"My screen is glitchy/ there's weird artifacts/ the screen is slow to update."

First signs Maya may be about to crash. Stop. Save your work. This could be a Maya issue, or it could be a graphics card/ hardware issue. I recommend shutting Maya and restarting the computer to see if it clears it up.

"There is something wrong with my playblast, I re-made it but it keeps happening."

There is a bug; if you make a playblast movie that gets corrupted, you need to delete it. If you keep rewriting over the same corrupted file, you will keep having issues. Make a completely new file.

"Parts of the rig are not casting shadows."

Select the geometry and go to the Attribute Editor, second tab. Go down to Render Stats and make sure Casts Shadows and Receive Shadows are checked.

"The shadows in the playblast are flickering."

Make the light a Spot Light, make sure the Cone Angle is less than 150°, change shadows to Depth Map, and increase Resolution and Filter.

"I'm on a Mac, I do not have the 'Home' or 'Insert' keys!"

On a Mac, you can hold down the d key to toggle into the mode that hold and insert activate.

Mac Option key = Alt key

"I'm working on a Mac and the teacher is using a PC and sometimes my files do not open?"

Go to Finder > Settings, click Advanced. Select Show all file names extension.

COMMON PROBLEMS

"I referenced a rig into a new scene and it's moving, but I can't delete the animation."

This is a situation where you need to open the rig file. Find the animation keys, delete them, and save the file without changing the name. Somehow there is animation on the master rig file and it will show up in any scene the rig is referenced into until it is removed.

"I did a constraint, but there's no Blend Parent option."

You must have one key on the constrained object in order for the Blend Parent channel to appear.

"I'm trying to constrain one part of the rig to another part of the rig, but it keeps giving me an error."

General rule: do not try to constrain two rig controls because you do not know what kind of constraints or connections already exist within the rig.

Instead, throw a locator into the relationship so that you are not directly constraining rig controls together.

"I can only playblast as .avi; how do I make a h264 video like I see online?"

You must install Quicktime to playblast from Maya. Close Maya and search for "Quicktime 7 Download". Install and restart Maya and .mov with h264 encoding should be an option when playblasting now.

"My background is black."

Hit Alt + B. You have a few choices when choosing a background color.
For this book, we like the gradient!

"My animation is playing too slow or too fast."

Right-click the Time Slider and check that Playback Speed is set to 'Real-time (24 fps)'. If caching is causing issues, turn off Cache Playback in Preferences > Animation.

"My animation is choppy even though I'm at real-time playback."

Disable Cache Playback, restart Maya, and try setting Viewport 2.0 to "Simple Shading" to improve performance.

"I deleted a keyframe, but the control still moves."

Check the Channel Box for any constraints or expressions driving the motion.

"I used the Euler Filter, but my rotations are still flipping."

Break up the animation on gimbal-prone axes (usually Y or X) by offsetting the keys on these channels slightly, and run the Euler Filter again.

"I can't see the rig's controls."

Make sure the Show menu > NURBS Curves is enabled.

"I keep selecting the geometry instead of the controls."

Use the Pick Mask (Top Menu Bar) to enable only NURBS Curves.

"The manipulator on this control is facing a weird direction."

Hold W + Left Click and set Move Axis to World.

"My limbs are drifting around slightly when the body moves."

Make sure you have fully set the IK switch to 1, and if it's keyed, there might be a smooth tangent on it making the value overshoot or undershoot the value of 1.

"My Time Slider is gone!"

You probably were maximizing or minimizing a window with Spacebar, and you accidentally held the key too long, dragging your mouse in the process and hiding it using the Hot Box. Hold Space, LMB click to the right of the Hot Box, and drag down.

"My Channel Box disappeared."

Press Ctrl + A to toggle between the Attribute Editor and Channel Box. Or, go to Display > UI Elements > Channel Box/Layer Editor.

"My Tool Settings window won't appear."

Double-clicking most tools in the Tool Box opens the Tool Settings window.

"I cannot dock a menu after tearing it off."

You are probably fighting Windows' window grouping functionality. Try reducing the Maya application window size so that it is not maximized, and try again.

"My Outliner is full of weird extra nodes."

Go to Outliner > Display > DAG Objects Only to hide non-transform nodes.

"I'm always selecting joints, even if I can't see them."

Joints have the highest selection priority, even through geometry. Animators rarely need to mess with a rig, so we recommend just always having Joints turned off in your Selection Mask.

"Maya crashes every time I open a specific file."

Start a new empty scene, then go to File > Import, instead of opening directly. It could be a hidden node with issues.

"Why is my character's geometry see-through?"

You are in wireframe mode! Press 5 to return to normal shading.

12 LAYERS

Animation layers are one of Maya's most powerful, yet often misunderstood tools. They allow animators to non-destructively adjust motion, test variations, and refine performances without ruining previous work. When used properly, animation layers provide the flexibility to iterate quickly and make adjustments that would otherwise require reanimating large portions of a shot. However, novice animators often misuse layers, either stacking too many or failing to manage blending properly. In this chapter, we'll demystify animation layers, showing when and how to use them efficiently to enhance your workflow, not complicate it.

WHAT ARE ANIMATION LAYERS?

Animation layers in Maya allow animators to modify animation non-destructively, meaning you can add, refine, or adjust motion without altering the base animation. They function similarly to layers in any other digital art paradigm; each layer adds, overrides, or blends into the animation beneath it.

This makes them one of the most powerful tools in an animator's workflow, allowing for polish, iteration, and alternative takes without committing to permanent changes.

HOW ANIMATION LAYERS WORK

At its core, an animation layer holds keyframes that are applied on top of existing animation. Maya blends the motion of the layers based on the layer type and weight.

Animation layers can be found in the Animation Layer Editor, accessible by going to Windows > Animation Editors > Animation Layer Editor, or by clicking the Animation Layer icon in the Channel Box (bottom-right corner of Maya's UI).

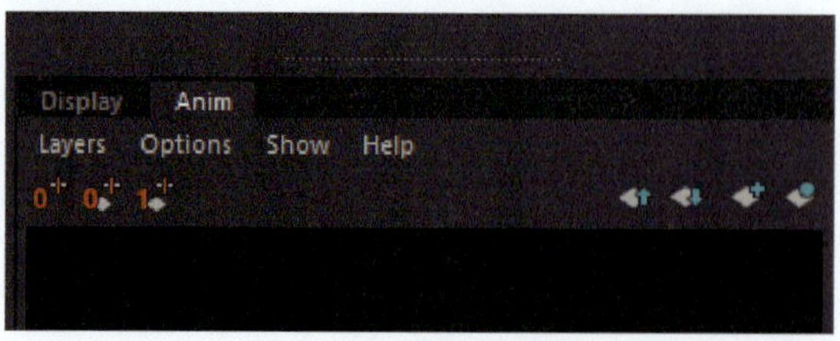

The Animation Layers Editor sits below the Channel Box on the right. Typically, you'll have only a few layers in a scene maximum, so there's no need for more room than this.

There are three types of animation layers:

1. **Base Layer:** This is your original animation. It exists by default and cannot be deleted.
2. **Additive Layers:** These apply additional motion on top of the Base Layer (e.g., adding secondary motion like head tilts or breathing).
3. **Override Layers:** These replace the Base Layer's movement entirely (e.g., trying a completely different version of an animation).

Each layer has a weight attribute (0 to 1), which controls how much influence it has. By keying this weight, you can fade animation layers in and out over time.

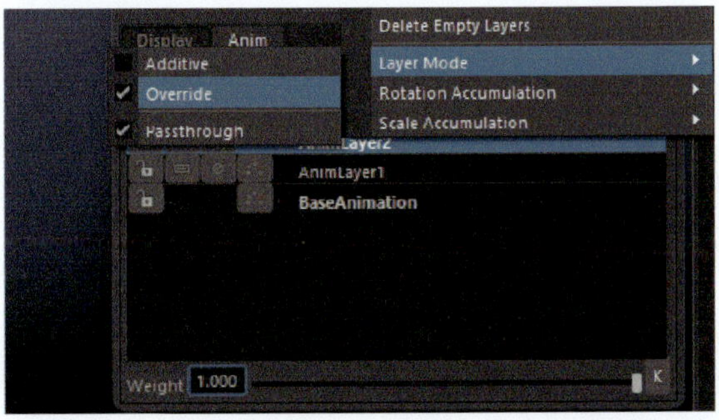

The Layer Modes, accessible by RMB clicking and hovering on Layer Mode, are useful for different effects of your animation layers.

The Base Layer is created automatically when a new Layer is made. All of the animation you create before creating the first Animation Layer will go into the BaseAnimation Layer.

By default, Layers are set to Additive Mode, with Passthrough enabled. This means all the layers additively combine with the ones below and then finally of course with the Base Layer.

Override means that any keys and curves on the objects in the layer will override the layers below. The "Passthrough" option changes whether or not Override layers animation stacks. With Passthrough off, the Override layer only affects the Base Layer.

12 LAYERS

These three buttons are used to affect the weight of the selected layer. From left to right, these buttons zero the weight, zero the weight and key the weight attribute, and set the layer weight to 1 and key the weight attribute, respectively.

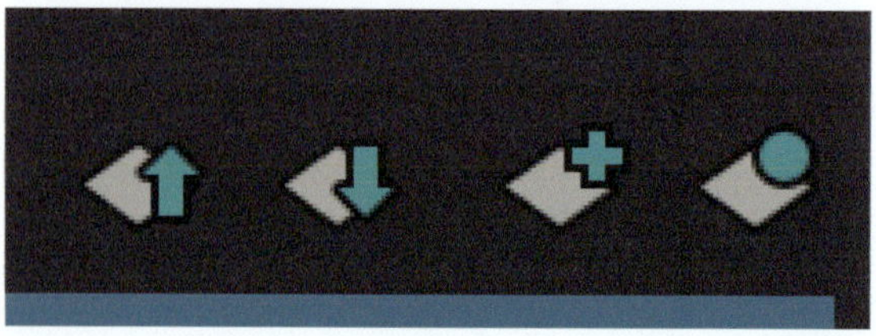

These four buttons are used to control and create layers. The two on the left move layers up and down, respectively. The third button creates a new empty Animation Layer. Finally, the last button creates a layer that contains selected objects.

CHEAT

It is by far most common to use the "Create Layer from Selected" button (far right) to create a new Animation Layer.

WHY USE LAYERS?

Layers serve many purposes, and when you progress as an animator, these use cases will start to jump out at you. It's best to learn to incorporate layers early in your study of Maya. The reason is that undoing and redoing animation that was messed up while editing is a big waste of time. If you can avoid messing up your animation altogether by using layers to make edits, the time savings are extreme.

The single most powerful use case for layers is by far the ability to adjust the scene non-destructively. Animation layers are also useful for:

- **Adding polish without affecting the base animation.** You can add subtle refinements without risking changing work you are happy with.
- **Testing alternative ideas.** Layers allow you to try out different timings or expressions without erasing previous work.
- **Blending animations smoothly.** Keying the layer weights allows you to transition between different motions.

- **Adding fine-tuned control of the influence of a motion on the scene.** For example, it is easy to adjust overlap on the spine of a character riding a horse in the Graph Editor, but even easier to adjust the overall size of the motion if it's on an Animation Layer.

However, overusing animation layers can lead to messy, unpredictable results. We'll cover when (and when not) to use them.

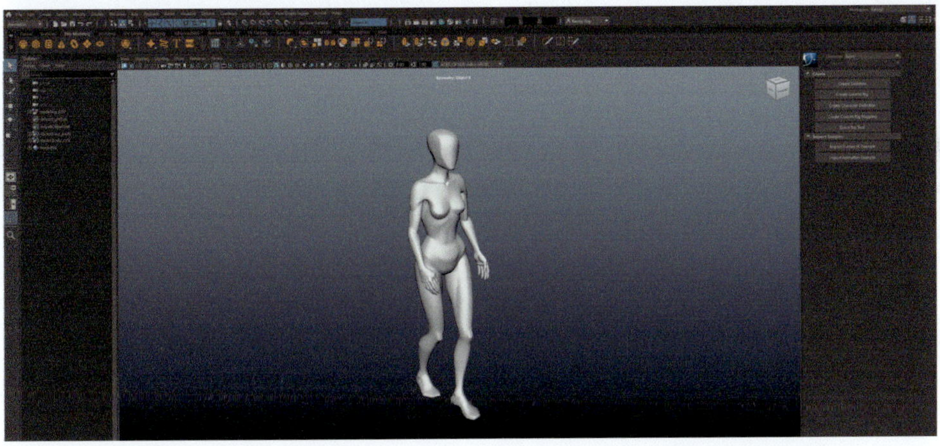

Open Layered_Walk_Start.ma. This rough animation has the trunk and legs moving in treadmill in place.

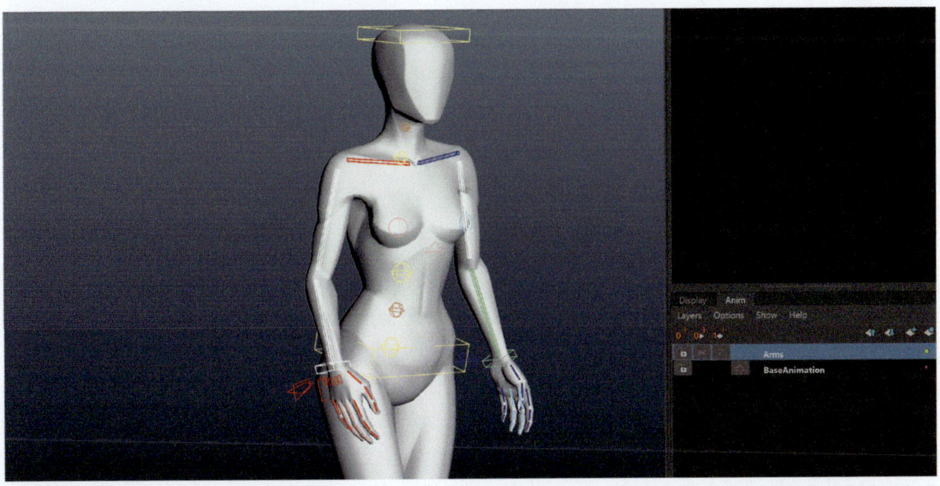

Select the arm controllers, and in the Animation Layers Editor (under the Channel Box), click the far right button to "Create Layer from Selected". The new Animation Layer appears.

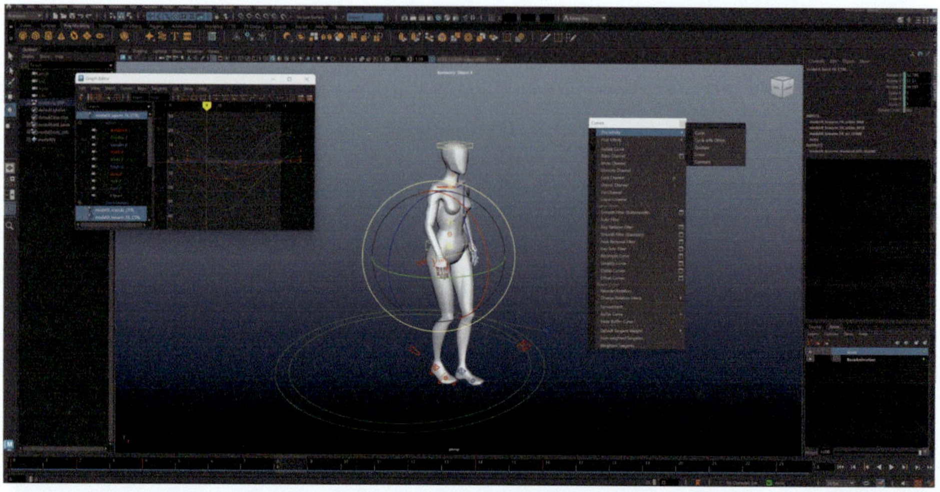

Create the swinging animation on the arms how you see fit. You will notice when you open Layer_Walk_Arms.ma that we placed sparse keys, and we used the Post-Infinity Curve type of Cycle to make it easy to offset the overlap on the elbow and wrist.

If at any time you want to add more objects to an animation layer, it is as easy as selecting them, right-clicking on the layer, and clicking Add Selected Objects. Do this with the clavicles, and add their movement yourself.

WATCH OUT!

If there are any keys on an attribute in the BaseAnimation Layer, keys on layers above may combine unexpectedly. When first starting, begin experimenting with layers with controls that have no animation on them. You'll learn to work with additive animation as you go.

LAYERING STRATEGIES

Animation layers in Maya allow you to refine movement without permanently altering the base animation. However, poor blending or excessive layering can lead to messy results. Understanding how layers interact ensures this powerful tool does not end up costing you time.

Maya calculates layers from the bottom up; the BaseAnimation is always evaluated first. Additive layers build upon existing motion, making them ideal for refining secondary movement like breathing or overlap. Override layers, on the other hand, replace animation on below layers entirely. This is quite useful for testing alternate versions of a shot.

When using layers, animators will separate whole parts of an animation (legs layer, spine layer, for example) when planning a scene, and only if it makes sense. A character delivering a line on horseback is a clear instance of when it would be wise to create the base animation of the body doing the dialogue delivery, and then add a layer of just the physicality of the bumpy horse ride on top of it. It is not nearly as common to animate segments of time and blend using the weight attributes, like blending mocap clips. If animators do use the weight attributes, it's much more common that we are dialing-in the size of a motion using layers, or are gradually introducing or fading out a layer that has some secondary or polish on it using the weight attributes.

Managing animation layers efficiently requires a structured approach. Too many layers can complicate an animation rather than improve it. Keeping separate layers for breathing, secondary, or overlap allows for easy adjustments without affecting the entire performance.

To illustrate this, let's continue to refine this layered walk cycle.

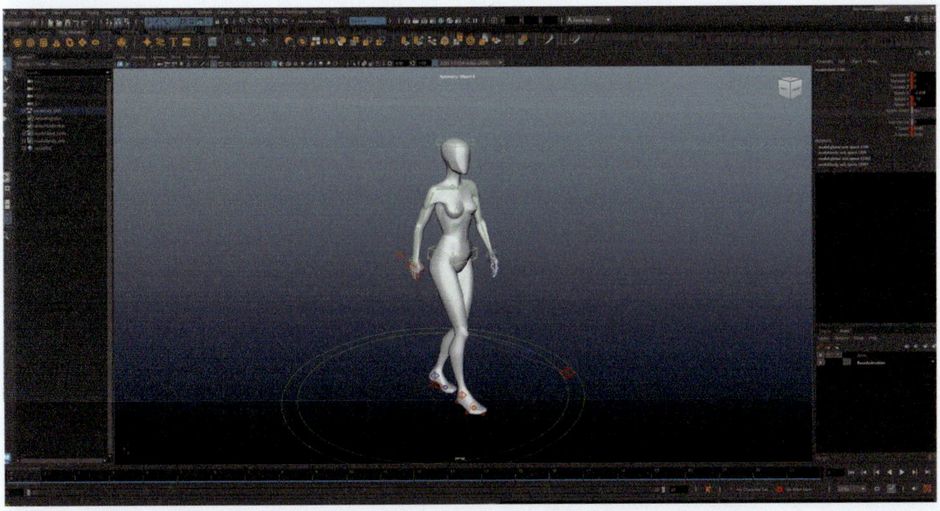

Open Layered_Walk_Spine.ma. We would like to now add some overlap to the spine, but as you can see, the spine is twisting with the arms and hips already.

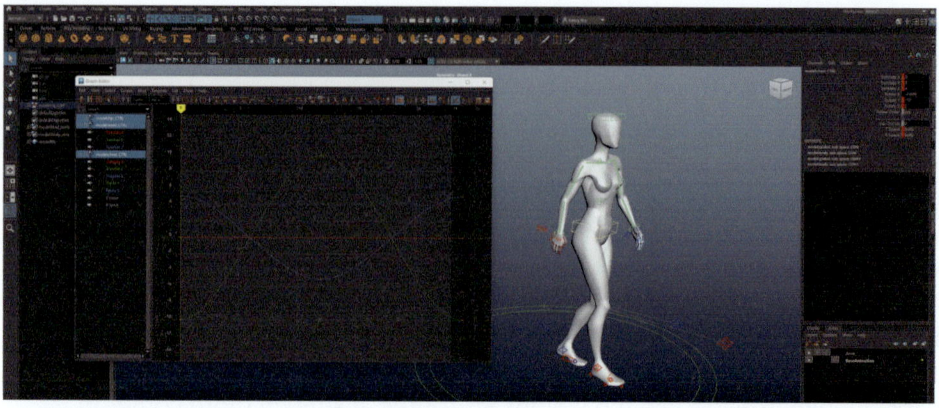

Open the Graph Editor, and in the Persp panel, select the three circular controllers that make up the spine. Notice how there is already animation on the spine, in the BaseAnimation Layer. This can lead to issues, so we'll "move" these curves to a new layer by extracting the motion.

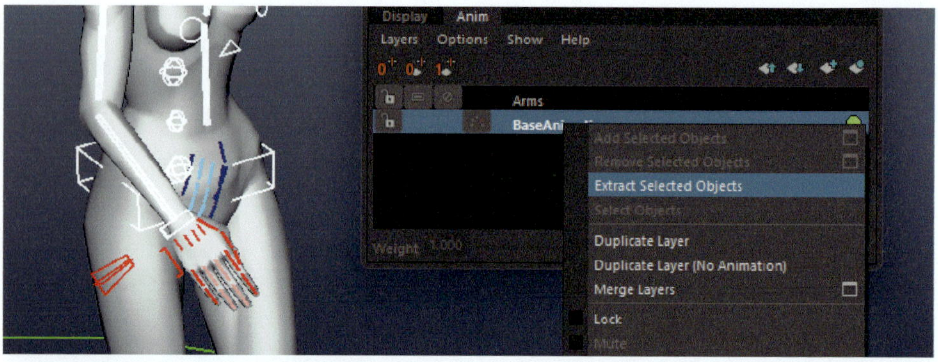

With the spine controls still selected, right click on the BaseAnimation Layer and choose Extract Selected Objects. Rename the new Layer "Spine." There is some Rotate Y and Z on the spine controls, but Rotate X (the "overlap" channel) is empty, ready for some work.

You are now free to experiment with the overlap in the spine with total confidence that nothing is going to be affected in other layers, or the base Layer. So, without fear of failure, go wild!

Remember to always go overboard when you are keying. Be fearless. When working with layers, using the weight attribute to fine-tune the size of an animation is by far the simplest method of honing the size of an animation in Maya. There's no danger of going too far when you have a slider to tone it down!

WHEN TO USE ANIMATION LAYERS (AND WHEN NOT TO)

Animation layers can speed up the workflow by allowing non-destructive refinements, but they are not a substitute for fixing poor animation. Knowing when to use layers and when to avoid them is as important as what you put into the layer itself.

Animation layers work best for small refinements rather than major structural changes. They are useful for adjusting timing, adding secondary motion, or testing subtle variations without modifying the base animation. For example, they are ideal for adding polish and texture, and secondary action like breathing without disturbing the original movement. They are also useful when you want to experiment with alternative takes, while keeping the ability to revert to the original.

However, using animation layers to fix broken animation is a mistake. If the base animation has fundamental issues, adding layers will only mask the problem rather than solve it. Similarly, stacking too many layers can lead to unintended motion buildup, making the final animation difficult or impossible to control.

To demonstrate an appropriate use of animation layers, let's add a look around to the walk cycle we've been working on.

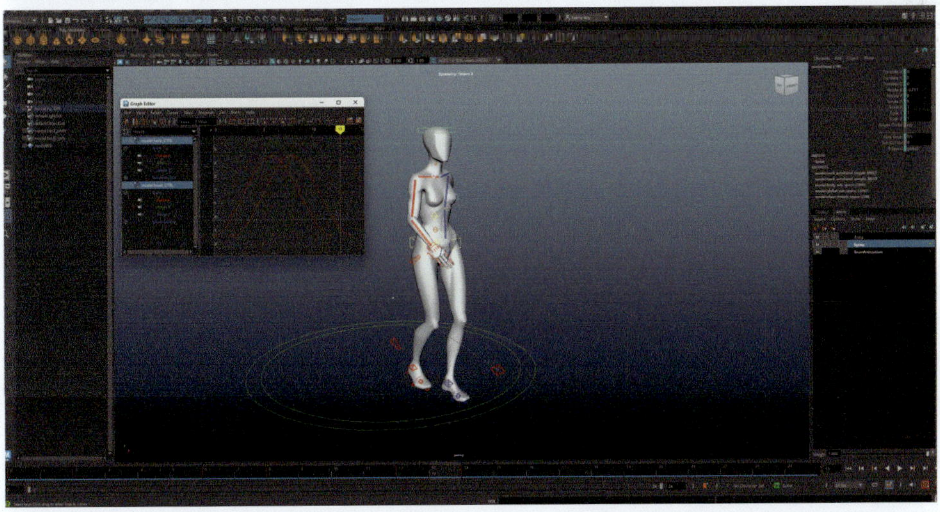

Open Layered_Walk_Look.ma. We're continuing on from the layered walk mentioned before, but we've gone ahead and added a little bit of overlap in the neck and head, too.

When using layers, it can be tempting to extract animation to a new layer every time you feel like isolating any motion. In this case, that would be a mistake; we're going to be adding a head turn to the walk as the character moves forward. The intention is to have the character seem like they are scanning ahead, looking for something. In this case, it is a better idea to let the purely physical motion of overlap on the neck and head remain on the Spine layer, so that if you change your mind about the head turn, or it needs a lot of finely detailed keys, the smoothness of the overlap remains.

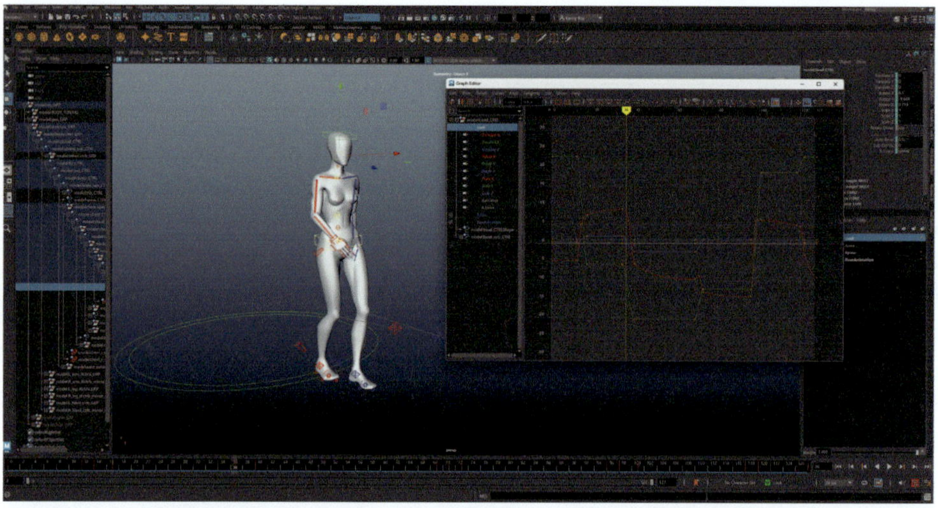

We've added a cycle on top of the walk, of the mannequin robotically looking around as it walks, almost as if it is scanning the room. Creepy! But more importantly, this Layer can be adjusted to your taste, and the overlap on the neck and head remains untouched.

This performance is coming together well, and how nicely editable it remains!

WATCH OUT!

When working with layers, pay attention to which layer is active! This is shown by the green dot next to it in the Layer Editor, or in the Graph Editor where the Layer's channels are expanded by default. Layers are a powerful time-saving tool, but NOT if you spend hours working on the wrong layer!

PRACTICAL APPLICATIONS IN PRODUCTION

Animation layers are a valuable tool in a production workflow, helping animators iterate quickly and make refinements without disrupting the base performance. Layers allow for non-destructive adjustments, which is particularly useful for polishing motion, and making last-minute changes per supervisor notes.

One of the most common uses for animation layers in production is adding subtle adjustments well after the primary animation is complete. For example, you may receive notes to add more impact on a character's landing, or to make a head turn feel more natural. Instead of redoing key poses, you can create an additive layer and apply the necessary refinements without altering the original motion. Animation layers are also frequently used in facial animation, to add micro-expressions, eye darts, or general texture while keeping the core performance intact.

Another practical application is separating different body parts into layers for better control. This is very common with game animation. A game character's run cycle might have the legs and trunk on the base layer and then create separate layers for arm swings, head motion, and breathing. Inside the game engine, these are combined for procedural effects, accounting for things like player look direction or other controller inputs. With broad motions like jumps, all of the world-space body movement is done on a layer to make it easy to export without, then reapply parametrically in-engine.

To round out our practice of layering, let's key the weight of the "Look" Layer for the exact effect we want.

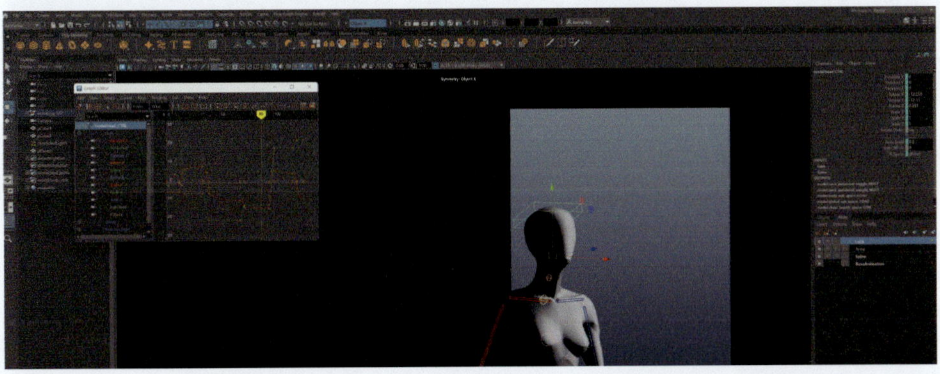

Open Layered_Walk_Weight.ma. This scene has been set up with a camera, and the character is no longer on a treadmill (the master control Translate Z channel has been muted).

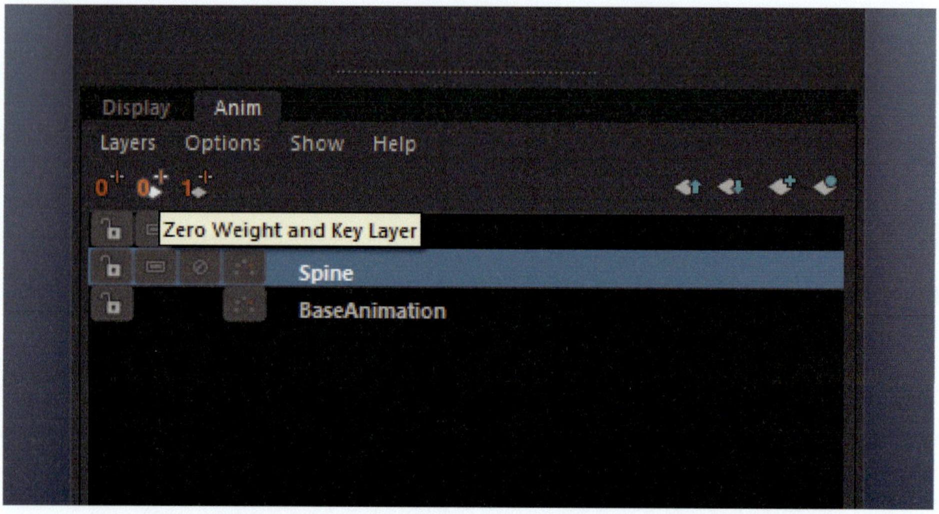

Somewhere between frames 30 and 40 (you get to play around with it!), click on the Look Layer, and click Zero Weight and Key Layer.

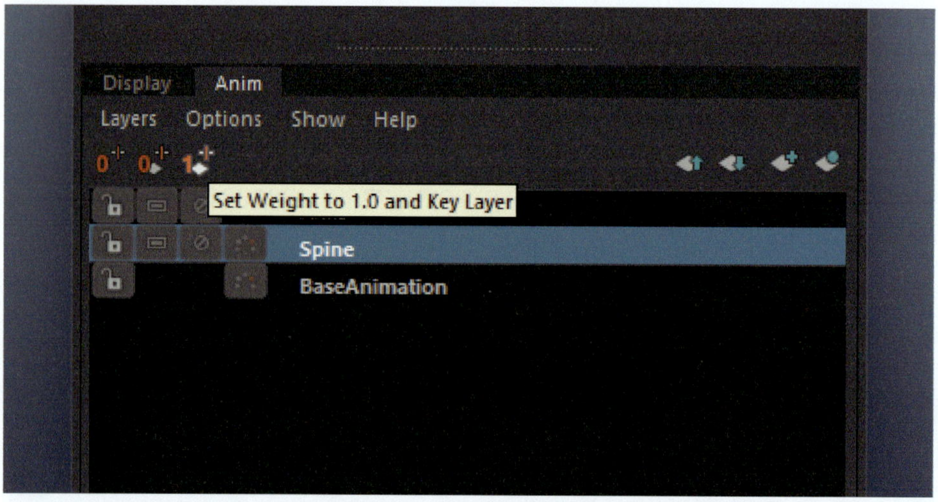

And around frames 50–55, Key the weight on.

Now the impression is given that this character emerges from a dark interior, and when met with the outside, begins to scan around for whatever, or whomever, it is pursuing. A simple, subtle performance was possible to craft merely by animating weight on animation layers!

KEY TAKEAWAYS

- Animation layers allow non-destructive adjustments to motion.
- Layers can be Additive (adjusting or enhancing movement) or Override (replacing movement).
- Layer weights can be keyed to fade motion in and out, and to fine-tune the size of animation.
- They are great for polish, experimenting, and secondary animation, but should not be overused!

Animation layers are a cheat, but like all cheats, they only work if you know how to control them. When used well, they let you iterate faster, tweak secondary motion efficiently, and refine performances without destroying your base animation.

Animation layers are not a crutch for bad animation. If your base layer isn't solid, no amount of layering will save it. But if used correctly, layers can be a powerful and time-saving tool in an animator's workflow.

13 POLISH

POLISH

Polishing animation is a skill of its own. The reason many animators have trouble polishing animation, especially in the beginning, is because typically, the workflow for beginning an animation is well-known and well-practiced. Gathering reference video can be fun and easy. Thumbnailing poses can be as well. However, coming to the end of an animation's lifecycle and putting the final touches on the work is a rare moment for beginners. Polishing is almost a privilege that only comes about when the first 95% of an animation has been done, and done correctly. In other words, we are good at what we practice, and novice animators have much more practice starting shots than finishing them.

The reality is film, visual effects (VFX), and game studios are only hiring animators who can finish their work. It is why, in general, we recommend that throughout the early part of your learning and career, you tackle small animations and really put in the work to finish them, rather than starting large animations but never quite getting enough practice polishing your work.

For this reason, in this chapter we will zero-in on the aspects of a shot that should be left for last, in a few broad categories. These categories are:

- Untwinning
- Secondary
- Smoothing
- Micro-adjustments
- Roughing/Texture

This list is ordered in the recommended workflow for minimal redoing of work, and maximum freedom for the animator.

UNTWINNING

Twinning, when both sides of a character move symmetrically, makes animation feel stiff and unnatural. To combat this, we go through a shot and ensure asymmetry in posing, timing, and spacing, making sure the character feels alive. Untwinning also applies to facial expressions and hand gestures, breaking mirrored movements to create a more organic and engaging performance.

This animation is extremely 'twinned'. There is very little interest in this pose because the entire body is nearly symmetrical.

While examining a shot, the first factor we look at during the polish phases is how interesting our poses ended up in motion. Quite often, our work will get a bit muddied as the shot progresses; this is a natural side-effect of working for a long time on a scene. What began as a scene chock-full of interesting poses ends up being somewhat watered-down as you near polish. It's an animator's duty to make sure the work continues to maintain the dynamic quality you determined in your reference, thumbnails, and blocking.

If there is twinning in the body, a good strategy to adjust the animation is to reimagine the pose as starting off-balance, and accounting for the shift in center-of-gravity throughout the motion. This may mean some sweeping changes to the work! Remember, what sets professional animators apart from beginners is not necessarily the ability to create perfect work the first time, but the ability to quickly iterate and edit work. Many times, students feel that an entire shot needs to be restarted because there are errant issues. This instinct is totally antithetical to the mindset pro animators are expected to bring to the workplace. To put it simply, being flexible, agile, and ready to roll with the punches is the type of animator you want to be.

Let's take a crack at untwinning this motion.

Much better! Just a different balance of weight, and suddenly the character feels like they are dynamic and alive!

The extent to which one must go back and re-block animation depends on just how symmetrical the posing and staging has become. This amount will lessen over time, as you learn to account for twinning in your blocking.

CHEAT

If you absolutely cannot re-block your shot, or a deadline is preventing you from putting more work into adjusting the posing, sometimes adjusting the camera so that it does not emphasize the twinning is a quick fix (camera framing that is straight-on is the worst in terms of emphasizing twinned poses!).

SECONDARY

Secondary motion (as opposed to the principle of Secondary Action) refers to the little movements that happen within the body, props, clothing, and environment as a result of the primary motion. If a scene is very simple, the secondary motion can be essential in maintaining visual interest. For realistic films and games, secondary is sometimes simulated rather than hand-keyed, but it's not uncommon for there to be broad controls on things like capes, hair, and hanging clothing to give the animator control over the silhouette. In games especially, real-time physics does a lot of heavy lifting, but don't rely on it!

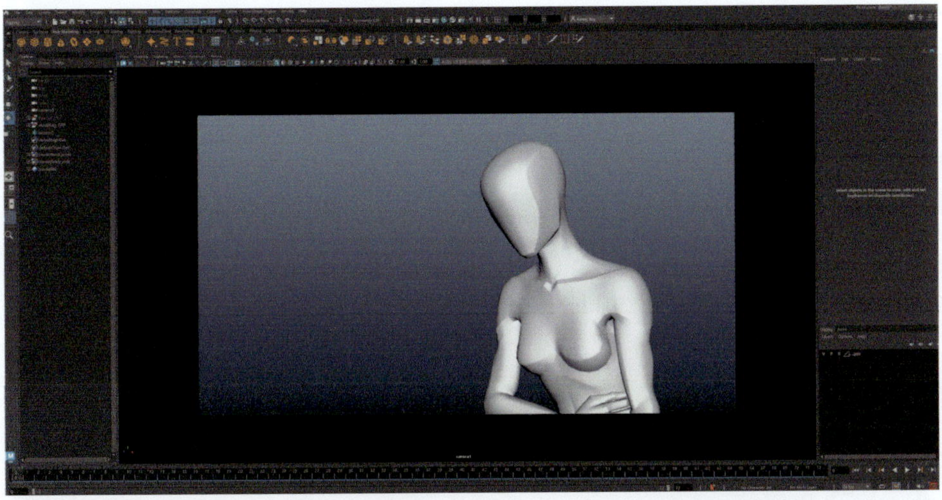

Open Breath.ma. Playing back the animation, you will see a simple scene in need of some polish. It's decent enough, but it's lacking interesting contrast. Secondary motion can give us that.

In this short scene, a wounded warrior takes a deep breath. When animating a shot such as this, it is crucial to understand the balance between slow, broad movement, and quick staccato motion. In other words, you are not done animating this until all of the elements work together to emphasize the main motion. This is an opportunity for some secondary motion.

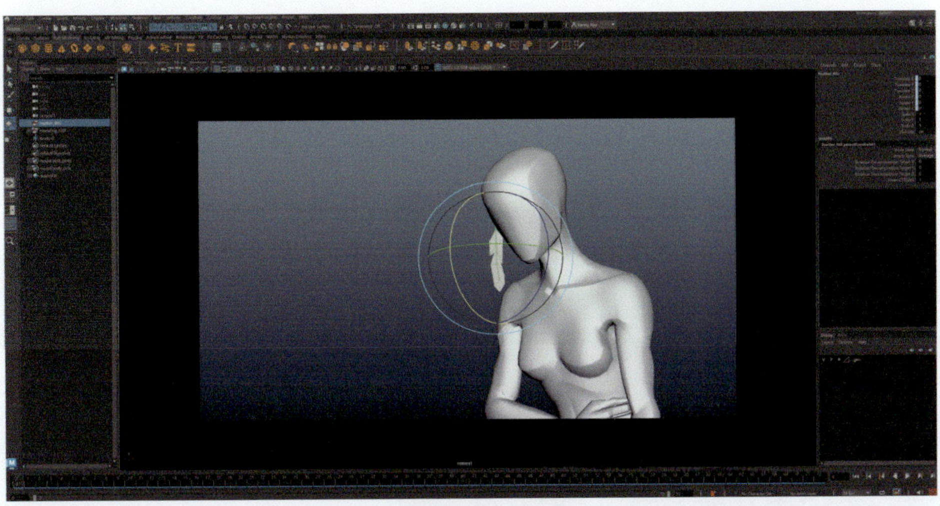

Select the object in the Outliner called "Feather_RIG", and press Shift+S to unhide it. Play the animation, and notice how it is subtly moving.

This new addition, though small, adds a huge amount of interest and dynamic to the shot. As with all animation, this will need to receive further polish to make it really shine. That said, look just how much the shot has changed with this addition of some secondary motion. Can you now imagine just how much more work is left to do after a shot enters the polish phase? This simple shot is a great example of the intricacies of secondary.

Spend a little time playing with the feather animation and see if you can come up with something you like even more.

CHEAT

You may have noticed there is a proper rig on the feather; we used an aim constraint to keep the feather's parent object facing the floor, so that all of the overlapping action could be achieved with VERY few keys as opposed to counter-animating it against the motion of the body/head!

SMOOTHING

Once the mechanics of the shot are in place, smoothing ensures fluidity and clarity. This step involves refining arcs, eliminating pops, and cleaning up transitions between poses. Using the Graph Editor, we check keys and tangents to prevent unwanted stuttering or erratic motion while maintaining the right level of texture and variation in timing. Smoothing should enhance the animation without making it feel overly soft or floaty.

There are telltale signs, artifacts if you will, of the keyframing process that can just be smoothed indiscriminately. Below is an example.

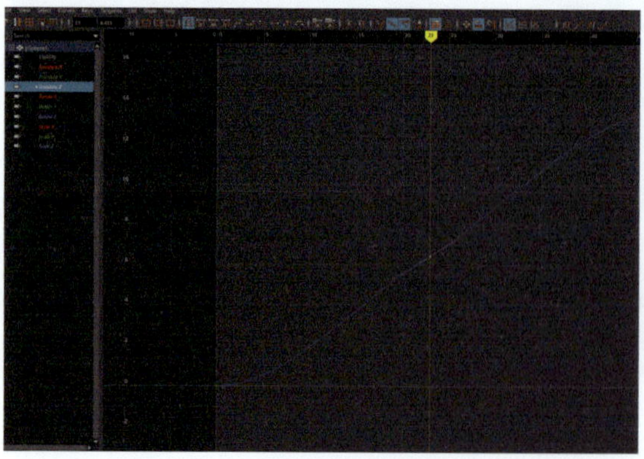

Look at this curve.
Notice anything strange?

Depending on your default interpolation, your workflow, and a bevy of other factors, setting a key in the midst of a motion can result in Maya misinterpreting the intention. This was obviously meant to be a smooth motion, and perhaps auto-keying inserted this errant key.

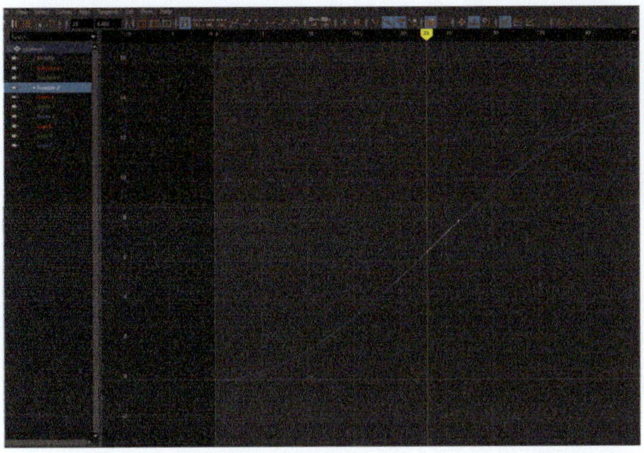

Much better, we've smoothed the key and restored the original intent. It is fairly safe to go through your animation and correct these types of bumps in the animation, even without knowing exactly what the curve represents.

This workflow of smoothing in the Graph Editor as part of your polish pass is a great workflow for discovering and correcting one of Maya's other annoying artifacts; unsnapped keys when working in the Time Slider.

Smoothing animation indiscriminately in the Graph Editor is a solid professional workflow. It may seem hazardous, but it is 10x faster than trying to find these pops by playblasting or framing through your scene. Remember, we're going to add back all of the GOOD bumps when we "Rough" it again.

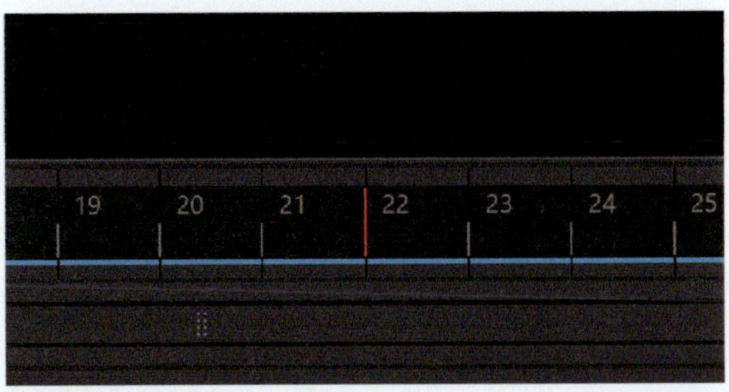

Look at this innocent little keyframe, sitting there so nicely. What is lurking beneath?

Just when you thought it was safe to polish without the Graph Editor! The Time Slider doesn't always display keys that are close together, so the Graph Editor is where you'll have to hunt down these problems.

As with the weird bumpy tangent, these smashed-together keys are a common occurrence in scenes that have a lot of work inside. It's just par for the course when there are long scenes, complex motion, and keys all over the place.

CHEAT

It is highly recommended to delete the key in the Graph Editor to fix this issue, rather than rely on Snap. Why? Well, snapping was probably how we got into this mess in the first place!

MICRO-ADJUSTMENTS

Micro-adjustments are the final refinements that push an animation from good to great. These are the tiny, often imperceptible tweaks that enhance realism, appeal, and clarity without fundamentally changing the shot.
At this stage, we fine-tune micro-poses, contact, and timing at a nearly frame-by-frame level; adjusting a fingertip that pops, softening an eye dart that feels too snappy, or adding a frame of drag to improve follow-through. Microaadjustments are not about big changes, but about subtlety; these are small refinements that make the movement feel polished, intentional, and effortless.

What kinds of adjustments should animators be thinking about?

- **Breath:** Add microscopic hitches in the chest, neck, and head during audible breaths to reinforce realism and layered body mechanics in dialogue shots.
- **Saccadic Eye Movement:** Instead of holding a gaze perfectly still, introduce tiny, natural eye micro-movements (called saccades) to simulate real-life focus shifts and prevent a dead-eyed look.
- **Fingertip Offsets:** When a hand comes to rest on a surface or an object, let the fingers settle one at a time rather than landing in perfect sync to add organic movement.
- **Lip Compression in Speech:** During dialogue, refine the press and release of the lips on consonants like "P" and "B" to add depth and realism to mouth shapes beyond simple phonemes.
- **Break up Movement of Attached Props:** Subtly delay the movement of hair strands, loose sleeves, or dangling props to add a touch of realism without over-complicating the animation.
- **Breathing Subtleties:** Introduce tiny shoulder or clavicle shifts during emotional beats, like nervous anticipation or relief.
- **Invisible Impact Delays:** On sudden stops (like a character slamming a door), add a 1–2 frame delay on parts like wrists, sleeves, or head recoil to reinforce energy transfer.
- **Micro-squash and Stretch in the Face:** Even outside of exaggerated cartoony animation, very subtle compression and release of the cheeks, eyelids, and nose bridge can add a natural texture to facial expressions.

Each of these refinements is subtle, often imperceptible at first glance, but collectively they elevate an animation from functional to professional.

If you remember that breathing animation from earlier, that was a really good example of how adding contrasting motion to an otherwise muted performance makes it more interesting and dynamic. Above, we mention breaking up the Movement of Attached Props; this is our chance for that technique.

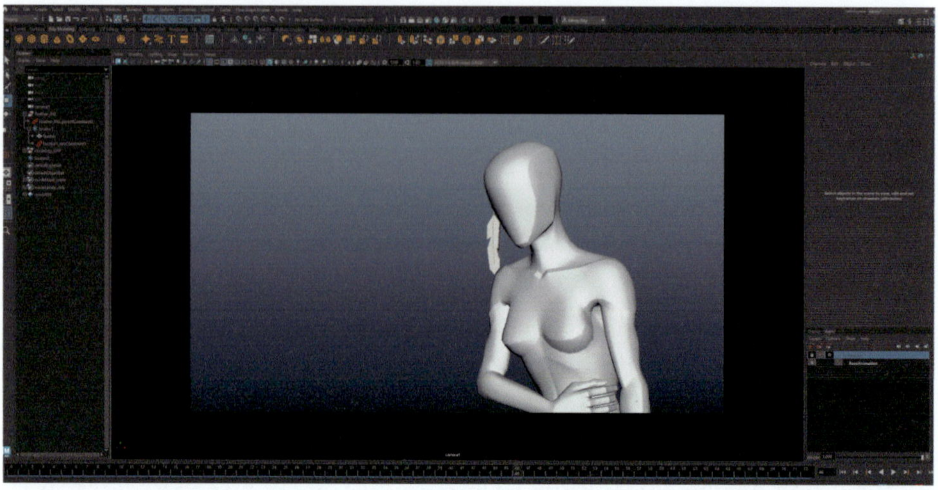

Open Breath.ma again. Watch the animation back a few times, paying close attention to how smooth the animation is.

Once you have played the animation a few times, let's take a look at the same shot with micro-adjustments added to the body on the breathing, and the feather (attached prop).

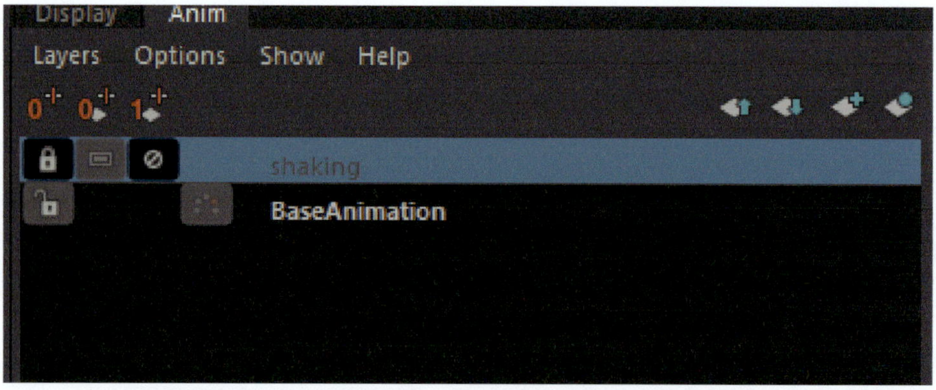

On the right side of the Maya window, find the Layer panel. Click on Anim to change to the animation layers. There is an animation layer saved into the scene, but it is muted; it's called "shaking." Unmute it by clicking the third button from the left.

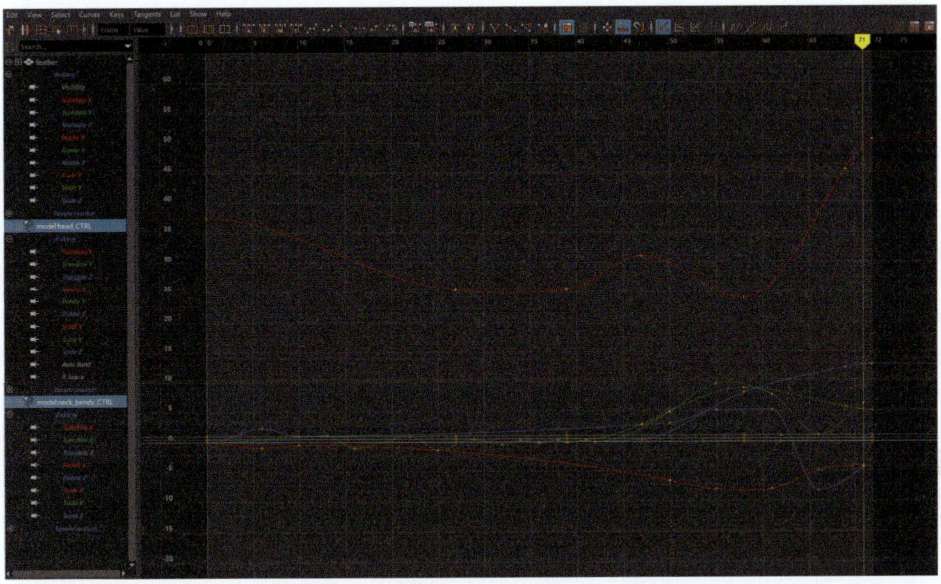

If you select the objects in the animation layer, and open the Graph Editor, you'll see there are only very tiny adjustments to the animation. The word "micro" is very fitting!

With time and practice, you can get very quick at adding these tiny adjustments to the animation.

CHEAT

We used animation layers to pepper in the final micro into this scene; this is a wonderful use of this powerful tool. It keeps the main animation clean and editable, while still giving the animator the option to use frame-by-frame straight ahead workflow to add interesting micro-movements to a shot.

13 POLISH

ROUGHING

Hey wait a minute, didn't we just smooth this animation!? Well, the final step in polishing is adding intentional texture back into the movement. A shot that is too smooth can lose its sense of realism, so we introduce controlled imperfections: micro-tuning the timing, slight offsets, or small, natural imperfections in movement. This gives the performance a more organic, believable quality and ensures it does not feel sterile or overly mechanical.

Maya has a bad habit of flattening tangents at the last keyframe, which can kill the sense of motion leading into the next shot. Even if the next shot is someone else's problem, the eye can perceive the slow-in before the cut. To counter this, always adjust the last keyframe's tangents as if the motion is continuing off-screen. Even if the character technically stops moving, the subtle hint of continuation makes the transition feel more natural.

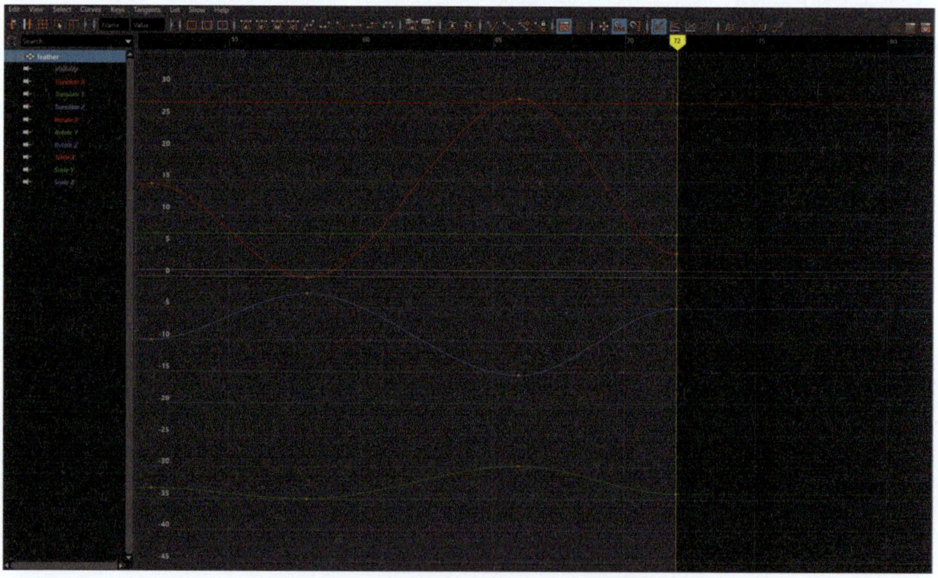

See how the default tangents all come to a dead stop on the last frame?
This is a big problem, because audiences can sense the energy dying as the shot concludes.

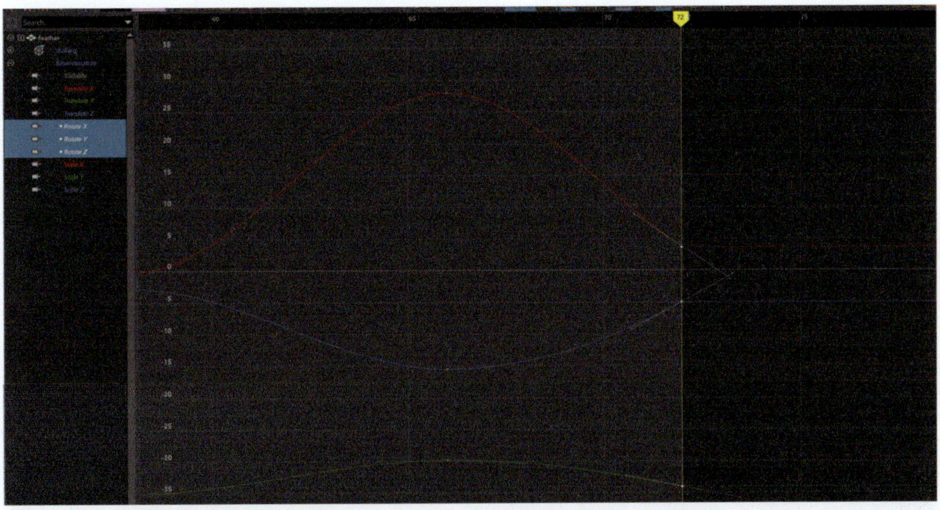

Notice how the tangents have been all adjusted to make sure the motion seems like it's continuing through the shot. It's subtle, but it all adds up.

A common problem when using Maya is leaving perfectly symmetrical curves in the Graph Editor. If your splines look too clean, so does your animation. When roughing, make sure the curves do not look like perfectly symmetrical mirrors of each other. This subtly textures the movement without adding unnecessary noise.

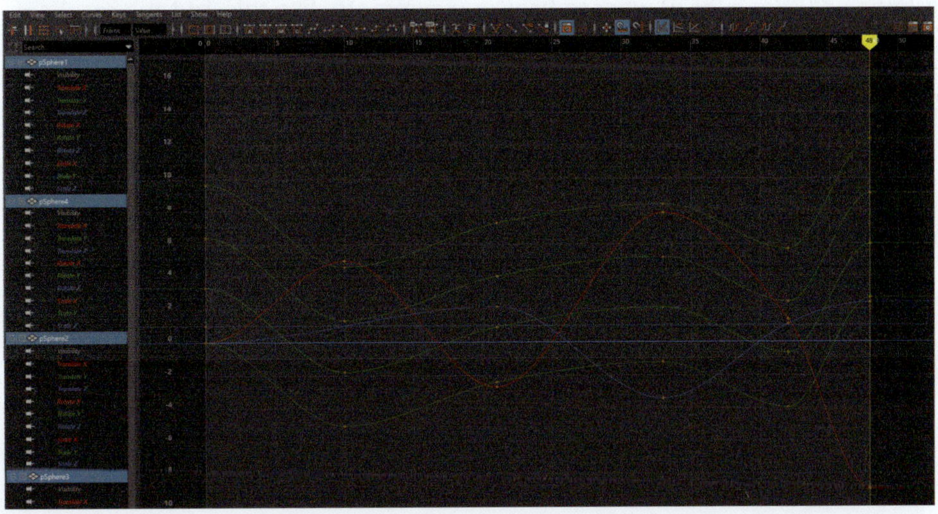

If keyframes like the above have survived to the end of your work on a shot, chances are it is the result of keying multiple controls all together at the same time and never going back and editing it.

It's not necessarily the case that this motion will always look bad, but it is also true that there is a likely problem if the entire scene's curves look like the above. In general, it is safe to subtly adjust these all during polish to remove an overly smooth and symmetrical look.

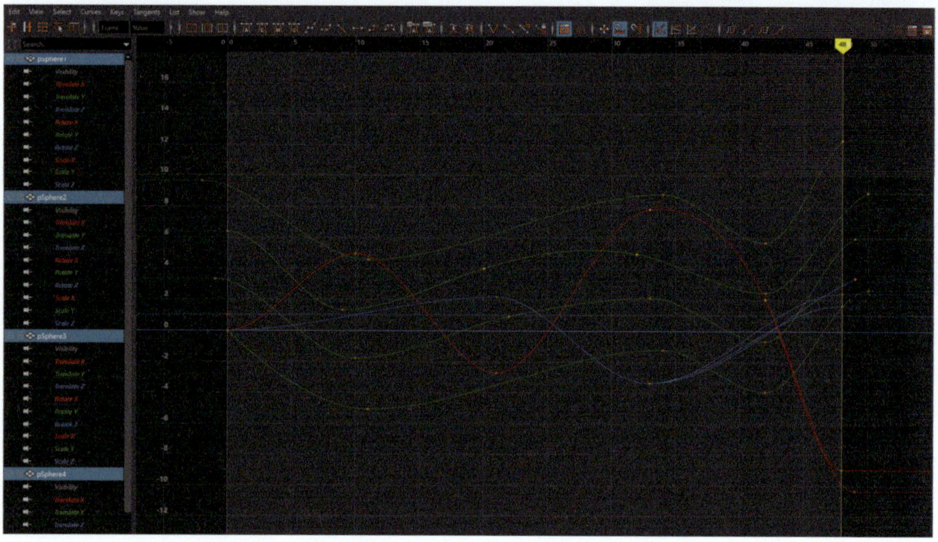

After just breaking the keys up slightly, the motion feels a lot more organic.

It does not take a lot of work to break up symmetry like this, but the results are important to polish. One might say that the effect of this kind of polish is more 'felt' than seen; audiences have great intuition, and it needs to be respected.

DON'T FORGET

If you are using the offset method of creating overlapping action (on a tail, for example), then you are guaranteed to encounter symmetrical curves in polish. As long as you remember that removing symmetrical keys is a part of your process every time, you'll be fine.

One of Maya's most underused tools for roughing is Animation Layers. Instead of manually tweaking every keyframe, add a subtle noise layer to introduce controlled imperfections. This can be useful for breath, tiny head corrections, or final looseness in secondary elements. In fact, using Animation Layers to add some jitter and roughness to the body can be done at any point in the shot and muted until you are ready for the polish phase.

Try this experiment: hold your hand in front of you and try to keep it as still as possible. Depending on how many cups of coffee you've had today, it will certainly not be perfectly still. Observe how the wrist moves, the fingers slightly twitch independently, and all the subtle, organic motion.

At the end of the day, roughing is not about making animation messy; it is about keeping it from feeling over-produced, too CG, or too predictable. Maya's tools are designed to give smooth movement, but as animators, we need to push back against the software's "perfection" to make something that feels real.

Conclusion

Animation is an art based on illusion. Despite all its quirks, crashes, and questionable default settings, Maya is the best tool to pull this illusion off. The real magic trick, though, is not just knowing which buttons to push, but how to push them efficiently. Every cheat, work-around, and optimization in this book exists to get you to the finish line faster, without sacrificing quality. Because, in the end, audiences don't care how clean your Graph Editor looks or how perfectly organized your Outliner is; they care about the performance.

The best animators are not the ones who fight the software, but the ones who bend it to their will. So go ahead, cheat the system, break the rules, and make your animation magic.

Index

A

B

C

D

E

F

G

H

I

K

L

M

O

P

R

S

T

V

W

Z

Glossary

180° Rule
Establishes clarity by keeping the camera on one side of the line, character A will always be on one side of the frame and character B on the other within the 180° range.

Accent
Parts of the dialogue that are stressed or exaggerated, parts of the dialogue that carry more emotion.

Acting Beats
Breaking down acting and actions into their smallest components. A change within a scene when mood or tone shifts.

Anatomical Posing
Animating characters with attention to realistic bone and muscle behavior to ensure believable performance.

Animation Layers
A non-destructive system that lets animators add, blend, and manage separate animation performances on top of base animation. Useful for polishing, additive motion, and complex performances.

Arcs
The visual path of motion, typically curved, followed by parts of the body. Naturalistic animation favors motion that follows arcs rather than straight lines.

Appeal
The quality of animation that makes characters and poses interesting, readable, and aesthetically pleasing. It applies to design, posing, and movement.

Anticipation — A small motion that prepares the audience for a larger action, improving clarity and enhancing the believability of the motion.

Arnold — The rendering software currently bundled with Maya.

Asymmetry — All living things are slightly asymmetrical in face and body. Perfect symmetry is unnatural except for inorganic objects like robots. For example, contrapposto is creating asymmetry by contrasting the angle of the hips, shoulders, and head.

Attribute Editor — A panel that lists all the attributes of the selected object.

Baking Animation — The process where Maya will place a key on every frame to preserve the curve shape. Sparse bake will repeat the existing keys across the frame range.

Bind Pose — The pose the character was modeled and rigged in. Everything is stiff and straight and set to default.

Blend Parent — The channel created when a constrained object is keyed. When the Blend Parent is set to 1 the constraint is on, 0 is set to off.

Blocking — The initial stage of animation where the key storytelling poses are placed, often using stepped or hold interpolation. Establishes structure and timing before refining.

Blocking Plus — An in-between stage of blocking with breakdown poses and timing refinements before transitioning to splining.

Blue Pencil a.k.a. Grease Pencil A tool that allows you to draw on the viewport (camera lens).

Body Mechanics Creating believable motion through weight and balance, conserving energy and obeying physics.

Bookends Securing a segment of animation by making sure every attribute is keyed at the start and end of the segment. This enables the segment of animation to be moved or scaled as a unit.

Breakdown Pose A pose in between two poses.

Breaking the Joints Term that describes how body parts drag behind each other. For example, slapping an arm down: bend at the elbow to drag the forearm behind and bend at the wrist to drag the hand behind the forearm.

Buffer Curve A snapshot of the current state of a curve in the Graph Editor. Used to compare curve edits and revert to a previous version if needed.

Center of Gravity (COG) Balancing the center of the mass over the support points so that the object doesn't fall over. For example, humans can stand upright by balancing their COG or pelvis over their two feet.

Channel Box A user interface (UI) element in Maya that displays keyable attributes for the selected object. Allows quick access to transform values and custom attributes.

Cliché An overused phrase, pose, reaction, antic, or acting choice that is predictable or stereotypical. Instead of avoiding cliché, start with it and then find ways to slowly make it different and unexpected.

Constraint

A relationship between two objects in which one drives certain attributes (like position, orientation, or scale) of the other. Common types include Parent, Point, Orient, Scale, and Pole Vector constraints.

Contrast

Emphasizing differences. Can be found in all aspects of animation: form, design, poses, movements, and acting. Contrast is important when crafting compelling, appealing animation.

Copied Pairs

Creating an animation hold by keying the pose and copying the key a few frames over.

Cycle

A looped animation, often used for repetitive motion such as walking, running, or flying.

Cycle with Offset

An animation pre- or post-infinity setting where curves repeat while progressively increasing or decreasing, often used in forward movement like walk cycles.

Display Layers

Layers that selected objects can be assigned to. V toggles visibility, P toggles object visibility during playback, T sets the layer objects to wireframe template and unselectable, and R sets the layer objects to referenced mode and unselectable.

Dope Sheet

An editor for managing keys and timing across multiple objects and attributes. Offers a high-level view and faster editing for timing changes than the Graph Editor.

Evaluation Mode

The way Maya evaluates the animation on the CPU and GPU for best performance. It is Parallel by default. Some older rigs need it switched to DG or Serial in the Animation preferences.

Encoding

This is the type of compression applied to the playblast to make the file size smaller but to still keep the visual quality of the movie high.

Euler Filter

A Graph Editor command that resolves rotation flipping issues (caused by gimbal lock) by adjusting Euler angles for cleaner animation curves.

Exaggeration

A principle of amplifying movement, poses, or timing to create more dynamic or expressive animation.

Extreme Pose

The extreme or most exaggerated poses during a motion.

Eyeline

The direction the character is looking, can be used to direct the audience's attention.

Favoring a Pose

Creating a breakdown pose that favors, or is closer to pose A or pose B. Used to create ease-in and ease-outs.

FK (Forward Kinematics)

A control method in which each joint is rotated individually from root down to the end of the chain. Ideal for natural, arc-based motion such as swinging arms or tails.

Flat Tangent a.k.a. Zero Slope

When the tangent handles are flat indicating the curve is neither increasing nor decreasing. A section of curve between two flat tangent handles is stopped and has no change in value.

Focal Length

The camera setting that affects perspective and depth in a shot; crucial for staging and composition.

Framing

When composing your shot, taking care to make the action clear, using angles and negative space to direct the audience's eye and tell a story.

Ghosting Editor

A visualization tool in Maya that displays the motion of an object across time as transparent outlines or snapshots.

Golden Pose

A key storytelling pose that defines the essence or emotion of a scene.

Graph Editor

Maya's primary interface for manipulating animation curves, controlling interpolation, tangents, and timing in a precise visual format.

Gimbal Lock

A situation in 3D rotation where two of the rotation axes align, causing loss of a degree of freedom and erratic behavior. Mitigated by using quaternion rotation or applying an Euler Filter.

Heads up Display (HUD)

Information displayed in the viewport camera like view axis, cube, stats, and camera name. The HUD should be hidden while playblasting.

Hierarchy

A system of organizing objects in a descending tree structure. Parents are at the top, and children 'inherit' transformations from their parent node.

IK (Inverse Kinematics)

A control method that lets the animator move the end of a joint chain, and Maya calculates the intermediate joint rotations. Ideal for planted feet or contact poses.

Infinity (Pre-/Post-)	Settings in the Graph Editor that determine how an animation curve behaves before the first keyframe and after the last. Options include Constant, Cycle, Cycle with Offset, Linear, and Oscillate.
Inner Monologue	a.k.a. What is the character thinking? Vital to know, since it will dictate all your animation decisions. The character's attitude will motivate the energy of their actions.
Insert Key Tool	A tool used to add keyframes across multiple selected channels or objects at the current frame.
Interpolation	The method Maya uses to calculate values between keyframes. Includes modes like Spline (smooth), Linear (constant speed), and Step (no interpolation).
Keyframe	A frame where a specific value is set for an attribute. Defines the timing and structure of animation.
Keyframe Animation	Animation that is 'handmade' by the animator setting the keys. As opposed to Motion Capture and Simulations that are generated by processing data.
Layered Animation	A blocking method where you key a body part and then go back and layer other body parts on top. For example, blocking the root and IK feet for the length of the shot first, then going back and adding the spine and arms.
Line of Action	The visual curve through a character's body used to establish strong, readable posing.

Locator A null object. A Locator is an empty shape that does not render but is very useful for grouping objects in hierarchies or organizing constraint relationships between rig controls.

MEL Maya's native scripting language.

Mesh The geometry that makes up your character or object. Usually polygons, but can be NURBS surfaces. Only animate the mesh during final polish.

Micro-expressions Seven universal emotions that all humans share and that unconsciously flash across the face in a fraction of a second giving away the person's true feelings.

Motion Trail Creates a curve showing the path of an object. If the object has translation keys, it will generate editable points on the motion trail path.

Moving Hold a.k.a. Keep Alive Adding very slight, minimal movement to a character while holding a pose to keep the illusion of life, also known as a 1 pixel drift.

Mute Channel Disables a keyed animation channel without deleting it, allowing temporary removal of motion.

Off Model To adjust controls in such a way that the physical characteristics or appearance of the character no longer resembles the design.

Normalize The ability of Maya to display various items as the same size in the display area, even if the object's true scales vary greatly. Never work in the Normalized view in the Graph Editor.

Options Box — Next to menu items is a square box icon called the Options Box. It contains different settings for the tool and the option to reset to default.

Outliner — A UI element, a hierarchical list view of all scene objects. Essential for organizing, parenting, and selecting assets and controls.

Overlap and Follow Through — Follow through is the continuation of motion after the main body stops. Overlap refers to offset timing of different parts of the body, creating fluidity.

Overshoot — A motion that goes past the intended target before settling, used to emphasize force or momentum.

Overshoot (curve) — Where the tangent handles make the curve go beyond the min and max keys. When the results are desirable, the new min and max should be secured by inserting a key on the curve.

Parent Constraint — A constraint that makes one object follow the translation and rotation (optionally scale) of another.

Phoneme — The smallest unit of speech that distinguishes one sound from another.

Playblast — A quick, preview-quality render used to check animation timing and spacing without committing to full rendering.

Plug-in Manager — A panel under settings/preferences to load and unload plug-ins.

Pole Vector — A control used in IK systems to direct the orientation of an elbow or knee joint.

Pose-to-Pose Animation	A technique where major poses are blocked first and refined with breakdowns. Contrasts with straight-ahead animation.
Python	A programming language, popular because it is considered to be easier to learn.
Quaternion	A type of smooth interpolation of rotations that is less likely to cause gimbal lock.
Reference	Photos, sketches, video, or film of action or acting that the animator studies and uses as a guide. It can be made by the animator and colleagues, or found footage.
Referencing (rig)	Instead of opening a rig file, we make a pointer to the file. This allows for easy reloading or swapping of updated rig files without loss of animation information.
Region Tool	Allows selective retiming of a portion of animation within a marked region on the timeline.
Rendering	Is the process of the software creating an image for every frame of animation. The sequence of resulting rendered frames must be loaded into a movie file to make a clip.
Retime Tool	A tool that lets the animator stretch or compress blocks of animation keys to adjust timing interactively.
Rig	The digital skeleton and controls that drive a character's movement in 3D animation.

Roughing a.k.a. Texture	Adding variation to timing, spacing, energy, and acting to make the polished performance unique and believable.
Root	The center control of the body, can also be the COG. The Root is the parent of the lower and upper body joints; therefore, it moves the entire rig.
Rule of Thirds	Divides the frame into thirds horizontally and vertically; place points of interest on the intersections for better shot composition.
Saccades (eyes)	A unconscious small eye adjustments that happen over one frame. The opposite eye movement would be tracking where the eyes follow a target over time.
Script Editor	Shows the history of commands and the input pane to enter commands or scripts.
Secondary Action	Supporting motion that adds complexity to the main action. Enhances realism and subtext.
Silhouette	The outline of a character or object from the camera's perspective. Clean silhouettes enhance clarity and staging.
Slow-In and Slow-Out a.k.a. Ease-In and Ease-Out	Gradually accelerating or decelerating an object's motion to make animation feel natural.
Space	A coordinate system for the position and translations of 3D objects. Examples include world space, local space, or a rig could have foot space, hip space, etc.

Spacing
How an object moves between keyframes. Refers to the distribution of positions across frames—whether evenly, with acceleration, or abrupt. Spacing affects the feel and style of motion.

Splining
The process of converting stepped blocking to spline interpolation. If the stepped blocking does not have enough holds, poses, and breakdowns, it may become mushy and lose its snappy timing.

Staging
The presentation of an idea so it is clear to the audience. Involves composition, timing, and motion.

Stepped Blocking
Blocking the shot with stepped interpolation where each pose is held to the next pose. Similar to 2D flipbooks. Take care to key the holds so they don't lose their snappy timing when they are splined.

Straight Ahead and Pose to Pose
Two animation workflows: straight ahead builds frame-by-frame in sequence, while pose to pose begins with key poses and refines the in-betweens.

Squash and Stretch
A deformation principle that preserves volume while exaggerating motion or force. Adds weight and flexibility.

Subtext
The underlying meaning of what is being said. It may differ from what is said out loud.

Tangent Handles
The handles on a key. The angle of the handle affects the slope of the curve. They can work together (unified) or separately (broken).

Tempo

A CG workflow principle that emphasizes establishing timing first before posing or rigging. By animating a primitive like a cube, animators can quickly experiment and iterate on the rhythm and pace of a shot without the complexity of full rigs. Once timing is locked, reference and performance choices are applied over that foundation.

Three-Light Setup

Simple light setup for film, photography, and animation consisting of a main key light, fill light, and rim light.

Thumbnails

Quick sketches to explore animation ideas. Keep them loose and rough, do not over-render.

Time Editor

A tool for clip-based workflow for non-linear animation editing.

Timing

When something happens. The number of frames an action takes. Affects the pacing and rhythm of a shot. Spacing is how the object moves between those times.

Time Slider a.k.a. Timeline

The visual control at the bottom of Maya's UI where you scrub through frames and place keyframes.

Trax Editor Functions

Like the Time Editor, but it also lets you drag-and-drop animation clips between mapped characters.

Twinning

When both sides of a character mirror each other too closely in pose or timing, reducing appeal.

Unsnapped (keys)

Keys between two whole frames that appear in stats box with a * or in the Time Slider as a dashed line. Often caused by scaling animation and could cause pipeline issues. Keys should be snapped to the nearest whole frame or deleted.

Viewport

The window in Maya used to view and interact with your 3D scene in real time. Also known as the Panel.

Visual Library

An animator's curated collection of drawings, photos, videos, and films that serve as inspiration and reference.

Volume

The amount of space an object takes up should stay consistent. For example, if you stretch an object vertically it, will get thinner; if squash it vertically, it will get wider.

Weight

The sense of mass conveyed by timing, spacing, and posing. Crucial for believable physics and performance.

Weighted Tangents

Animation curve tangents that can be both rotated and scaled for fine control over easing and curve shaping. Non-Weighted Tangents can only be rotated, limiting the control over their influence on curve shape.

Zero the Controls

Reset all the controls to zero to set the rig back to its default bind pose.

For Product Safety Concerns and Information please contact our
EU representative GPSR@taylorandfrancis.com Taylor & Francis
Verlag GmbH, Kaufingerstraße 24, 80331 München, Germany